Civil Litigation

Connecticut, Massachusetts, New Jersey, New York, and Rhode Island

Kimberly A. Peterson

PRENTICE HALL PARALEGAL SERIES

Prentice Hall
Upper Saddle River, New Jersey 07458

Library of Congress Cataloging-in-Publication Data

Peterson, Kimberly A.
Civil litigation in Connecticut, Massachusetts, New Jersey, New York, and Rhode Island / Kimberly A. Peterson.
p. cm. — (Prentice Hall paralegal series)
Includes index.
ISBN 0-13-787938-5
1. Civil procedure—Connecticut. 2. Civil procedure—Massachusetts. 3. Civil procedure—New Jersey. 4. Civil procedure—New York (State) 5. Civil procedure—Rhode Island. I. Title. II. Series.
KF8841.P48 1999
347.74'05—dc21 98-34334
CIP

Acquisitions Editor: Elizabeth Sugg
Director of Production and Manufacturing: Bruce Johnson
Managing Editor: Mary Carnis
Editorial/Production Supervision and Interior Design: Inkwell Publishing Services
Cover Director: Miguel Ortiz
Manufacturing Buyer: Edward O'Dougherty
Marketing Manager: Danny Hoyt

Simon & Schuster / A Viacom Company
Upper Saddle River, New Jersey 07458

Printed in the United States of America

10 9 8 7 6 5 4 3 2 1

ISBN 0-13-787938-5

PRENTICE-HALL INTERNATIONAL (UK) LIMITED, *London*
PRENTICE-HALL OF AUSTRALIA PTY. LIMITED, *Sydney*
PRENTICE-HALL CANADA INC., *Toronto*
PRENTICE-HALL HISPANOAMERICANA, S.A., *Mexico*
PRENTICE-HALL OF INDIA PRIVATE LIMITED, *New Delhi*
PRENTICE-HALL OF JAPAN, INC., *Tokyo*
PRENTICE-HALL OF SOUTHEAST ASIA PTE. LTD., *Singapore*
EDITORA PRENTICE-HALL DO BRASIL, LTDA., *Rio de Janeiro*

CONTENTS

3
The Prelitigation Stage: Determining Causes of Action 19

4
The Prelitigation Stage: The Plaintiff's Complaint 33

5
The Prelitigation Stage: Commencing a Lawsuit 57

6
The Pretrial Stage: Responsive Pleadings to the Plaintiff's Complaint 81

17
Defaults, Nonsuits, and Dismissals: When Parties Do Not Comply with Court Rules 305

18
Prejudgment Remedies 325

19
The Trial Stage: Preparations for Trial 337

20
The Trial Stage: The Trial 361

PREFACE

Nothing in life can prepare us for practicing civil litigation. We can watch the fictional legal programs on television, but actually litigating a case is an entirely different matter. In real life, we deal with real people, on opposite sides, who have their own ideas of black and white, right and wrong. These differing ideas lead to a dispute. If they can't resolve the dispute themselves, they hire attorneys to "prove" the "truth" as they see it.

To illustrate this point, I often use an example involving a dispute over a simple shade of blue. When you think about it, blue can be labeled sapphire, cobalt, navy, royal, dark, or even sky blue, depending upon one's perception and the direction of the lighting. If this issue were to go to trial to be decided by a jury, you can only image how many different opinions the jurors would express, before finally determining, based upon the evidence presented, the "real" shade of blue. Therefore, always remember that—no matter how simple or trivial a matter may seem, or how right or wrong, or how black or white—in law there are absolutely no absolutes.

With all this ambiguity in mind, I set out to write this text to provide students, paralegals, and new attorneys with a practical guide to civil litigation in Connecticut, Massachusetts, New Jersey, New York, and Rhode Island. While we can't control people's perceptions and opinions that lead to disputes brought to a courtroom, we can control, to a certain extent, the litigation process. The first step is figuring out what the first step is. To accomplish that task, I created Litigation Checklist Summaries that apply to each state. These checklists spell out each stage of the litigation process from beginning to end. In addition, most chapters contain individual state summaries that address the topic discussed in the main chapter and cite specific state requirements and relevant court rules.

Examples of pleadings, motions, and other court papers begin in Chapter 4. The end of that chapter contains five sample complaints, each depicting a common type of civil litigation case. These cases are revisited over and over again to demonstrate the various documents that are commonly filed in each stage of the litigation process. Although these documents are from different states, their formats can be easily adapted to meet other states' requirements.

Keep in mind that this text is to be used as a *guide* to maneuver through a maze of uncertainty. Court rules and statutes change constantly and must be thoroughly researched before being relied upon. In addition, individual courthouse procedures differ throughout each state. As a result, there are no guarantees or expectations that the reader will be an expert litigation paralegal or attorney after reviewing this text or that all the information is 100 percent accurate. Instead, I embarked on this project to provide a solid foundation and understanding of the litigation process that will enable readers to confidently enter a law firm and know what to do with the litigation files handed to them.

Civil litigation never ceases to amaze me. It's exciting and invigorating. It can also be nerve-racking and even torturous at times. This text, when used in conjunction with the applicable court rules, statutes, and case law, dispels a lot of the mystery regarding litigation procedures, allowing time to address the various shades of blue.

Kimberly A. Peterson
Attorney at Law

Acknowledgments

This book is dedicated to my family, students, friends, and clients. In addition, there are numerous people I wish to thank for assisting me make this text a reality. They include but are not limited to Elizabeth Sugg and Dana Meltzer at Prentice Hall for their constant encouragement and enthusiasm for this project as well as many others: my husband Alan for his ongoing support, assistance and perseverance as the spouse of a writer; Lucy Michaud, Esq. from Connecticut, Bruce Sattin, Esq. from New Jersey, Joseph Conway, Esq. and Anna Lembo, Esq. from Massachusetts, and Mark Benjamin, Esq. from Rhode Island for their time in contributing information and ideas; paralegals William Carowick James Holcomb and Barbara Riley for their research; and Fred Dahl and his editors and staff at Inkwell Publishing Services for producing this text.

Connecticut Litigation Checklist Summary

I. The Prelitigation Stage (P: Plaintiff, D: Defendant)

P and D:	Identify all possible parties.
P and D:	Determine all causes of action.
P and D:	Determine statute of limitations.
P and D:	Investigation and settlement discussions
P:	Draft Summons and Complaint.
P:	Serve Defendant: Contact proper officer to serve copy of Summons and Complaint to all Defendants.
P:	File lawsuit: File original Summons, Complaint, Return of Service, and entry fee in proper Superior Court.

II. The Pretrial Stage: Pleadings and Discovery Occur Simultaneously

D:	File Appearance in Court.

A. Pleadings

D: File one or more of the following three *optional* responsive pleadings, one at a time:

Motion to Dismiss — P: Objection to Motion to Dismiss

	Request to Revise	P: Comply or file Objection
	Motion to Strike	P: Comply or file Objection
D:	File Answer which is mandatory if the case survives the pleadings listed above. Presume there are no Special Defenses or Counterclaim.	
Either or both parties:	File Motion for Summary Judgment and Objection.	
Either party:	File Certificate of Closed Pleadings (and Claim for Jury if applicable) to place case on Trial List.	
Both parties:	Attend Pretrial Conferences: scheduled by the court.	

B. Discovery

P and D:	Interrogatories, Objections, and Compliance
P and D:	Requests for Production, Objection, and Compliance
P and D:	Request for Inspection, Objection, and Compliance
D to P:	Request for Physical or Mental Exam, Objection, and Compliance
P and D:	Requests for Admission, Objection, and Compliance
P and D:	Disclosure of Expert Witnesses
P and D:	Depositions of parties and nonparties, Motions to Quash and Objections

III. The Trial Stage

Both parties:	Preparation, Motions in Limine and Offers of Judgment	
Both parties:	Jury selection	
P:	Opening statement and Case in Chief: witnesses and exhibits	
P:	Direct examination	D: Cross examination
P:	Redirect examination	D: Recross examination
D:	Motion for Directed Verdict or Dismissal	P: Objection
D:	Opening statement and Case: witnesses and exhibits. (In some cases, both the Plaintiff and the Defendant give their opening statements before any evidence is introduced.)	
D:	Direct examination	P: Cross examination
D:	Redirect examination	P: Recross examination
D:	Rebuttal	
P and D:	Closing Arguments	
P:	Rebuttal Closing Argument	

Bench Trial:	Judge's decision; or
Jury Trial:	Both parties: Requests to Charge, Charge Conference Judge: Jury Instructions

Jury deliberations, Jury verdict, Judge accepts verdict

After the Trial: P or D or both: Motion to Set Aside Verdict and other motions that challenge the verdict

IV. The Appeal Stage (AP: Appellant, AE: Appellee)

A. Appellate Court

AP:	File Appeal
AP	Brief
AE:	Opposing Brief
AP:	Reply Brief
Both parties:	Preargument Settlement Conference at court
Both parties:	Oral Argument

Appellate Court's Decision

B. Supreme Court (P: Petitioner, OP: Opposing Party)

P:	Petition for Certification	OP: Objection
P:	Brief	
OP:	Opposing Brief	
P:	Reply Brief	
Both parties:	Preargument Settlement Conference at court	
Both parties:	Oral Argument	

Supreme Court's Decision

Massachusetts, New Jersey, and Rhode Island Litigation Checklist Summary

I. The Prelitigation Stage (P: Plaintiff, D: Defendant)

P and D:	Identify all possible parties.
P and D:	Determine all causes of action.
P and D:	Determine statute of limitations.
P and D:	Investigation and settlement discussions
P:	Draft Summons and Complaint.
P:	File lawsuit: File original Summons, Complaint, and entry fee in proper Superior Court.
P:	Serve Defendant: Contact proper officer to serve copy of Summons and Complaint to all Defendants.
P:	File Return of Service in court.

II. The Pretrial Stage: Pleadings and Discovery Occur Simultaneously

A. Responsive Pleadings and Motions

D: File Motion or Answer, at Defendant's option.

Optional Motions:

Motion to Dismiss	P: Objection to Motion to Dismiss
Motion for More Definite Statement	P: Comply or file Objection
Motion to Strike	P: Comply or file Objection
NJ: Motion to Dismiss for Improp. of Plead.	P: Comply or file Objection

File Answer, which is mandatory if case survives the above listed motions.

Alone or, if no motions listed above are filed, include grounds for a Motion to Dismiss as Affirmative Defenses if applicable. Presume no Counterclaims, Cross Claims, etc.

Either or both parties:	File Motion for Summary Judgment and Objection.
Both parties:	Attend Pretrial Conferences scheduled by the court.

B. Discovery

P and D:	Interrogatories, Objections, and Compliance
P and D:	Requests for Production, Objection, and Compliance
P and D:	Request for Inspection and Examinations, Objection, and Compliance
D to P:	Request for Physical or Mental Exam, Objection, and Compliance
P and D:	Requests for Admission, Objection, and Compliance
P and D:	Disclosure of Expert Witnesses
P and D:	Depositions of parties and nonparties, Motions to Quash, Objections

III. The Trial Stage

Both parties:	Preparation, Motion in Limine, Objection, and Offers of Judgment	
Both parties:	Jury selection	
P:	Opening statement and Case in Chief: witnesses and exhibits	
P:	Direct examination	D: Cross examination
P:	Redirect examination	D: Recross examination
D:	Motion for Direct. Verdict or Judge.	P: Objection
D:	Opening statement and Case: witnesses and exhibits. (In some cases, both the Plaintiff and the Defendant give their opening statements before any evidence is introduced.)	
D:	Direct examination	P: Cross examination
D:	Redirect examination	P: Recross examination

D:	Rebuttal
P and D:	Closing Arguments
P:	Rebuttal Closing Argument
Bench Trial:	Judge's decision; or
Jury Trial:	Both parties: Requests to Charge, Charge Conference Judge: Jury Instructions

Jury deliberations, Jury verdict, Judge accepts verdict

After the Trial: P or D or both: Motion for New Trial and other types of motions that challenge the verdict and objections

IV. The Appeal Stage (AP: Appellant, AE: Appellee)

A. Appellate Court

AP:	File Appeal
AP	Brief
AE:	Opposing Brief
AP:	Reply Brief
Both parties:	Preargument Settlement Conference scheduled by court
Both parties:	Oral Argument

Appellate Court's Decision

B. Supreme Court (P: Petitioner, OP: Opposing Party)

P:	Petition for Certification	OP: Objection
P:	Brief	
OP:	Opposing Brief	
P:	Reply Brief	
Both parties:	Preargument Settlement Conference scheduled by court	
Both parties:	Oral Argument	

Supreme Court's Decision

New York Litigation Checklist Summary

I. The Prelitigation Stage (P: Plaintiff, D: Defendant)

P and D:	Identify all possible parties.
P and D:	Determine all causes of action.
P and D:	Determine statute of limitations.
P and D:	Investigation and settlement discussions
P:	Draft Summons and Complaint.
P:	File lawsuit: File original Summons, Complaint, and entry fee in proper Superior Court.
P:	Serve Defendant: Contact proper officer to serve copy of Summons and Complaint to all Defendants.
P:	File Return of Service in court.

II. The Pretrial Stage: Pleadings and Discovery Occur Simultaneously

A. Responsive Pleadings and Motions

D: File Motion or Answer, at Defendant's option.

Motions:

Motion to Dismiss	P: File Objection
Motions to Correct Pleadings:	
Motion for More Definite Statement	P: Comply or File Objection
Motion to Strike	P: Comply or file Objection
Demand for Bill of Particulars	P: Responses

Answer: Mandatory if case survives the above listed motions.

D:	File the Answer alone which is mandatory if case survives the motions listed above, or, if no motions listed above are filed, include grounds for a Motion to Dismiss as Affirmative Defenses, if applicable. (Presume no Counterclaims, Cross Claims, etc.)
Either party:	Note of Issue, Certificate of Readiness and if applicable, Jury Demand, to place case on Trial List
Either or both parties:	File Motion for Summary Judgment and Objection.
Both parties:	Attend Pretrial Conferences scheduled by the court.

B. Discovery

P and D:	Interrogatories, Objections, and Compliance
P and D:	Notice to Produce, Objection, and Compliance
P and D:	Notice to Inspect or Examine, Objection, and Compliance
D to P:	Notice for Physical or Mental Exam, Objection, and Compliance
P and D:	Notice to Admit, Objection, and Compliance
P and D:	Disclosure of Expert Witnesses
P and D:	Depositions of parties and nonparties, Motions to Quash, Objections

III. The Trial Stage

Both parties:	Preparation, Motions in Limine, Objections and Offers of Compromise	
Both parties:	Jury selection	
P:	Open. statement and Case in Chief: witnesses and exhibits. (In some cases, both the Plaintiff and the Defendant give their opening statements before any evidence is introduced.)	
P:	Direct examination	D: Cross examination
P:	Redirect examination	D: Recross examination
D:	Mot. for Judge. or Direct. Verdict	P: Objection
D:	Opening statement and Case: witnesses and exhibits. (In some cases, both the Plaintiff and the Defendant give their opening statements before any evidence is introduced.)	
D:	Direct examination	P: Cross examination
D:	Redirect examination	P: Recross examination
D:	Rebuttal	

P and D:	Closing Arguments
P:	Rebuttal Closing Argument
Bench Trial:	Judge's decision; or
Jury Trial:	Both parties: Requests to Charge, Charge Conference Judge: Jury Instructions

Jury deliberations, Jury verdict, Judge accepts verdict

After the Trial: P or D or both: Motion for New Trial and other types of motions that challenge the verdict and objections

IV. The Appeal Stage (AP: Appellant, AE: Appellee)

A. Appellate Court

AP:	File Appeal
AP	Brief
AE:	Opposing Brief
AP:	Reply Brief
Both parties:	Preargument Settlement Conference scheduled by court
Both parties:	Oral Argument

Appellate Court's Decision

B. Supreme Court (P: Petitioner, OP: Opposing Party)

P:	Petition for Certification	OP: Objection
P:	Brief	
OP:	Opposing Brief	
P:	Reply Brief	
Both parties:	Preargument Settlement Conference scheduled by court	
Both parties:	Oral Argument	

Supreme Court's Decision

Index of Sample Documents

I. Complaints

II. Serving Defendants and Filing the Lawsuit

III. Responsive Pleadings

IV. Motions Relating to Complaint

V. Discovery

VI. Defaults

VII. Prejudgment Remedies

VIII. Motions/Offers Before Trial

IX. At Trial and After Verdict

1

The Legal Profession and Practice

Terminology

Litigation	Suit	Intern
Civil Litigation	Parties	Case Law
Litigants	Et Seq.	Law Clerk
Statute of Limitations	Plaintiff	Pro Se
Case	Defendant	Malpractice
Statute	Damages	Court Rules
Diarying	Criminal Litigation	Lawsuit

I. Litigation: The Art of Persuasion

Welcome to the legal profession and to **litigation,** specifically. As you can see from the Table of Contents and Litigation Checklist Summaries found at the beginning of this book, you will have plenty of work to do, challenging work with results that will never cease to astound you.

From now on, when you hear the word litigation, immediately picture a courtroom in your mind. Ultimately, that's where litigation takes place. It begins when two or more people disagree about something and one decides to bring the other to court to have a judge or jury settle their dispute.

I believe the easiest way to describe the litigation process is to think of it as a game. The game is entitled, "The Art of Persuasion." The object is for each side to persuade the judge or jury that his or her version of the facts best describes the truth. Sounds simple, doesn't it? After all, the truth is the truth, right? Just wait. It's amazing how many versions of the truth you will encounter.

As you delve into this game, you will discover that litigation is a unique animal. Nothing in life can compare or prepare you to play. Almost immediately, you will realize that the rules change as you go along, and 20/20 hindsight constantly causes you to second-guess yourself. To sum it all up, what's right today can be wrong tomorrow, but may be quite acceptable the following day. Just like in any game, no matter how talented the attorneys and staff on each side are, when it's finished, one side must lose.

Civil litigation typically involves disputes in which one side is seeking **damages** from the other. These damages are usually money. **Criminal litigation,** on the other hand, involves the state government which charges individuals with committing crimes and seeks to punish them with criminal penalties such as prison sentences, fines, etc.

This text is designed to provide you with a concise guide to the game of civil litigation in five states: Connecticut, Massachusetts, Rhode Island, New Jersey, and New York. Each of these states has its own distinct court procedures, with Connecticut and New York differing the most. Fortunately, however, they all follow the litigation process described below.

I have divided the litigation process into four stages: the ***Prelitigation Stage;*** the ***Pretrial Stage,*** which encompasses *pleadings, motions,* and *discovery;* the ***Trial Stage;*** and the ***Appeal Stage.*** These stages are detailed throughout Chapters 3 to 22 of this text. If at anytime you become confused, simply refer to the Litigation Checklist Summaries on pages xv–xxx after the Acknowledgments to determine what stage you are working in. In addition, Appendix A contains a checklist to be photocopied and placed in each litigation file you are working on. This will save you time in answering questions about a file and keeping it organized.

Recently, I took a poll among a group of my attorney friends. They all agreed that successful paralegals and law clerks must demonstrate the same characteristics as successful lawyers: Each must be extremely conscientious and persistent, detail oriented, dependable, and creative. A good sense of humor never hurts either. Remember, you're dealing with human beings, all of whom have their own quirks and agendas. In most cases, clients find themselves in law offices because they have problems. They want to be able to rely upon the people in that office to help solve those problems. That's a huge responsibility to undertake.

It's important that you do your absolute best to remain flexible and go with the flow. When you practice litigation, your life will revolve around deadlines you can't control. That means no matter how far in advance you prepare, there will always be "one last thing" to do. And nothing ever takes "just five minutes." Remember that sense of humor? It will definitely come in handy.

Anybody who works in this profession can tell you that photocopiers break down just when you need to make that final copy of a twenty-page brief due at court within the next half hour. Or your computer will freeze you out of the one file you absolutely must access, now! Then there's the laser printer that simply refuses to print a document you desperately need. And finally, don't forget the stapler that runs out of staples at the most inopportune moment, making you want to fling it and yourself right out the nearest window.

We won't get into lapses of electricity, traffic jams, flat tires, dead batteries, and blizzards. Trust me. The author of Murphy's Law knew what he was talking about. If it can happen, it will. So don't start questioning your intelligence or wondering if you chose the wrong profession. You didn't. At times like these, the best you can do is take a deep breath, smile, and plunge forward. So let's do it!

II. Admission to the Bar: State and Federal Courts

Every state in the United States operates its own unique court system, according to its laws and court procedures. In addition, there is a federal court system which operates under its own set of laws and court procedures. Each person in this country is required to follow all applicable state and federal laws.

Attorneys who practice law must first be granted a license or permission by the specific state or federal court they choose to work in. This license, or permission, is referred to as an "admission to the bar" of that state or federal court. Such admission is obtained once the attorney passes the applicable state's bar exam: a written exam that is held around the country every July and February. In addition, each person is subject to a personal background investigation regarding specific educational requirements and moral character.

Understandably, the bar exam is cause for much concern. It's made worse by the fact that the results are usually not released until three or more months after the exam is given. Paralegals and other law office staff are not subject to such admission requirements.

Most states permit law students and graduates who have not yet passed the bar to work for licensed attorneys as **law clerks** or **interns.** They may also obtain permission to appear before a specific court, under the guidance and direction of their employers.

It is possible for attorneys to work in more than one state or federal court at the same time, as long as they are admitted in those state or federal courts. At times, a court will permit an out-of-state attorney who is not admitted to its bar to appear in court to handle a specific case. This is called being admitted **Pro Hac Vice:** temporarily, under the guidance of an in-state attorney.

Most law firms practice in the state court where they are located. Others prefer the federal court system, or practice in both systems. This, of course, requires the attorneys, paralegals, law clerks, and other office staff to juggle both sets of complicated laws and rules at the same time.

III. The Parties to a Lawsuit

As you will learn, the terms **case, file, action,** and **suit** are often used interchangeably with **lawsuit.** Attorneys are never named in a lawsuit in which they represent a client. Instead, they file such suits and defend them in the names of their clients.

Just as there are at least two sides to every argument, there are at least two sides to every lawsuit. The individuals or groups on each side are known as **parties.** Parties named in a lawsuit include individuals, corporations, partnerships, associations, governmental agencies, etc.

Once a lawsuit is filed in court, these parties become the **Plaintiff** and the **Defendant.** Together, they are also known as **litigants.** (After a lawsuit is filed in court, the terms **parties** and **litigants** are often used interchangeably.)

A **Plaintiff** is the party who brings a lawsuit against someone. Plaintiffs are often identified by the pi symbol.

A **Defendant** is the party being sued and is often identified by a triangle.

In addition, *individuals* may represent themselves in court, instead of hiring an attorney. These individuals are called **pro se** parties and are still known as Plaintiffs and Defendants. (Please note that many states prohibit corporations, partnerships, and associations from representing themselves as pro se parties. Instead, these entities must hire an attorney.)

IV. Statutes and Case Law

Laws are enacted by the legislature in each state and in the federal government. These laws are often called **statutes.** The statutes enacted are assigned a number and may be referred to as **sections.** They can be found in a series of published volumes such as the *Massachusetts General Laws*, or *Connecticut General Statutes*, etc.

The courts in each state interpret their statutes by deciding cases that are brought before them. Such decisions are published and are referred to as **case law.** Attorneys and courts rely upon such case law as *precedent:* examples and authority for dealing with future cases that are similar in nature. (See Section II in Chapter 2.)

V. Statewide and Local Court Rules

While statutes address some litigation procedures, the majority of these procedures are found in each state's **court rules.** These court rules are established by a rules committee that consists of judges and possibly other judicial staff. Their purpose is to provide instructions and requirements regarding courthouse and litigation procedures that are expected to be complied with on a statewide basis.

In addition to statewide court rules, many individual courthouses have their own specific procedures that must be followed on their own or in conjunction with other applicable court rules and statutes.

Like statutes, each rule is assigned a number and may be referred to as a section or a rule. The rules are published in one or more volumes called a practice book or rules book of some type. At times you will see a statute or rule followed by the term, **et seq.** Et seq. refers to the numbered section (or rule) and those that immediately follow.

Civil Litigation is intended to be used in conjunction with court rules and state statutes, not as a replacement. In addition, some rules will cite a statute at the end. These statutes may contain language that is identical to the rule, or slightly different. Therefore, be sure to have access to both sets of materials.

VI. The Statute of Limitations

I can't stress enough the importance of the **statute of limitations** in civil litigation. The statute of limitations is a specific time limit any potential Plaintiff has to bring a lawsuit against someone. If the time limit expires, the Plaintiff will not be able to recover damages from the Defendant. These time limits are found in the state's statutes.

For example, Connecticut General Statute Section 52-584 requires that most personal injury lawsuits be brought within two years of the date of the incident that caused the Plaintiff's alleged injuries. If a lawsuit is brought after that two-year time period, the Defendant will claim the statute of limitations has expired and ask the court to grant judgment in his or her favor, in other words, throw the case out of court. If the court agrees and the Plaintiff's attorney is at fault for missing the deadline, there is a strong likelihood that the Plaintiff will then turn around and sue the attorney for **legal malpractice.**

The term legal malpractice makes everyone in an office uncomfortable. Essentially, the phrase means that an attorney made a mistake in handling a client's case. As a result of that mistake, the client was prevented from recovering damages from the Defendant. In a suit for legal malpractice, the client sues his or her former attorney, hoping to recover from the attorney the damages he or she would have received from the original Defendant.

Chapters 3 and 5 will address the statute of limitations in conjunction with preventing malpractice by **diarying** (also known as calendaring) these important dates and other court-imposed deadlines that arise once a lawsuit is filed in court. For now, suffice it to say that there are no exceptions to the statute of limitations—none. Paralegals, interns, and other office staff are expected to play a large role in making sure all deadlines are met. This role includes realizing their importance and cooperating to the fullest extent possible.

Always make certain someone in your office is available to handle your files in your absence. Prepare ahead of time to address issues that may arise while you're on vacation or out due to illness. Inform others of potential problems and any impending deadlines. Being prepared might mean staying late at the office a few nights before you're scheduled to be away. You won't be alone. This same conscientious conduct is expected of everyone, including attorneys. To do otherwise could result in your being out of a job when you return and compromising an attorney's professional career. It's an awful situation, one which is best avoided at all costs.

VII. Conclusion

You've been exposed to a lot of terminology in this chapter. Don't fret. There is a glossary at the end of the text and the terms will be used over and over again throughout the following chapters. Soon, they will become part of your everyday vocabulary. With all of this in mind, review the material listed below. Then move on to Chapter 2 and explore the court systems.

Key Issues in This Chapter

1. There are four stages in the litigation process: *Prelitigation, Pretrial* (which includes *pleadings, motions,* and *discovery*), *Trial,* and *Appeal.*
2. The *Plaintiff* brings the lawsuit against the *Defendant.*
3. Plaintiffs and Defendants are called *parties.*
4. *Pro se* parties can be individual Plaintiffs or Defendants. These parties do not have attorneys. Instead, they represent themselves.
5. *Civil litigation* typically involves disputes about money *damages*. It does not involve criminal cases in which fines and prison terms are used as punishment.
6. *Statutes of limitations* are found in the state's *statutes* and are established time limits to file specific civil actions.
7. *Court rules* explain courthouse and litigation procedures.
8. Be sure to *diary* (or calendar) deadlines such as the date the statute of limitations expires for every new litigation case assigned to you that has not yet been filed in court.
9. *Legal malpractice* occurs when an attorney negligently handles a client's case, causing the client to suffer damages.

STATE SUMMARIES

The court rules and statutes cited throughout the remainder of this text are from the sources stated below.

Connecticut

Connecticut's civil court rules can be found in the ***Connecticut Practice Book.*** In this text, they are abbreviated ***Pbs,*** followed by the applicable number. In addition, some of Connecticut's litigation procedures are found in the ***Connecticut General Statutes,*** abbreviated, ***C.G.S. sec.,*** followed by the applicable number.

Massachusetts

Civil court rules in Massachusetts can be found in the ***Massachusetts Rules of Civil Procedure,*** abbreviated as ***Rule,*** followed by the applicable number. In addition, other applicable rules can be found in the ***Superior Court Rules,*** abbreviated ***Sup. Ct. Rule,*** and in ***Standing Orders of the Superior Court,*** abbreviated ***Standing Orders*** in this text.

New Jersey

Civil court rules in New Jersey can be found in the ***Rules of General Application,*** which encompass Rules 1:1 and subparts, and ***Civil Practice Rules,*** which start at Rule 4:1. Both are abbreviated as ***Rule,*** followed by the applicable number.

New York

Civil court rules in New York can be found in the ***Civil Practice Laws and Rules,*** abreviated ***CPLR,*** followed by the applicable number, and in the ***Uniform Civil Rules of the Supreme Court and the County Court,*** abbreviated ***Unif. Rule.*** in this text.

Rhode Island

Civil court rules in Rhode Island can be found in the ***Superior Court Rules of Civil Procedure,*** abbreviated ***Rule,*** followed by the applicable number, and ***Superior Court Rules of Practice,*** abbreviated ***R.P.***

2 The Court System

Terminology

Supreme Court	Appellate Court	Trial
Superior Court	District Court	Appeal
Trier of Fact	En Banc	Brief
First Impression	Transcript	Jury
Record	Bench Trial	Precedent

Introduction

Before you begin practicing litigation, you will need a clear understanding of the state court system you are working in. I have divided the court system into three tiers that are described below.

I. A Multilevel System

Each state labels its courts differently. At minimum, each state has a **trial court** and an **appellate court** that usually includes two levels: an intermediate appellate level and a final appellate level.

A. The Trial Court and the Trier of Fact

The trial court is the lowest court in each state. There are usually several trial courts located throughout a state to handle the numerous lawsuits filed each year. Several judges are assigned to this level of the court system, many of whom rotate from one trial court location to another during their terms.

Trials are conducted only at the trial court level. A trial gives both parties their sole opportunity to explain their side of the story firsthand, call witnesses, and provide evidence directly to a judge or **jury**. The trial judge or the jury, consisting of between six and twelve members who listen and decide the case, is referred to as the **trier of fact.** The trial judge or jury observes and determines the credibility of each witness, including the parties, and weighs the evidence presented, in order to discover the relevant facts of a case, i.e., the truth. Next, the trial judge or jury makes a decision based upon those facts and the law.

Chapter 19 discusses reasons to choose a trial to only a judge (called a **bench trial**) versus a trial to a jury. For now, suffice it to say that some cases are more appropriate for a judge to decide, while in others, your client may obtain a better result with a jury. In any event, this choice must be made. Only one or the other will hear and decide a case, not both.

Assume the parties want a jury to decide their dispute. Does this mean a judge isn't needed? No. In those situations, a judge must still be present to preside over the case. He or she will keep order in the courtroom and decide issues based upon the law, as these issues arise during the trial. The jury, on the other hand, is solely responsible for determining the facts and applying the law, *as the law is explained to it by the judge.* By contrast, judges who decide a case without a jury are responsible for both tasks: determining the facts and applying the law.

Don't be confused if you read a case or hear an attorney referring to a judge as "the Court," or "Your Honor." The three titles are often used interchangeably.

Trial courts (except in New York) are usually referred to as **district courts** or superior courts or both. The difference often involves the value of a case and whether it will be a bench trial or a jury trial. For instance, in Massachusetts, trials involving cases valued at $25,000 or under, tried to a judge rather than a jury, usually take place in district court. Civil cases over $25,000 tried to a jury take place in superior court. Connecticut, on the other hand, does not have a district court. Instead, all civil trials take place in the superior court.

In this text, we will address litigation procedures applicable to each state's superior court (except in New York where the trial court is called the supreme court). Please note, however, that state agencies usually have an internal court system that does not permit a jury trial. Appeals from that system usually begin in the state's trial court.

B. The Appeals Courts

Each state has some type of higher court the parties may go to in order to challenge decisions made in the trial court. This challenge is known as an **appeal.** A party who believes the trial court made a mistake during the trial may appeal to the state's appellate level court.

As stated earlier, most states have two levels of appeals courts. (**Note:** Rhode Island has only one for civil cases in its superior court.) The first level is called the Appeals Court or Appellate Court or Appellate Division. The final level is the highest court in the state and is called the **Supreme Court** (except New York, which reverses the titles and called its highest court the Court of Appeals). In dramatic terms, this court is often referred to as the "court of last resort," or "the maker of the law of the land."

Appellate courts and supreme courts consist of a small number of judges who hear and decide appeals as a group, called a *panel.* For instance, Connecticut's appellate court consists of nine judges who are divided into panels of three. Its supreme court consists of seven judges who are divided into panels of five. In some situations, the entire appellate court or the entire supreme court will hear and decide a case. This is called sitting **en banc.**

There are no juries, no witnesses, no new exhibits or other evidence presented to an appellate or supreme court. Instead, these courts base their decisions upon the lower court **record:** They review the case by reading the **transcript** of the proceeding and the parties' **briefs,** and by listening to the parties' oral arguments. They then decide whether or not an error was made in the lower court, based upon this information and the applicable law.

II. Precedent

Decisions made by each state's highest court (usually the Supreme Court) must be followed by the lower courts in that state. These decisions are published in the form of cases based upon the names of the parties and are referred to as case law. As mentioned in Chapter 1, the concept of following the decisions made in these cases is known as **precedent**. Following precedent is essential to ensure that issues that arise over and over again in different cases are decided consistently. Otherwise, it would be impossible to determine what the law was on a specific issue, to adequately advise a client, or to prepare a case for trial.

If the Supreme Court has not addressed an issue, the lower courts should look to decisions made by the appellate level court in that state. These decisions are also published in the form of case law. If no appellate court or supreme court decision on the issue is available, the issue becomes one of **first impression.** The lower courts may then look for guidance from other state and federal court decisions and decide the issue using their best judgment.

III. Filing an Appeal

In many states, there is no right to appeal a trial court decision directly to the supreme court. Instead, appeals usually begin in the appellate court (except in Rhode Island; see page 18). If the appellate court determines that the trial court made an error, it could order the case to be sent back to the trial court for a new trial or completely reverse the trial court's decision. If no error is found, the trial court's decision will stand.

A party who wishes to appeal an appellate court decision to the supreme court must first ask permission by filing a *Petition for Certification* to the state's supreme court. If the Petition for Certification is granted, the party wishing to appeal will file the appropriate appeal documents, including a new brief. In addition, they will be permitted to present an oral argument.

If the Supreme Court finds an error in the appellate court's decision, it will send the case back to the appellate court with specific instructions which could include reversing the decision and ordering a new trial in the trial court. On the other hand, if a Petition for Certification is denied, there is no further appeal and the appellate court's decision stands as law.

IV. Conclusion

A. Key Issues in This Chapter

1. Litigation begins in the *trial court,* which is usually called the *superior court.*
2. All states have at least one court the parties may go to in order to challenge a trial court decision. This challenge is called an appeal.
3. Most states have two levels of appellate courts: an *appellate court* and a *supreme court* (except New York which reverses the titles and Rhode Island which only has a supreme court).
4. All lower courts in a state must follow the law that has been decided by the highest court in that state. This is called following *precedent.* If an issue has not yet been decided, it is known as an issue of *first impression.*

For more information on appellate court litigation see Chapter 22.

B. Additional Comments

Some law firms practice *administrative law.* This type of law is highly specialized and is not addressed in this text, except for this brief mention. The cases involve disputes that arise between state citizens and state agencies. Most agencies have an internal court system to handle these disputes. The procedures are determined by applicable state statutes and regulations that tend to vary from one agency to another. Citizens who wish to appeal a decision usually begin by filing a lawsuit in the state's trial court. From there it is often possible to appeal a trial court's decision to the state's appellate level courts.

The following is a brief description of the five states' court systems.

STATE SUMMARIES

The Connecticut Court System

Connecticut has a three-level court system: the **Superior Court,** the **Appellate Court,** and the **Supreme Court.** The judges on the Superior Court and the Appellate Court are referred to as "judges." The judges on the Supreme Court are referred to as "justices."

I. The Superior Court

The Superior Court is Connecticut's trial court. Instead of counties, the Superior Court system is divided into twelve Judicial Districts. (In 1998, it is anticipated that the Hartford/New Britain Judicial District will separate into two judicial districts.) Each Judicial District (JD) has one or more courthouses where the Superior Court is located.

There are five types of Superior Courts:

1. JD courts, which handle all civil and family cases and serious criminal cases;
2. Geographical Area (GA) courts, which handle small claims and less serious criminal offenses, and sometimes housing matters;
3. Housing Matters, which handle landlord and tenant disputes, etc.;
4. Juvenile Matters, which handle cases involving children such as care and protection, delinquency, and criminal cases;
5. Tax court.

Though these courts are separate, they may be located in the same building, or nearby. Only the juvenile courts are required to have their own facilities.

This text will address civil cases filed in the JD court.

II. The Connecticut Appellate Court

Connecticut has one appellate court that addresses appeals pertaining to superior court decisions. All litigants have a right to appeal a superior court decision to this court. It is located at 95 Washington Street in Hartford and consists of nine judges, including a chief judge. In most cases, a panel of three judges will hear and decide a case. One of the three judges will write the majority decision (called the opinion) that will be published in the *Connecticut Appellate Reports.* The remaining two judges may write a *concurrence* or *dissent* which will also be published with the opinion.

The Appellate Court shares a clerk's office with the Connecticut Supreme Court. It is located at 231 Capitol Avenue in Hartford.

III. The Supreme Court

Connecticut's highest court is the Connecticut Supreme Court. Most of its cases are appeals from Connecticut Appellate Court decisions that the Supreme Court has agreed to take pursuant to granting a petition for certification. A very small number of specific types of cases may be appealed directly to the Supreme Court from the Superior Court.

The Connecticut Supreme Court consists of one court which is located at 231 Capitol Avenue in Hartford. There are seven justices in total, including a chief justice. In most cases, a panel of five will sit and decide a case. As in Appellate Court, one of the five justices will write the majority opinion which will be published in the *Connecticut Reports,* along with any *concurrence* or *dissent.*

IV. Probate Courts

In Connecticut, *probate* matters are handled in probate courts. These courts are located in most cities and towns throughout the state and their judges (who do not have to be attorneys) are elected by the city or town they serve. There are no juries. Appeals from the probate court are brought to the Superior Court and could eventually end up at the Supreme Court.

THE MASSACHUSETTS COURT SYSTEM

The Massachusetts court system consists of three departments: The **Trial Court,** the **Appeals Court,** and the **Supreme Judicial Court.** All Massachusetts judges in this system are called justices, though they may be referred to as "judge" in the Trial Court Departments.

I. Trial Court Departments

The Trial Court Departments consists of seven different departments where trials take place:

1. The District Court Department
2. The Superior Court Department
3. The Housing Court Department
4. The Probate and Family Court Department
5. The Juvenile Court Department
6. The Land Court Department
7. The Boston Municipal Court Department

Though these departments are separate, they may be located in the same building or in separate facilities nearby. This text addresses issues in civil cases that are filed and decided in the Superior Court Department. In these cases, the Plaintiff is seeking more than $25,000 in damages and has notified the court that he or she has exercised the right to demand a jury trial. Note, however, that civil cases may also be filed and decided in District Court. Typically, these cases are valued at $25,000 or less and are decided by a judge. At the time this text was printed, District Courts did not conduct jury trials in civil cases. If a party wants a jury trial, the case could be transferred to the Superior Court. Last, cases valued at $2,000 or less are called small claims cases and should also be filed in the District Court.

II. The Appeals Court

Massachusetts has one Appeals Court that addresses appeals pertaining to Trial Court Department cases as mentioned above. It is considered an intermediate appellate court. It is located at New Court House, Pemberton Square in Boston and consists of 13 associate justices and one chief justice. The justices will, however, travel to other parts of the state to handle appeals.

In most cases, the justices hear and decide cases in panels of three. They rotate writing the majority decision (called an opinion) for each case they hear. The remaining justices on the panel are free to write a concurrence or dissent. All *opinions* and any *concurrences* and *dissents* are published in the *Massachusetts Appeals Court Reports.*

III. The Supreme Judicial Court

The Supreme Judicial Court (often abbreviated SJC) is the highest court in Massachusetts. In most instances, it decides appeals from decisions made by the Massachusetts Appeals Court. A very small number of specific types of cases may be appealed directly to the Supreme Court from the trial court.

Massachusetts has one Supreme Judicial Court. It is located at New Court House, Pemberton Square in Boston. Although numerous appeals are heard at this location, the court will sit, at its discretion, in other locations throughout the state.

The court consists of six associate justices and one chief justice. In the past, panels of four or five justices often heard and decided cases. Recently, however, all seven justices have been sitting at the same time. Like the Appeals Court, the members of the panel rotate writing the majority opinion for each case they hear. It will be published in the *Massachusetts Reports,* along with any *concurrence* and *dissent.*

The New Jersey Court System

The New Jersey court system consists of the Superior Court and the Supreme Court. The Superior Court contains six court divisions and an appellate division.

I. The Trial Court Divisions in the Superior Court

The trial courts are separated into the following divisions:

1. Law Division Civil Part
2. Law Division Special Civil Part
3. Law Division Criminal Part
4. Chancery Division Family Part
5. Chancery Division General Equity Part
6. Tax Court

Though these departments are separate, they may be located in the same building or in separate facilities nearby.

In this text we will focus on cases filed in the Civil Part. Plaintiffs who file these civil cases are seeking damages that exceed $10,000. Each of New Jersey's 21 counties has a Civil Part.

II. The Appellate Division of the Superior Court

The Appellate Division, which is also part of the Superior Court system, is the first level of New Jersey's appellate system. It consists of more than 30 judges who address appeals from the trial courts in the law and chancery divisions. The judges sit in panels of two, three, or four to hear and decide cases. The clerk's office is located at the Hughes Justice Complex, 25 W. Market Street in Trenton. The panels sit in various locations throughout the state including Trenton, Atlantic City, Hackensack, Morristown, Newark, and Elizabeth.

The judges on each panel rotate writing the majority decision (called an opinion) for each case they hear. The remaining justices on the panel are free to write a concurrence or dissent. All *opinions* and any *concurrences* and *dissents* are published in the *New Jersey Superior Court Reports.*

III. The Supreme Court

New Jersey's court of last resort is located at the Hughes Justice Complex, 25 W. Market Street in Trenton and consists of seven justices. In most instances, Supreme Court cases are heard and decided at this location in Trenton. Most Supreme Court cases are appeals from decisions made by the Appellate Division.

Like the Appellate Division, the members of the panel rotate writing the majority opinion for each case they hear. These *opinions,* along with any *concurrences* and *dissents,* are published in the *New Jersey Reports.*

The New York Court System

New York divides its counties into 12 Judicial Districts. These districts are divided among four judicial departments. The system as a whole differs from the remaining states in the following ways:

1. It uses the title Supreme Court much differently from the other states. Instead of being the state's highest court, it is actually one of the state's trial courts. The highest court is called the Court of Appeals.
2. It allows its litigants at least one opportunity to challenge the ***facts,*** as well as the law applied in a trial, on appeal.
3. Its judges, except those who sit on the Court of Appeals, are elected, rather than appointed.
4. Its judges, except those who sit on the Court of Appeals, are called justices.

I. The Trial Courts

A large percentage of civil trials in New York are conducted in the Supreme Court. There is one Supreme Court courthouse in each county. In addition, civil trials may also be conducted in the following courts:

1. Court of Claims: if the case is against the State of New York or if the State of New York is the Plaintiff.
2. County Courts: cases valued at up to $25,000.
3. District Courts and City Courts: cases valued at up to $15,000.

4. Justice Courts: town and village courts; less serious criminal matters and lower valued civil cases.

Other types of cases are filed in the following trial courts:

1. Surrogate's Court: probate and guardianship cases.
2. Family Court: divorces, etc.

This text will address civil cases filed and decided in a Supreme Court.

Note: In addition to being a trial court, the Supreme Court also consists of the state's intermediate Appellate Division.

II. The Appellate Division and the Appellate Term

As stated above, unlike the other states addressed in this text, New York's intermediate appellate courts, the Appellate Division and the Appellate Term, allow the parties to appeal the ***facts*** found in the trial court, as well as the trial court's legal rulings.

A. The Appellate Division

Each of the state's four Judicial Departments contains one Appellate Division. These divisions are actually part of the Supreme Court but they are not trial courts. The judges must first be elected to the Supreme Court. The governor may then appoint them to sit on the Appellate Division.

Cases that are decided in the following courts may be appealed to the Appellate Division in that same Judicial Department:

Supreme Court
Court of Claims
County Courts
Surrogate's Court
Family Court
Appeals from the Appellate Term

The Appellate Division justices in each department sit in panels of five. They rotate writing the majority decision (called an *opinion*) for each case they hear. The remaining justices on the panel are free to write a *concurrence* or *dissent.* All opinions and any concurrences and dissents are published in the *Appellate Division Reports.*

B. The Appellate Term

The Appellate Term only exists if the Appellate Division in a Judicial Department creates it. Currently, the first and second departments each have an Appellate Term. This court will hear appeals that challenge both the facts found and the law applied in trials to the lower courts such as the district court, city courts, town and village courts, etc. Selected decisions are published in the *Miscellaneous Reports.*

III. The Court of Appeals

New York's court of last resort is located at Court of Appeals Hall in Albany. It consists of a chief judge and six associate judges, all of whom are appointed by the governor and ratified by the Senate. Like the appellate division, the members of the panel rotate writing the majority opinion for each case they hear. These opinions, along with any concurrences and dissents, are published in the *New York Reports.*

The majority of cases heard by the Court of Appeals are appeals from the Appellate Division. These appeals are based solely upon the law determined by the Appellate Division.

Note: Murder cases involving the death penalty that are tried in the trial court may be appealed directly to the Court of Appeals. Because New York permits the parties at least one opportunity to appeal both the facts and the law applied, the Court of Appeals will review both types of challenges in these cases.

The Rhode Island Court System

Rhode Island is a two-level system for the types of civil cases we are addressing in this text: a trial court level and one appellate court level.

I. The Trial Court

The trial court level consists of the Superior Court, the Family Court, and the District Court. In addition, there is a workers' compensation court and an administrative adjudication court. The judges in the Superior Court are called justices. This text will address civil cases filed and decided in the Superior Court.

II. The Supreme Court

Parties who wish to challenge a trial court's decision may appeal to Rhode Island's Supreme Court. It consists of four associate justices and a chief justice. All of the justices sit at one time to hear and decide a case. They rotate writing the majority decision (called an *opinion*) for each case. The other members of the court may write a *concurrence* or *dissent* which will also be published. All decisions, including concurrences and dissents, are published in the *Rhode Island Reports.* The court itself is located at the Frank Licht Judicial Complex, 250 Benefit St., in Providence.

3 The Prelitigation Stage: Determining Causes of Action

Terminology

Tort	Tortfeaser	Negligence
Claims Adjuster	Judgment Proof	Clients' Funds
Intake Sheet	Prelitigation Stage	Breach
Intentional Tort	Personal Injury	Retainer Letter
Notice Requirement	Sovereign Immunity	Contingency Fee
Cause of Action	Liability	

Introduction

Welcome to the **prelitigation stage.** This is the time period between the date of the incident that created the dispute and the date the lawsuit begins. In this chapter, we will address various **causes of action,** investigating a case, and settlement discussions. Chapters 4 and 5 will address how to begin a lawsuit by drafting a *complaint,* filing it in court, and serving a Defendant.

As you enter the legal profession and begin meeting clients, keep the following in mind: People go to lawyers because they need help. It's only the degree of help that varies. At one end of the spectrum, a client may seek help buying or selling a home. In many situations, residential real estate closings are quick and involve little if any argument. Everybody leaves the law office relatively happy. On the other end, you may have a client who became a quadriplegic while a passenger in a compact car that faced a head-on collision with a tractor trailer. Obviously, the stakes are much higher in these types of cases and emotions run high.

I. Causes of Action, Liability, and Damages

A Plaintiff must have a **cause of action** against a Defendant in order to win a lawsuit. Causes of action are legally recognized situations (disputes) that may be resolved in court. They may be found in each state's statutes and in its case law. In civil cases, most causes of action involve *torts* and contract disputes, which are described below.

At trial, a Plaintiff must prove the Defendant's **liability** for one or more specific causes of action that are detailed in the Plaintiff's Complaint. (See Chapter 4.) In addition, the Plaintiff must prove the amount of **damages** he or she should receive from the Defendant as a result of that liability. **Caution:** When interviewing clients be sure to keep in mind that it is possible to have 100 percent liability and no damages. In these situations, a trier of fact will be compelled to find in favor of the Defendant.

II. Torts Generally

Torts are injuries or wrongs suffered by a Plaintiff's person, property, rights, or economic relationships with others. Individuals who commit torts are called **tortfeasers.**

Tort cases are based on the principle of fairness: Individuals harmed by torts should be compensated for their damages by tortfeasers. In addition, tort cases act as a deterrent by causing most people to behave carefully in order to reduce their chances of being sued.

III. Types of Torts

Generally speaking, there are two common types of torts cases: those involving unintentional torts and those involving intentional torts.

A. Unintentional Torts: Negligence

Negligence cases presume a Defendant did not intend to harm a Plaintiff. Instead, the harmful act was accidental. Often, negligence is described as the failure to act as a reasonable, prudent, and careful person would under the same (or similar) circumstances.

Negligence cases are the most common type of civil cases found in a courthouse. Most often they involve situations in which a Plaintiff is physically injured during an automobile accident or from falling on a patch of ice on a sidewalk or down a cluttered stairway.

For example: John Doe drove his car through a red light at an intersection and smashed into a car driven by Jane Smith. During the collision, Jane broke her leg in two places and a piece of glass from the windshield cut her cheek, causing a three-inch scar. Jane sued John for these **personal injuries** she suffered as a result of the collision. At trial, in order to prevail, Jane needs to prove the following:

1. that John owed her a duty to operate his car in a safe and reasonable manner; and
2. that John negligently operated his car (i.e., he operated his car in an unsafe and unreasonable manner); and
3. that John breached his duty, and as a result of that breach (known as proximate cause), she was harmed and suffered damages; and
4. the amount of damages she suffered. (**Note:** In most states, Plaintiffs are not permitted to ask for a specific sum. They can, however, provide a formula to assist the trier of fact in determining the amount.)

In addition, there are other types of more complex cases that often allege negligence as a cause of action. They include:

1. product liability
2. medical malpractice
3. legal malpractice
4. architectural malpractice

B. Intentional Torts

Many **intentional torts** are difficult to prove. In essence, the Plaintiff is accusing the Defendant of purposely causing the Plaintiff harm. Some examples include:

1. assault
2. battery
3. intentional infliction of emotional distress
4. tortious interference with business relations
5. libel
6. slander
7. defamation of character

Again, keep in mind that the Plaintiff must prove liability and damages.

IV. Breach of Contract Cases

Breach of contract cases often involve some type of business deal. In general terms, a contract is an agreement between two or more parties. It can be in writing or oral. Under the terms of this agreement, both parties should benefit in some way.

A breach of contract occurs when one party does not follow through with his or her part of the agreement and the other party is harmed. This harm is usually financial.

Like tort cases, breach of contract actions are based on fairness and compensation for damages. In our society, it is imperative that parties be able to rely upon each other's promises. Otherwise, we would be in a state of chaos.

V. Sovereign Immunity

Many states, their agencies and employees, as well as cities, towns, and boroughs are protected from being sued by **sovereign immunity.** This means that government entities may not be sued by any Plaintiff unless they consent to a lawsuit pursuant to a specific statute, or some other designated department or office authorizes such a suit. Those that consent to being sued usually have some type of **notice requirement** that Plaintiffs must comply with.

Sending notice of a pending suit entails sending a letter to the government entity that identifies the Plaintiffs, the cause of action, and the date and location of the incident at issue. In most cases, the deadline for meeting this notice requirement is much shorter than the statute of limitations. As a result, Plaintiffs who delay contacting an attorney may miss the deadline and their case may be eventually thrown out of court. Be sure to consult the applicable state statutes for specific details if you handle any cases against a municipality. In most instances, missing the notice deadline is equivalent to missing the statute of limitations.

VI. Medical Malpractice Claims: Good Faith Certificate

Some states require Plaintiffs who wish to bring a medical malpractice action, in tort or contract, to produce a **certificate of good faith** or other type of offer of proof. The purpose of this certificate or offer of proof is to require the Plaintiff to make a reasonable inquiry, before bringing suit, to determine if there are grounds for a good faith belief that the doctor or other health care provider had been negligent in caring for or treating the Plaintiff.

VII. Different Types of Law Firms

Parties involved in civil disputes often attempt to settle their matters without hiring an attorney. This makes sense. After all, attorneys cost money and it could take years before the court assigned the case for trial. Nevertheless, if the parties' efforts to settle fail, the Plaintiff will have no choice but to sue.

Many firms specialize in the types of cases they handle. For instance, some firms practice only Plaintiff's personal injury law. They do not represent insurance companies, nor do they handle breach of contract cases, real estate, criminal, or family cases.

Other firms devote themselves to personal injury defense. In fact, it is quite common for insurance companies to hire specific attorneys or firms to represent them exclusively. Finally, there are firms that bring and defend personal injury cases as well as practice other areas of the law.

Many potential clients prefer to shop around for an attorney before hiring anyone in particular. Some firms provide free consultations. Others charge a fee for this time, regardless of whether the client hires the firm. Remember, practicing law is a business as well as a service. Time is valuable.

It is not uncommon to find complete strangers calling your firm expecting free legal advice over the telephone. Don't give it. You don't know the entire story and you don't want to be blamed later for providing someone with faulty advice. Nor do you have time to listen to their entire situation. Don't worry, you're not being rude. Depending upon your location in the telephone book, you can bet that the caller has already called, or will call, at least half a dozen other firms seeking the same advice.

VIII. Reasons Attorneys Decline Cases

A law firm may have many reasons to decline a case. For instance:

1. The potential client may not have sufficient financial resources to hire the firm and properly pursue the case.
2. The cost of litigating the case may outweigh the results. For instance, the Defendant may be **judgment proof:** He or she may not have insurance to cover the incident or may have filed bankruptcy or may not have sufficient assets to pay a judgment. Therefore, even if the Plaintiff wins the case, there won't be any damages to collect.
3. The case may be too time-consuming for the firm.
4. The firm may lack expertise in the area and prefer to do other types of cases.
5. There may be personality clashes with the client. Some clients can be extremely difficult to deal with and unreasonable in their expectations. In those situations, it's often better not to accept the case.
6. The attorney may decide not to risk a legal malpractice suit because the statute of limitations will expire before the attorney can realistically and properly prepare the case for suit.
7. There is a conflict of interest or a potential conflict of interest because the attorney or the law firm currently represents or previously represented the opposing party.

The list goes on and on.

IX. Agreements for Representation

A. Written Agreements

Once a party decides to hire a law firm and the attorney agrees to take the case, the party will become a client and will need to sign an agreement with the firm. This agreement is often called an **agreement for representation.** (It may also be called a retainer letter.) In most situations, this agreement should be obtained before an attorney begins working on the case. Most firms already have a standard agreement form. It states the name of the client, the type of case at issue, and the applicable legal fee arrangements. In many states, attorneys who file suit against their clients for nonpayment of legal fees will lose if they do not have a written agreement.

B. Plaintiffs and Contingency Fee Cases

Attorneys who handle Plaintiff's personal injury claims and debt collection cases do not usually require any payment from their clients until the case ends. Instead, the attorneys work on a **contingency** basis.

Under a contingency agreement, in many cases, the Plaintiff's attorney's fees will be no more than one-third of the entire amount of damages paid by the Defendant. In addition, the Plaintiff will be required to pay all the costs incurred during the lawsuit, such as the court entry fee, sheriff's or constable's fees, witness fees, report fees, etc. If there is no settlement and the Defendant wins at trial, the Plaintiff will not owe his or her attorney any legal fees. Note, however, that these Plaintiffs are still responsible for the above-mentioned costs.

C. Defendants: Insurance Company Attorneys

Most Defendants in negligence cases are covered by auto or homeowners' insurance. As a result, any payments for damages are usually paid by their insurance companies who hire attorneys to represent them.

Insurance companies have claim departments to address potential and actual lawsuits against the people they insure. Individuals who work in these departments are called **claims adjusters.** Their responsibilities include determining how much a case is worth and negotiating a settlement on behalf of the insurance company and its insureds.

Presume for a moment that a case falls within the two-year statute of limitations for negligence cases and the Plaintiff retains an attorney a week after the accident. That attorney and the insurance company's claims adjuster will probably spend the next year attempting to settle the case. If settlement attempts fail, the Plaintiff's attorney will then file suit before the statute of limitations expires. Once the lawsuit starts, the insurance company must hire its own attorney to represent its interests, including its insured, in court.

D. Other Types of Cases

If the attorney does not take the case on a contingency basis and does not typically represent an insurance company, he or she will usually require the client (either a Plaintiff or a Defendant) to pay a **retainer** before he or she begins work on the case.

A retainer is an advance payment for legal fees. It may range anywhere from a few hundred dollars to several thousand dollars. It is placed in the attorney's **clients' funds** bank account and is drawn on when work is performed on the file.

Retainers ensure that attorneys will be paid for their work and expenses, regardless of the outcome of a case. In addition, they demonstrate how much clients are committed to proving their claims or defending themselves in court. People have no trouble fighting for their rights or defending themselves, as long as little or no money is involved. Once money is required, they tend to reevaluate and reprioritize.

X. Obtaining Information and Diarying

When reviewing new files or meeting clients to discuss their cases, determine the following information:

1. Identify the parties: Who is the Plaintiff and who is the Defendant?
2. Determine the cause of action: tort, contract, etc.
3. Has legal action started, and if not, what is the applicable statute of limitations? Is there a notice requirement for a government Defendant?
4. If the client is the Plaintiff, what are his or her damages? If the client is the Defendant, what is the maximum exposure he or she faces? In other words, what is the worst-case scenario?

A. The Intake Sheet

Most firms have an **intake sheet** they use to list the above-stated information. This intake sheet is usually kept in the client's file and the information is often entered into the firm's computer system.

An intake sheet for a personal injury case will probably request the following information:

1. The client's complete name, address, and telephone numbers where he or she can be reached;
2. Whether the client is the Plaintiff or the Defendant;
3. The date of the incident in dispute;
4. Next of kin;

5. Emergency contact numbers;
6. Social security number;
7. Client's version of how the accident occurred:
    a. description of the accident;
    b. the client's role: a driver or passenger in a motor vehicle;
    c. location of the accident;
    d. name and address of the opposing party, if known;
    e. what the client remembers happened immediately prior to the accident or incident;
8. Other people involved in the accident: driver or passengers in Plaintiff's car and in Defendant's car;
9. Witnesses on behalf of both parties;
10. Client's health issues prior to the accident;
11. Injuries sustained from the accident: scars, broken bones, sprains, strains, etc.
12. List of all hospitals, clinics, doctors, chiropractors, and therapists involved in treating the client before the accident for any reason;
13. List of all hospitals, clinics, doctors, chiropractors, and therapists involved in treating the client's injuries caused by the accident;
14. Amount of wages, if any, the client lost as a result of the accident;
15. Any impairment to the client's earning capacity as a result of the accident;
16. Amount and type of property damage to the vehicle the Plaintiff was in;
17. Amount and type of property damage to the vehicle the Defendant was in;
18. Amount and type of other property damage caused during the accident, such as trees, guard rails, other vehicles, etc., and who caused the damage;
19. The make, model, and year of each vehicle involved and who owned them;
20. Plaintiff's auto insurance company's name and policy numbers;
21. Defendant's auto insurance company's name and policy numbers, if known;
22. If either insurance company was notified yet;
23. Client's motor vehicle driving history;
24. Client's history of any previous litigation;
25. Any other information the client has about the case.

B. Diarying

Every law firm should have a diary system. It usually consists of *at least two or more calendars* in the office that list important deadlines. These calendars are the regular type you can buy in any store. To diary, simply state the name of the case and the purpose of the date on the appropriate date on the calendar.

1. Calendars should be located in the following areas:

a. the attorney's desk calendar; and

b. the paralegal's desk calendar; and

c. a large master calendar that hangs in a visible place for everyone in the office to see; and

d. on a computer program for diarying, if available at the law firm.

2. Diarying the Statute of Limitations

a. Diary the actual deadline for the statute of limitations; and

b. Diary the one-year anniversary of the date of the accident or date the cause of action occurred, i.e., one year prior to the expiration of the statute of limitations.

In addition, Plaintiffs and some Defendants add the following:

c. Diary the date that falls six months before the statute of limitations expires; and

d. Diary the date that falls three months before the statute of limitations expires; and

e. Diary the date that falls one month before the statute of limitations expires.

This may seem excessive, but it's one of the best ways to avoid malpractice. As we move forward in this text, you will discover the other important dates to diary. Fortunately, they won't be as complicated and are usually limited to the attorney and office staff working on a particular file.

C. Who May Be a Party

1. Individuals and Entities

An individual over the age of eighteen can be a party. (See Jones v. City of Massachusetts on page 46 where the Plaintiff is a child.) In addition, parties can be corporations, partnerships, voluntary associations, municipalities, the State of Connecticut, etc. For Plaintiffs, this information is important to determine in order to contact the appropriate individual who has authority to discuss settlement and, if necessary, to sue.

2. Owners and Operators or Managers

In many personal injury cases involving a motor vehicle accident, the individual Defendant who drove the vehicle at the time of the accident may not own the motor vehicle involved in the accident. Note, however, that both the owner's and the operator's insurance will usually cover the operator's acts. Therefore, Plaintiffs must identify the owner as well as the operator and contact both insurance companies to make a claim, and sue, if necessary. (See *Martin v. Tyler*, et al., Complaint on page 55.)

The same holds true when a Plaintiff is injured falling on a piece of property. The manager of the property may differ from the owner, yet both insurance policies may cover the claim. As a result, be sure to identify and bring a claim against the owner, as well as any party who may lease, manage, or use the property.

XI. Investigation and Analysis

A. The Police Report

Once you have the preliminary information, take all necessary steps to obtain as much additional information about the opposing party and the cause of action as possible. If the police were called to the scene of the incident at issue, the police report will often provide useful information.

A police report involving a motor vehicle accident will often contain the following:

1. the parties' names, including the owners of the vehicles, if known;
2. addresses;
3. dates of birth;
4. operators' license numbers;
5. make, model, and year of each vehicle;
6. names of insurance companies and policy numbers;
7. if possible, a diagram of the accident;
8. the names and addresses of any witnesses and other people involved in the accident.

A copy of the police report may be obtained simply by calling the records department of the police station that responded to the incident. Someone there will make a copy for you to pick up or to mail to you. It usually doesn't cost more than a few dollars per report. It's faster if you pick up the report in person.

In most situations, once the Plaintiff's attorney has confirmed that the Defendant was insured at the time of the accident, he or she will want to contact the Defendant's insurance company and apprise it of the claim. The case will be assigned to a claims adjuster, if it hasn't been already, who has authority to discuss the matter.

If the Defendant was not insured, the Plaintiff may make a claim under the Uninsured Motorist Coverage portion of the Plaintiff's insurance policy. This portion enables Plaintiffs to collect damages under their policies and sue their insurance companies if their claim cannot be settled.

B. When There Is No Police Report

The parties will need the above-stated information in any personal injury case, with or without a police report. If no such report exists, a thorough investigation will definitely be needed.

C. Obtaining Other Information: The Plaintiff

During the Prelitigation Stage, the following actions should be taking place:

1. The Plaintiff client should be sending the attorney all bills relating to the accident.
2. The Plaintiff's attorney's office should prepare forms entitled "Authorization to Release Information" for the Plaintiff to sign. These forms permit the office to obtain the Plaintiff's medical and employment information.
3. The Plaintiff's attorney's office should be contacting the Plaintiff's physicians to obtain an opinion regarding the extent of the Plaintiff's injuries, the need for future treatment, permanent disability, if any, etc. Much of this information is sent to the claims adjuster in an effort to encourage settlement.
4. The Plaintiff's attorney's office should be contacting the Plaintiff's employers to obtain information regarding the Plaintiff's lost wages, etc., incurred due to the accident.
5. The opposing party and the accident must be investigated.
   - **a.** What do the witnesses say about the accident?
   - **b.** What does the opposing party say about the accident?
   - **c.** Was either party under the influence of alcohol or drugs at the time of the accident?
   - **d.** Did one of them fall asleep at the wheel?
   - **e.** Did either of them fail to wear prescription eyeglasses?
   - **f.** Was either one of them talking on a cellular phone?
   - **g.** Did either car's brakes give out?
   - **h.** What were the weather conditions at the time of the accident?
   - **i.** What were the driving conditions at the time of the accident?
   - **j.** Was the sun in either of the parties' eyes?
   - **k.** Obtain all of this information and identify any discrepancies.

XII. The Prelitigation File

Every firm has its own method of maintaining client files. To stay organized, many offices label various manila folders and place them all in a larger file.

A. Personal Injury Cases

In personal injury cases, these file labels often include but are not limited to:

1. Correspondence: all written communications regarding the file, including the retainer letter if it is not in a separate file;
2. Authorizations: signed by the client to obtain necessary information that is relevant to the case from third parties such as medical providers, employers, etc.
3. Medical reports and list of injuries client suffered and/or will continue to suffer;
4. Medical bills: with a summary sheet on top listing all of the bills and whether they have been paid;
5. Proof of lost wages and/or reduced earning capacity;
6. Police accident reports and any other reports regarding the incident such as accident reconstruction, etc.;
7. Legal billing and/or expenses incurred;
8. Witness information and other statements by client, opposing party, etc.;
9. Plaintiff's insurance information;
10. Defendant's insurance information;
11. Settlement negotiations, with notes describing conversations, offers, demands, etc.;
12. Attorney's notes;
13. Evidence;
14. If representing the Plaintiff, drafts of the potential Complaint.

B. Contract Cases and Others

Select all of the above that are applicable and add others, including a documents file containing *copies* of the contract, etc. In most circumstances the *original* documents are kept elsewhere for safekeeping. In the event of litigation, the original documents will be needed to obtain a judgment against the Defendant. **Do not lose the originals or give them to anyone!**

XIII. Settlement Discussions

A. Analyzing the Information

Remember, there are always two or more sides to every story. Proper analysis requires the parties to determine their own strengths and weaknesses as well as those of their opponents. Don't overlook anything. Even the smallest detail could come back to haunt you when you least expect or want it to.

B. Settlement Discussions

The purpose of obtaining information and analyzing it is to enter into effective settlement negotiations. The more you know about the case, the more prepared you are to use your own persuasion tactics.

Do not rely on anyone when discussing settlement. If you represent the Plaintiff and you are down to six months before the statute of limitations will expire, I suggest starting litigation proceedings as described in Chapter 5. Remember, Defendants have everything to gain by convincing Plaintiffs to delay. They have their own diary system to remind them when the statute will expire. Statements like, "I'll see what I can do" or "We won't need to go to court on this one" will not stop the statute from running. Unless you receive a check for the Plaintiff from the Defendant and that check has cleared the bank, there is no settlement. Don't wait until the last minute and risk a legal malpractice suit. Start litigation no later than at the six-month mark. Sooner is even better.

XIV. Preparing to Bring Suit

A. Steps to Take

If your office represents the Plaintiff and you have been instructed to bring a lawsuit, I suggest you take the following steps:

1. Draft the Complaint, as described in Chapter 4;
2. Take steps to verify the Defendant's current home and business addresses;
3. Diary the deadline for the Complaint and all other necessary documents to be completed, as explained in future chapters;
4. Add the following individual files to the client's file:
   - **a.** Complaint and officer's Return of Service;
   - **b.** Defendant's appearance;
   - **c.** Defendant's pleadings;
   - **d.** Plaintiff's pleadings;
   - **e.** Plaintiff's discovery;

f. Defendant's discovery;
g. Court calendars;
h. Defendant's Answer and, if applicable, Special Defenses, Counterclaim;
i. Plaintiff's response to Defendant's Answer, Special Defenses, Counterclaim.

Each of these items will be discussed later in the text.

XV. Conclusion

The lists in this chapter are not exhaustive. Instead, they should be used as guidelines and adapted to fit the circumstances of each case.

As we move into litigation itself, you will note that I refer to the Plaintiff and the Defendant, instead of directing my comments to the reader. These titles are directed to the role of Plaintiffs' attorneys and their staff, and the role of Defendants' attorneys and their staff. They do not apply to pro ses or individual clients unless otherwise specified.

Key Issues in This Chapter

1. The Plaintiff must promptly identify all possible causes of action at issue in each case. Specific causes of action can be found in a state's statutes and case law.
2. Both parties should determine the *statute of limitations* for each cause of action in each case and *diary* these dates.
3. Both parties should obtain an *Agreement for Representation* from their clients prior to working on a case. Obtain a *retainer,* if appropriate.
4. Prior to suit, if time permits, both parties should obtain as much information about the case as possible in order to conduct appropriate settlement discussions.
5. Create a *prelitigation file* to keep information organized and expand the file if litigation is necessary.

4 The Prelitigation Stage: The Plaintiff's Complaint

Terminology

Complaint	Venue	Case Caption
Counts	Pleadings	Et Al.
Jurisdiction	Case Number	

Introduction

Once a Plaintiff decides to sue a Defendant, he or she must draft a **Complaint.** A Complaint is a printed document that is divided into numbered paragraphs that contain the facts which support the Plaintiff's cause of action against the Defendant.

A Complaint serves three purposes:

1. It notifies the Defendant that he or she is being sued by the Plaintiff;
2. It states the grounds for such a lawsuit; and
3. It is (usually) the first **pleading** filed in court in each lawsuit.

In many states, if the case goes to trial, the trier of fact will receive a copy of the Complaint when it begins deliberations.

When the Plaintiff finishes drafting the final version of the Complaint, he or she must then make arrangements to serve a copy of the Complaint to file the lawsuit in court and serve each Defendant named in the lawsuit. This process will be addressed in Chapter 5. For now, we will concentrate on the Complaint itself.

I. The Four Parts of a Complaint

I've divided the Complaint into four parts:

1. the case caption;
2. the body of the Complaint;
3. the relief requested;
4. the jury claim.

A. The Case Caption

As you can see from the sample Complaints found at the end of this chapter, the case caption is located at the top third of the first page of the Complaint. Though the style of a case caption may differ from state to state, typically it consists of the following:

1. the names of the Plaintiff(s) and the Defendant(s);
2. the type of court and location of the courthouse where the lawsuit is filed; and
3. the title of the document.

1. The Names of the Parties

The names of the parties are self-explanatory. The Plaintiff's name goes first. The Defendant's name is placed underneath. **Note:** Typically, if a Complaint is against more than one Defendant, the Complaint will state all the Defendants' names. Afterward, all other documents involved with the case will list only one Defendant's name, followed by the term **et al.** *Black's Law Dictionary* defines it as "and another."

2. Jurisdiction and Venue

The type of court and the location of a courthouse involve **jurisdiction** and selecting the proper **venue.**

a. Jurisdiction

Jurisdiction is a court's authority to decide a case and enforce a judgment. This concept is addressed in more detail in Chapter 8. For our purposes now, keep in mind that many states have more than one type of court that has jurisdiction over civil lawsuits, e.g., district court vs. superior court, etc. The differences may involve the amount of damages a Plaintiff is seeking, or the type of civil lawsuit being filed, or both. Therefore, a Plaintiff must be sure to select the proper court that is appropriate for his or her case. Otherwise, the case may be dismissed or transferred, or the Plaintiff may obtain an inadequate or worthless judgment.

For example, many states have a specific court to address landlord and tenant matters or land and zoning disputes. Likewise, divorces and custody cases are usually handled separately in a family court. As a result, a family court judge has no jurisdiction to handle a personal injury lawsuit or a landlord and tenant case, and vice versa. Any judgment would be worthless because it could not be enforced.

b. Venue

Venue involves the proper location of the courthouse where a lawsuit may be filed. Selecting the proper venue requires selecting the proper county within a state to file a lawsuit.

For instance, if an automobile accident occurred in Mercer County, New Jersey and all the Plaintiffs and all the Defendants involved in the accident resided in Mercer County, the proper venue to file the lawsuit is in Mercer County, not Hunterdon County or Bergen County because neither of them have any relationship to the accident or to the parties. If this lawsuit was filed in Hunterdon or Bergen County, the Defendant could attempt to have the case dismissed for improper venue.

All states have statutes that address venue. In general, our five states agree that as long as one or both of the parties lives in the state, the Plaintiff may file the lawsuit where either of them lives in the state. It's the Plaintiff's choice.

At times, a party (usually a Defendant) may attempt to change the venue where a case is filed because he or she believes there has been too much publicity over the incident at issue in that county. As a result, he or she will claim that it is impossible to select an impartial jury and to have a fair trial. This situation arises more frequently in criminal cases that receive significant media coverage than in civil cases. If the court agrees with the party, the case will be transferred to another venue within the state.

Last, some counties (or in Connecticut, judicial districts) have more than one courthouse location that has jurisdiction over a civil lawsuit. In most states, the Plaintiff is permitted to select the location he or she prefers.

3. A Case Number

At the time a Complaint is filed in court, the clerk will assign it a **case number.** This number is called a *docket number, index number, civil action number,* etc., depending upon the state. It will be used to identify the case and will be entered into the courthouse's computer system. Therefore, be sure to leave space in the case caption for the clerk to fill in it. **Note:** This number must be placed on all future documents filed in court.

4. Title of the Document

The title, "Complaint," should appear in the case caption or directly above the body of the document.

B. The Body of the Complaint

The body of a Complaint contains the allegations the Plaintiff claims against the Defendant.

1. Content

The body of the Complaint sets forth the allegations (the Plaintiff's version of the facts) that lead up to the cause of action a Plaintiff claims against a Defendant. Each allegation should be listed separately in paragraph form in a concise statement and numbered consecutively.

My first offer of advice here is not to reinvent the wheel. Your time is precious. If your law firm handles a lot of litigation, there's a good chance it has a similar type of Complaint that recites the cause of action you are working on already in a forms file in the computer system, or in another case file. All you have to do is change the case caption and insert the specific facts of your case.

In addition, check the numerous forms books that are available in law libraries. In most instances, you will find at least one example of the type of cause of action you are working on. I personally try to find as many different versions as possible and compare them, borrowing certain parts from one and combining and deleting from others.

If you can't find what you are looking for, don't just sit there wracking your brain and feeling incompetent. Take a deep breath and give it your best shot. Remember what I said earlier: Nothing in life prepares you to excel in the legal profession. It's a matter of trial and error, patience and experience.

2. Counts of a Complaint

A **count** is used to separate a Complaint into parts. For instance, a Complaint that involves more than one cause of action should contain a count for each cause of action. A Complaint that involves more than one Plaintiff or Defendant should contain a count for each of them.

The Martin Complaint (Rhode Island) found at the end of this chapter provides an example of a Complaint that alleges two separate causes of action. As you can see, the counts are easily separated by the words, "count one" and "count two." In addition, it demonstrates a Complaint against multiple Defendants.

The same format applies when there are two Plaintiffs, for example, when the Plaintiffs are the driver and a passenger in the Plaintiffs' car. Both were seriously injured in the crash they claim was caused by the Defendant who was operating his own car. Each Plaintiff has a different role in the accident: driver and passenger. In addition, each Plaintiff suffered different injuries. Therefore, the first count of the Complaint should focus on the Plaintiff driver's role and injuries. The second count should focus on the Plaintiff passenger's role and injuries. Much of the remaining part of each count will include the same information such as the time and place of the accident and the same alleged negligent conduct role of the Defendant.

C. The Relief Requested

The type of damages a Plaintiff hopes to recover in a lawsuit is found at the end of the Complaint or after each count. Typically, it begins with the word, "Wherefore ..." and includes money damages, though no specific amount is stated, and possibly interest and attorney's fees.

D. The Jury Claim

As you can see from the sample Complaints at the end of this chapter, Plaintiffs filing New Jersey, Massachusetts, and Rhode Island lawsuits should indicate at the end of the Complaint, or after each count, that they want a jury trial. In addition, they may include this information in the case caption under the title of the document. See the state summaries in Chapter 19 for additional information.

II. The Format of a Complaint and Signature

The Complaint should be should be typed or computer printed, double spaced, on one side of 8.5" x 11" white paper, with no less than a 1" margin on the left side. The name of the law firm and its address and telephone number must appear on either the first or last page. Many firms have preprinted pleading paper that includes this information and provides red lines for margins. Furthermore, their computer systems are already programmed to address the margins and other requirements.

The last requirement involves signing the Complaint. An individual attorney should place his or her signature at the end of the Complaint and all other papers filed in court. Underneath the signature, the attorney's name should be typed or printed. This signature acts to verify that the attorney has read the paper and that its contents are true to the best of his or her knowledge. Most states have a cause of action that permits parties to bring suit against someone who files a frivolous lawsuit against them. If they win, the damages can be quite substantial and include attorney's fees.

III. Verified Complaints

A verified complaint is a Complaint, as described above. The only difference is that the individual party, i.e., the (Plaintiff) client, signs the Complaint and swears that the allegations stated therein are true. The signature of the Plaintiff's attorney is usually placed below the client's signature.

Verified complaints are not common. Each state has specific rules dictating when a verified complaint may be required.

IV. Conclusion

A. Key Issues in This Chapter

1. The Complaint is the first pleading filed in court in each lawsuit.
2. The Complaint contains three parts:

   a. the case caption
   b. the body
   c. the relief requested.
3. Be sure to select a court that has jurisdiction over your case and determine the proper venue.
4. Be sure to comply with the format the applicable state requires for Complaints and all other papers filed in court.
5. An individual attorney must sign the Complaint and all other papers filed in court as verification that he or she has read the paper and that its contents are true to the best of his or her knowledge.

B. Examples of Complaints

The list below and the following pages present example Complaints and comments pertaining to lawsuits that will be referred to throughout the remainder of this text.

1. ***Donahue vs. Andrew:*** A Connecticut Complaint used for a negligence action involving a two-car accident with one Plaintiff and one Defendant.
2. ***Jones vs. City in Massachusetts:*** A Massachusetts Complaint used for a negligence action against a city in Massachusetts that provided special education classes to the Plaintiff child. During a seizure in the classroom, the Plaintiff fell against a hot radiator and was burned.
3. ***Birch Realty Co. vs. Safety Ins. Co.:*** A New Jersey Complaint against a Defendant insurance company that refused to pay the proceeds of a fire insurance policy to the Plaintiff because it suspects the Plaintiff cased the fire through arson.
4. ***Wilkenson vs. Ryan:*** A New York Complaint that alleges a negligence action involving a slip and fall that took place on the Defendant's property.
5. ***Martin vs. Tyler, et al.:*** A Rhode Island Complaint used for a negligence action involving a two-car accident with one Plaintiff and three Defendants.

STATE SUMMARIES

Don't forget that all complaints as well as all other pleadings, motions, objections, memorandums of law, etc. that are filed in court should be double-spaced and typed on one side only. The format used in the examples in this text is necessary in order to conserve space.

A CONNECTICUT COMPLAINT

I. The Case Caption: Pbs 4-1

The case caption appears at the top third of the first page of the Complaint. It contains the following:

1. the return date;
2. the parties' names and title of the court;
3. the location of the court where the Complaint will be filed; and
4. the date of the Complaint.

A. The Return Date: C.G.S. sec. 52-48(a) and (b)

Connecticut is the only state addressed in this text that uses a return date. The return date is located above the Plaintiff's name at the top left corner. Note that this May 28, 1998 return date is approximately three weeks after the May 1, 1998 date that is the date of the document. (I know this sounds confusing. Just bear with me.) It acts as an anchor date for future events to take place. These future events include the following:

1. the deadline by which all Defendants in a case must be served a copy of the Complaint;
2. the deadline by which the Plaintiff must file the Complaint in court; and
3. the deadline by which the Defendant must file his or her *Appearance* in the case in court. (The other states do not have this requirement.)

Each of these events will be discussed in detail in future chapters. For now, keep in mind the following:

1. All Complaints must contain a return date.
2. All return dates in civil cases (other than Summary Process cases) must be ***Tuesdays.***
3. When drafting a case caption for a Complaint, a Plaintiff must select a Tuesday return date that is approximately three weeks and not more than two months in the future, from the date of the Complaint.

Last, note that the return date will be replaced with a *docket number* by the clerk when the case is filed in court.

B. The Parties' Names

The Plaintiff's name goes first, under the return date. Place the Defendant's name a few lines below. Also include the title, "Superior Court," on the other side of the page.

C. Venue and Location of the Court: C.G.S. sec. 51-345

As stated in Chapter 2, Connecticut consists of 12 (soon to be 13) Judicial Districts. Each has its own clerk's office in the courthouse where lawsuits are filed.

Most of the JDs have only one superior house location. Four, however, have two locations.

When choosing the proper venue to file a case, concentrate on the applicable JD. Most Plaintiffs have a choice between the JD where they live or the JD where the Defendant lives. The location within that JD is also the Plaintiff's choice. The name of the proper JD, followed by the name of the town or city where the courthouse is located, should be stated in the case caption.

D. Date of Complaint

The date of the Complaint should be the date it is ready to be served to the Defendant. It should be approximately three weeks before the return date. (**Note:** As you will learn in Chapter 5, Defendants in Connecticut are served before the Complaint is filed in court. In the other states, the Defendant is served after the Complaint is filed in court.)

II. The Body of the Complaint: Pbs 10-20

Under the case caption, center the name of the document. The body of the Complaint follows. Divided into paragraphs, it consists of the names of the parties, the date of the incident at issue, and the allegations that establish the Plaintiff's cause of action against the Defendant.

III. The Relief Requested: Pbs 10-20 and C.G.S. sec. 52-91

In Connecticut, the **Wherefore page** and the **Statement of Amount in Demand page** address the relief requested.

Note the following:

1. At minimum, the Wherefore page requests money damages and "such other just relief as this Court deems fair, just, and equitable."
2. Both the Wherefore page and the Statement of Amount in Demand page should appear on separate sheets of paper after the body of the Complaint.
3. The Statement of Amount in Demand requires a case caption at the top of the page.
4. Neither the Wherefore page nor the Statement of Amount in Demand should state a specific sum the Plaintiff seeks.
5. Pursuant to C.G.S. sec. 52-91, the Statement of Amount in Demand must include one of the following:
    a. The amount, legal interest, or property in demand is fifteen thousand dollars or more, exclusive of interest and costs; or
    b. The amount, legal interest, or property in demand is two thousand five hundred dollars or more, but is less than fifteen thousand dollars, exclusive of interest and costs; or
    c. The amount, legal interest, or property in demand is less than two thousand five hundred dollars, exclusive of interest and costs. (Usually, these cases are filed in small claims division of the superior court.)

IV. Attorney's Signature: Pbs 4-2

Both the Wherefore page and the Statement of Amount in Demand page should include the signature of the Plaintiff' attorney and the law firm's name, addresses, telephone number, and **juris number.** The juris number is a number attorneys (and law firms) are assigned by the state of Connecticut after they pass the bar exam and are admitted to practice. Only one such number is required. In most instances, the law firm's number is used unless the attorney is a solo practitioner.

V. The Jury Demand: Pbs 14-10

Connecticut does not requires the Plaintiff to indicate if he or she wants a jury trial at this time. The decision is made later when the *pleadings are closed.* See Chapter 19.

Example 4-1. Connecticut, Personal Injury, Motor Vehicle, One Plaintiff, One Defendant

RETURN DATE: MAY 26, 1998	:	SUPERIOR COURT
SARAH A. DONAHUE	:	JUDICIAL DISTRICT
	:	OF TOLLAND
VS.	:	AT ROCKVILLE
RICHARD P. ANDREW	:	MAY 1, 1998

COMPLAINT

(1) On September 13, 1996, at approximately 8:15 a.m., the Plaintiff, Sarah A. Donahue, was traveling in her automobile in a westerly direction along Manor Avenue, a public highway in Vernon, Connecticut, near its intersection with Wolcott Street, and stopped in preparation for making a right-hand turn onto said Wolcott Street.

(2) At said time and place, the Defendant, Richard P. Andrew was operating his automobile in a westerly direction along said Manor Avenue when suddenly and without warning, he collided his automobile into the rear of the Plaintiff's automobile, causing her to suffer serious injuries and losses that are set forth below.

(3) The Defendant was negligent and careless in one or more of the following ways:

(a) In that he failed to keep a reasonable and proper lookout and pay attention to where he was going;

(b) In that he operated said automobile at a greater rate of speed than the circumstances warranted;

(c) In that he failed to sound his horn to give timely warning, or any warning whatsoever, of the impending collision;

(d) In that he operated said automobile with defective or inadequate brakes or failed to apply his brakes in time to avoid said collision;

(e) In that he failed to keep and operate said automobile under proper control;

(f) In that he failed to turn said automobile to the left or to the right to avoid said collision;

(g) In that he violated Connecticut General Statutes Sections 14-219 and 14-222 by operating said automobile without regard to the width, traffic and use of the highway, the intersection of streets and the weather conditions;

(h) In that he violated Connecticut General Statutes Section 14-218a. by operating said automobile at a rate of speed greater than was reasonable, without having regard to the width, traffic and use of the highway, the intersection of streets and the weather conditions;

(i) In that he violated Connecticut General Statutes Section 14-240 by following the Plaintiff's automobile too closely.

(4) As a direct and proximate result of the aforesaid negligence and carelessness of the Defendant, the Plaintiff suffered a cervical strain and damage to her lower back, spine, neck, chest, shoulders, right leg, right knee, right ankle and both feet, together with aggravation of preexisting fibromyalgia. In addition, the Plaintiff suffered headaches and a severe shock to her entire nervous system. From all of the aforesaid injuries, or effects thereof, the Plaintiff has suffered and will continue to suffer pain, mental anguish, and nervousness, some of which injuries or effects thereof are, or are likely to be, permanent.

(5) As a further result of the Defendant's negligence and carelessness, as aforesaid, the Plaintiff has lost wages and her earning capacity has been impaired.

(6) As a further result of the Defendant's negligence and carelessness, as aforesaid, the Plaintiff has incurred expenses for ambulance, hospital care, medical care, x-rays and physical therapy, and it will be necessary for her to incur additional expense for such items in the future.
(7) As a further result of the Defendant's negligence and carelessness, as aforesaid, the Plaintiff's ability to enjoy life's offering has been impaired, and will continue to be impaired.

(Separate Sheet)

WHEREFORE, the Plaintiff claims:

(1) Money damages,
(2) Such other relief as the Court deems fair, just and equitable.

THE PLAINTIFF
SARAH A. DONAHUE

BY ______________________

Christine Kulas, Esq.
Law Offices of Christine Kulas,
her attorney
P.O. Box 2005
Ellington, CT 06066
Tele. #(860) 222-2222
Juris # 989898

(Separate Sheet)

SARAH A. DONAHUE	:	JUDICIAL DISTRICT
	:	OF TOLLAND
VS.	:	AT ROCKVILLE
RICHARD P. ANDREW	:	MAY 1, 1998

STATEMENT OF AMOUNT IN DEMAND

The amount, legal interest or property in demand is FIFTEEN THOUSAND DOLLARS or more, exclusive of interest and costs.

THE PLAINTIFF
SARAH A. DONAHUE

BY ______________________

Christine Kulas, Esq.
Law Offices of Christine Kulas,
Her attorney
P.O. Box 2005
Ellington, CT 06066
Tele. #(860) 222-2222
Juris # 989898

A Massachusetts Complaint

I. The Case Caption

The case caption appears in the top third of the first page of the Complaint. It contains the following:

1. the state and division of the court;
2. the county where the case is filed;
3. title of Court;
4. space for the civil action number;
5. the parties' names and designation; and
6. the title of the document and jury claim.

A. The State and Division of the Court

Both "Commonwealth of Massachusetts" and "Trial Court Division" should be centered at the top of the first page of the Complaint.

B. Venue: The County of the Courthouse: Massachusetts General Law, Chapter 233 sec. 1

Massachusetts has numerous superior court locations. The Plaintiff may file a lawsuit in the following locations: where either the Plaintiff or Defendant lives, or where the Defendant has a usual place of business. State the name of the county that contains the courthouse where the lawsuit will be filed in the case caption.

C. Name of Court: See Rule 10

As stated in Chapter 2, civil lawsuits that are valued at $25,000 or under, tried to a judge rather than a jury, may be filed in the district court. Cases over $25,000 should be filed in the superior court. State the applicable court in the case caption.

D. The Case Number See Rule 10

The case number in Massachusetts is called a civil action number or docket number. Be sure to designate a place for it in the case caption.

E. The Parties' Names and Designations: See Rule 10

State the Plaintiff's name first, followed by the designation, Plaintiff. The Defendant's name goes below, followed by the designation, Defendant.

Note that the Plaintiff in the Massachusetts Complaint found on page 46, is a minor. These types of cases are designated as such by adding "by his father and next friend, George Jones, Sr." Every state requires this or a similar type of designation.

F. The Title of the Document and Jury Claim: See Rules 7a, 10, and 38

Type "COMPLAINT" and, if applicable, "CLAIM FOR JURY TRIAL."

II. The Body of the Complaint: See Rules 8 and 10

The body of the Complaint begins after the case caption. Divided into paragraphs, it consists of the names of the parties, the date of the incident at issue, and the allegations that establish the Plaintiff's cause of action against the Defendant.

III. Relief Requested: Rule 8

In Massachusetts, at the end of the body of the Complaint, the Plaintiff states that he or she demands judgment against the Defendant in a just and proper amount including general damages, medical and special damages, and the cost of the suit.

IV. The Jury Demand: Rule 38

In addition to being stated in the case caption, the Plaintiff should include a demand for a trial by jury at the end of the document, after the relief requested.

V. Signatures: Rule 11

The Plaintiff or his or her attorney must sign the end of the Complaint and include the address, telephone number, and BBO number. The BBO is the **Board of Bar Overseer's number** that attorneys are assigned once they pass the state's bar exam and are admitted to practice. Note that the Complaint is dated at the end of the document.

Example 4-2. Massachusetts, Personal Injury, a Child Plaintiff Who Is Injured at School

COMMONWEALTH OF MASSACHUSETTS
TRIAL COURT DIVISION

HAMPDEN, SS. SUPERIOR COURT
CIVIL ACTION NO.
(insert number if known)

GEORGE JONES, Jr.,)
by his father and next friend,)
GEORGE JONES, SR.,)
Plaintiff)
vs.)
) ***COMPLAINT AND CLAIM FOR JURY TRIAL***
CITY IN MASSACHUSETTS)
Defendant)
)

COUNT I

(1) The Plaintiff is GEORGE JONES, JR., at all times a minor child who brings this action by his father and next friend, GEORGE JONES, SR., all of whom reside at 67 Monroe Street, Springfield, Hampden County, Massachusetts.
(2) The Defendant, CITY IN MASSACHUSETTS, is at all times mentioned, a municipal corporation organized and existing under the laws of the Commonwealth of Massachusetts with executive offices located at 36 Court Square, Springfield, Hampden County, Massachusetts.
(3) At all times mentioned, the Plaintiff was a duly admitted pupil attending Little People School, a public school managed, operated and controlled by the Defendant.
(4) The Plaintiff gave written notice of the claimed referred to in this Complaint to the executive officer of the Defendant on May 19, 1996, within the statutory period required by law and received no response to the notice. The Plaintiff confirmed notice of said claim to the Defendant and attempted to arbitrate, settle or compromise the claim and received no response.
(5) On or about April 27, 1996, the Plaintiff was being supervised in a very small "special education room" by school employees at a school facility, operated, managed, maintained and controlled by the Defendant.
(6) While the Plaintiff was in said "special education room" he suffered a seizure episode and fell from a chair onto a hot, stand up, old, metal type radiator, and fell onto the floor.
(7) The radiator was dangerous and capable of inflicting serious injuries to students, including the Plaintiff as it was in close proximity to the area where the students were seated and lacked any adequate guard or safety shield.
(8) The teacher charged with supervision of the Plaintiff failed and neglected to warn the Plaintiff or take any precautions whatsoever to protect the Plaintiff from the foreseeable probability of contacting the radiator.
(9) At all relevant times, the Defendant was charged with the control, maintenance and supervision of students and facilities and committed the following negligent acts and/or omissions:

(a) it acted in such a manner as to proximately cause injury to the Plaintiff;
(b) it failed to provide adequate supervision of the school facility;
(c) it allowed the Plaintiff to be taught in a facility wholly inadequate;
(d) it permitted an exposed, hot, stand up, old metal type radiator to be approximately three feet from the Plaintiff, thereby creating a dangerous and unsafe condition;
(e) it failed to warn the Plaintiff of the unsafe condition;
(f) it allowed the Plaintiff to be taught in a "special education room" when it knew, or should have known of the dangerous condition;
(g) it failed to install appropriate protectors to the exposed radiator.

(10) As a proximate result of one or more of the above mentioned negligent acts or omissions of the Defendant, the Plaintiff was bodily injured and suffered great pain and suffering and will suffer in the future great discomfort and has suffered permanent scars on his chest and arm.

(11) As a result of the Defendant's actions, as aforesaid, the Plaintiff suffered injuries and was otherwise injured and suffered great pain of body and mind, and incurred expenses for medical attention and hospitalization.

WHEREFORE, the Plaintiff demands judgment against the Defendant in the amount he deems just and proper, including general damages, medical and special damages and the costs of this suit.

JURY DEMAND

The Plaintiff demands a trial by jury on all issues triable to a jury.

The Plaintiff,
GEORGE JONES, JR., ET AL.
By His Attorneys:

____

Ann Lambert, Esq.
Lambert and Smith, P.C.
529 Corporate Place
Agawam, MA 04540
Tele. #(413) 777-7777
BBO # 45454

Dated: ______________

A New Jersey Complaint

I. The Case Caption: Rule 1:4-1

The case caption appears at the top third of the first page of the Complaint. It contains the following:

1. identity of Plaintiff's attorney;
2. the parties' names and title of the court;
3. space for docket number;
4. civil action designation, title of document, and jury demand.

A. Identity of Plaintiff's Attorney: Rule 1:4-1(b)

At the top of the document, state the name of the Plaintiff's law firm and its address and telephone number.

B. The Parties' Names and Designations and Title of Court: Rule 1:4-1

State the Plaintiff's name first, followed by the designation, Plaintiff. The Defendant's name goes below, followed by the designation, Defendant.

Next to the parties' names, place the title of the court, Superior Court, Law Division, and the county where the lawsuit will be filed.

C. The Docket Number: Rule 4:100

As in Connecticut, the case number is called a docket number. Leave a space for it in the case caption.

D. Civil Action Designation, Title of Document and Jury Demand: Rule 1:4-1, 4:35-1

As stated in Chapter 2, New Jersey is divided into law divisions and chancery divisions. The types of cases we are addressing in this text will be filed in the Civil Law Division.

Under the civil action designation, place the title of the document and indicate that you want a jury trial.

II. The Body of the Complaint: Rule 1:4-2

Label each count. After filling in the various paragraphs, end each count with a Wherefore clause.

III. Signatures, the Date, and Jury Demand: Rules 1:4-5, 1:4-6, 4:35-1

The Plaintiff's attorney who drafted the Complaint must place his or her signature at the end of the document. In addition, designate a jury demand and provide another signature as well as the date of the document.

Example 4-3. New Jersey, Breach of Contract and Insurance, Failure to Pay Policy

MARSH & MARSH
2719 Bergen Street
Wayne, New Jersey 07470
(201) 696-9523
Attorney for Plaintiff

SUPERIOR COURT OF NEW JERSEY
LAW DIVISION: BERGEN COUNTY

Plaintiff	
BIRCH REALTY COMPANY	
vs.	DOCKET NO. (insert if known)
Defendant	
SAFETY INSURANCE CO.	Civil Action
	COMPLAINT AND JURY DEMAND

FIRST COUNT

Plaintiff, having offices at 2700 Main Street, Upper Saddle River, New Jersey, through its attorneys, Marsh & Marsh, says by way of Complaint against Defendant therein as follows:

(1) At all times relevant hereto Plaintiff was the owner of certain premises commonly known as 34 Lake Road, Newark, New Jersey, consisting of improved real estate ("Subject Premises") and Defendant was an insurance carrier license to provide coverage within the State of New Jersey.

(2) On October 1, 1997, Defendant wrote its policy #00000 insuring the Plaintiff in consideration of premiums to be paid, against loss, injury or damage to the Subject Premises by reason of fire or other casualty during the policy period October 1, 1997 to October 1, 1998 in the amount of $500,000.

(3) On January 15, 1998, within the said policy period, the building on the Subject Premises was totally consumed by fire.

(4) The actual cash value of the building thus destroyed was equal to the amount of coverage provided, to wit, $500,000.

(5) The Plaintiff has complied with all policy conditions precedent to the Defendant's objection to pay the said loss.

(6) Notwithstanding the foregoing, Defendant has failed, refused and neglected to pay the said loss.

WHEREFORE, the Plaintiff demand judgments against the Defendant in the amount of $500,000 together with interest from the date of loss until the date of payment, costs of Court and such other or further sums as Plaintiff's proofs may show it to be entitled.

SECOND COUNT

(1) Plaintiff repeats and restates all of the allegations contained in the First Count with as full force and effect as if set out at length.
(2) The said policy of insurance also provided Plaintiff coverage for loss of income from the Subject Premises resulting from casualty up to a maximum of $60,000.
(3) The Plaintiff has sustained loss of income from the subject premises in excess of said amount.
(4) The Plaintiff has complied with all policy conditions precedent to the Defendant's objection to pay said claim.
(5) Notwithstanding the foregoing, the Defendant has failed, refused and neglected to pay said claim or part thereof.

WHEREFORE, the Plaintiff demands judgment against the Defendant upon this Count of the Complaint in the amount of $60,000 together with interest and costs.

THIRD COUNT

(1) The Plaintiff repeats and restates all of the allegations contained in the First and Second Counts with as full force and effect as if set out at length.
(2) Said policy written by the Defendant provides, in addition to the coverages which are the subject of the First and Second Counts hereof, benefits to reimburse the Plaintiff for certain debris removal costs incurred as a result of a covered casualty.
(3) The Plaintiff incurred such costs as a result of the fire at the Subject Premises on January 15, 1998.
(4) The Plaintiff has complied with all policy conditions precedent to the Defendant's objection to pay said claim.
(5) Notwithstanding the foregoing, the Defendant has failed, refused and neglected to pay said claim or any part thereof.

WHEREFORE the Plaintiff demands judgment against the Defendant in the amount of $100,000 together with interest and costs.

MARSH & MARSH
Attorney for Plaintiff

Dated: ________________

By: ________________________
Robert A. Hathaway

JURY DEMAND

Plaintiff hereby demands a trial by jury as to all issues.

MARSH & MARSH
Attorney for Plaintiff

By: ________________________
Robert A. Hathaway

Dated: ________________

A New York Complaint

I. The Case Caption: CPLR 2101

The case caption appears at the top third of the first page of the Complaint. It contains the following:

1. Supreme Court and County designation;
2. the parties' names and title of the court;
3. designation and space for index number (the label for New York's docket or case number);
4. title of document: Complaint.

II. The Body of the Complaint: CPLR 3013, 3014

Note that New York uses an introductory sentence before setting forth the paragraphs: "Plaintiff, by its attorneys, (insert name of firm), complaining of the Defendant, alleges the following:" etc.

Label each count as follows: "AS AND FOR A FIRST CAUSE OF ACTION."

III. Demand for Relief: CPLR 3017(a)

Of the five states addressed in this text, it appears that New York is the only state that permits a Plaintiff in personal injury actions to state the exact amount of damages he or she is seeking from the Defendant. Note, however, that it is not mandatory to state an amount.

IV. Identifying Information: CPLR 2101(d)

At the end of the Complaint, the attorney will date it and include his or her name, address, and telephone number. It does not appear that a signature is required, but nor is it prohibited.

V. Jury Demands: CPLR 4102

As in Connecticut, a jury demand in New York is not necessary until later in the litigation process. See Chapter 19 for details.

Example 4-4. New York, Personal Injury, Fall Down

SUPREME COURT OF THE STATE OF NEW YORK
COUNTY OF NEW YORK

---X	Index No. (insert number if known.)
SHEILA WILKENSON, Plaintiff,	
-against-	COMPLAINT
RYAN KEEGAN Defendant.	
---X	

Plaintiff, by her attorneys, PETERS, McROY & SILVER, complaining of the Defendant, alleges the following:

AS AND FOR A FIRST CAUSE OF ACTION

(1) At all times hereinafter mentioned, Plaintiff was and still is a resident of Dublin, Ireland.
(2) At all times hereinafter mentioned and upon information and belief, Defendant, Ryan Keegan, was and still is a resident of the County, City and State of New York.
(3) At all times hereinafter mentioned and upon information and belief, Defendant owned, occupied and controlled the premises known as 43 East Center Street in the County, City and State of New York.
(4) Upon information and belief, in September 1995, Defendant purchased said 43 East Center Street in the County, City and State of New York and personally made several renovations to the house located on the premises in which he lived and continues to live. These renovations included adding a second story upstairs, complete with two bedrooms and a bathroom on that second story.
(5) Pursuant to Defendant's invitation, in May 1996, Plaintiff arrived from Ireland to New York with her two children to visit Defendant for one week at his home at said at 43 East Center Street.
(6) Plaintiff and her family arrived at Defendant's said home on May 20, 1996. That night, Plaintiff and her family were directed to sleep in the two upstairs bedrooms.
(7) During that first night, Plaintiff left the bedroom in an attempt to utilize the bathroom facilities.
(8) Plaintiff was unable to find and turn on the hall lights due to the switch being placed at an unusual position at the bottom of the stairwell.
(9) While Plaintiff attempted to open the bathroom door, which opened out into the hallway, she was compelled to step backward and fell down the stairway which was opposite the bathroom door.
(10) As a result of this fall, Plaintiff suffered serious injuries and was transported by ambulance to the hospital.

(11) Plaintiff's fall was caused by reason of the carelessness and negligence of Defendant and consisted of the following, among others:

(a) Defendant failed to construct the bathroom in accordance with applicable building codes and created a hazard for Plaintiff and others who he invited into his home to visit and to use said bathroom.

(b) Defendant failed to locate light switches in accordance with applicable building codes and created a hazard for Plaintiff and others who sought to use the light for the hallway.

(c) Defendant knew or should have known that the light switch in the hallway adjacent to the bathroom connected to a light found on the porch outside of the house and did not illuminate the upstairs.

(d) Defendant failed to warn Plaintiff of the above-mentioned hazards and failed to make and keep his property safe for persons, such as the Plaintiff, who he invited onto the property.

(12) As a result of the Defendant's negligence and carelessness, the Plaintiff suffered an epidermal hematoma, multiple skull fractures involving the left skull base, the right temporal bone, nerve deafness, a traumatic brain injury and numerous other injuries involving muscles, ligaments, nerves, torn tissues, bones, joints, and discs. All of the aforesaid injuries and the affects thereof are, or are likely to be, permanent in nature.

(13) As a further result of the Defendant's negligence and carelessness, as aforesaid, the Plaintiff incurred and will continue to incur expenses for medical care and attention, hospitalization, medication, x-rays, physical therapy, etc., all to her further financial loss.

(14) As a further result of the negligence and carelessness of the Defendant as aforesaid, the Plaintiff has lost time and wages from her employment and her earning capacity has been greatly impaired, all to her further financial loss.

(15) As a further result of the Defendant's negligence and carelessness as aforesaid, the Plaintiff has suffered great physical and mental pain and suffering.

WHEREFORE, the Plaintiff demands judgment against the Defendant in an amount to be determined at the time of trial of this action, together with the costs and disbursements of this action.

Dated: New York, New York

____

Yours, etc.,

ALAN F. PETERS, ESQ.
PETERS, McROY & SILVER
Attorneys for Plaintiff
2700 E. Broad Street
New York, NY 04540
Tele. #(212) 232-2323

A Rhode Island Complaint

I. The Case Caption: Rule 10(a)

The case caption appears at the top third of the first page of the Complaint. It contains the following:

1. the date of the Complaint;
2. the state and city courthouse location where the lawsuit will be filed;
3. the title of court;
4. the names of the parties;
5. space for the Civil Action Number (the docket or case number).

Most of the above is self-explanatory. Note that all civil cases we are discussing will be filed in the Superior Court. Rhode Island has four Superior Court locations throughout the state. In addition, as in Massachusetts, the case number is called a civil action number.

II. The Body of the Complaint and Relief Requested: Rule 10(b)

Center the title, "COMPLAINT" and "COUNT I," under the case caption. After filling in the various paragraphs, end each count with a Wherefore clause.

III. Identifying Information and Signatures: Rule 11

End the Complaint with a jury demand. In addition, include the attorney's signature, the **bar number** that is assigned to all attorneys who pass the Rhode Island bar exam and are admitted to practice, and the attorney's address. **Note:** I've seen the jury demand designation in the case caption in some cases.

IV. Jury Demand: Rule 38

Many Plaintiffs include their Jury Demand in their Complaint. Rule 38 also permits the jury demand to be made no later than ten days after the last pleading involving an issue to be tried to a jury is served. This may apply to Affirmative Defenses, Counterclaims, etc., in situations when the Plaintiff did not include a jury demand.

Example 4-5. Rhode Island, Motor Vehicle, One Plaintiff, Three Defendants

January 5, 1998	:	
STATE OF RHODE ISLAND	:	SUPERIOR COURT
PROVIDENCE, SC.	:	
	:	
JOHN MARTIN	:	
VS.	:	C.A. NO: (insert number if known)
	:	
	:	
JAMES TYLER,	:	
PETER SMITH and	:	
LUCY SMITH	:	

COMPLAINT
COUNT I

(1) Plaintiff, John Martin, is a resident of the City of Cranston, County of Providence, State of Rhode Island.
(2) Defendant, James Tyler, is a resident of the Town of Glocester, County of Providence, State of Rhode Island.
(3) Defendant, Peter Smith, is a resident of the City and County of Providence, State of Rhode Island.
(4) Defendant, Lucy Smith, is a resident of the City and County of Providence State of Rhode Island.
(5) That on August 20, 1996, Defendant, James Tyler, was the owner and operator of a motor vehicle being operated along and upon Route 10 South, a public highway, located in the City and County of Providence, State of Rhode Island.
(6) That on the same date, Plaintiff, John Martin, was riding as a passenger in the motor vehicle owned and operated by Defendant James Tyler.
(7) That on the same date, Defendant Lucy Smith, was the owner of a motor vehicle operated by her agent, servant or employee, Defendant Peter Smith, along and upon Route 10 south, a public highway, located in the City and County of Providence, State of Rhode Island.
(8) That on the same date, Defendant, Lucy Smith, by and through her agent, servant or employee, Defendant Peter Smith, negligently caused their motor vehicle to collide with the vehicle of Defendant, James Tyler in which the Plaintiff, John Martin was riding as a passenger.
(9) As a result whereof, Plaintiff, John Martin, sustained severe and permanent injuries and a shock to his nervous system; he suffered and will suffer great pain and agony for a long period of time; he was and will be unable to perform his usual work and affairs for a long period of time, thereby causing him to lose large sums of money; he was and will be obliged to receive medicines and medical treatment for a long period of time in an endeavor to cure or relieve said injuries and to expend large sums of money therefore; and the Plaintiff was otherwise greatly injured and damnified.

WHEREFORE, Plaintiff, John Martin, demands judgment against the Defendants in a monetary amount sufficient to establish the jurisdiction of the Superior Court.

COUNT II

(1) Paragraphs 1, 2, 3, 4, 5, 6 and 7 of Count I are hereby incorporated by reference into Count II with the same force and effect as if they were set forth in full.
(2) Defendant, James Tyler, negligently caused the motor vehicle he was operating to collide with Defendants Lucy Smith and Peter Smith's vehicle.
(3) As a result whereof, Plaintiff, John Martin, sustained severe and permanent injuries and a shock to his nervous system; he suffered and will suffer great pain and agony for a long period of time; he was and will be unable to perform his usual work and affairs for a long period of time thereby causing him to lose large sums of money; he was and will be obliged to receive medicines and medical treatment for a long period of time in an endeavor to cure or relieve said injuries and to expend large sums of money therefore; and the Plaintiff was otherwise greatly injured and damnified.

WHEREFORE, Plaintiff, John Martin, demands judgment against the Defendants in a monetary amount sufficient to establish the jurisdiction of the Superior Court.

THE PLAINTIFF
JOHN MARTIN,

PLAINTIFF HEREBY CLAIMS
A TRIAL BY JURY

By His Attorney,

____

CHARLENE M. MURPHY, ESQ.
Bar # 1111
MURPHY & SABLE
333 Landing Ave.
Providence, RI 02910
(401) 946-1111

5 The Prelitigation Stage: Commencing a Lawsuit

Terminology

Summons	Entry Fee	Process
Service	In Hand	Abode
Sheriff	Court Stamped Copy	Constable
Proper Officer	Proof of Service	Order of Notice
Foreign Corporation	Domestic Corporation	Agent for Service

Introduction

Commencing a lawsuit involves two steps: filing a Complaint and an **entry fee** in court and serving each Defendant in the lawsuit with a copy of the Complaint. In addition, each state includes other slightly different documents in the process. These differences are discussed below and in the state summaries at the end of this chapter.

I. When Does a Lawsuit Begin?

In Massachusetts, New Jersey, New York, and Rhode Island, a lawsuit begins and the statute of limitations stops running when a Plaintiff files an original Complaint and other items in court. Afterward, the Plaintiff must takes steps to have each Defendant served with a copy of a Complaint and other items within a specific period of time.

Connecticut follows a different course. There, the first step is to serve each Defendant with a copy of the Complaint and other items. At that point the lawsuit technically begins and the statute of limitations stops running. Afterward, the Plaintiff must file the Complaint and other items in court within a specific period of time.

Why the difference? I have no idea. Rather than try to figure it out, keep the general idea of filing and serving in mind and move forward to the next section. The relevant details are outlined for you in the state summaries at the end of the chapter.

A. The Entry Fee

Each Plaintiff who wishes to file a lawsuit in court must pay the court an entry fee. This fee often ranges somewhere between $100 and $200. The clerk's office will usually accept a law firm's check, a money order, a certified check, or cash. There may, however, be restrictions on personal checks. If necessary, be sure to call the applicable clerk's office regarding this, and the amount of the entry fee. **Note:** Many states have provisions to authorize the court to waive the entry fee for indigent Plaintiffs.

B. The Summons

Each of our five states requires a Summons to be served with a copy of the Complaint. A **Summons** is a court-issued document that at minimum contains the name and address of the Plaintiff, the applicable court, and each Defendant(s) who must be served a copy of the Complaint. In addition, it includes specific instructions directed to Defendants regarding steps they must take in order to defend themselves in court. In some states, such as Connecticut, the word Summons is used interchangeably or in addition to the word **Writ,** for instance, **Writ of Summons.**

C. A Court Issued Case Form

The time period between filing a lawsuit and the actual trial can often be quite lengthy, especially if a jury trial is requested. The wait can be three years or more in some states. Our courts are overloaded with cases and there are just so many judges and courtrooms available at one time.

To reduce delays, most states have implemented tracking systems that set deadlines, including a trial date. In Massachusetts, cases valued at more than $25,000 should be tried (meaning a trial should take place), settled, or otherwise disposed of no later than 36 months after they are filed. Cases valued below that amount have 24 months after the date they are filed. New Jersey has a similar schedule.

To assist in tracking their cases, Massachusetts and New Jersey require Plaintiffs to complete a court-issued form, to be filed with the Complaint and a copy served to each Defendant in a case. New Jersey calls its form a *Civil Case Information Statement.* In Massachusetts, it's called a *Civil Action Cover Sheet.*

D. Filing a Lawsuit in Court

1. Documents Generally

In most instances, only *original* documents should be filed in court. To **file** a document means that the clerk's office in a particular courthouse *stamps* it or uses some other method to verify the date it was received. In future chapters you will discover why filing dates can be extremely important in a case.

Filing documents in court can be accomplished by mailing them or by hand delivery. Many Plaintiffs prefer to hand deliver their documents (especially their Complaints) to the applicable clerk's office in the courthouse. This can be accomplished by anyone: an attorney, any staff member, the client, a *proper officer,* etc. Usually, the person doing the filing will also bring a copy of the document for the clerk to stamp. He or she will then bring it back to the office and place it in the client's litigation file. That way, if the Defendant challenges the filing date, the Plaintiff can use the **court stamped copy** to verify when the Complaint was filed.

Plaintiffs who mail documents to the courthouse usually include a copy and a self-addressed stamped envelope with a brief written request to stamp the copy and mail it back.

2. Filing a Lawsuit

Once a Complaint, entry fee, and any other required documents are filed in court, the clerk will assign the case a number such as a case number, docket number, index number, etc., then enter it into the computer system. The Complaint and other documents will then be placed in some type of folder with the parties' names and the case number. All future documents pertaining to the case will be placed there. This is known as the court's file. It will be filed alphabetically or numerically in a room that most courthouses call a vault.

II. Serving Defendants

To serve a Defendant means to provide him or her with a copy of the Complaint. The purpose of serving Defendants is to ensure that they have notice of the lawsuit commenced against them and the opportunity to present a defense. Typically, mailing the Complaint to a Defendant is not enough. Instead, there are specific instructions regarding service. If the Defendant is not properly served, he or she may file a Motion to Dismiss the Plaintiff's case from court. See Chapter 8.

A. Legal Process and Proper Officers

Each state, by court rule or law, authorizes certain individuals to serve **legal process:** the Summons and Complaint. These individuals are often referred to as **proper officers.** These individuals usually include, but are not always limited to, a **sheriff,** a **deputy sheriff,** or a **constable.** They are usually elected or appointed by a specific county or city or town. In addition, their authority to serve legal process may be restricted to that county, city, or town, unless specific conditions are met.

When selecting an officer to serve legal process, the Plaintiff must find someone who is competent and capable of properly performing this function. Many firms have a specific list of officers they prefer to work with. In addition, each courthouse usually has a list of officers who are authorized to make service in the county where the courthouse is located.

B. Types of Service

This section will address serving an individual who is a state resident Defendant, rather than a corporation, business, municipality, or out-of-state Defendant.

In many states, mailing a Summons and Complaint is not sufficient to make service. Instead, a proper officer must hand deliver it directly to the Defendant (called **in hand service**) or leave it *inside* his or her place of **abode.**

In hand service, also called personal service, is exactly what it sounds like: The officer personally meets the Defendant and hands him or her a copy of the Summons and Complaint.

Abode service is made when a copy of the Summons and Complaint is left inside the Defendant's home or other place where he or she is most likely to have knowledge of a service. Abode service can be accomplished by handing the documents to someone other than the Defendant who opens the door to the Defendant's abode, or, in some states, by simply slipping the copies under the Defendant's door. Abode service cannot be made by leaving the copies in a mailbox or by nailing them to the Defendant's door unless the court orders otherwise.

Plaintiffs prefer in hand service. That way, Defendants are less likely to claim they never received the Summons and Complaint.

C. Providing Instructions to the Proper Officer

Once the sheriff or constable is contacted, the Plaintiff should do the following:

1. Make arrangements for the officer to receive the original documents and necessary copies.
2. Specify what type of service the Plaintiff wants, in hand or abode.
3. Be sure the officer is aware of the deadline to make service.

Many law firms include the information listed above in a letter to the sheriff or constable. Officers who frequently work for a Plaintiff's office usually come to the office to pick up the documents. Out-of-county sheriffs or out-of-town constables may ask the Plaintiff to mail them the documents or hand deliver them. This decision depends on how quickly service must be made. If I'm working with an officer for the first time, I may hand deliver the documents and meet him or her personally to discuss how service should be made and who will be filing the documents in court. That way, there is less chance for error.

Provide the officer with as much information about the Defendant as possible, for instance, his or her age, sex, physical description, where he or she works and the hours, what kind of car he or she drives, date of birth, social security number, etc. If the case involves a police report, the Plaintiff should give the officer a copy. It provides a lot of this information, and possibly more.

If the officer is having difficulty serving the Defendant, the officer can use the information mentioned above to request the Department of Motor Vehicles to verify the Defendant's address and type of vehicle that is registered to him or her. The officer can then drive by the home or place of employment and keep an eye out for the Defendant's car.

D. The Proper Officer's Proof of Service

After the Defendant is served, the officer must provide written confirmation that service was made. This written documentation is often called a **Return of Service** or **Proof of Service.** It may also be called an affidavit of service, or a Sheriff's Return, a Constable's Return, etc.

The purpose of the Return of Service is to prove that a Defendant was properly served. As a result, the Defendant has received proper notice of the lawsuit and is aware of his or her responsibilities as stated on the Summons.

At minimum, the contents of a Return of Service should include:

1. the name of each Defendant served and the address where each Defendant was served;
2. the type of service made: in hand or abode;
3. a list of the type of documents served on each Defendant;
4. a statement that the documents served were accurate copies of the original documents;
5. the officer's signature.

Some states provide a specific location for this information on the Summons. Other states require the officer to complete a form or provide the information in a specific format. Once service is made, the Return of Service must be filed in court. (In Connecticut, it is filed with the Summons, the Complaint, and the entry fee.)

E. Fee for Service

Consult specific state laws for allowable fees and expenses officers may charge to make service. Serving a Summons and Complaint often averages between $20 and $45 per Defendant. **Note:** Many states have provisions authorizing the court to waive service fees for indigent Plaintiffs.

F. Waiving Service

Note that some states such as Rhode Island follow the Federal Rules of Civil Procedure and permit the Plaintiff to request the Defendant to waive service by a proper officer. In these situations, service begins by mailing a copy of the Complaint, without the Summons, to the Defendant, along with instructions. The Defendant, if he or she agrees, will sign the wavier of service enclosed and mail it to the Plaintiff, who will file it in court. If the Defendant disagrees, the court may order him or her to pay the proper officer's costs for making service.

G. Amending Process

If it appears an error was made in serving the defendant, many states allow the Plaintiff to correct the error pursuant to a Motion to Amend Process

III. Serving Domestic and Foreign Corporations and Municipalities

When serving Defendants who are not being sued as individuals, check the laws and court rules in your state to determine how to properly serve in-state corporations and municipalities. In addition, the following information may be helpful.

A. Domestic Corporations

A domestic corporation is an *in-state* corporation: It is being sued in the state in which it was formed. Each of the five states we are addressing in this text direct their corporations to appoint an **agent for service** to accept legal process on its behalf. On the other hand, the Plaintiff may elect to serve the officers of the corporation directly.

1. Agents for Service

An agent for service may be any of the following:

- **a.** a natural person who is a resident of the state; or
- **b.** an in-state (referred to as a *domestic*) corporation; or
- **c.** a corporation not organized under the laws of the state, but that has a certificate of authority to transact business or conduct its affairs in that state.

The name of a corporation's agent for service should be available at the state's Secretary of State's Office, usually located in the state's capital. It is common for a corporation's attorney or one of its officers or directors to be appointed as an Agent for Service.

Agents for service may usually be served in hand or at their abode as described above. In addition, if the agent is a corporation, some states permit service by leaving the Summons and Complaint at the corporate office. Check your state's rules. Once served, the agent will notify the corporation of the lawsuit.

2. Serving Corporation Officers

If the Plaintiff prefers, he or she may have the officers of the corporation served, rather than the Agent for Service. In most states, this can be accomplished by serving the officer in hand or at his or her abode.

B. Foreign Corporations

Foreign corporations are corporations that are formed in one state, but operate in others.

1. Suing a Foreign Corporation

Many states will allow citizens to sue a foreign corporation if the corporation has some ties such as:

- **a.** The foreign corporation currently transacts business in the state or has transacted business in the state; or
- **b.** The foreign corporation is exclusively engaged in interstate or foreign commerce and if the cause of action arises out of the following:
  - **i.** A contract was made in the state or to be performed in the state;
  - **ii.** Business is solicited in the state by mail or otherwise;
  - **iii.** The corporation distributed, produced, or manufactured goods that are to be used or consumed in state and are so used or consumed, regardless of how and where they were produced, manufactured, marketed, or sold; or
  - **iv.** The corporation conducted tortious conduct in the state.

2. The Agent for Service of a Foreign Corporation

A Plaintiff, through a proper officer, may serve the Agent for Service of a foreign corporate Defendant. This agent may be one of the following:

- **a.** an individual who resides in the state and whose business office is identical with the registered office; or
- **b.** a domestic corporation or not-for-profit domestic corporation; or
- **c.** a foreign not-for-profit corporation authorized to transact business in the state whose business office is identical to the registered office; or
- **d.** in many states, the **Secretary of State's Office** acting as agent for service of a foreign corporation.

C. Municipalities

Municipalities often include towns, cities, townships, counties, boroughs, school districts, etc. Again, check the applicable laws and court rules. In most cases, the town or city clerk or assistant clerk may be served.

IV. Serving Other Types of Defendants

A. Serving Partnerships and Associations

If your state does not require partnerships and associates to appoint an Agent for Service, the Plaintiff should probably serve the presiding officer, secretary, or treasurer.

B. Serving the State

If the Plaintiff is suing the state or one of its agencies, the proper officer should usually serve the relevant state's Attorney's General's Office.

C. Deceased Defendants

If a Defendant dies before the Plaintiff brings suit, most states direct the Plaintiff to name and serve the Defendant's executor or administrator, or other person appointed by the court. In some cases, this may entail opening the Defendant's probate estate.

D. Suing an Insurance Company: Serving the Insurance Commissioner

In many states, if the Defendant is an insurance company, the law requires the Defendant to serve a copy of the Summons and Complaint to the state's Insurance Commissioner.

E. When a Defendant Cannot Be Located

At times, an officer may not be able to find a Defendant. This can be intentional on the Defendant's part, or the Defendant may have moved out of the county or state without leaving a forwarding address. Nevertheless, the Plaintiff is still required to serve the Defendant.

1. Secretary of State's Office and Orders of Notice

Some states allow proper officers to serve the Secretary of State's Office when they cannot locate a Defendant. In addition, the Plaintiff may be required to file a motion asking the court for an **Order of Notice.** If granted, this order will allow the Plaintiff's proper officer to make service by placing notice of the lawsuit in newspapers where it is believed the Defendant will most likely learn of the lawsuit.

2. Motor Vehicle Accidents

In many states, if the lawsuit involves a motor vehicle accident and the Defendant cannot be located, the officer may serve a copy of the Summons and Complaint to the state's Department of Motor Vehicles, who will attempt to track down the Defendant in other states. In addition, the officer will send another copy by certified or registered mail to the Defendant's last address on file at the Motor Vehicle Department.

F. Serving Nonresident Defendants

A nonresident Defendant is an individual who does not live in the state where the lawsuit will take place.

1. Motor Vehicle Accidents

In many states, service is handled the same way as if the Defendant cannot be located: The proper officer may serve the Department of Motor Vehicles in the state where the suit is or will be filed and send, by certified or registered mail, the Summons and Complaint to the Defendant at his or her last known address on file. Again, the Department of Motor Vehicles will attempt to track down the Defendant.

2. Other Types of Cases

In non–motor vehicle accident involving nonresidents cases, service may often be made at the Secretary of State's Office in the state where the suit is or will be filed. Note that this type of service may not be sufficient. In those instances, the Plaintiff should ask the court for an **Order of Notice** to permit a proper officer to make service by certified mail to the out-of-state Defendant.

V. Conclusion

Key Issues in this Chapter

1. A proper officer's authority to serve Defendants is limited to his or her precinct. These officers often include sheriffs, their deputies, and constables.
2. Most service upon individuals is made in hand or at their usual place of abode.
3. As you may have noticed, an Order of Notice is appropriate in most situations in which a Defendant cannot be served in the usual manner permitted by a state's court rules and statutes. If granted, the order could permit a proper officer to send service out of state, and/or authorize notice of the lawsuit to be published in an appropriate newspaper.

4. I strongly suggest reviewing the proper officer's Return of Service before it is filed in court to make certain it contains the required information. If it does not, request that the officer amend it before filing it in court. **Note:** If an erroneous Return of Service is filed in court, don't worry. Under most circumstances, each state allows an amended return to be filed.
5. Each state has specific rules and statutes regarding serving corporate and government Defendants. Make sure the proper officer follows these, and all other requirements pertaining to service, exactly.

STATE SUMMARIES

COMMENCING A CONNECTICUT LAWSUIT

As stated in the main chapter, Connecticut differs from the remaining states addressed because the Defendant must be served a copy of the Summons and Complaint before the originals can be filed in court.

I. Serving Defendants

A. Documents Needed: Pbs 8-1

Each Defendant must be served the following documents:

1. a copy of the Summons,
2. a copy of the Complaint.

B. Who May Make Service: Proper Officers: C.G.S. sec. 52-50

Proper officers include sheriffs, their deputy sheriffs, constables, **borough bailiffs,** and in very limited situations, **indifferent persons.** Typically, sheriffs, their deputies, and constables are called upon to make service. They may be contacted directly to make service. See the *Connecticut State Register and Manual* for a list, or contact the Sheriff's Office or clerk's office located in the courthouse of the applicable county.

C. How to Serve Defendants: C.G.S. sec. 52-46

All Defendants named in a Complaint must be served no later than ***12 days*** before the Return Date. If the proper officer cannot meet this deadline, he or she will contact the Plaintiff's attorney's office for permission to change the Return Date.

Note: Pursuant to C.G.S. sec. 52-593a, if a Plaintiff waits until the last minute and the statute of limitations is in danger of expiring before the officer can make service, the Plaintiff can save the case as long as he or she delivers the Summons and Complaint to the officer ***before the statute of limitations expires.*** If this is done, the proper officer has ***15 days*** from the date he or she received the documents to make service. (I do not suggest that any law office make a habit of using this statute. It's much too stressful and too many things can go wrong.)

D. Types of Service: C.G.S. sec. 52-57(a)

Individual Defendants may be served in hand or at their usual place of abode. In Connecticut, abode service is sufficient if the documents are placed inside the dwelling. This can be accomplished by sliding them under a door, throwing them through an open window, etc., or simply handing them to someone other than the Defendant who opens the door of the dwelling and is standing inside.

See the remainder of C.G.S. sec. 52-57 et. seq., C.G.S. sec. 33-660 et. seq., and C.G.S. sec. 33-920 et seq. regarding serving other types of Defendants or when a Defendant cannot be located.

E. The Return of Service

In Connecticut, the proper officer must prepare his or her own Return of Service. As stated in the text, it must include the name of the person served, the type of service and location, the date of service, and the officer's signature.

II. Filing the Lawsuit in Court: C.G.S. sec. 52-46a

The Plaintiff must file the following in court ***six days*** before the Return Date:

1. the original Summons and Complaint;
2. the entry fee;
3. the Return of Service from the proper officer.

Hint: This filing deadline falls on the Wednesday prior to the Return Date.

Once a case is filed in court, the clerk will assign it a docket number. If the filing is done by hand and a clerk is available, the Plaintiff may receive the docket number at that time. Otherwise, the Plaintiff will be informed of the number by mail.

As stated in Chapter 4, once assigned, the docket number replaces the Return Date on all future documents filed in court, unless otherwise requested.

Example 5-1. Connecticut, Letter to Deputy Sheriff

CHRISTINE KULAS
ATTORNEY AT LAW
P.O. BOX 2005
ELLINGTON, CT 06066
(860) 222-2222

May 1, 1998

Deputy Sheriff Alex J. Porter
P.O. Box 545
Vernon, CT 06340

RE: Sarah A. Donahue vs. Richard P. Andrew
(Defendant's Operation #1111111)

Dear Deputy Sheriff Porter:

Enclosed please find the original Summons and Complaint, along with a copy of each to be served upon the Defendant, Richard P. Andrew, in the above captioned case.

As stated on the Summons, Mr. Andrew lives at 329 Lakeside Blvd., Rockville, CT. Please try to make in hand service. Service should be made by Thursday, May 14, 1998.

This case involves an automobile accident between the Plaintiff and the Defendant. I have attached a copy of the Police Accident Report which will provide you with additional information about Mr. Andrew.

After serving the Defendant, please return the original Summons and Complaint to me, along with your Return of Service, by Monday, May 18, 1998.

Thank you for your assistance with this matter. Do not hesitate to contact me should you have any questions or concerns.

Sincerely,

Christine Kulas

Commencing a Lawsuit in Massachusetts

In Massachusetts, a lawsuit is begun by filing the Complaint and other necessary items in court. Afterward each Defendant in the case must be served within ***90 days*** from the date the case was filed.

I. Filing the Lawsuit in Court: Rule 3

A. Items Needed

The Plaintiff must file the following:

1. the original Complaint;
2. the proper entry fee; and
3. a *Civil Action Cover Sheet.* (Rule 29 of the Superior Court Rules and Standing Order 1-83.)

B. Filing the Case

Filing a lawsuit may occur in one of two ways:

1. by sending the original Complaint and Civil Action Cover Sheet, with the entry fee, by certified or registered mail to the court clerk's office; or

   Note: If the Plaintiff convinces the clerk that the statute of limitations will expire before he or she can complete and file a Civil Action Cover Sheet, the clerk will permit the Complaint to be filed alone and the Civil Action Cover Sheet must be filed within ***10 days.*** (See Standing Order 1-83.)
2. by hand delivering the above to the court clerk at the clerk's office.

Most Plaintiff's attorneys prefer to file lawsuits in person. It's faster and there is no danger of delay or mistake that could occur by mail.

C. After the Lawsuit Is Filed: The Civil Action Number and Tracking Sheet

1. The Civil Action Number

Once the case is filed, the clerk will assign it a civil action number (which is also referred to as a docket number). If the Complaint and other items are filed in person, rather than by certified or registered mail, the clerk can provide the number at the time of filing. Otherwise, it will be sent to the Plaintiff by mail.

2. The Tracking Sheet: Standing Order 1-88

The tracking sheet is unique to Massachusetts. It coincides with the court rule that requires civil cases filed in Superior Court (valued more than $25,000) to be tried, settled, or otherwise disposed of within 36 months after they are filed.

The tracking sheet is generated by the clerk usually within a few days after the case is filed. It provides deadlines for the parties to address various litigation procedures (that are discussed in future chapters) to ensure that the case is ready for trial within the 36-month deadline. See Standing Order 1-88 for more details and how to request permission to extend deadlines. An example of a tracking sheet is found on page 71.

II. Serving Defendants: Rule 4

Rule 4 of the Rules of Civil Procedure requires each Defendant named in a Complaint to be served ***within 90 days*** from the date the lawsuit was filed in court with the following:

1. a copy of the Summons;
2. a copy of the Complaint; and
3. a copy of the Civil Action Cover Sheet.

A. The Summons

Plaintiffs may obtain a Summons at the clerk's office in Superior Court for $2.00. They must complete the Summons by filling in the names of the parties, etc.

B. Proper Officers

Service may be made by a sheriff, deputy sheriff, special sheriff, or other person legally authorized or appointed by the court. See the *Massachusetts Lawyer's Diary and Manual* or contact the clerk's office in the courthouse for information if your office does not have a list of proper officers.

C. Types of Service

Service upon individuals should be made personally (in hand) or by leaving a copy of the Summons and Complaint at the Defendant's "last and usual place of abode...." In Massachusetts, abode service is sufficient if the documents are placed inside the dwelling. This can be accomplished by sliding them under a door, throwing them through an open window, etc., or simply handing them to someone other than the Defendant who opens the door of the dwelling and is standing inside.

See the remainder of Rule 4 regarding serving corporations, municipalities, and out-of-state Defendants, and regarding when a Defendant cannot be located.

D. Return of Service: Must Be Filed in Court

The proper officer's Return of Service is located on the back of the original Summons. The officer must fill in the requested information. Then the Summons must be filed in court no later than the time the Defendant is required to respond to the lawsuit (which is ***20 days*** after the Defendant is served).

Although the officer may file the Summons and Return of Service in court, many Plaintiffs' attorneys prefer to review each Return of Service before it is filed. That way any errors may be corrected, including reserving the documents if necessary.

Example 5-2. Massachusetts, Tracking Sheet

HAMPDEN COURT FOR CIVIL BUSINESS
PRESUMPTIVE DATE UPDATE

DOCKET 9822222 PLAINTIFF JONES, GEORGE ET AL
DEFENDANT CITY IN MASSACHUSETTS

DOCKET NO	ENTRY DATE	CASE TYPE	TRACK	SESS	
9822222	012198	F	A		(Dates will be listed below)

O2 SERVICE COMPLETED ....

05 ANSWER FILED ....

10 RULES 12, 15, 19, 20 MOTIONS HEARD ....

20 DISCOVERY COMPLETED ....

30 RULE 56 MOTIONS HEARD ....

40 PRETRIAL CONFERENCE ....

APPROXIMATE DATE AS TO EVENT 40. NOTICE WILL BE SENT.

60 TRIAL ....

60 TRIAL CONTINUED ....
LAST CONTINUANCE ....

Commencing a Lawsuit in New Jersey

In New Jersey, a lawsuit is begun by filing the necessary items in court. Afterward, each Defendant in the case must be served with a copy of specific documents listed below.

I. Filing the Lawsuit in Court: Rule 4:2-2 et seq.

A. Items Needed

The Plaintiff must file the following:

1. the original Complaint;
2. the original *Civil Case Information Statement* (Rule 4:5-1); and
3. the proper entry fee.

B. Filing the Case

Filing a lawsuit may occur in one of two ways:

1. by sending all of the above-listed items by mail to the court clerk's office; or
2. by hand delivering the above-listed items to the court clerk.

Most Plaintiffs' attorneys prefer to file lawsuits in person. It's faster and there is no danger of delay or mistake that could occur by mail.

C. After the Lawsuit Is Filed: The Docket Number

Once the case is filed, the clerk will assign it a docket number. If the Complaint and other items are filed in person rather than mailed, the clerk can usually provide the number at the time of filing. Otherwise, it will be sent to the Plaintiff by mail.

II. Serving Defendants: Rule 4:4-1 et seq.

Each Defendant named in a Complaint must be served a copy of the following:

1. the Complaint;
2. the Civil Case Information Statement, attached to the Complaint; and
3. the Summons.

Note: Rule 4:4-3 requires the proper officer to receive an extra copy of the items to be served.

A. The Summons: Rule 4:4-1 and 4:4-2

The Plaintiff must deliver sufficient copies of the Complaint, the Civil Case Information Statement, and the Summons to the proper officer for service within ***10 days*** after filing the lawsuit. Otherwise the case could be dismissed. (See Rule 4:37-2(a).)

B. Proper Officers: Rule 4:4-3

Proper officers include sheriffs or other persons "specially appointed by the court for that purpose...." See the *New Jersey Lawyer's Diary and Manual* or contact the clerk's office in the courthouse for information if your office does not have a list of proper officers. (**Note:** In New Jersey, it does not appear that the Plaintiff has a choice regarding who will actually make service. Instead, the documents are forwarded to the appropriate sheriff's office where they are distributed to the available individuals who are authorized to make service.)

C. Type of Service: Rule 4:4-4

Individual Defendants may be served in hand or "by leaving a copy thereof at the individual's dwelling place or usual place of abode with a competent member of the household of the age of 14 or over then residing therein...." It is not enough to slide the documents under the door of the Defendant's abode. See the remainder of Rule 4:4-3 et seq. to serve other types of Defendants and those who cannot be located.

D. Deadline to Serve Defendants: Rule 4:4-3(b)

Rule 4:4-3 states that if the sheriff returns the documents unserved or if ***40 days*** have passed since the documents were forwarded to the sheriff's office, the attorney, his or her agent, or "any other competent adult, not having a direct interest in the litigation," may make service as provided in the rule.

E. Return of Service: Rule 4:4-7

New Jersey refers to a Return of Service as a *Proof of Service.* The proper officer who made service must complete the information requested on the back of the original Summons and on the extra copy referred to above and file them both in court no later than the time the Defendant is required to respond to the lawsuit (which is ***35 days*** after the Defendant has been served). **Note:** If service is made to someone other than the Defendant, the officer must include the name of the person served or a physical description of the person.

Commencing a Lawsuit in New York

In New York, a lawsuit is begun by filing the Complaint and other necessary items in court. Afterward, each Defendant in the case must be served within ***120 days*** from the date the case was filed.

I. Filing the Lawsuit in Court: CPLR 304

A. Items Needed

The Plaintiff must file two copies (or a copy and the original) of the following:

1. the Summons;
2. the Complaint;
3. the proper entry fee; and
4. *Application for Index Number* (CPLR 8018 and Unif. Rule 202.5(a)). This is a court-issued form the Plaintiff completes regarding some information

about the case and to request an Index Number. There is a cost for obtaining an Index Number. In addition, once received, the Plaintiff must immediately give all parties in the action written notice of the number.

Note: In addition to the above, the Plaintiff must obtain a *litigation back,* also known as a blue back. Similar to a cover sheet, it is a sheet of heavyweight blue paper that contains a case caption and other information. The Plaintiff must staple it to the back of the Summons and Complaint with the information facing the outside if you were to turn the package over. (See example on page 77.)

B. Filing the Case

1. Send all of the above-listed items by mail to the court clerk's office; or
2. Hand deliver the above-listed items to the court clerk.

Most Plaintiffs' attorneys prefer to file lawsuits in person. It's faster and there is no danger of delay or mistake that could occur by mail. Once the items are filed, the clerk will return one copy to the Plaintiff and eventually, if not right away, assign the case an Index Number.

II. Serving Defendants: CPLR 308

Each Defendant named in a Complaint must be served within ***120 days*** from the date the lawsuit was filed in court with the following:

1. a copy of the Summons;
2. a copy of the Complaint.

A. The Summons

An example of a Summons can be found on page 76.

B. Proper Officers

New York allows sheriffs, constables, and anyone 18 years old or older who is not a party in the case to serve Defendants. See the *New York Lawyer's Manual* or contact the clerk's office in the courthouse for more information if your office does not have a list of proper officers.

C. Types of Service: CPLR 308

1. In hand: Service upon individual Defendants should be made personally; or
2. Abode: This type of service requires two steps:
   a. delivering to a person of suitable age and discretion at the Defendant's business, dwelling, or usual place of abode; and
   b. mailing the documents to the Defendant's last known residence or place of work within ***20 days*** after abode service.

See CPLR 311 for additional information regarding serving corporations, etc.

D. Deadline to Serve Defendants

As stated above, the deadline to serve all Defendants named in a Complaint is within ***120 days*** of filing the lawsuit in court.

E. Return of Service

The Proper Officer's Return of Service (called Proof of Service) must be filed within ***20 days*** after serving the Defendants named in a Complaint. **Note:** It appears, however, that the latest date to file a Proof of Service is within ***120 days*** after the lawsuit was filed. If the officer makes abode service, he or she must include the name of the person served or a physical description.

Example 5-3. New York, Summons

SUPREME COURT OF THE STATE OF NEW YORK
COUNTY OF NEW YORK

<table>
<tr><td>---X
SHEILA WILKENSON,)
)
Plaintiff)
)
-against-)
)
)
RYAN KEEGAN)
)
Defendant)
)
)
---X</td><td>Index No.
Plaintiff designates
NEW YORK
County as the place of trial
Date Summons filed:
The basis of the venue is
Defendant's residence

SUMMONS

43 East Center Street
New York, NY 66666
County of NY</td></tr>
</table>

To the above-named Defendants

YOU ARE HEREBY SUMMONED to answer the complaint in this action and to serve a copy of your answer, or, if the complaint is not served with this summons, to serve a notice of appearance, on the Plaintiff's Attorney(s) within 20 days after this summons, exclusive of the day of service (or within 30 days after the service of complaint if this summons is not personally delivered to you within the State of New York); and in case of your failure to appear or answer, judgment will be taken against you by default for the relief demanded in the complaint.

Dated: New York
____

Yours, etc.

ALAN F. PETERS, ESQ.
PETERS, McROY & SILVER
Attorneys for Plaintiff
2700 E. Broad Street
New York, NY 04540
Tele. #(212) 232-2323

Defendant's address:

RYAN KEEGAN
43 East Center Street
New York, NY 66666

Example 5-4. New York, Litigation (Blue) Back

SHEILA WILKENSON,
Plaintiff,
-against-
RYAN KEEGAN
Defendant.

SUMMONS AND COMPLAINT

PETERS, McROY & SILVER
Attorney for Plaintiff
2700 E. Broad Street
New York, NY 66666
(212) 232-2323

To

Attorney(s) for

Service of a copy of the within is hereby admitted.

Dated

Attorney(s) for

Sir: Please take notice

NOTICE OF ENTRY
that the within is a (certified) true copy of a
duly entered in the office of the clerk of the within named court on

NOTICE OF SETTLEMENT
that an order of which the within is a true copy will be presented for
settlement to the HON. one of the judges of the within named Court at
on the day of 19 at m.

Dated, Yours, etc.

PETERS, McROY & SILVER
Attorney(s) for Plaintiff
2700 E. Broad Street
New York, NY 66666
(212) 232-2323

Commencing a Lawsuit in Rhode Island

In Rhode Island, a lawsuit is begun by filing a Complaint and other necessary items in court. Afterward each Defendant in the case must be served within ***120 days*** from the date the case was filed.

I. Filing the Lawsuit in Court: Rule 3

A. Items Needed

The Plaintiff must file the following:

1. the original Complaint; and
2. the proper entry fee.

B. Filing the Case

Filing a lawsuit may occur in one of two ways:

1. by sending the original Complaint and proper entry fee by regular mail to the court clerk's office; or
2. by hand delivering the original Complaint and entry fee to the court clerk at the clerk's office.

Most Plaintiffs' attorneys prefer to file lawsuits in person. It's faster and there is no danger of delay or mistake that could occur by mail.

C. After the Lawsuit Is Filed: The Civil Action Number

Once the case is filed, the clerk will assign it a civil action number. If the Complaint and other items are filed in person rather than mailed, the clerk can usually provide the number at the time of filing. Otherwise, it will be sent to the Plaintiff by mail.

II. Serving Defendants: Rule 4

Rule 4 requires each Defendant named in a Complaint to be served within ***120 days*** from the date the lawsuit was filed in court with the following:

1. a copy of the Complaint;
2. a notice of Lawsuit and Request for Waiver of Service of Summons;
3. a waiver; and
4. a self-addressed stamped envelope.

A. Waiver of Service

Rhode Island strongly encourages Defendants to waive service by a proper officer. Rule 4 directs Plaintiffs to notify each Defendant in a case that a lawsuit has been filed against him or her, and request the Defendants to waive their right to be served a copy of the Summons by a proper officer.

The Plaintiff begins this process by sending by mail or other "reliable means" a copy of the Complaint and a Notice of Lawsuit and Request for Waiver of Service of Summons that should include the following:

a. Identify the court where the Complaint has been filed;

b. Inform the Defendant that he or she has ***30 days*** from the date the notice was sent to comply with this request;

c. Inform the Defendant that if service is waived, he or she will have ***60 days,*** rather than ***20 days,*** to respond to the Complaint;

d. Inform the Defendant that if he or she fails to waive service the court will order him or her to pay all the proper officer's service fees;

e. State the date the notice/request was sent.

As stated above, include the waiver itself and a self-addressed stamped envelope.

If the Defendant waives service, the Plaintiff must file the waiver in court. If the Defendant refuses to waive service, the Plaintiff must make arrangements for the Defendant to be served a copy of a Summons and Complaint by a proper officer.

B. The Summons

A Summons is needed only if the Defendant does not waive service. It is a court form that may be obtained from the clerk's office and filled out by the Plaintiff.

C. Proper Officers

Proper officers include a sheriff, deputy sheriff, constable, or any other person who is not a party to the action and is at least 18 years old. Contact the clerk's office in the courthouse for more information.

D. Types of Service

Individual Defendants may be served in hand or the documents may be left at the "individual's dwelling house or place of abode *with someone of suitable age and discretion who lives there.*" It is not enough to slide the Summons and Complaint under the door of the Defendant's abode.

See the remainder of Rule 4 to serve other types of Defendants and those who cannot be located.

E. Deadline to Serve Defendants

Each Defendant named in a Complaint should be served within ***120 days*** of the date the original Summons and Complaint were filed in court. Otherwise, the case could be dismissed.

F. Return of Service

The proper officer's Return of Service is located on the back of the original Summons. The officer must fill in the requested information. Then the Summons must be filed no later than the time the Defendant is required to respond to the lawsuit (which is within ***20 days*** after the Defendant has been served).

Although the officer may file the Summons and Return of Service in court, many Plaintiffs' attorneys prefer to review each Return of Service before it is filed. That way any errors may be corrected, including reserving the documents if necessary.

Example 5-5. Rhode Island, Proof of Service

STATE OF RHODE ISLAND AND PROVIDENCE PLANTATIONS

______________, SC

PROOF OF SERVICE

I hereby certify that on the ______ day of __________ I served a copy of this summons and a copy of the complaint received therewith upon __________ in the following manner:

By delivering a copy of the summons and complaint to him personally.

By leaving a copy of the summons and complaint at his dwelling house, __________, with a person of suitable age and discretion then residing therein.

By leaving a copy of the summons and complaint at his usual place of abode with a person of suitable age and discretion then residing therein.

By delivering a copy of the summons and complaint to an agent authorized by appointment or by law to receive service of process, namely __________.

Such agent being one designated by statute to receive service, further notice as the statute requires was given as follows:

Sheriff's Fees

Travel... $

Service... $

____

Total... $

____

Deputy Sheriff

6

The Pretrial Stage: Responsive Pleadings to the Plaintiff's Complaint

Terminology

Defenses	Answer	Counterclaim
Cross Claim	Appearance	Contested Issues
Certification of Service	Third-Party Complaint	Trial List
Third-Party Plaintiff	Third-Party Defendant	
Amended Pleadings	Responsive Pleadings	

Introduction

Up until now, we have been addressing the Prelitigation Stage. During this time, all of the litigation burdens have been placed exclusively upon the Plaintiff: He or she drafted the Complaint, filed all the proper documents and the entry fee in the proper court, and made certain the Defendant was properly served. Having accomplished all of that, the Prelitigation Stage ends and the **Pretrial Stage** begins.

The Pretrial Stage involves **pleadings, motions,** and **discovery.** It encompasses that period of time between the beginning of the lawsuit and the actual trial. During this time, the majority of the litigation burdens shift to Defendants. This is their opportunity to respond to the Plaintiff's Complaint and attempt to have the case thrown out of court without the need for a trial. Fortunately or unfortunately, they have plenty of time to accomplish this goal. The stage usually involves several months or even years, depending upon the complexity of the case and the court's backlog.

I. The Defendant's Response to a Complaint: Responsive Pleadings and Motions

Each state discussed in this text requires a Defendant to respond to a Plaintiff's Complaint. This response is called a **responsive pleading.** A responsive pleading is a typewritten (or computer generated) document, prepared by the Defendant, that is filed in court as well as served to all other parties in the case. There are five different types of responsive pleadings. Only one, however, called an **Answer,** is mandatory.

To highlight the importance of an Answer, turn to the example of a Summons used in New York on page 76. Notice that the document informs the Defendant, Ryan Keegan, that within 20 days of being served the Complaint, he must serve the Plaintiff's attorney with an Answer. Other types of responsive pleadings include **Affirmative Defenses** (called Special Defenses in Connecticut), **Counterclaims, Cross Claims,** and **Third Party Actions.** Each will be discussed later in this chapter.

Prior to serving and filing an Answer, the Defendant may attempt to convince the court to dismiss the Plaintiff's Complaint or to order the Plaintiff to revise the Complaint in a specified manner. To accomplish any or all of these goals, the Defendant may file and serve any or all of the following: a **Motion to Dismiss,** a **Motion for More Definite Statement,** or a **Motion to Strike.** If the Plaintiff's case survives the court's rulings on the motions, the Defendant must then file an Answer.

Because of the mandatory nature of the responsive pleadings listed above, we will first address them in this chapter. Chapters 7 and 8 will discuss motions in detail.

II. The Defendant's Answer

A. The Purpose of the Defendant's Answer

The Defendant's Answer is extremely important because it defines specifically what allegations (also called claims) in the Plaintiff's Complaint he or she must prove at trial to meet his or her burden of proof and win the case. Each allegation a Defendant admits to will be treated as true by the trier of fact. Therefore, both parties need to concentrate only on those allegations a Defendant denies (or claims to have insufficient knowledge of). These denied allegations are often referred to as the **contested issues.**

B. Drafting the Defendant's Answer

Turn to page 91 et seq. for examples of Answers. In comparison to other responsive pleadings we will address later in this chapter, the Answer is an uncomplicated document. It should be direct, precise, and specific. When drafting an Answer, a Defendant must read all the allegations set forth in each paragraph of the Plaintiff's Complaint and respond in one of the following ways:

1. **admit** the entire truth of each paragraph that is true; or
2. **deny** the entire truth of each paragraph that is false; or
3. claim to have **insufficient knowledge or belief to either admit or deny the truth of the paragraph and leave the Plaintiff to his or her burden of proof.** This response is treated as a denial.

In addition:

4. If a Defendant finds one portion of a paragraph true and another portion untrue, this should be explained in the Answer to that paragraph.
5. If a Defendant finds he or she has insufficient knowledge or belief to admit or deny a portion of a paragraph, this should be stated. The remainder of the paragraph should be either admitted or denied.
6. If a Defendant intends to deny each paragraph in the Complaint, the Answer may consist of one sentence: "The Defendant hereby denies each and every paragraph in the Plaintiff's Complaint." The same holds true if the Defendant intends to admit every paragraph in the Complaint: "The Defendant hereby admits each and every paragraph in the Plaintiff's Complaint." (Of course this rarely occurs.)

III. The Defendant's Affirmative Defenses

As you can see from your review of the Answers on page 91 et seq. and the explanation above, Defendants are not permitted to elaborate on their responses to the Complaint. To address this deficiency, after they have drafted the Answer, they may, at their option, then raise **Affirmative Defenses.** These defenses are *legally recognized reasons* Defendants may rely upon to claim that they should not be found liable for all or some of the Plaintiff's injuries, or that such liability should be decreased.

While defenses are optional, in many instances, if they are not included as part of the Defendant's Answer or shortly thereafter, the Defendant may not be permitted to raise them later at trial. At trial, the Defendant has the burden to prove that the defenses are true. As a result, they permit a Defendant to take an offensive rather than a solely defensive position in the case.

A. Types of Affirmative Defenses

Many states recognize the following Special Defenses or Affirmative Defenses:

i. **Accord and Satisfaction:** The parties previously reached an agreement that wiped out a cause of action adjacent to their original agreement.

ii. **Arbitration and Award:** A prior proceeding took place that resolved the issues.

iii. **Duress:** The Defendant was forced by the Plaintiff to enter into the agreement (usually applies in contract cases).

iv. **Fraud:** The Plaintiff used false or illegal information or methods to cause the Defendant to enter into the contract (usually applies in contract cases).

v. **Illegality not apparent on the face of the pleading:** For instance, if a promissory note that is being sued on does not state that the interest charged was higher than legally permitted.

vi. **Infancy:** The Defendant was not legally old enough to enter into the agreement and therefore the agreement cannot be enforced.

vii. **Non Compos Mentis:** The Defendant was not of sound mind while involved in the incident.

viii. **Payment (even though the Plaintiff alleges nonpayment):** The Plaintiff already received any payment due.

ix. **Release:** The parties already resolved this issue and the Plaintiff agreed that the Defendant is no longer responsible

x. **Set-Off:** If the Plaintiff owes money to the Defendant, the Defendant may claim he or she is entitled to a credit for that sum, against the sum the Plaintiff is seeking in the Complaint.

xi. **Statute of Limitations:** The deadline to file this lawsuit against the Defendant expired before this action was brought.

xii. **Res Judicata:** The issue has already been decided by the court in a prior proceeding.

xiii. **Statute of Frauds:** The terms of the contract are not in writing as required (in contract cases).

xiv. **Title in a Third Person to What the Plaintiff Sues upon or Alleges to Be His or Her Own:** The Defendant does not own or have what the Plaintiff wants.

xv. **Contributory Negligence:** The Plaintiff's actions contributed to his or her injuries in some way. In this defense, the Defendant will want the trier of fact to determine a percentage that reflects the Plaintiff's negligence, if any. If such percentage is determined, the trier of fact will deduct that percentage from the verdict. If the trier of fact finds that the Plaintiff was more than 50 percent negligent, it must find in favor of the

Defendant and not award any damages to the Plaintiff. (Some states call this **comparative negligence.**)

xvi. **Assumption of the Risk:** The Plaintiff understood the risks before engaging in the conduct that allegedly caused his or her injuries.

B. Drafting Affirmative Defenses

As stated above, Defendants must plead their defenses as part of their Answers. In addition, if more than one defense is applicable, each must be set forth in separate paragraphs. If a Plaintiff's Complaint contains more than one count, the Defendants must indicate which count the Special Defense(s) applies to, for instance, *FIRST AFFIRMATIVE DEFENSE TO FIRST COUNT.*

C. Plaintiff's Response to Affirmative Defenses

Connecticut is the only state that requires a Plaintiff to respond in writing to each of a Defendant's defenses. In the remaining states, it is presumed that the Plaintiff denies them.

IV. The Defendant's Counterclaim

In addition to Affirmative Defenses, Defendants have the right to bring their own lawsuit against the Plaintiff. This lawsuit is called a **Counterclaim** and should be included as part of a Defendant's Answer.

When a Counterclaim is brought, the Plaintiff's role and the Defendant's role are reversed: The Defendant bears the burden of proving the Counterclaim and the Plaintiff will present a defense.

A. Two Types of Counterclaims: Compulsory and Permissive

Compulsory Counterclaims relate to the events that are the subject of the Plaintiff's Complaint. If they are not brought during the action, the Defendant may be prevented from raising the issues in a separate lawsuit against the Plaintiff at a later time.

The following example comes to mind: An attorney sues a former client for failing to pay legal bills. In response, the client turns around and files a Counterclaim against the attorney for legal malpractice pertaining to legal work the attorney wants to be paid for. The Plaintiff must now file an Answer to the Counterclaim, which can include Defenses. The Defendant must then reply to these defenses.

By contrast, there is no requirement that allegations asserted in a **Permissive Counterclaim** relate to the allegations raised in the Plaintiff's Complaint. It can be any type of action against the Plaintiff.

B. The Plaintiff's Response to a Counterclaim

A Plaintiff must respond to a Counterclaim in the same way that a Defendant must respond to a Complaint. This means that the Plaintiff must file an Answer. In addition, he or she may include any of the Affirmative Defenses stated above.

V. More Complicated Cases: Cross Claims and Third-Party Actions

The more Plaintiffs and Defendants that are involved in a case, the more complicated it may become. As a result, in addition to filing an Answer, with or without Affirmative Defenses and Counterclaims, Defendants may include a **Cross Claim** or bring **Third-Party Complaints** against individuals who are not parties in the case.

A. Cross Claims

A Cross Claim is a claim brought by one Defendant against a Co-Defendant in the case. It's purpose is to attempt to place the blame for the Plaintiff's claims and injuries on the Co-Defendant in hopes of reducing or extinguishing the Defendant's liability to the Plaintiff. In addition, Cross Claims may be used to idemnify the Defendant. In essence, this means that if the jury finds against the Defendant, the Co-Defendant should be required to reimburse the Defendant for the amount of the damages it paid to the Plaintiff or pay that amount directly to the Plaintiff.

Most states require the Co-Defendant who is served with a Cross Claim to respond in writing to the claims alleged.

B. Third-Party Actions

If a Defendant believes a third person who is not named in the Plaintiff's Complaint is liable for the Plaintiff's injuries, the Defendant may summon this third person into the lawsuit by serving a **Third-Party Complaint.** If this occurs, the Defendant will become a **Third-Party Plaintiff** and the third person will become a **Third-Party Defendant.** (Third-party actions may be called *Interpleader* actions.)

Third-party Defendants have all the rights and responsibilities of a Defendant in the case. As a result, they must serve and file an Answer. In addition, however, they may assert Affirmative Defenses, Counterclaims, Cross Claims, and their own Third-Party Actions.

VI. Closing the Pleadings

As stated above, the purpose of an Answer is to narrow down the contested issues that will be focused on at trial. Once all the parties' responsive pleadings are served and filed, the pleadings are closed and the case is placed on the Trial List.

As I'm sure you can imagine, Affirmative Defenses and Counterclaims are bad enough. Tossing in Cross Claims and Third Parties can really turn a case into a circus. Therefore, paralegals and lawyers must make sure they calendar all deadlines pertaining to each party in the case in order to ensure that the pleadings are closed within the deadlines established by the court. Otherwise, the parties may face penalties such as the court dismissing the Plaintiff's case or defaulting the Defendant. See Chapter 17 for more details.

VII. Content of Responsive Pleadings

Each responsive pleading must contain the following:

1. a case caption, including the title of the document;
2. identifying information from the attorney filing the pleading, called the Appearance; see Section VIII below;
3. the content of the document;
4. the drafting attorney's signature, above the printed name;
5. the date the document was signed;
6. Certification of Service; see Section IX below.

The above-stated requirements have already been addressed except for the Appearance and the Certification of Service.

VIII. The Appearance

Every party in a lawsuit must have his or her attorney file an Appearance in court.

A. The Plaintiff's Appearance

As stated in Chapter 5, a Plaintiff's Complaint must contain the name, address, telephone number, bar number, etc., of the attorney who drafted the document. In addition to holding the attorney responsible for the content of the pleading, in many states, this is considered the Plaintiff's **Appearance:** It tells the court who represents the Plaintiff and how to contact him or her. This same requirement applies to all other documents filed in court in any case by any party.

B. The Defendant's Appearance and Pro Se Parties

The Defendant's Appearance is included in the Answer, which must contain the name, address, telephone number, bar number, etc. of the attorney who represents him or her. Parties who represent themselves as pro ses are also held responsible for supplying this information and should also indicate their pro se status under their name.

C. Attorney of Record

Once a party's attorney files an Appearance, he or she is called the attorney of record. This becomes important when a certification of service is needed. See Section IX.

D. When a New Appearance Is Needed

If any of the parties in a case change attorneys or if a pro se party decides to hire an attorney (or vice versa), the new attorney must notify the court. Usually this is accomplished by filing a court-issued Appearance form or drafting a brief notice explaining the change (no reason is needed) and providing all the required identifying information.

Note: As the State Summaries demonstrate, in Connecticut, in addition to including the attorney's information at the end of all documents filed in court, the Plaintiff's Appearance is included in the Summons. Furthermore, Defendants and any new attorneys who become involved later in the case must file a court-issued form entitled *Appearance.*

IX. Certification of Service

As you should recall, in order to begin a lawsuit, a Complaint must be filed in court and every Defendant listed in the Complaint must be served a copy by a proper officer. This requirement of serving copies of documents continues throughout the remainder of the lawsuit (except for *ex parte* matters) and extends to all parties in the case. For instance, when a Defendant prepares to file an Answer in court, he or she must serve a copy of that Answer to the Plaintiff's attorney and every other attorney of record (or pro se) in the case. Fortunately, however, a proper officer is usually no longer needed. Instead, copies of most types of documents filed after the Complaint may be served by:

1. hand delivery to each attorney of record or to the person in charge of his or her office; or
2. delivery by the regular mail.

A. Serving Pro Se Parties

If the party being served is pro se, the copy may be hand delivered or mailed directly to him or her. Otherwise, never contact or serve a party if he or she is represented by an attorney. See Rule 5(b) if there is no address or office to serve a pro se party.

B. Content of a Certification of Service

To prove that each party has received a copy of any documents filed in court, the drafting party must include a **Certification of Service** at the end of each document. (See examples on pages 97, 102, 111, 113, 114, 127, 128, 130, and 131.) At minimum, each state requires this certification to include the following:

1. that a copy was served on all parties of record;
2. the names of each party;
3. the method (hand delivery or mail) used to serve each attorney or pro se party of record;
4. the location of service: address mailed or delivered to;
5. the date of service;
6. at the bottom, the attorney's signature who performed such service.

C. When Service Is Complete

Hand Delivery: If service is made by hand delivery, it is complete upon that delivery.

Mail: If service is made by mail, the states differ as to when service is complete. Some say it is complete upon mailing. Others state that it is presumed completed within three days after mailing.

D. Deadlines to Respond to Documents Served by Mail

If a party intends to respond to a pleading such as an Answer to a Counterclaim, etc., some states allow extra time to respond if the initial document was served by mail. For instance, Rhode Island gives parties an additional day to respond to a document that was served by mail. Massachusetts gives parties three additional days. Be sure to check the applicable state's court rules when faced with this issue.

E. Numerous Parties

If there are several parties in a case, the court may reduce the number of copies to be served, either on its own initiative or pursuant to a *motion* by one of the parties.

X. Deadlines to File Responsive Pleadings

If a Defendant fails to comply with such deadlines, he or she risks being *defaulted* and having judgment entered in favor of the Plaintiff. See Chapter 17 for more details.

A. Deadlines Vary from State to State

Each state has specific rules that set forth the time period a Defendant has to file his or her Answer and any of the other pleadings mentioned above. See the State Summaries at the end of this chapter for more information.

B. Computing Deadlines

Fortunately, each of the five states discussed in this text agrees with the following when calculating deadlines:

1. When counting the days to determine when a pleading or other type of paper is due to be served or filed, do not count the date that begins the deadline period. Instead, begin counting on the next day and continue to count to the last day permitted. Be sure to include all Saturdays, Sundays, and legal holidays.
2. If the last day of the deadline falls on a Saturday, Sunday, or legal holiday, the deadline is extended until the end of the next day that is not a Saturday, Sunday, or legal holiday.

   For example: If a Defendant has 20 days to serve an Answer to a Complaint, the 20 days starts to run the day after he or she was served.

   If the twentieth day falls on a Saturday, Sunday, or legal holiday, the Answer must be served no later than the end of the next day that is not a Saturday, Sunday, or legal holiday.

XI. Amended and Supplemental Pleadings

Each state has court rules that permit the parties to amend or supplement their pleadings, including allowing the Plaintiff to amend the Complaint or allowing a Defendant to amend the Answer by adding Defenses or a Counterclaim.

In most circumstances, there is a specific time period in which parties may serve and file such **amended pleadings** or supplemental pleadings without the other party's consent or the court's permission. After that deadline, they will need consent or permission. This is accomplished by serving and filing a motion or request and attaching the new pleading that contains the additional information, corrects mistakes, etc. In most cases the court will grant permission as long as:

1. There is no strenuous objection from the opposing party claiming they will be unfairly prejudiced by the new pleading; or
2. The new pleading will not unduly delay the trial.

XII. Conclusion

Key Issues in This Chapter

1. The *Pretrial Stage* begins once the Complaint is filed in court and the Defendant is served with a copy.
2. The Pretrial Stage consists of *pleadings, motions,* and *discovery.* They take place simultaneously and involve specific procedures and numerous deadlines that keep both parties on their toes.
3. During the Pretrial Stage, the burden switches to the Defendant to respond to the Plaintiff's Complaint and determine what motions and requests should be filed to weaken the Plaintiff's case and possibly have it thrown out of court without a trial.
4. The Plaintiff's Complaint is the first pleading filed in a lawsuit.
5. The Defendant ***must*** respond to the Plaintiff's Complaint by a responsive pleading. At minimum, the Defendant must file an *Answer.*
6. Along with the Answer, the Defendant may file *Defenses,* a *Counterclaim,* a *Cross Claim,* or a *Third-Party Complaint.*
7. Most states require Plaintiffs to respond to a Defendant's Defenses that are listed in the Answer.
8. If a Defendant files a Counterclaim, the Plaintiff must respond by filing an Answer to the Counterclaim. The Plaintiff may also file defenses to such Counterclaim which the Defendant must respond to.
9. A Cross Claim is directed from one Defendant to another for damages the Plaintiff is claiming.
10. If a Defendant files a Third-Party Complaint, he or she is bringing a new party into the action and claiming damages that are related to the Plaintiff's Complaint.
11. Defendants must file their Answers, along with any defenses, Counterclaims, etc., within the deadlines stated in each state's court rules. Otherwise, they risk being *defaulted* and having judgment enter in favor of the Plaintiff.
12. Any party who files a pleading (or almost any other type of document) in court must send the opposing party(s) copies at the time of filing. In addition, the pleading or document must contain a *Certification of Service* that states such copy was sent.

STATE SUMMARIES

As you review the material found below, do not forget that each state requires the documents to contain a case caption, identifying information, and Certification of Service.

Responsive Pleadings in Connecticut

I. Connecticut vs. the Remaining Four States

As you will soon discover, Connecticut requires Defendants to file an Appearance, and its responsive pleadings and deadline calculations differ significantly from the remaining states.

II. Calculating Deadlines

Connecticut calculates most deadlines by the date a document is filed in court. The other states, however, calculate their deadlines based upon the date the parties are served a copy of a document from the opposing party. Examine the difference by reviewing this summary, then comparing it to the others in this chapter.

III. A Defendant's First Response: An Appearance: Pbs 3-2

In addition to the above, Connecticut differs from the remaining states in that instead of a pleading, the first document a Defendant must file in court after being served is called an *Appearance.* This is a simple court-issued form that must be filed within ***two days*** after the return date. The Plaintiff's Appearance is officially part of the Summons.

IV. Types of Responsive Pleadings: Pbs 10-6, 10-10, 10-11, and 10-54

Pbs 10-6 permits the pleadings listed below. Like the remaining states, however, only the Answer is mandatory.

1. *Defendant:* Motion to Dismiss — *Plaintiff:* Objection
2. *Defendant:* Request to Revise — *Plaintiff:* Objection or Compliance
3. *Defendant:* Motion to Strike — *Plaintiff:* Objection or Compliance
4. *Defendant:* Answer, with or without Special Defenses
5. *Plaintiff:* Request to Revise Defendant's Answer — *Defendant:* Objection or Compliance
6. *Plaintiff:* Motion to Strike Defendant's Answer — *Defendant:* Objection or Compliance
7. *Plaintiff:* Reply to Special Defenses (See also Pbs 10-56.)

The format and significance of motions, requests, and objections are discussed in detail beginning in Chapter 7. In addition, the grounds for each of the above are discussed in Chapter 8. At this point, I suggest reading the information on these topics but focusing on Answers, Counterclaims, Cross Claims, and Third-Party Actions addressed below.

Pbs 10-54 permits:

8. *Defendant:* Counterclaims — *Plaintiff:* Like the Defendant, the Plaintiff has the option to file a Motion to Dismiss, Request to Revise, or Motion to Strike, but must eventually file an Answer.

Pbs 10-10 permits:

9. *Defendant:* Cross Claims against Co-Defendants. It appears no response is necessary.

Pbs 10-11 permits:

10. *Third-party actions.* — *Third-Party Defendant:* Like any Defendant, a Third-Party Defendant may file a Motion to Dismiss, Request to Revise, or Motion to Strike, but must eventually file an Answer. He or she may also assert claims against Plaintiff and vice versa, etc.

Pbs 10-58 permits:

11. *Subsequent Pleadings:* A party who wishes to file additional pleadings should obtain permission from the court.

V. Deadlines for Responsive Pleadings Prior to the Answer: Pbs 10-6, 10-7, and 10-8

The deadlines to file motions, requests, and objections are found in Chapters 7 and 8 where each is specifically addressed. For now, remember that they are optional. Only the Answer is mandatory. In addition, please note that these motions and the request must be filed in the specific order listed. For example, if a party files a Motion to Strike as the first pleading and loses, he or she cannot then file a Motion to Dismiss or a Request to Revise. The only option is to file an Answer (with or without special defenses, etc.). Further, if his or her first pleading is an Answer, he or she cannot later file a Motion to Dismiss, Request to Revise, or Motion to Strike.

VI. Defendant's Answer: Pbs 10-6, 10-7, 10-8, and 10-46 et seq.

In Connecticut, if a Defendant does not intend to file a Motion to Dismiss, a Request to Revise, or a Motion to Strike, he or she must file an Answer within ***30 days*** from the return date. (See Pbs 10-8.) Along with the **Answer,** a Defendant may file:

1. **Special Defenses;** and/or
2. a **Counterclaim.**

The Special Defenses (called Affirmative Defenses in other states) permitted are listed in the main chapter and in Pbs 10-51 et seq.

VII. Plaintiff's Response to an Answer, Special Defenses, and Counterclaims: Pbs 10-6, 10-7, 10-8, and 10-54

A Plaintiff has the options listed below when a Defendant files an Answer, with or without Special Defenses and/or a Counterclaim.

A. The Answer, without Special Defenses or a Counterclaim

After an Answer is filed, the Plaintiff may attack the Answer by filing a Request to Revise Answer and/or Motion to Strike Answer within ***15 days*** after the Answer is filed in court. In most cases, however, the Plaintiff will simply close the pleadings by filing a court-issued form entitled Certificate of Closed Pleadings (see Chapter 19). The court will then place the case on a waiting list for trial. In the meantime, the parties will continue to conduct discovery as needed.

B. Special Defenses: Mandatory Reply to Special Defenses

Like the Answer filed by itself, a Plaintiff may attack the Special Defenses by filing a Request to Revise Special Defenses and/or Motion to Strike Special Defenses. Again, this must be done within ***15 days*** after the Answer and Special Defenses are filed in court. On the other hand, Plaintiff may simply file the ***mandatory*** Reply to Special Defenses and close the pleadings.

C. Counterclaim: Mandatory Answer to Counterclaim

When filing the Answer, a Defendant may file a Counterclaim against the Plaintiff as long as the action arises out of allegations stated in the Plaintiff's Complaint. If the Defendant files a Counterclaim, the Plaintiff must eventually respond by filing a mandatory **Answer to Counterclaim.** Beforehand, however, he or she has the option of filing all the motions and the request found in Pbs 10-6 as if he or she were the original Defendant. The ***15-day*** interval rule found in Pbs 10-8 applies.

D. Cross Claims: Pbs 10-10

Two different types are permitted:

1. Cross Claims against Co-Defendants: if the Cross Claim "arises out of the transaction" that is addressed in the Plaintiff's Complaint; or
2. Cross Claims against Any Party: to prove that party is liable to the Defendant for all or part of the damages the Plaintiff claims against Defendant.

No specific deadline is stated in this section.

E. Third-Party Actions: Pbs 10-11

A Defendant may file a motion at ***any time before trial*** asking the court for permission to bring a Third-Party action by serving a nonparty with a Writ Summons and Complaint. If granted, the Third-Party Defendant may file any of the pleadings discussed in this summary, as if he or she were an original Defendant, as well as make a claim against the original Plaintiff or bring other nonparties into the case if the claim arises out of the original Complaint.

Within ***20 days*** after a Third-Party Defendant appears, a Plaintiff may bring a claim against him or her. Again, the Third-Party Defendant has the same rights and responsibilities as if he or she were an original Defendant.

VIII. Certification of Service: Pbs 10-12 et seq.

Connecticut's requirements for certification of service are substantially the same as stated in this chapter. Note, however, that each party is expected to serve a copy of a document to all opposing parties in the case at the same time they file the original document in court. As stated in the beginning of this summary, all deadlines are calculated from the date the original document is court stamped.

IX. Amended and Supplemental Pleadings

These types of pleadings have been addressed in the main chapter. See Pbs 10-59 et seq. for specific details.

Example 6-1. Connecticut, Answer and Special Defenses

DOCKET NO. CV 98-0333333 S	:	SUPERIOR COURT
SARAH A. DONAHUE	:	JUDICIAL DISTRICT
	:	OF TOLLAND
VS.	:	AT ROCKVILLE
RICHARD P. ANDREW	:	(date)

ANSWER

(1) The Defendant admits that the Plaintiff was traveling in a westerly direction along Manor Avenue as stated in Paragraph 1 of the Plaintiff's Complaint. The Defendant has insufficient knowledge as to the remainder of Paragraph 1 and leaves the Plaintiff to her proof.
(2) The Defendant admits that he was traveling in a westerly direction along Manor Avenue as stated in Paragraph 1 of the Plaintiff's Complaint. The Defendant denies the remainder of Paragraph 1.
(3) The Defendant denies Paragraphs 3 through 7 of the Plaintiff's Complaint.

DEFENDANT'S SPECIAL DEFENSES
DEFENDANT'S FIRST SPECIAL DEFENSE

(1) Any injuries, losses or damages sustained by the Plaintiff were caused by her own negligence and/or carelessness in one or more of the following ways:

(a) She failed to maintain her automobile in a safe and reasonable manner to prevent the automobile from stalling out in the middle of the road while in operation.
(b) She operated her automobile on Manor Avenue and Wolcott Street, which are public highways, although she knew or should have known that it was in need of repairs and/or it was unsafe to operate on said public highways.
(c) She operated her automobile in a negligent and in an unsafe manner on said public highways.

DEFENDANT'S SECOND SPECIAL DEFENSE

(1) The Plaintiff was contributorily negligent in causing the collision and any injuries she claims in that she:

(a) failed to maintain her automobile in a safe and reasonable manner to prevent the automobile from stalling out in the middle of the road while in operation;
(b) operated her automobile on a public highway, although she knew or should have known that it was in need of repairs and/or it was unsafe to operate on said public highways;
(c) operated her automobile in a negligent and unsafe manner.

THE DEFENDANT

BY ______________________________
Neil E. Clifford, Esq.
Michaels, Sabrina & Alexander, P.C.,
his attorneys
259 Sage Road, Suite 200
West Hartford, CT 08080
Tele. # (860) 111-1111
Juris #626262

CERTIFICATION

I hereby certify that a copy of the above was mailed on (date) to all counsel and pro se parties of record, namely: Attorney Christine Kulas, Esq., P.O. Box 2005, Ellington, CT 06066.

____
Commissioner of Superior Court

Example 6-2. Connecticut, Reply to Special Defenses

DOCKET NO. CV 98-0333333 S	:	SUPERIOR COURT
SARAH A. DONAHUE	:	JUDICIAL DISTRICT
	:	OF TOLLAND
VS.	:	AT ROCKVILLE
RICHARD P. ANDREW	:	(date)

REPLY TO SPECIAL DEFENSES

The Plaintiff hereby denies each of the Defendant's Special Defenses, dated _____________.

THE PLAINTIFF

BY ____________________________
Christine Kulas, Esq.
Law Offices of Christine Kulas,
her attorney
P.O. Box 2005
Ellington, CT 06066
Tele. # (860) 222-2222
Juris #989898

CERTIFICATION

I hereby certify that a copy of the above was mailed on (date) to all counsel and pro se parties of record namely: Attorney Neil E. Clifford, of Michaels, Sabrina and Alexander, 259 Sage Road, Suite 200, West Hartford, CT 08080.

____
Commissioner of Superior Court

Responsive Pleadings in Massachusetts

I. Deadlines to File Responsive Pleadings: Rule 12(a)(1)

The responsive pleadings listed below must be served on all attorneys of record within *20 days* of being served with any pleading that requires a responsive pleading as stated below.

II. Types of Responsive Pleadings

Massachusetts' responsive pleadings include:

a. **Defendant's Answer,** including if applicable:
   1. Affirmative Defenses;
   2. Counterclaim;
   3. Cross Claim

   Deadline: Serve within ***20 days*** after service of Complaint.

b. Plaintiff's **Reply to Counterclaim** including Affirmative Defenses if applicable:

   Deadline: Serve within ***20 days*** after service of Answer with Counterclaim.

   (**Note:** At this point, Plaintiff may also serve a Third-Party Complaint, if applicable. See d. and e. below.)

c. **Co-Defendant's Answer to Cross Claim**

   Deadline: Serve within ***20 days*** after service of Answer with Cross Claim.

d. **Third-Party Complaint**

   Deadline: May be served by any party ***any time*** after an action starts. However, if it is brought later than ***20 days*** after the Defendant serves the Answer, the party needs the court's permission.

e. **Third-Party Answer** (with Affirmative Defenses, Counterclaim, Cross Claim, or Third-Party Complaint if applicable).

   Deadline: Serve within ***20 days*** after service of the Third-Party Complaint. (See d. above for Third-Party Complaint.)

   Note: Follow the same ***20-day*** deadlines if a Plaintiff files a Cross Claim in response to a Counterclaim or if a Third-Party Defendant files a Counterclaim and/or a Cross Claim.

   In addition, a party may ask permission to serve a **Reply to Answer** or a **Reply to Third-Party Answer.** If permission is granted, the court will determine the deadlines.

III. Types of Affirmative Defenses: Rule 8(c)

Massachusetts permits the following Affirmative Defenses to be included as part of a Defendant's Answer to a Complaint, a Plaintiff's Answer to Counterclaim, or a Third-Party Defendant's Answer to a Third-Party Complaint:

a. accord and satisfaction
b. arbitration and award
c. contributory negligence
d. discharge in bankruptcy
e. duress
f. failure of consideration
g. fraud
h. illegality
i. injury to fellow servant
j. laches
k. license
l. payment
m. release
n. res judicata
o. statute of frauds
p. statute of limitations
q. waiver
r. contributory negligence
s. assumption of the risk
t. that a signature or endorsement on a document is not authentic
u. any other matter that addresses avoidance or an Affirmative Defense

IV. Counterclaims: Rule 13

Massachusetts recognizes two types of Counterclaims:

a. **Compulsory Counterclaims:** claims against the Plaintiff that arise out of the subject matter of the Plaintiff's Complaint; or
b. **Permissive Counterclaims:** claims against the Plaintiff that are not related to the subject matter of the Plaintiff's Complaint.

   If the Defendant fails to file a Counterclaim, he or she may be precluded from raising such claims against the Plaintiff in a later lawsuit. **Note:**

   1. If this failure occurs and the Defendant realizes it, he or she may ask the court for permission to file the Counterclaim by filing a Motion to File Supplemental Pleading. In the motion, the Defendant should explain that this failure was due to oversight, inadvertence, or excusable delay, or that justice requires it to be filed.
   2. If this failure occurs because the claim did not arise until after the Defendant filed an Answer, he or she should file the Motion to File Supplemental Pleadings and explain the situation.

V. Cross Claims: Rule 13 and Third-Party Actions: Rule 14

These responsive pleadings were addressed in this chapter. In addition, see Rules 13 and 14 for more details.

VI. Serving and Filing Responsive Pleadings: Rule 5 and Super. Ct. Rule 9B.

Serving copies of documents (after the Complaint) to all attorneys (and pro se parties) of record may be accomplished by hand delivery or regular mail as discussed in this chapter.

A. Completed Service: Rule 5(b)

Service is complete upon one of the following:

1. date of hand delivery; or
2. date of mailing

B. Additional Time to Respond to Documents Served by Mail: Rule 6(d)

If service is made via the mail, the party who receives the copies may ***add three additional days*** to the deadline stated in the rules.

For example: If a Defendant serves an Answer by mail that contains a Counterclaim against the Plaintiff, the Plaintiff may add three days to the 20-day deadline to serve his or her Reply to Counterclaim.

C. Filing Documents in Court: Rule 5(d) and 5(f)

The parties are expected to file their original documents in court either before service or within a reasonable time after service. If for some reason a party fails to do so ***within five days*** after a copy was served, the court on its own, or pursuant to a motion by the opposing party, may order that the document be filed by a specific date. If the order is disobeyed, the document will be stricken and the service will be void.

D. The Certification of Service: Super. Ct. Rule 9B

Although Rule 5(d) mentions serving copies of all documents filed in court to all opposing parties, Super. Ct. Rule 9B specifically states that a Certification of Service is required.

VII. Amended and Supplemental Pleadings

These types of pleadings have been addressed in the main chapter. See Rule 15 for specific details.

Example 6-3. Massachusetts, Answer and Affirmative Defenses

COMMONWEALTH OF MASSACHUSETTS
TRIAL COURT DIVISION

HAMPDEN, SS. SUPERIOR COURT
CIVIL ACTION
NO. 98-0000

GEORGE JONES, JR., by his father and next friend, GEORGE JONES, SR., Plaintiff vs. CITY IN MASSACHUSETTS, Defendant	DEFENDANT, CITY IN MASSACHUSETTS **ANSWER**

COUNT I

Now comes the Defendant City in Massachusetts and hereby answers the Plaintiff's complaint as follows:

(1) The Defendant does not have sufficient knowledge or information to either admit or deny the allegations set forth in paragraph 1 of the Plaintiff's complaint.
(2) The Defendant admits the allegation set forth in paragraph 2 of the Plaintiff's complaint.
(3) The Defendant does not have sufficient knowledge or information to either admit or deny the allegations set forth in paragraph 3 of the Plaintiff's complaint.
(4) The Defendant admits receipt of written notice of the claim as set forth in paragraph 4 of the Plaintiff's complaint but denies the balance of the allegations.
(5) The Defendant does not have sufficient knowledge or information to either admit or deny the allegations set forth in paragraph 5 of the Plaintiff's complaint.
(6) The Defendant does not have sufficient knowledge or information to either admit or deny the allegations set forth in paragraph 6 of the Plaintiff's complaint.
(7) The Defendant denies the allegation set forth in paragraph 7 of the Plaintiff's complaint.
(8) The Defendant denies the allegation set forth in paragraph 8 of the Plaintiff's complaint.
(9) The Defendant denies the allegation set forth in paragraph 9 of the Plaintiff's complaint.
(10) The Defendant denies the allegation set forth in paragraph 10 of the Plaintiff's complaint.

AFFIRMATIVE DEFENSES

First Defense

The Plaintiff's complaint fails to state a claim upon which relief can be granted.

Second Defense

The alleged defect was not of such nature that the Defendant knew or should have known of its existence.

Third Defense

If the Plaintiff sustained any damages as alleged in his complaint, they were caused by his own negligence and as such the Plaintiff cannot recover against the Defendant.

Fourth Defense

The duty owed to the Plaintiff by the Defendant is one of public duty which is a duty owed to the public as a whole and not to private individuals.

Fifth Defense

Further answering the Defendant says that the Plaintiff was negligent, which negligence was greater than the Defendant's negligence, and therefor the Plaintiff is not entitled to recover, as provided under the terms and provisions of M.G.S.A. chapter 231, section 85.

Sixth Defense

The Plaintiff has failed to comply with the requirements of M.G.L.A. chapter 258 in that no notice of claim was sent to the executive officer of the City of Springfield within two years of the alleged damage.

Seventh Defense

The Plaintiff has failed to comply with the statutory requirements of M.G.L.A. chapter 258, section 1 et seq.

Eighth Defense

The alleged actions of the Defendant were not the proximate cause of the Plaintiff's damages.

Ninth Defense

If the Plaintiff, George Jones, Jr., has suffered any damages as alleged, such damages were caused in whole or in part by the acts or omissions of parties other than the Defendant.

Tenth Defense

The claim alleged by the Plaintiff is based upon the exercise or performance or the failure to exercise or perform a discretionary function or duty on the part of the public employee, acting within the scope of his office or employment, whether or not the discretion involved is abused.

THE DEFENDANT DEMANDS A TRIAL BY JURY OF ALL ISSUES.

THE DEFENDANT,

Dated:_______________ By:_______________________

Martha Pierson, Esq.
City Solicitor
Law Department
932 Center Street
Citytown, MA 04444
(413) 787-9090
BBO #898980

CERTIFICATE OF SERVICE

Ann Lambert, Esq.,
Lambert & Smith, P.C.
529 Corporate Place
Agawam, MA 04540

I, Martha Pierson, hereby certify that I caused the within document to be filed within the tracking time standards or by leave of the Regional Administrative Justice and further that I caused a copy of the foregoing document to be served on the parties by mailing, postage pre-paid, a copy to the above named on _________.

____

Martha Pierson
COMMONWEALTH OF MASSACHUSETTS
TRIAL COURT DIVISION

HAMPDEN, SS.

SUPERIOR COURT
CIVIL ACTION NO. 98-0000

GEORGE JONES, JR. By his Father and Next Friend, GEORGE JONES, SR., Plaintiff	
vs.	**NOTICE OF WITHDRAWAL OF APPEARANCE**
CITY IN MASSACHUSETTS, Defendant	

TO THE CLERK OF THE ABOVE-NAMED COURT:

Please withdraw my appearance as attorney for Plaintiff, George Jones, Jr., et al. in the above-entitled case. This notice is accompanied by the appearance of my successor counsel, Shetland and Morris. There are no motions currently pending before the court, no trial date has been set, and proof of service on my client and all other parties of said record is attached hereto.

Dated ____________

____
Ann Lambert, Esq.
Lambert and Smith, P.C.
529 Corporate Place
Agawam, MA 04540
BBO #33333

CERTIFICATION OF SERVICE

I, Ann Lambert, Esq., hereby certify that on this ____________, I served a copy of the foregoing NOTICE OF WITHDRAWAL OF APPEARANCE and attached NOTICE OF APPEARANCE to the Defendant by mailing a copy of the same to its attorneys of record, Martha Pierson, Esq., City Solicitor, Law Department, 932 Center Street, Citytown, MA 04444.

____
Ann Lambert, Esq.

COMMONWEALTH OF MASSACHUSETTS
DEPARTMENT OF THE TRIAL COURT

HAMPDEN, ss.

SUPERIOR COURT
CIVIL ACTION NO.: 98-0000

GEORGE JONES, JR. By his Father and Next Friend, GEORGE JONES, SR., Plaintiff) vs.) CITY IN MASSACHUSETTS, Defendant)	**NOTICE OF APPEARANCE**

TO THE CLERK OF THE ABOVE-NAMED COURT:

Please enter my appearance as attorney of the Plaintiff, George Jones, Jr. by his Father and Next Friend, George Jones, Sr., in the above-entitled case. Plaintiff's prior counsel has advised me that they have filed, or are in the process of filing a disappearance.

THE PLAINTIFF
GEORGE JONES, JR., BY HIS FATHER
AND NEXT FRIEND, GEORGE JONES, SR.

BY THEIR ATTORNEY

Date: ____________

____
Samuel Shetland, Esq.
Shetland and Morris
60 Main Street
E. Longmeadow, MA 04340
Tele. # (413) 456-7877
BBO # 45454

Notes to readers:

(1) Mass. Sup. CT. Rule 48 requires a withdrawing attorney to obtain a Military Affidavit regarding his or her client if no successor counsel has filed an appearance.
(2) Mass. R. Civ. P. Rule 11 (c) requires a party to file a Motion to Withdraw, instead of this notice, if all of its requirements are not met.
(3) A similar form may be obtained at the clerk's office.

Responsive Pleadings in New Jersey

I. The Case Information Statement: Rule 4:5-1

As you should recall, Plaintiffs in New Jersey must complete and attach a court-issued form entitled the ***Case Information Statement*** to the Complaint when filing it in court. In addition, a copy of this form must be attached to the copy of the Summons and Complaint to be served to each Defendant in the case. Likewise, Defendants must complete their own Case Information Sheet and attach it to the first document they file in court and attach a copy to the copies of documents that will be served to the Plaintiff and all other parties in the case. If any information stated in the form changes, the party must notify the opposing parties and the court.

II. Types of Responsive Pleadings and Deadlines: Rule 4:5 et seq.

New Jersey's responsive pleadings include:

a. **Defendant's Answer,** including if applicable:

  1. Affirmative Defenses;

  2. Counterclaim;

  Deadline: Serve within ***35 days*** after service of Complaint.

b. Plaintiff's **Answer to Counterclaim,** including Affirmative Defenses, if applicable: Rule 4:6-1.

  Deadline: Serve within ***35 days*** after service of Answer with Counterclaim.

c. Defendant's Cross Claim: Rule 4:7-5(c)

  Deadline:

  1. Serve any time within ***90 days*** of service of the original Complaint or ***90 days*** after service of the Complaint upon the party against whom the Cross Claim is asserted, whichever is later.

  2. If the 90-day deadline is missed, the party may ask the court's permission, "which shall be freely given."

d. Co-Defendant's **Answer to Cross Claim:** Rule 4:6-1

  Deadline: Serve within ***35 days*** after service of Answer with Cross Claim.

e. Defendant's **Third-Party Complaint:** Rule 4:8-1

  Deadline:

  1. Serve on new party (include a copy of Plaintiff's Complaint) within ***90 days*** after serving his or her Answer; and

  2. Serve a copy of the Third-Party Complaint to the Plaintiff within ***five days*** of serving the Third-Party Complaint.

  If a Defendant misses the 90-day deadline, he or she may file a motion asking the court for permission to bring the Third-Party action.

Note: Within ***four days*** after being served a copy of the Third-Party Complaint, a Plaintiff may amend his or her Complaint to add the Third-Party Defendants, or within ***45 days*** of a court's order allowing the Defendant to file a Third-Party Complaint.

f. **Third-Party Defendant's Answer,** including if applicable:

Affirmative Defenses, Counterclaim, Cross Claim, or Third-Party Complaint.

Deadline: Serve within ***35 days*** of service of the Third-Party Complaint.

In addition, a party may ask the court's permission to file a **Reply to Answer to Counterclaim** or a **Reply to Answer to Cross Claim.** If permission is granted, the pleading must be served within ***20 days*** of service of the Answer he or she is responding to. Rule 4:6-1

III. Types of Affirmative Defenses

New Jersey permits the following Affirmative Defenses to be included as part of a Defendant's Answer to a Complaint, a Plaintiff's Answer to a Counterclaim, or a Third-Party Defendant's Answer to a Third-Party Complaint:

a. accord and satisfaction
b. arbitration and award
c. contributory negligence
d. discharge in bankruptcy
e. duress
f. estoppel
g. failure of consideration
h. fraud
i. injury to fellow servant
j. laches
k. license
l. payment
m. release
n. res judicata
o. statute of frauds
p. statute of limitations
q. waiver
r. denying the authenticity of a signature or endorsement
s. assumption of the risk
t. any other matter that addresses avoidance or an Affirmative Defense

Note: The Plaintiff is not required to respond to these Affirmative Defenses. Instead, they are treated as if the Plaintiff denies them and the Defendant must prove them at trial.

IV. Counterclaims: Rule 4:7 et seq.

New Jersey recognizes two types of Counterclaims:

a. **Mandatory Counterclaims:** claims against the Plaintiff that arise out of the subject matter of the Plaintiff's Complaint; or

b. **Permissive Counterclaims:** claims against the Plaintiff that are not related to the subject matter of the Plaintiff's Complaint.

If the Defendant fails to file a Counterclaim, he or she may be precluded from raising such claims against the Plaintiff in a later lawsuit. **Note:**

1. If this failure occurs and the Defendant realizes it, he or she may ask the court for permission to file the Counterclaim by filing a Motion to File Supplemental Pleading. In the motion, the Defendant should explain that this failure was due to oversight, inadvertence, or excusable delay, or that justice requires it to be filed.
2. If this failure occurs because the claim did not arise until after the Defendant filed an Answer, he or she should file the Motion to File Supplemental Pleadings and explain the situation.

V. Cross Claims and Third-Party Actions: Rules 4:7 and 4:8

These types of responsive pleadings have already been addressed in this summary and the main chapter.

VI. Serving and Filing Responsive Pleadings: Rule 1:5-4

Serving copies of documents (after the Complaint) to all attorneys (and pro se parties) of record may be accomplished by regular mail or hand delivery as discussed in this chapter. In addition, New Jersey makes special provisions for delivery by courier services.

A. Completed Service: Rule 1:5-4

Service of responsive pleadings is complete upon one of the following:

1. date of ordinary mailing;
2. if certified mail or registered mail: service is complete upon date of acceptance of such mail (the date on post office card);
3. date of hand delivery by person who is not a commercial courier;
4. if a commercial courier is used, service is complete upon courier's receipt from the sender of the document to be served, as long as:
   a. the courier is in the business of providing delivery services; and
   b. the courier "guarantees delivery to the addressee by the end of the next business day following the courier's receipt from the sender."

B. Filing Documents in Court: Rule 1:5-6

All documents that are served should be filed in court either before they are served or "promptly thereafter" unless a court rule or order provides otherwise.

C. The Certification of Service: Rules 1:5 and 4:6 -1(d)

Rule 4:6-1(d) addresses certification of service regarding responsive pleadings specifically. Rule 1:5 addresses this topic generally relating to all documents filed in court. In addition, it mentions three types of proof of service, all of which are intended to confirm that service has been made on all parties (through their attorneys or pro ses) of record:

1. a written acknowledgment, by the party or attorney who received service; or

2. an affidavit by the person making service (a statement made and sworn to under oath to a notary public); or
3. a certification by the attorney's party making service: see page 111. New Jersey has its own requirements which are more involved than stated in the sample pleadings from other states.

VII. Amended and Supplemental Pleadings

These types of pleadings have been addressed in the main chapter. See Rule 4:9 for specific details.

Example 6-4. New Jersey, Answer, Affirmative Defenses, Counterclaim, and Third-Party Complaint

GRAVEY, MADISON AND PAUL, P.C.
190 Court Street
Newark, New Jersey 07102-5497
(201) 623-0000
Attorneys for Defendant/Third-Party Plaintiff,
Safety Insurance Co.

SUPERIOR COURT OF NEW JERSEY
LAW DIVISION: BERGEN COUNTY

Plaintiff	
BIRCH REALTY COMPANY vs.	DOCKET NO.: BER-L-11111-98
Defendant	
SAFTEY INSURANCE CO. Defendant/Third- Party Plaintiff	Civil Action ANSWER, AFFIRMATIVE DEFENSES, COUNTERCLAIM, THIRD-PARTY COMPLAINT, DESIGNATION OF TRIAL COUNSEL AND JURY DEMAND
vs.	
Third-Party Defendant	
JOSEPH DEXTER	

The Defendant, Safety Insurance Company, in answer to the Complaint, alleges and says:

FIRST COUNT

(1) Admitted.
(2) Admitted, except that each coverage was subject to the terms and conditions of the policy.
(3) Admitted.
(4) Admitted.
(5) Denied.
(6) Admitted that the Defendant has not paid. Denied that Defendant has any obligation to make payment.

SECOND COUNT

(1) Defendant repeats and realleges all of the responses contained in the First Count as if set forth at length herein.
(2) Admitted, except that each coverage is subject to the terms and conditions of the policy.
(3) Denied.
(4) Denied.

(5) Admitted that Defendant has not paid. Denied that defendant has any obligation to make payment.

THIRD COUNT

(1) Defendant repeats and realleges all of the responses contained in the First and Second Counts as if set forth at length herein.
(2) Admitted, except that each coverage is subject to the terms and conditions of the policy.
(3) Defendant is without sufficient information to admit or deny the third paragraph.
(4) Denied.
(5) Admitted that Defendant has not paid. Denied that Defendant has any obligation to make payment.

FIRST AFFIRMATIVE DEFENSE

The Complaint fails to state a claim upon which relief may be granted against this Defendant.

SECOND AFFIRMATIVE DEFENSE

The policy is subject to a mortgagee clause requiring that payment be made to any mortgagee to the extent of its interest before any payment to the insured. Accordingly, any payment due to the Plaintiff is to be reduced by any payment made or to be made to the mortgagee.

THIRD AFFIRMATIVE DEFENSE

Plaintiff is barred by the doctrine of unclean hands. The damages allegedly sustained by the Plaintiff resulted from an act of arson caused, solicited or procured by the Plaintiff.

COUNTERCLAIM

Defendant, Safety Insurance Company, by way of Counterclaim, alleges and says,

(1) Defendant is an insurance company licensed to provide insurance coverage within the State of New Jersey.
(2) Defendant provided Plaintiff with a policy of insurance providing $500,000 worth of coverage for damages to property.
(3) Such policy contained a mortgage provision insuring any mortgagee's interest up to the amount of the mortgage interest.
(4) On or about January 15, 1998, the insured premises were destroyed by fire.
(5) Such fire was, on information and belief, an act of arson by the insured or someone acting on behalf of the insured.
(6) Notwithstanding the act of arson, under the policy, and by operation of law, Defendant became obligated to the mortgagee who had no apparent involvement in the arson up to the amount of their mortgage interest.
(7) In satisfaction of this obligation, the Defendant has paid, or imminently will pay, the mortgagee up to the amount of their mortgage interest in the property.
(8) The Plaintiff's action, in committing arson to the premise, directly and proximately caused the Defendant to become obligated to the mortgagees.
(9) As a result of having caused the Defendant to become obligated to the mortgagees, Plaintiff is liable to Defendant/Counterclaimant.

WHEREFORE, the Defendant demands judgment against the Plaintiff for all sums paid and to be paid to Plaintiff's mortgagee together with interest, costs of suit, attorney's fees, and such other relief the court deems appropriate.

THIRD-PARTY COMPLAINT AGAINST JOSEPH DEXTER

Defendant/Third-Party Plaintiff, Safety Insurance Company, by way of a Third-Party Complaint against Third-Party Defendant, Joseph Dexter, alleges and says:

(1) The Defendant/Third-Party Plaintiff is an insurance company licensed to underwrite business within the State of New Jersey.

(2) Third-Party Defendant, Joseph Dexter, who resides at 367 Osgood Avenue, Edison, New Jersey, is a one-third shareholder of Plaintiff, Birch Realty Company.

(3) Third-Party Plaintiff issued a policy of insurance insuring the Plaintiff, Birch Realty Company, against damages, including damages resulting from a fire.

(4) On or about January 15, 1998, a fire occurred at the premises owed by the Plaintiff.

(5) As a result of the fire, Defendant/Third-Party Plaintiff became obligated to Plaintiff's mortgagees.

(6) By operation of law and the terms of the policy Defendant/Third-Party complainant is subrogated to the rights of the insured and its mortgagees.

(7) On information and belief, the Third-Party Defendant, Joseph Dexter, for personal gain and/or benefit of the Plaintiff, directly or indirectly caused such fire to occur.

(8) Alternatively, the Third-Party Defendant, Joseph Dexter, without exercising due care, negligently caused the fire.

(9) Third-Party Defendant is libel to the Defendant/Third-Party Plaintiff for having proximately caused Defendant/Third-Party Plaintiff to become liable to the Plaintiff and to its mortgagees.

WHEREFORE, Defendant/Third-Party Plaintiff, Safety Insurance Company, demands judgment against Third-Party Defendant, Joseph Dexter, for all sums paid and to be paid to Plaintiff and/or its mortgagees together with interest, costs of suit, attorney's fees, and such other relief the Court deems appropriate.

JURY DEMAND

Defendant/Third-Party Plaintiff hereby demands a trial by jury on all issues.

Safety Insurance Company
Attorneys for Defendant/Third-
Party Plaintiff
Gravey, Madison & Paul, P.C.

Dated: ______________ By: ______________________
Walter M. Madison

CERTIFICATION

I hereby certify that the Answer, Counterclaim and Third-Party Complaint in this matter were filed within the time period provided by Court Rule and that a copy was served by regular mail, postage prepaid, upon all counsel of record on the date set forth.

I hereby further certify that pursuant to R. 4:5-1, to our knowledge and based on the information available to us at this time, the matter in controversy is not the subject of any other action pending in any court or of pending arbitration proceeding and that no additional parties are known at this time who should be joined in this action.

Attorney for Defendant

Dated: ______________ By: ______________________
Walter M. Madison

Example 6-5. New Jersey, Answer to Counterclaim

MARSH & MARSH
2719 Bergen Street
Wayne, New Jersey 17470
(201) 696-9523
Attorney for Plaintiff

Plaintiff	SUPERIOR COURT OF NEW JERSEY LAW DIVISION: BERGEN COUNTY
BIRCH REALTY COMPANY	
vs.	DOCKET NO.: BER-L-11111-98
Defendant/Third-Party Plaintiff	
SAFTEY INSURANCE CO. Defendant/Third- Party Plaintiff	Civil Action ANSWER TO COUNTERCLAIM
vs.	
Third-Party Defendant	
JOSEPH DEXTER	

Plaintiff, having offices at 2700 Main Street, Upper Saddle River, New Jersey, through its attorneys, Marsh & Marsh, says by way of its Answer to Defendant's Counterclaim against Plaintiff as follows:

FIRST COUNT

(1) Admitted.
(2) Admitted.
(3) Admitted.
(4) Admitted.
(5) Denied.
(6) Third-Party Defendant is without sufficient information to admit or deny the sixth paragraph.
(7) Third-Party Defendant is without sufficient information to admit or deny the seventh paragraph.
(8) Denied.
(9) Denied.

WHEREFORE, Plaintiff, Birch Realty Company, demands judgment against the Third-Party Plaintiff, No Cause for Action, and for costs and counsel fees.

MARSH & MARSH
Attorney for Plaintiff

Dated: ______________ By: ____________________
Robert A. Hathaway

CERTIFICATION

I hereby certify that the Answer to Counterclaim in this matter was filed within the time period provided by Court Rule and that a copy was served by regular mail, postage prepaid, upon all counsel of record on the date set forth.

I hereby further certify that pursuant to *R.* 4:5-1, to our knowledge and based on the information available to us at this time, the matter in controversy is not the subject of any other action pending in any court or of pending arbitration proceeding and that no additional parties are known at this time who should be joined in this action.

MARSH & MARSH
Attorney for Plaintiff

By: ____________________
Robert A. Hathaway

Example 6-6. New Jersey, Answer to Third-Party Complaint

MARSH & MARSH
2719 Bergen Street
Wayne, New Jersey 07470
(201) 696-9523
Attorney for Third-Party Defendant

Plaintiff	SUPERIOR COURT OF NEW JERSEY LAW DIVISION: BERGEN COUNTY
BIRCH REALTY COMPANY	
vs.	DOCKET NO.: BER-L-11111-98
Defendant/Third-Party Plaintiff	
SAFTEY INSURANCE CO. Defendant/Third- Party Plaintiff	Civil Action
	ANSWER TO THIRD-PARTY COMPLAINT
vs.	
Third-Party Defendant	
JOSEPH DEXTER	

Third-Party Defendant, Joseph Dexter, residing at 367 Osgood Avenue, Edison, New Jersey, through his attorney Marsh and Marsh, says by way of answer to the Third-Party Complaint herein as follows:

(1) This Defendant admits the allegations of paragraphs 1, 2,3,4,5,6 of the Third-Party Complaint.
(2) This Defendant denies the allegations of paragraphs 7, 8, and 9 of the Third-Party Complaint.

WHEREFORE, this Defendant, Joseph Dexter, demands judgment against the Third-Party Plaintiff, No Cause for Action, and for costs and counsel fees.

MARSH & MARSH

Date: ___________ By: ________________________
Robert A. Hathaway

CERTIFICATION

I hereby certify that the Answer to Third-Party Complaint in this matter was filed within the time period provided by Court Rule and that a copy was served by regular mail, postage prepaid, upon all counsel of record on the date set forth.

I hereby further certify that pursuant to R. 4:5-1, to our knowledge and based on the information available to us at this time, the matter in controversy is not the subject of any other action pending in any court or of pending arbitration proceeding and that no additional parties are known at this time who should be joined in this action.

MARSH & MARSH
Attorney for Third-Party Defendant

By: ______________________
Robert A. Hathaway

Responsive Pleadings in New York

I. Types of Responsive Pleadings and Deadlines: CPLR 3011-3019, 1007-1011

New York's responsive pleadings include:

a. A **Defendant's Answer,** including if applicable:
   1. Affirmative Defenses;
   2. Counterclaim;
   3. Cross Claim;

   Deadline: File within ***20 days*** after service of Complaint.

b. **Plaintiff's Response to Affirmative Defenses**

   No response is needed. They are deemed automatically denied.

c. **Plaintiff's Reply to Counterclaim**

   Deadline: File within ***20 days*** after service of Counterclaim.

d. **Answer to Cross Claim: Required Only if Demanded in Document**

   Deadline: File within ***20 days*** after service of Cross Claim. If no demand is made, the Cross Claim is treated as denied.

e. **Defendant's Third-Party Complaint**

   Deadline: A Third-Party Complaint, along with a Summons and all other pleadings filed in the case, may be served on a Third-Party Defendant after the Defendant files an Answer. In addition, serve a copy of all the documents to the Plaintiff.

f. **Third-Party Defendant's Answer,** including Affirmative Defenses, Counterclaim, etc.

   Deadline: File within ***20 days*** of service of Third-Party Complaint.

II. Types of Affirmative Defenses: CPLR 3018 and 1411

New York permits the following Affirmative Defenses to be included as part of a Defendant's Answer to a Complaint, a Plaintiff's Answer to Counterclaim, a Third-Party Defendant's Answer to a Third-Party Complaint, etc.:

contributory negligence

assumption of the risk

arbitration and award

collateral estoppel

cupable conduct claimed in diminution of damages in Article 14A

discharge in bankruptcy

facts demonstrating Plaintiff's illegal acts pursuant to statutes or common law

fraud

infancy or any other disability of the party defending

payment

release

res judicata

statute of frauds

statute of limitations

any other similar type claim that would rise to the level of an Affirmative Defense

III. Counterclaims: CPLR 3019

A Defendant in New York may assert two types of Counterclaims against the Plaintiff:

1. **Compulsory Counterclaim:** a cause of action that relates to the subject matter set forth in the Complaint; or
2. **Permissive Counterclaim:** a cause of action that is unrelated to the subject matter set forth in the Plaintiff's Complaint.

In addition, New York adds a twist: If a Defendant brings a Counterclaim against a Plaintiff, he or she may also, if applicable, serve a Counterclaim against a nonparty, that asserts a cause of action against that nonparty. **Note:** This must be done together. It cannot be brought against the nonparty alone. That type of action is a Third-Party action.

IV. Cross Claims: CPLR 3019

As stated in the main chapter, Cross Claims are claims against Co-Defendants. New York, however, adds the same twist that applies to Counterclaims:

If a Defendant asserts a cause of action against a Co-Defendant through a Cross Claim, he or she may also, if applicable, serve a Cross Claim against a nonparty, that asserts a cause of action against that nonparty. **Note:** This must be done together. It cannot be brought against the nonparty alone. That type of action is a Third-Party action.

V. Third-Party Claims: CPLR 1007-1011

New York's Third-Party actions are substantially similar to what is discussed in the main chapter.

VI. Serving Responsive Pleadings: CPLR 2103

Serving copies of documents (after the Complaint) to all attorneys (and pro se parties) of record may be accomplished by regular mail or hand delivery as discussed in this chapter. In addition, New York makes specific provisions for delivery by courier services.

A. Completed Service: CPLR 2103

Service of pleadings is complete upon one of the following:

1. Service by mail is complete upon mailing. If, however, a party must respond to the document mailed, calculate the deadline to respond by adding *five additional days.*
2. Service by overnight delivery is complete at the time the document is in custody of overnight delivery service. If a party must respond to the document delivered in this way, calculate the deadline to respond by adding *one additional day.*
3. Service by hand delivery by other than overnight delivery is complete upon delivery.
4. Service by fax is complete at time sender receives confirmation that transmission is sent. In addition, mail a copy to the party.

B. The Certification of Service: Proof of Service: CPLR 306, 2101

New York follows substantially the same procedure for a Proof of Service as stated in the main chapter. See CPLR 306 for specific details. Be sure to include it when filing any documents in court.

C. Filing Documents in Court: CPLR 2102

The parties are expected to file their documents in court when serving them to the parties in the case.

VII. Amended and Supplemental Pleadings: CPLR 3025

These types of pleadings have been addressed in the main chapter. See CPLR 3025 for specific details.

VIII. Bill of Particulars: CPLR 3041 et seq.

In addition to responsive pleadings that are required, a Defendant or any party who is served Affirmative Defenses, a Counterclaim, a Cross Claim, or a Third-Party Complaint *may* serve a document entitled ***Demand for Bill of Particulars*** to the drafter of the pleading.

A. Purpose of Demand for Bill of Particulars

The purpose of this document is to require the party who bears the burden of proof to disclose detailed information regarding his or her claims. Hence, a Defendant who is served a Complaint may serve a Demand for Bill of Particulars to the Plaintiff, asking the Plaintiff to provide a more detailed picture of the allegations set forth in the Complaint. The Plaintiff's responses will amplify the Complaint, thereby preventing the Defendant from being surprised at trial.

B. Examples of Requested Information

The content of a Demand for a Bill of Particulars will vary, depending upon the facts of a case. Note, however, that each request should correspond to a paragraph in the Complaint (or other pleading).

CPLR 3043 assists in cases involving automobile accidents and personal injury cases by setting forth the types of information that may be requested. Such requests may include:

1. the date and approximate time of the occurrence;
2. the approximate location;
3. a general statement of the negligent acts or omissions;
4. if notice of a condition is a prerequisite, whether the Plaintiff is claiming actual or constructive notice; if actual notice, when and who received it;
5. a list of the Plaintiff's injuries;
6. a description of the alleged permanent injuries;
7. the length of time the Plaintiff was confined to bed and the home;
8. the length of time of loss of employment;
9. the total amount of specific damages: physicians, hospitals, nursing services, medicines, lost wages, etc. Include the names and addresses of all.

C. Responding to a Demand for Bill of Particulars

A party should serve the requested information within ***30 days*** of the date the demand was served. Any objections should also be made during that time, directed to the specific request, and include the grounds for the objection.

If the Plaintiff fails to comply with the demand, the Defendant may serve and file a Motion to Compel Compliance. Also, remember that an affirmation will be needed that states that a good faith effort was made to resolve the matter before filing the motion. (Unif. Rule 202.7.)

D. Amending and Supplementing Responses

The information provided, pursuant to a Demand for Bill of Particulars, may be amended one time, prior to the time the Note of Issue is filed. (See page 358.) However the new information must be served to the Defendant at least ***30 days*** before trial in order to prevent surprise.

Example 6-7. New York, Answer

SUPREME COURT OF THE STATE OF NEW YORK
COUNTY OF NEW YORK

--X	Index No. 22222
SHEILA WILKENSON, Plaintiff,)	
-against-)	
)	ANSWER
RYAN KEEGAN)	
Defendant.)	
--X	

The Defendant, Ryan Keegan, by his attorneys, MARKS, JEROME and PENNY, answering the Complaint of the Plaintiff herein, respectfully alleges:

AS AND FOR AN ANSWER TO THE FIRST CAUSE OF ACTION

FIRST: Deny each and every allegation contained in the paragraphs designated as "11," "12," "13," "14," and "15" of the Plaintiff's Complaint.

SECOND: Deny knowledge or information sufficient to form a belief as to all the allegations contained in the paragraphs designated as "1," "7," "8," "9," and "10" of the Plaintiff's Complaint.

WHEREFORE, the Defendant, Ryan Keegan, demands judgment dismissing the Plaintiff's Complaint, with the costs and disbursements of this action, together with such other and further relief as to this court may seem just and proper in the premises.

Yours, etc.

Dated: _______________
New York, New York

HERMAN S. MARKS, ESQ.
MARKS, JEROME & PENNY
Attorneys for Defendant
206 Salem Street
New York, NY 10007
Tele. #(212) 888-0101

To:
Alan F. Peters, Esq.
Peters, McRoy & Silver
2700 E. Broad Street
New York, NY 14540

Example 6-8. New York, Defendant's Demand for a Bill of Particulars

SUPREME COURT OF THE STATE OF NEW YORK
COUNTY OF NEW YORK

---X	Index No. 22222
SHEILA WILKENSON,)	
Plaintiff,)	
-against-)	
)	DEMAND FOR A BILL
RYAN KEEGAN)	OF PARTICULARS
)	
Defendant.)	
---X	

SIRS:

PLEASE TAKE NOTICE, that the answering Defendant, Ryan Keegan, hereby demands that you serve upon the undersigned within thirty (30) days from the date of service hereof, a Bill of Particulars with respect to the allegations contained in the Complaint against the answering Defendant.

(1) Set forth the specific "applicable building codes" the Plaintiff alleges the Defendant violated in paragraphs 11(a) and 11(b) of the Complaint.
(2) Set forth the names and addresses of each hospital the Plaintiff was treated at or was confined to as a result of injuries alleged in paragraph 12. Include the dates of each treatment and/or confinement and describe each treatment and/or the purpose of confinement.
(3) Set forth a list of all physical injuries claimed in paragraph 12 and describe any claimed permanency.
(4) Set forth the dates in which the Plaintiff alleges she was confined as a result of her claimed injuries:

- (a) hospitals
- (b) bed
- (c) home

(5) Set forth all amounts of claimed special damages alleged in paragraph 14 of the Complaint that are causally connected to this instant action for:

- (a) hospitals
- (b) physicians
- (c) nursing
- (d) medical supplies
- (e) lost earnings
- (f) all other special damages claimed

(6) Set forth the loss of earnings claimed:

- (a) The length of time the Plaintiff claims she was incapacitated from employment;
- (b) The last date the Plaintiff worked prior to incident alleged in the Complaint;
- (c) The first date on which the Plaintiff returned to work after the incident alleged in the paragraph 14 of the Complaint;
- (d) The names and addresses of the Plaintiff's employers as of the dates stated in her responses to b. and c. above.
- (e) Describe in detail the nature of the Plaintiff's employment as of the dates stated in her responses to b. and c. above.

(f) Any other special damages claimed.

Dated: _______________
New York, NY

Yours, etc.

HERMAN S. MARKS, ESQ.,
MARKS, JEROME & PENNY
Attorneys for Defendant
206 Salem Street
New York, NY 10007
Tele. #(212) 888-0101

To:
Alan F. Peters, Esq.
Peters, McRoy & Silver
2700 E. Broad Street
New York, NY 14540

Responsive Pleadings in Rhode Island

I. Types of Responsive Pleadings and Deadlines: Rules 7, 8, 12, 13, 14, 15

A. Answer, Affirmative Defenses, Cross Claims, and Counterclaims: Rule 12

1. *Service by Summons and Complaint*

   If a Defendant was served with a Summons and Complaint his or her Answer, including Affirmative Defenses, a Cross Claim, and a Counterclaim, if any, is due within ***20 days*** of being served, unless the court orders otherwise.

2. *Waiver of Service: Rule 12(a)(1)*

   If a Defendant waives service as described in Chapter 5, the Answer, including Special Defenses and a Counterclaim, if any, is due within ***60 days*** after the date the Plaintiff's Request for Waiver was sent (***90 days*** if the Defendant's address is out of the United States).

3. *Service by Publication of Order of Notice Rule 12(a)(1)(a)*

   If a Defendant is served by publication because he or she cannot be located to serve in hand or abode, the Defendant's Answer, including Special Defenses, and/or a Counterclaim is due within ***20 days*** after the last publication.

B. Reply to Counterclaim: Rule 12(a)(2)

Deadline: Serve within ***20 days*** of service of Answer with Counterclaim

C. Answer to Cross Claim: Rule 12(a)(2)

Deadline: Serve within ***20 days*** of service of Answer with Cross Claim.

D. Third-Party Complaint or Additional Party Complaint under Rule 14

Deadline: Serve within ***ten days*** of serving Answer. Otherwise, obtain the court's permission.

E. Answer to Third-Party Complaint

Serve within ***20 days*** of service of Third-Party Complaint.

In addition, a ***Reply to Answer*** (including a Reply to Third-Party Answer) may be permitted if the court grants permission.

II. Types of Affirmative Defenses: Rule 8

Rhode Island permits the following Affirmative Defenses to be included as part of a Defendant's Answer:

a. accord and satisfaction
b. arbitration and award
c. assumption of the risk
d. discharge in bankruptcy
e. duress
f. estoppel
g. failure of consideration
h. fraud
i. illegality
j. injury to fellow servant

k. laches
l. payment
m. release
n. statute of frauds
o. statute of limitations
p. waiver
q. that a signature or endorsement on a document is not authentic
r. contributory negligence
s. assumption of the risk
t. any other matter that addresses avoidance or an Affirmative Defense

III. Counterclaims: Rule 13

Rhode Island recognizes two types of Counterclaims:

a. **Compulsory Counterclaims:** claims against the Plaintiff that arise out of the subject matter of the Plaintiff's Complaint; or
b. **Permissive Counterclaims:** claims against the Plaintiff that are not related to the subject matter of the Plaintiff's Complaint.

   If the Defendant fails to serve and file a Counterclaim, he or she may be precluded from raising such claims against the Plaintiff in a later lawsuit.
   Note:

   1. If this failure occurs and the Defendant realizes it, he or she may ask the court for permission to file the Counterclaim by filing a Motion to File Supplemental Pleading. In the motion, the Defendant should explain that this failure was due to oversight, inadvertence, or excusable delay, or that justice requires it to be filed.
   2. If this failure occurs because the claim did not arise until after the Defendant filed an Answer, he or she should file the Motion to File Supplemental Pleadings and explain the situation.

IV. Cross Claims and Third-Party Actions: Rules 13 and 14

These responsive pleadings were addressed in this chapter. In addition, see Rules 13 and 14 for more details.

V. Serving and Filing Responsive Pleadings: Rule 5

Serving copies of documents to all attorneys (and pro se parties) of record may be accomplished by hand delivery or regular mail, as discussed in this chapter.

A. Completed Service: Rule 5(b)

Service is complete upon the following:

1. the date of hand delivery; or
2. the date of mailing.

B. Additional Time to Respond to Documents Served by Mail: Rule 6(b)

If service is made by the mail, the party who receives the copies may add ***one additional day*** to the deadline stated in the rules.

For example: If a Defendant serves an Answer by mail that contains a Counterclaim against the Plaintiff, the Plaintiff may add one day to the 90-day deadline to file a Reply to Counterclaim.

C. Certification of Service: Rule 5(d)

Rhode Island's requirements for a certification of service are substantially similar to what is stated in the main chapter.

D. Filing Documents in Court: Rule 5(d) and 5(f)

The parties are expected to file their original documents in court within a reasonable time after the copies are served. If, for some reason, a party fails to do so within ***five days*** after a copy was served, the court on its own or pursuant to a motion by the opposing party may order that the document be filed by a specific date. If the order is disobeyed, the document will be stricken and the service will be void.

VI. Amended and Supplemental Pleadings: Rule 15

These types of pleadings have been addressed in the main chapter. See Rule 15 for specific details.

Example 6-9. Rhode Island, Answer

(date)

STATE OF RHODE ISLAND	:	SUPERIOR COURT
PROVIDENCE, SC	:	
	:	
JOHN MARTIN	:	
	:	C.A. NO. PC 98-0000
vs.	:	
	:	
JAMES TYLER,	:	
PETER SMITH and	:	
LUCY SMITH	:	

ANSWER OF DEFENDANT JAMES TYLER
COUNT I

(1) Admitted.
(2) Admitted.
(3) Defendant neither admits nor denies the allegations in Paragraph 3 and leaves the Plaintiff to his proof.
(4) Defendant neither admits nor denies the allegations in Paragraph 4 and leaves the Plaintiff to his proof.
(5) Admitted.
(6) Admitted.
(7) Defendant neither admits nor denies the allegations in Paragraph 7 and leaves the Plaintiff to her proof.
(8) Admitted.
(9) Defendant neither admits nor denies the allegations in Paragraph 9 and leaves the Plaintiff to his proof.

WHEREFORE, Defendant James Tyler demands Judgment in his favor against the Plaintiff and further requests that the Plaintiff's within action be dismissed with prejudice and that said Defendant be awarded his costs and reasonable attorney's fees.

COUNT II

(1) Paragraphs 1-7 of Count I are hereby incorporated by reference.
(2) Denied.
(3) Denied.

WHEREFORE, Defendant James Tyler demands Judgment in his favor against the Plaintiff and further requests that the Plaintiff's within action be dismissed with prejudice and that said Defendant be awarded his costs and reasonable attorney's fees.

Defendant James Tyler
By his attorneys,

____

Lucus Moore, Esq., B C #7777
Law Offices of Lucus Moore
89 Willow Street
Pawtucket, RI 02860
(401) 555-6666

Defendant hereby claims a trial by jury.

____

CERTIFICATION

I hereby certify that on the __________, I mailed a true copy of the within Answer to Attorney Charlene M. Murphy, Esq., 333 Landing Avenue, Providence, RI 02910 and Attorney Ronald Jacob, 67 Market Street, Providence, RI 02910

____

Example 6-10. Rhode Island, Cross Claim

(date)

STATE OF RHODE ISLAND	:	SUPERIOR COURT
PROVIDENCE, SC	:	
	:	
JOHN MARTIN	:	
	:	C.A. NO. PC 98-0000
V.	:	
	:	
JAMES TYLER,	:	
PETER SMITH and	:	
LUCY SMITH	:	

JAMES TYLER'S CROSS CLAIM AGAINST PETER SMITH

(1) Plaintiff, John Martin, has filed a Complaint against Defendants James Tyler, Peter Smith and Lucy Smith.

(2) Defendant, James Tyler, without admitting any liability in such Complaint and expressly denying the allegations of his negligence alleged in such Complaint, says that if he is found liable in any manner for injuries sustained by John Martin, such liability would have been brought about by the negligence of Co-Defendant Peter Smith, and a consequence thereof, Defendant James Tyler is entitled to contribution and/or indemnification from the Co-Defendant, Peter Smith.

WHEREFORE, Defendant James Tyler demands Judgment for contribution and/or indemnification against Co-Defendant Peter Smith for all sums, if any, John Martin may recover from him, together with interest and costs and that he be afforded a trial by jury on all issues.

Defendant James Tyler
By his attorneys,

____

Lucus Moore, Esq., BC#7777
Law Offices of Lucus Moore
89 Willow Street
Pawtucket, RI 02860
(401) 555-6666

CERTIFICATION

I hereby certify that on the ________________, I mailed a true copy of the within Cross Claim against Peter Smith to Attorney Charlene M. Murphy, Esq., 333 Landing Avenue, Providence, RI 02910 and Attorney Ronald Jacob, 67 Market Street, Providence, RI 02910

____

Lucus Moore

Example 6-11. Rhode Island, Answer

(date)

STATE OF RHODE ISLAND	:	SUPERIOR COURT
PROVIDENCE, SC.	:	
JOHN MARTIN	:	
	:	C.A. NO. PC 98-0000
vs.	:	
	:	
JAMES TYLER,	:	ANSWER OF PETER SMITH and
PETER SMITH and	:	LUCY SMITH, CLAIM FOR
LUCY SMITH	:	JURY TRIAL AND ENTRY OF
	:	APPEARANCE

ANSWER AS TO COUNT I

(1) Defendants Peter Smith and Lucy Smith admit paragraphs 1, 2, 3, 4, 5, 6, and 7.
(2) Defendants Peter Smith and Lucy Smith deny paragraph 8, but admit that at the time and place alleged, a collision occurred between their motor vehicle and the motor vehicle of Defendant James Tyler.
(3) Defendants Peter Smith and Lucy Smith are without knowledge or information sufficient to form a belief as to the truth or falsity of paragraph 9 and leave the Plaintiff to his proof thereof.

WHEREFORE, the Defendants, Peter Smith and Lucy Smith, ask the court to discharge them from all liability in the action and award them their costs.

ANSWER AS TO COUNT II

(1) Insofar as paragraphs 1 through 9 of Count I are incorporated by reference into Count II with the same force and effect as if they were set forth in full, Defendants make the same answer thereto.
(2) The Defendants admit paragraph 2.
(3) The Defendants deny any negligence on their part, and as to the remaining allegations of paragraph 3 they say they are without knowledge or information sufficient to form a belief as to the truth or falsity thereof and they leave the Plaintiff to his proof thereof.

WHEREFORE, the Defendants, Peter Smith and Lucy Smith, ask the court to discharge them form all liability in the action and award them their costs.

ANSWER TO CROSS CLAIM

(1) Defendant, Peter Smith, hereby denies all the allegations asserted against him in the Cross Claim filed by Defendant, James Tyler.

PETER SMITH AND LUCY SMITH,
DEENDANTS
By Their Attorney

____

Ronald Jacobs, Esq., BC#0999
Jacobs and Ruddle
67 Market Street
Providence, RI 02910
(401) 521-3333

CLAIM OF JURY TRIAL

The Defendants, Peter Smith and Lucy Smith, hereby claim a right to a trial by jury as to all counts.

PETER SMITH AND LUCY SMITH,
DEFENDANTS
By Their Attorney

____
Ronald Jacobs, Esq., B C#0999

ENTRY OF APPEARANCE

I, Attorney Ronald Jacobs, Bar No. 0999, of Jacobs and Ruddle, hereby enter my appearance for the Defendants, Peter Smith and Lucy Smith.

JACOBS & RUDDLE
Attorneys for Defendants Peter Smith
and Lucy Smith

CERTIFICATION

I hereby certify that on ___________, I mailed a true copy of the within Answer to Attorney Charlene M. Murphy, Esq., 333 Landing Avenue, Providence, RI 02910 and Attorney Lucus Moore, 89 Willow Street, Pawtucket, RI 02860

____
Ronald Jacobs

Example 6-12. Rhode Island, Motion to Amend Complaint

(date)

STATE OF RHODE ISLAND SUPERIOR COURT
PROVIDENCE, SC.

JOHN MARTIN	:	
	:	C.A. NO. PC 98-0000
V.	:	
	:	
JAMES TYLER,	:	
PETER SMITH and	:	
LUCY SMITH	:	

MOTION TO AMEND COMPLAINT

Plaintiff, John Martin, hereby moves this Honorable Court for leave to file the Amended Complaint in the manner and form attached hereto.

JOHN MARTIN
Plaintiff
By his Attorney

____
Charlene M. Murphy, Bar # 1111
Murphy & Sable
333 Landing Ave.
Providence, RI 02910
Tele. (401) 946-1111

NOTICE OF HEARING

Please take notice that the within motion shall be called for hearing before a Justice of the Providence County Superior Court on the ____ day of ____ at 9:30 a.m. or as soon thereafter as counsel may be heard; if objection be timely filed pursuant to Rule 7(b)(3) to the Rhode Island Superior Court Rules of Civil Procedure, otherwise this motion will be deemed granted by Rule of Court.

____
Charlene M. Murphy

CERTIFICATION

I hereby certify that I caused a true and accurate copy of the within document to be mailed by regular mail, postage prepaid, from the law office of Murphy & Sable of 333 Landing Ave., Providence, RI to ______________on this ___ day of __ 19__.

____
Charlene M. Murphy

Note to readers: Don't forget to attach the Amended Complaint.

7 THE PRETRIAL STAGE: MOTIONS AND OBJECTIONS

TERMINOLOGY

Motion	Request	Objection
Oral Argument	On the Papers	Continuance
Sustain	Brief	Memorandum of Law
Overrule	Hearing	Order
With Prejudice	Without Prejudice	Enlargement
Adjournment	Notice of Hearing	

INTRODUCTION

In the last chapter we discussed responsive pleadings. At minimum, a Defendant must serve and file an Answer to the Complaint. When reviewing the sample Answers and other responsive pleadings, notice that no court action is required. These pleadings merely contain a series of replies, some defenses and allegations of additional disputes between the parties. When all the responsive pleadings have been filed, the pleadings are closed.

In addition to pleadings, the parties in a lawsuit often file numerous *motions* at various times during the litigation process. The purpose of a motion is to ask the court or the opposing party to take a specific course of action.

The majority of motions rarely address the actual dispute between the parties. Instead, they address technicalities involving court rules and statutes relating to specific litigation procedures and ask a judge (never a jury) to make a decision. While some of these issues arise during and after trial, most arise during the Pretrial Stage when the Defendant is attempting to have the court dismiss the Plaintiff's case.

Before we move on, don't forget that every time any party files a document in court (except an *ex-parte* matter), he or she must send a copy to all the other attorneys of record (or pro ses) in the case and state that this occurred in the *certification of service*. This rule applies to pro se parties as well as attorneys. Failure to comply can result in disciplinary action from the court.

I. Motions and Objections

In simplistic terms, **motions** are written documents drafted by any party that ask the court to decide a particular issue pertaining to a lawsuit. **Objections** are written documents that are drafted by a party who receives a motion and is opposed to it.

A. Types of Motions

I have divided motions into two types:

1. motions that are directed to the Complaint, Cross Claim, or Counterclaim; and
2. motions that are directed to discovery, pretrial, trial, and post-trial procedures.

For instance, in the first type, if a Defendant is not properly served a copy of a Complaint, he or she may file a Motion to Dismiss. In the second type, either party may file a motion against an opposing party who fails to comply with required discovery deadlines or if they want to prevent certain evidence from being introduced at trial. The list of other possible motions seems endless and many states label their motions differently. Nevertheless, they tend to accomplish the same purpose.

This chapter focuses on motion practice, which entails drafting, serving, filing, objecting, and arguing in court. Specific types of commonly drafted motions are discussed beginning in Chapter 8 and continuing throughout the remainder of the text.

B. Memorandums of Law and Briefs

Many motions and objections are short and to the point. Others are more lengthy and contain a **memorandum of law** or a **brief,** depending upon your state's terminology. The purpose of a memo of law or a brief is to provide legal arguments in the form of analysis, case law, and other legal authority such as statutes and court rules to support a party's motion or objection. Each state's rules indicate when the motion or objection must be accompanied by a memo of law or a brief.

C. Responding to Motions

When a party receives a motion from the opposing party, he or she has three options:

1. File an **objection** to the motion, with or without a memorandum of law; or
2. Attempt to correct the issue raised in the motion; or
3. Do nothing and wait for the court's ruling on the motion.

An objection is the most common type of response. Essentially, it is a written response, filed in court, that challenges the claims, arguments, and case law contained in the motion and asks the court to disregard them. If a party fails to file an objection or fails to attempt to correct the issues raised in the motion, a court may interpret this as the party's consent for it to grant the motion. Other courts will review the motion and deny it if it is contrary to the law even if an objection is not filed.

II. Requests, Compliance, and Objections

Typically, requests are written documents from one party asking his or her opponent to take a specific type of action. In most states, a request is treated as automatically granted by the court unless the opposing party files an objection within a specific period of time. If an objection is filed, a judge will decide the issue. If no objection is filed or the deadline is missed, the party who received the request must comply with what is being asked. Requests are less common than motions and often involve various types of discovery procedures.

III. How Courts Decide Motions and Objections

In most states, the party serving and filing a motion will simply call the clerk's office and ask for the next available *motion date,* time, and courtroom location in which the motion will be decided by a judge. This date, time, and location will then be included in the motion, usually under the heading, **Notice of Hearing,** to inform both the court and the other parties. (Connecticut has a different procedure. See the State Summaries.)

Upon receiving a copy of the motion, the opposing party must be sure to serve and file an objection within a specific time period before the assignment date. This deadline will be stated in the applicable court rules. As a result, the judge will have the opportunity to review both the motion and the objection before making a decision. (In some situations, the party who filed the motion may be permitted to file a written reply to the objection before the judge makes his or her decision.)

Requests are a bit different. Because they are automatically granted if no objection is filed, they are not assigned a date to be decided by a judge. Instead, the objection is assigned a date to be decided, as described above.

A. A Hearing vs. No Hearing

Written motions and objections filed in court during the Pretrial Stage are decided in one of two ways: After a **hearing,** or **on the papers.**

Before we go further, keep in mind that only judges decide motions and objections. A jury's only function is to decide *at trial* the actual dispute that led to the lawsuit between the parties.

If a motion arises during a trial, the jury is usually not present in the courtroom when it is brought to the attention of the judge. Objections to evidence, as seen on television and in the movies, differ in that they may be briefly addressed in front of the jury. However, if the issue becomes hotly contested or complicated, the jury will be removed from the courtroom, out of earshot of the attorney's arguments and the judge's decision. They will return when the issue has been resolved and are sometimes given a brief explanation or instruction by the judge.

1. Hearings

In many states, only specific types of motions and objections are entitled to a hearing. In addition, a hearing is usually only needed if there is an objection to a motion.

A hearing is like a mini trial. It enables both parties to explain to the judge, through **oral argument** (and **testimony** if needed), why the judge should rule in their favor. After the hearing and after the judge has the opportunity to review the parties' written documents, one of two things will occur:

a. The judge will announce the decision to the parties *from the bench;* or

b. The judge will *take the papers.* This means the judge wants more time to make a decision. In this instance, the parties will be notified of the decision by mail or by a telephone call from the judge's clerk. This can take days, weeks, or sometimes months.

2. Motions and Objections Decided without a Hearing

Motions and objections that are resolved without a hearing are decided by a judge after he or she reviews the parties' documents. The decision is then sent by mail or through a telephone call from the clerk.

Note: If a party wants a hearing on a motion or objection but is not entitled to one under the court rules, most courthouses have a procedure that allows the party to ask permission for a hearing by filing a motion or contacting the clerk's office, etc. Many times, permission is granted.

B. Rulings on Motions and Objections

Motions may be ***granted*** or ***denied.*** These definitions are self-explanatory. Objections may be **sustained** or **overruled.** This can get a bit confusing. Try to remember it this way:

1. If a judge sustains an objection, the party who made the objection wins. As a result, the motion or request objected to is denied.
2. If a judge overrules an objection, the party who made the objection loses. As a result, the motion or request objected to is granted.

In addition, a judge may make a ruling *with prejudice* or *without prejudice,* or reserve the ruling until the time of trial.

a. A ruling **with prejudice** means that the ruling is final and neither party should raise the issue again.
b. A ruling **without prejudice** has the opposite effect. Either party may raise the motion or objection at a later time in the case and the judge will reconsider it.

Last, some issues are more appropriately decided at the time of trial, after the parties have completed discovery, etc. Therefore, a court may decide to delay ruling on a motion or objection until a later time when the contested issues in the case are more defined and/or parties have additional information to provide to the judge to assist him or her in reaching a decision.

C. The Judge's Order

The judge's ruling or decision on a motion or objection is called an **order.** If an order has the effect of ending a lawsuit before it reaches trial, such as granting a Motion to Dismiss, the party who disagrees with the order may immediately challenge it by appealing it to that state's appellate court. If, on the other hand, the order does not end the case, the disagreeing party will usually have to wait to appeal it later, after the case is resolved by a trial. If the case is settled, the order becomes moot and no appeal is allowed. (See Chapter 22 for more details on appeals.)

Other types of orders are less crucial in that they may direct a party to comply with a particular overdue discovery request or to file a specific overdue responsive pleading by a certain deadline, etc. If the deadline is directed to a Plaintiff who misses it, the case could be dismissed. If it is directed to a Defendant who misses it, a *default* may enter against him or her. In addition, the judge could order the noncomplying party to pay the opposing party's attorney's fees for having to bring the motion in the first place.

IV. Continuances, Adjournments, Extensions, and Enlargments

There will be times when a party's attorney will need to postpone a hearing date or the deadline date to respond to a motion. Fortunately, each state recognizes this reality and provides court rules to address the situation. Note, however, that instead of using the word "postponement," the words continuance, adjournment, extension, or enlargement may be used, depending upon the state you are working in.

A. Continuances and Adjournments

A Motion for Continuance or Motion for Adjournment asks the court to postpone a court event such as a hearing on a motion or objection, a pretrial conference, or even the trial itself and includes the reason for the requested postponement. In many instances, if the opposing party in the case agrees, the court will usually grant the motion (though postponing a trial date may be more difficult). As a result, when drafting the motion, be sure to include the consent and the agreed upon date for compliance as well as the reason for the delay.

If an opposing party does not consent to the postponement, file the motion anyway. Most courts will usually grant them if there is an adequate reason to justify the postponement and it does not unduly delay the case.

B. Extensions and Enlargements

A Motion for Extension of Time or Motion for Enlargement of Time (depending upon your state) asks the court to give a party more time to take a specific course of action such as respond to discovery, etc. Like a Motion for Continuance or Adjournment, it is more likely to be granted if the opposing party has no objection.

Note: It is good practice to file the motion before the deadline has passed.

V. Format of Motions, Requests, and Objections

Like pleadings, the majority of motions, requests, and objections contain the following:

1. a case caption, including a title that states the type of document;
2. content of the document including the grounds relied upon and the relief requested;
3. the attorney's identifying information such as name, law firm, address, telephone number, and license number to practice law;
4. the drafting attorney's signature above the printed name;
5. the date the document was signed;

6. a memorandum of law or brief; and
7. a certification of service stating that a copy of the document(s) was mailed or hand delivered to all other attorneys of record in the case on a specific date. Include the attorneys' names and the date and type of service, followed by the serving attorney's signature. See other required information in the applicable court rules.

Furthermore, in many states, *motions* and *objections* must contain the following:

1. An Order

Some states require the order to set forth how the party wants the court to rule on the document. In other states, such as Connecticut, the party must provide a space on the document for the judge to insert the ruling.

2. Notice of Hearing

As stated earlier, in most states, a party filing a motion or objection to a request may call the court to verify the specific date, time, and location for the matter to be decided. This information should then be included in the document.

Remember, requests do not need an order or a notice of hearing because they will not be addressed by the court unless a party files an objection.

VI. Affidavits, Affirmations, and Certifications

In addition to a motion or objection, a party may include other documents that support his or her argument.

A. Affidavits

An affidavit is a written statement that sets forth specific information that a party or nonparty swears is accurate to a third party such as a Notary Public or other individual the court authorizes to administer oaths. (See examples on pages 171 and 316.)

B. Affirmations and Certifications

In addition to or in lieu of affidavits, some states recognize affirmations. Similar to an affidavit, it is a written statement that sets forth specific information. The difference is that usually there is no need for a third party to acknowledge the person's oath. Instead, the person signing the affirmation acknowledges that he or she could be charged with committing perjury if it is later determined that the affirmation is untrue.

VII. Motions for Reconsideration

After a motion is decided by a judge, most states permit the party who lost the argument to ask the judge to reconsider his or her decision. In many instances, such a Motion for Reconsideration or Motion to Reargue may be based upon new information or case law that was not previously available, etc.

VIII. Conclusion

In addition to pleadings, the majority of the Pretrial Stage consists of motions, requests, objections, and discovery. As a result, their requirements and deadlines will keep both sides of any lawsuit extremely busy. To help you stay organized, you may find it helpful to photocopy the applicable state checklist found in Appendix A.

Key Issues in This Chapter

1. *Motions* are written documents that are filed by either party asking the court to decide issues that relate to litigation procedures in a particular case. These issues usually do not address the actual dispute between the parties.
2. *Requests* are written documents that ask a party to comply with a specific course of conduct. Though requests are usually filed in court, they are treated as automatically granted unless the party who received the request files an objection within the applicable deadline stated in the court rules.
3. Some motions and objections are comprised of a simple format. Others require the parties to attach a memorandum of law or a brief that contains legal analysis, case law, etc., to support their claims.
4. Motions are *granted* or *denied.*
5. Objections are *sustained* or *overruled.*
6. Motions and objections are decided only by a judge. The jury's only role is to decide the dispute between the parties that led to filing the lawsuit.
7. Some types of motions and objections are decided by a judge after a *hearing.* A hearing is a mini trial that permits each party to present oral argument and testimony, if necessary, to support their claims. Other types of motions and objections are decided *on the papers,* meaning without a hearing. In those instances, the judge will make a decision after reviewing each party's documents.
8. In addition to a case caption and the attorney's identifying information, etc., each motion and objection should contain a *notice of hearing* and possibly an *order.*

STATE SUMMARIES

Beginning in Chapter 8, you will find numerous examples of motions, requests, and objections in this text. In addition, page xxvii lists these documents as they relate to the five lawsuits found at the end of Chapter 4. These are the more common types of documents filed and provide good examples of how parties in each of the five states should address the issues they discuss.

Connecticut's motion practice procedures differ from the other states and are detailed in the Connecticut summary. The remaining states follow the Notice of Hearing system. Note also that New Jersey's method for determining the date of service of motions differs from its method for determining the date of service of responsive pleadings.

Motion Practice in Connecticut

I. Motions and Pleadings

As stated in Chapter 6, Connecticut's pleadings practice is combined with specific motions and a request that are listed in Pbs 10-6. The deadlines for those motions/pleadings are found in Pbs 10-8 and are recited in Chapter 8 where similar motions recognized by other states are discussed.

In addition to the motions and the request found in Pbs 10-6, there are many other types of motions that may be filed at any time before (or possibly during and after) trial. Several of them are discussed in this text. Any deadline restrictions are found in the applicable practice book sections.

At this juncture, we will address how motions, requests, and objections reach the court to be decided by a judge.

II. Short Calendar Instead of a Notice of Hearing

Connecticut civil motions and objections do not contain a Notice of Hearing as mentioned in this chapter. Instead, motions and objections are assigned a date, usually two or three weeks after they are filed. The parties get notice of the date by receiving a copy of a ***Short Calendar*** in the mail.

A. Short Calendar

Short Calendar is a computer-generated list of all motions and objections that are scheduled to be decided on a specific date that is stated on the calendar. In most courthouses, this date is usually a Monday.

The list is generated weekly and differs depending upon which documents are currently pending. It is sent by mail to all law offices that have cases on the list. The law firms usually receive it on the Tuesday prior to the Monday court date.

The term Short Calendar is also used to describe the court appearance that is necessary if the parties wish to present oral arguments and possible testimony. For instance, you may hear the following phrases: "I've got Short Calendar on Monday" or, "That motion was decided last week at Short Calendar."

B. Contents of a Short Calendar

You will find an example of a Short Calendar at the end of this State Summary. As you can see, it contains a lot of very important information.

In the top left-hand corner, you will find:

1. The name and address of the court where the matter will be decided.
2. The date of the Short Calendar: This means the date the matter will be assigned to a judge to hear oral argument or consider the motion or objection without oral argument.
3. The time court opens to address the motion or objection listed on the Short Calendar.
4. Special instructions pertaining to that courthouse.
5. The name of the judge and the courtroom; if not included here, you can obtain this information in court the day of Short Calendar.

For each case listed on the Short Calendar, you will find:

1. The docket number.
2. The name of the case: Plaintiff's name at the top and the Defendant's name below.
3. The name of the motion or objection, under the case name.
4. The number assigned by the court to the motion or objection. It can be found directly in front of the document. See Pbs 4-3.
5. The Plaintiff's attorney's law firm on the left and the Defendant's attorney's firm on the right.
6. The **position number** in parentheses (this number assists in locating a case on the Short Calendar).
7. The **column number** at the bottom of each column (this number also assists in locating a case on the Short Calendar).
8. In the bottom left corner, either "N/A" for **nonarguable** (taken on the papers) or "Arg" for **Arguable** (oral argument and possible testimony) appears.

C. To Find Your Motion or Objection

The position number of your case(s) can be found on the envelope the Short Calendar was mailed in. Usually, it is directly above the law firm's address. Find your case by simply following the list of position numbers.

D. Oral Argument As a Right: Pbs 11-18

The parties are *entitled* to oral argument and, if necessary, to present witnesses to testify in the following situations:

1. A Motion to Dismiss, with or without an objection;
2. A Motion to Strike, with or without an objection;

3. A Motion for Summary Judgment, with or without an objection;
4. A Motion for Judgment of Foreclosure, with or without an objection.

Pursuant to Pbs 4-1, the party who drafted any of the above and wants oral argument must take two steps to notify the court:

1. Type: ORAL ARGUMENT REQUESTED
TESTIMONY (NOT) REQUIRED

   on the bottom left-hand corner of the first page of the pleading; and
2. Inform the court by "marking the motion or objection ready" according to the directions found on the applicable Short Calendar. (See Section F below.)

E. When Oral Argument Is Not Requested

If the party who drafted any of the above-listed motions does not want oral argument, he or she should state the following on the bottom left-hand corner of the first page of the motion:

ORAL ARGUMENT NOT REQUESTED
TESTIMONY NOT REQUIRED

F. When an Opposing Party Wants Oral Argument

The opposing party who files an objection to any of the above-listed motions will still have the opportunity to argue or present testimony by filing a **Notice of Intent to Argue,** pursuant to Pbs 11-18.

G. Deadline to File Notice of Intent to Argue

This notice must be filed no later than the ***third day*** before the date the motion is scheduled to be decided. In addition, some courts request the party filing the notice to also inform the court clerk by telephone. Once the clerk (or the judge assigned to the case) is aware of the Notice of Intent to Argue, the case will be scheduled for argument. (Some courthouses permit oral argument that same day. Others will reschedule the case to be heard on another day.)

H. Oral Argument for Other Motions or Objections

Each court has specific instructions that are stated on the Short Calendar for parties to follow if they want oral argument on a motion or objection not listed above. The decision rests solely within the court's discretion.

I. Marking Cases

The party who files a motion or objection that appears on a Short Calendar has the option of **marking** it "ready" or "off." It doesn't matter if the pleading is Arguable or Not Arguable. **Marking** simply means to inform the court, pursuant to the instructions on the Short Calendar, whether or not the party wants the pleading assigned to a judge on the Short Calendar date. A ***ready*** marking means yes. An ***off*** marking means no. The opposing party cannot contact the court and mark a pleading ready or off without the consent of the party who filed it.

J. Short Calendar List Claim/Reclaim Slip: Pbs 11-13

A **Short Calendar List Claim/Reclaim** is a yellow, court-issued form that serves two purposes:

1. to **reclaim** a motion or objection to the Short Calendar that has been previously marked off: This means to ask the court (by filing the slip) to reprint the case on the next Short Calendar; or
2. to **claim** a motion or objection to the Short Calendar: In most instances, motions and objections will automatically appear on a Short Calendar two to three weeks after they are filed in court. Some, however, do not, for instance, a Motion for Nonsuit and Motion for Default pursuant to Pbs 17-31. Therefore, the drafting party must notify the court (by filing the slip) that the document should be printed on the next Short Calendar.

In addition, only the party who drafted a motion or objection should be able to claim or reclaim it.

III. When a Memorandum of Law Is Required: Pbs 11-10

As stated in this chapter, some motions and objections are very short and to the point. Others require the parties to attach a **memorandum of law.** A memorandum of law is a document in which a party presents the facts of the case, the applicable statutes, rules, and case law, and his or her supporting legal arguments.

In Connecticut, the following motions must be accompanied by a memorandum of law.

1. Pbs 9-18: Motions to Add or Substitute Parties;
2. Pbs 10-11: Motions to Implead a Third-Party Defendant;
3. Pbs 10-30: Motions to Dismiss, except those filed pursuant to Pbs 14-3;
4. Pbs 10-39: Motions to Strike;
5. Pbs 17-4: Motions to Set Aside Judgment;
6. Pbs 17-44: Motions for Summary Judgment.

Turn to pages 169–170 for an example of the format of a motion with a memorandum of law.

IV. Content of the Order

Refer to page 169 and examine the order. Notice that it simply asks the court to circle whether the motion is granted or denied and sign below. In many instances, at the judge's request, his or her clerk will actually sign the order. By contrast, turn to the New Jersey motion and order on pages 214–216. Here, the party drafting the motion is expected to draft the terms of the order he or she wants the court to grant.

V. Motions for Reconsideration: Pbs 11-12

Connecticut calls a Motion for Reconsideration a Motion to Reargue. Consult Pbs 11-12 for details.

HHB$$$$sh1

New Britain
SUPERIOR COURT
Short Calendar—Law

Hon. Bernard D. Gaffney (A.A.J.)
Hon. Robert L. Holzberg (P.J.)
Hon. Sandra V. Leheny
Hon. James T. Graham
Hon. Joseph H. Goldberg
Hon. Harry N. Jackaway
Hon. Julius J. Kremski
Hon. Max H. Reicher
177 Columbus Boulevard
Courtroom 202
9:30 A.M.

NOTICE

MARKINGS: Markings are taken by telephone only on the Thursday and Friday preceding the Calendar. Call (860) 827-7133.

The Clerk's Office accepts only "Off by Agreement" or "Take the Papers by Agreement" markings for arguable motions. Motions not marked "Off" are considered ready: "Ready" markings are not

(Notice Continued on Last Column)

TABLE OF CONTENTS

SHORT CAL. NO. 1

PREJUDGMENT REMEDIES 05/04/98 09.30
NON FAMILY 05/04/98 09.30

05/04/98 09.30
PREJUDGMENT REMEDIES

PJR 0486702 S BRIAN-THOMAS CANDY
CV-98 V. PATEL,SANAT ET AL
(1)
REINER R & B PC C.P. DIFAZIO
N/A 103.00 MOTION TO STRIKE

PJR 0485323 S YANKEE GAS SERVICES
CV-98 V. WEINSTEIN,ROBERT,H.
(2)
PEPE & HAZARD WEINSTEIN & ASSO
ARG * 101.00 PJR HEARING-ATTACHMENT
ARG 102.00 MOT PJR ASSET DISCLOSURE

PJR 0486925 S PEOPLE'S BANK
CV-98 V. SPYROS,EDWARD,J.
(3)
GESMONDE P S & P PRO SE
ARG 101.00 PJR HEARING-ATTACHMENT

PJR 0486926 S PEOPLE'S BANK
CV-98 V. CLOUTIER,JOSEPH,R.
(4)
GESMONDE P S & P NO APPEARANCE
ARG 101.00 PJR HEARING-ATTACHMENT

PJR 0472829 S SCHOONMAKER,WILLIAM ET AL
CV-96 V. LAWRENCE BRUNOLI ET AL
(5)
T.BRIGNOLE CRANMORE F & MEA
GORDON,M & F
N/A 172.00 OBJECTION TO MOTION

PJR 0486233 S PRIME HOMES,INC.
CV-98 V. BUCKEY,ARLENE S.
(6)
MORAN S C & KNIE P.A.KEILY
ARG * 101.00 PJR HEARING-ATTACHMENT
ARG 102.00 MOT PJR ASSET DISCLOSURE

PJR 0479536 S PRESUTTI,JOSEPH
CV-97 V. COATMAN,MICHAEL
(7)
T.BRIGNOLE GOLDNER ELLEN PE
N/A 108.00 MOT FOR NONSUIT-DISCVERY

PJR 0486550 S GARRETT,KELLI
CV-98 V. REOME,KEITH
(8)
ZIEGLER R A WEBER & M.
N/A 105.00 MOTION TO STRIKE

PJR 0487059 S PODHAJSKI,VIRGINIA ET AL
CV-98 V. MO-NO-POLE REST.
(9)
TABELLIONE T P P NO APPEARANCE
ARG 101.00 PJR HEARING-ATTACHMENT

PJR 0485368 S COLLOCK,YVONNE
CV-98 V. ZUBROWSKI,CASMIER
(10)
WEBER & M. FUREY D E K T &
ARG 101.00 PJR HEARING-ATTACHMENT

PJR 0486979 S HARTFORD TELEPHONE
CV-98 V. KARMELOWICZ,LINDA,M.
(11)
EISENBERG A M & NO APPEARANCE
ARG 101.00 PJR HEARING-ATTACHMENT

PJR 0482596 S LINN,VERONICA
CV-97 V. MCNAMEE,THOMAS,G.
(12)
EISENBERG A M & FORD O M & H PC
ARG 101.00 PJR HEARING-ATTACHMENT

05/04/98 09.30
NON FAMILY
NON-SUIT/DEFLTS NON-ARG

0485207 S HARDY,DANIEL
CV-98 V. TRAVELERS PROPERTY ET AL
(13)
JD JELLY CLENDANIEL W & L
HARRIGAN C L L O
N/A 106.00 MOT FOR NONSUIT-DISCVERY

0485807 S KELLEY,ROSALEE,B.
CV-98 V. WEINSTEIN,ROSLYN
(14)
W. BUMSTER LEONE T & NAGLE
N/A 104.00 MOT FOR NONSUIT-DISCVERY

0484909 S MUCCINO,NANCY
CV-97 V. HARTFORD,CITY OF ET AL
(15)
F.P. O'SULLIVAN CLENDANIEL W & L
N/A 106.00 MOT FOR NONSUIT-DISCVERY

0485412 S ABELL,MICHELE,M.
CV-98 V. MURPHY,STEPHEN ET AL
(16)
BUTLER N & GOLD DUBORG G J L OFF
N/A 104.00 MOT FOR NONSUIT-DISCVERY

0484216 S WILLIAMS,HARRY ET AL
CV-97 V. LAJOIE,MARY,A. ET AL
(17)
S.P.SZTABA L.H. LEWIS
HOWD & L.
N/A 106.00 MOT FOR NONSUIT-DISCVERY

0482318 S CHUDZIK,ALBERT ET AL
CV-97 V. MONTELEONE,FRENANDO
(18)
WEBER & M. CARTAFALSA & SHI
N/A * 109.00 MOT FOR NONSUIT-DISCVERY
N/A 110.00 MOT FOR NONSUIT-DISCVERY

0485618 S DIBELLA,BRENDA A.
CV-98 V. PROCACCINI,SARAH M. ET AL
(19)
JEPSON & F LLC CLENDANIEL W & L
N/A 103.00 MOT FOR NONSUIT-DISCVERY

0485923 S CASALE,BRIAN ET AL
CV-98 V. JANKOWSKI,ROBERT,J.
(20)
GORDON,M & F NUZZO & R LLC
N/A 104.00 MOT FOR NONSUIT-DISCVERY

0486124 S COMPLEX CARE,INC.
CV-98 V. LAUREL WOODS,INC. ET AL
(21)

---CONTINUED

RL KITTREDGE A.J.ZULLO
BROWN W & V PC
N/A 105.00 OBJECTION TO DEFAULT
N/A * 105.25 MOT FOR NONSUIT-DISCVERY

0484925 S HERZIG,MICHAEL,J. ET AL
CV-97 V. EATON,JAMES,R. ET AL
(22)
G.A.DELPIANO KENNY & B
N/A 107.00 MOT FOR NONSUIT-DISCVERY

0486032 S CLEVELAND,ERSKIN ET AL
CV-98 V. TREVETHAN,ANDREA ET AL
(23)
NAMNOUM KENNETH L.H. LEWIS
N/A 102.00 MOT FOR NONSUIT-DISCVERY

0484842 S DZIURDZIAK,TOMASZ ET AL
CV-97 V. BELIVEAU,MICHAEL,S.
(24)
D.LUEDERS CLENDANIEL W & L
N/A 108.00 MOT FOR NONSUIT-DISCVERY

0485747 S WATTS,RUTH
CV-98 V. MCCANN,WILLIAM J. ET AL
(25)
JD JELLY GORDON,M & F
ROSENBAUM N S L FRANKFORTER LOIS
N/A 117.00 MOT FOR NONSUIT-DISCVERY

0475548 S DEBELLA,ANN MARIE
CV-96 V. DEBELLA,MICHAEL
(26)
JI HAYMOND SYLVESTRE DAVID
N/A 119.00 OBJ EXTND DISCOVERY TIME
N/A * 120.00 MOT FOR NONSUIT-DISCVERY
N/A 121.00 MOT ORDER RE DISCOVERY

0485262 S GORDON,MARVELLA
CV-97 V. DOUGLAS,GLORIA
(27)
MCCARTHY & S. CLENDANIEL W & L
N/A 103.00 MOT FOR NONSUIT-DISCVERY

0476864 S FUSCO,CHERYL A. ET AL
CV-96 V. LAFRANCE,ARMAND
(28)
EISENBERG A M & KERNAN & HENRY
N/A 121.00 MOT EXTEND TIME
N/A * 123.00 MOT FOR NONSUIT-DISCVERY

0482996 S TARICANI STILES,J.
CV-97 V. GOLD STAR MED.SER. ET AL
(29)
SWEENET & GRIFFE MILLER G H J L O
N/A 105.00 MOTION TO COMPEL
N/A * 105.25 MOT FOR NONSUIT-DISCVERY

05/04/98 09.30
NON FAMILY
MISCELLANEOUS ARG.

0480801 S LAWLER,GEORGE V.,EXE
CV-97 V. LUNDBORG,WILFRID G.
(30)
GV LAWLER PRO SE
ARG 111.00 PJR HEARING-ATTACHMENT

0479801 S PEOPLES BANK
CV-97 V. CATANZARO,PAUL,D.
(31)
GESMONDE P S & P NO APPEARANCE
ARG 108.00 PET EXAMINE JT DEBTOR

0481816 S VALLEY TEACHERS' FED
CV-97 V. BENITES,JESUS
(32)
EISENBERG A M & NO APPEARANCE
ARG 104.00 PET EXAMINE JT DEBTOR

FL* 0465117 S BRACKETT,WALLACE ET AL
CV-94 V. CALO,MICHAEL,P. ET AL
(33)
MARINELLI S & H NO APPEARANCE
ARG 102.00 APPL EXAMINE JGMT DEBTOR

COLUMN 1
NEW BRITAIN SHORT CAL NO. 1
COLUMN 2
COLUMN 3

```
0485042 S       RICKARD,KYLE W.
CV-97        V. JOHNSON,ERNEST R.     ET AL
                 ( 153)
JI HAYMOND              MORRISON M & MIL
 N/A   108.00 MOT ORDER RE DISCOVERY
-------------------------------------------
0481443 S       SAGLIMBENI,JERRYR
CV-97        V. ROSSIER,JOHN W.
                 ( 154)
KRAWIECKI & DORV        PRO SE
 N/A   113.00 MOT ORDER RE DISCOVERY
-------------------------------------------
0484655 S       MALLOOKIS,GEORGE
CV-97        V. AUTOTOTE ENTERPRISES
                 ( 155)
MARINELLI S & H         DANAHER T L & N
 N/A   110.00 MOT ORDER RE DISCOVERY
-------------------------------------------
0477361 S       CHATEAUNEUF,ROBERT
CV-96        V. VELASQUEZ,JAIME,A.    ET AL
                 ( 156)
GAFFNEY K R & S         GORDON,M & F
                        L.H. LEWIS
 N/A   119.00 REQ EXTND DISCOVERY TIME
-------------------------------------------
0485374 S       ARAUJO,GREGORY        ET AL
CV-98        V. BASSELL,CHRISTIAN
                 ( 157)
NEISTAT & MASON         DUBORG G J L OFF
 N/A   102.00 MOT ORDER RE DISCOVERY
-------------------------------------------
0483277 S       SIEMBAB,LAUREN
CV-97        V. SAMUEL-HODGE,ROSIE
                 ( 158)
KC FERRY                KENNY & B
 N/A   113.00 MOT ORDER RE DISCOVERY
-------------------------------------------
0468877 S       CLARKE,ANTWAIN J.     ET AL
CV-95        V. FOUNTAIN,KEVIN        ET AL
                 ( 159)
APPLETON & APPLE        CLENDANIEL W & L
 N/A   120.00 MOT DETERMINE ADMISSION
-------------------------------------------
MED 0459377 S   FERONE,MARY ANN
CV-93        V. NEW BRITAIN,CITY OF   ET AL
                 ( 160)
MCELENEY & M.           NEW B C COUNSEL
 N/A   125.00 AFFIDAVIT RE OBJECTION
-------------------------------------------
0485783 S       MICHAUD,TAMMY
CV-98        V. MURRAY,PAUL W.        ET AL
                 ( 161)
D. KOSKOFF              KENNY & B
 N/A   105.00 MOT ORDER RE DISCOVERY
-------------------------------------------
LPL 0477290 S   CARRERO,JENNIFER      ET AL
CV-96        V. HOPKO,ROBERT S.       ET AL
                 ( 162)
NEISTAT & MASON         PRO SE
                        P.M.BLOCK
                        MORRISON M & MIL
                        MCNAMARA F T PC
                        REGNIER,T. C & E
                        PICKETT J M L OF
 N/A * 115.00 MOT ORDER RE DISCOVERY
 N/A   116.00 MOT ORDER RE DISCOVERY
-------------------------------------------
0485394 S       SHAPIRO,DENISE,T.
CV-98        V. ST. EDWARD,ANGE
                 ( 163)
RISCASSI & D PC         ROSENBLATT & S L
 N/A   108.00 MOT ORDER RE DISCOVERY
-------------------------------------------
0482695 S       LABROAD,JOHN W.
CV-97        V. MCELENEY,MICHAEL      ET AL
                 ( 164)
COONEY, S. & D.         HOWARD,K,S & F
                        DANAHER T L & N
 N/A   112.00 MOT ORDER RE DISCOVERY
-------------------------------------------
0486197 S       KOLODZIEJ,MARZENA,E.
CV-98        V. BLAMBERG,ROBERT,R.    ET AL
                 ( 165)
WEIN & P LLC            CLENDANIEL W & L
                        REGNIER,T. C & E
 N/A   107.00 MOT ORDER RE DISCOVERY
-------------------------------------------
0479997 S       NORWEST BANK IOWA
CV-97        V. BOREK,WALTER E.       ET AL
                 ( 166)
WEINSTEIN & ASSO        ROSENZWEIG C M L
                           ---CONTINUED

NEW BRITAIN      COLUMN 13     SHORT CAL NO. 1
```

```
 N/A   107.00 MOT ORDER RE DISCOVERY
-------------------------------------------

           05/04/98  09.30
             NON FAMILY
        QUESTIONS OF LAW ARG.

-------------------------------------------
0469213 S       OSTERLING,MICHELLE
CV-95        V. VAN,RICHARD
                 ( 167)
WILLCUTTS T P &         HOWD & L.
                        WILLCUTTS T P &
 ARG   134.25 MOT FOR SUMMARY JUDGMENT
-------------------------------------------
0485714 S       FORD,DAVID M.         ET AL
CV-98        V. SERIGNESE,P. & Z.     ET AL
                 ( 168)
DM FORD                 UPDIKE, K.&S.
                        G.A.DELPIANO
 ARG * 120.00 MOTION TO STRIKE
 N/A   121.00 MOT PROTECTIVE ORDER
 N/A   121.25 MOTION FOR SANCTIONS
-------------------------------------------
0485328 S       WILSHIRE CREDIT CORP
CV-98        V. SCHWARTZ,SCOTT,M.
                 ( 169)
SULLIVAN B & WIN        RM SOLAZZO
 ARG   108.00 MOTION TO STRIKE
-------------------------------------------
0478432 S       MAINELLI,GARY
CV-97        V. LAZ PARKING LTD
                 ( 170)
MARINELLI S & H         SMITH K & MUSCO
                        HARTFORD C COUNS
 ARG   114.00 MOTION TO STRIKE
-------------------------------------------
0484135 S       KALINOWSKI,DANIEL     ET AL
CV-97        V. WADDELL & REED,INC.   ET AL
                 ( 171)
WILLCUTTS T P &         C BOTTICELLI
TF BUTLER               LYNCH T K & E PC
                        DAY,B & H
                        CUMMINGS & LOCK
 ARG * 118.00 MOTION TO STRIKE
 ARG   119.00 MOTION TO STRIKE
-------------------------------------------
0479341 S       FLANNERY,NANCY
CV-97        V. FORMICA & DOBKIN
                 ( 172)
ZIEGLER R A             SWEENET & GRIFFE
 ARG   117.00 MOT FOR SUMMARY JUDGMENT
-------------------------------------------
0483349 S       PEOPLES BANK
CV-97        V. LINDO,BARBARA P.,AKA
                 ( 173)
GESMONDE P S & P        I.E.HARE,JR.
 ARG   107.00 MOT FOR SUMMARY JUDGMENT
-------------------------------------------
0484365 S       BARBER-COLMAN
CV-97        V. MANCHESTER,TOWN OF    ET AL
                 ( 174)
PEPE & HAZARD           MANCH. CRP. CSL.
                        TYLER, C. & A.
 ARG   117.00 MOTION TO DISMISS
-------------------------------------------
0481266 S       NORTH AMERICAN MRKT
CV-97        V. MACHINERY VALUES
                 ( 175)
SOROKIN S G H &         WA SNIDER
 ARG   107.00 MOT FOR SUMMARY JUDGMENT
-------------------------------------------
0483674 S       JACKSON,CLARENCE
CV-97        V. CONN. LOTTERY CORP.
                 ( 176)
JACOBS & J PC           CARMODY & T
 ARG   103.00 MOT FOR SUMMARY JUDGMENT
-------------------------------------------
0485797 S       ADAJIAN,REGINA P.
CV-98        V. POULOS,DICK T.        ET AL
                 ( 177)
A.A. KORZENIK           ZULTOWSKY H L OF
 ARG   101.00 MOTION TO STRIKE
-------------------------------------------

CHIEF CLERK

                 COLUMN  14
```

NOTICE (continued from Column 1)

taken. N/A (non-arguable) motions are automatically taken on the papers, if they are not marked off; no telephone call is required. NO motions are marked over. Reclaim slips should be filed to reschedule calendar matters that have been marked off. Moving parties must notify adverse parties that they will be proceeding.

NEW: In accordance with Practice Book Sec. 211, as amended 10/1/95, Sec. 211 requests for argument on all non-arguable (N/A) matters must be filed no later than 5 p.m. on the Wednesday preceding the Monday short calendar. The Presiding Judge will review the requests. Counsel for cases for which argument will be allowed will be notified on Friday to appear for argument at the following Monday's short calendar on which the motion appears. (Faxed requests will not be accepted.)

NOTE: The only "As of right" motions for argument are motions to dismiss, motions to strike, and motions for summary judgment.

PROCEDURES: All PJR motions, applications for show cause orders, temporary injunctions, restraining orders, or discharge of mechanic's liens, must be claimed by counsel at the short calendar. NOTE: COUNSEL MUST BE PRESENT AT CALENDAR CALL TO CLAIM THE MATTER. When being claimed for the first time on short calendar, unless agreement can be reached, the following procedure will apply:

1. The case will be marked over by the COURTROOM CLERK when claimed by counsel at calendar call. No reclaim slip is required.

2. The parties must file an offer of proof (written summary of the testimony of each witness offered to prove facts in issue) to the court and each other within one week from date of the first short calendar date.

3. Cases appearing on the short calendar, after exchanging offers of proof, will be heard on factual issues determined by the court to be in dispute and subject to the availability of the court to hear the matter.

ALL PAPERS FILED WITH THE COURT MUST BE PUNCHED IN ACCORDANCE WITH P.B. § 118.

SHORT CALENDAR NOTICE FOR LAW AND FORECLOSURE CALENDARS

(New) Motions for extension of time filed after April 15, 1997 (except motions for extension of time to file a brief or an appeal) will not appear on short calendar. These motions are deemed to be requests. All parties shall consider such motions granted for a period of 30 days from the date of their filing. Objections to such motions must be filed within 10 days and will be placed on short calendar. This rule does not apply to motions filed in cases with return dates over 12 months old. Motions in these cases will be placed on short calendar for action by the court.

Whenever matters are listed in the Dormancy by Court Order section of the calendar, they are NON-ARGUABLE.

Hon. Robert L. Holzberg

HHBSSSSsh1

Example 7-1. Connecticut, Notice of Intent to Argue

DOCKET NO. CV 98-0333333 S	:	SUPERIOR COURT
SARAH A. DONAHUE	:	JUDICIAL DISTRICT
	:	OF TOLLAND
VS.	:	AT ROCKVILLE
RICHARD P. ANDREW	:	(date)

NOTICE OF INTENT TO ARGUE

The Plaintiff hereby gives notice that she intends to appear at the Short Calendar to argue against the Defendant's Motion to Dismiss, dated _______________.

Said Motion to Dismiss appears on the (date) Short Calendar #6, position number 5, column 1.

THE PLAINTIFF
BY________________________
Christine Kulas, Esq.
her attorney
Law Officers of Christine Kulas
P.O. Box 2005
Ellington, CT 06000
Tele. #(860) 222-2222
Juris #989898

CERTIFICATION

I hereby certify that a copy of the foregoing was mailed on (date) to all counsel and pro se parties of record, namely: Neil Clifford, Esq., of Michaels, Sabrina and Alexander, P.C., 259 Sage Road, Suite 200, West Hartford, CT 08080.

____
Commissioner of the Superior Court

Example 7-2. Connecticut, Short Calendar Envelope

NAME AND ADDRESS OF COURT

FST/SC01/## 144
CHRISTINE KULAS, ESQ.
P.O. BOX 2005
ELLINGTON, CT 06000

(The pleading that appears on the Short Calendar inside the envelope will be found at position number 144.)

Motion Practice in Massachusetts

I. The Contents of Motions and Objections: Super. Ct. Rule 9A

As stated previously, all motions and objections must contain a case caption, the drafting attorney's signature and identifying information, notice of hearing, and a certification of service. (See Rule 5(g).) Note, however, that the filing requirements for motions and objections differ from what is stated in the main chapter. See Section III below for details.

A. The Form of Motions, Objections, and Memorandums of Law

Super. Ct. Rule 9A(b)(4) contains the physical requirements for these documents, including paper size, page limits, etc. For instance, unless the court rules otherwise, a memorandum of law should be no longer than ***20 double-spaced pages.*** See the rule for more details.

B. The Body of Motions and Objections

Super Ct. Rule 9A(a)(1) and (2) address the body of motions and objections by requiring that they include or be accompanied by a "statement of reasons, including supporting authorities, why the motion should be granted." If applicable, also include affidavits or other documents that support the facts stated in the motion.

II. Hearings: Super. Ct. Rule 9A

As mentioned in the main chapter, a Notice of Hearing does not guarantee that there will actually be a hearing on that day. Instead, the motion may simply be scheduled to be decided by a judge that day.

A. Hearings and Specific Motions

The court will usually permit a hearing to address the following types of motions:

Attachments
Trustee Process
Motion to Dismiss
Adopt Master's Report
Motion for Summary Judgment
Motions for Injunctions
Motions for Receivers
Motions for Lis Pendens

B. Requesting a Hearing

Hearings for other types of motions should be requested according to Super Ct. Rule 9A(c) (1) and (2). As stated in the main chapter, if there is no hearing, the motion will be decided on the papers. (Super. Ct. Rule 9A (d).)

C. Enlargements of Time: Postponing a Hearing: Rule 6(b)

As stated in the main chapter, there are times when a motion is scheduled for a hearing but the attorneys involved are not available to attend. As a result, the party who filed the motion may notify the court that the motion hearing should be postponed. If this occurs, the party who filed the motion does not need to file the same document again. Instead, he or she may file a Notice of Hearing that indicates the next hearing date, and serve a copy to all the attorneys of record in the case.

III. Serving and Filing Motions and Objections: Rule 6(c) and Super. Ct. Rule 9A

According to Rule 6(c), a copy of a motion and Notice of Hearing must be served ***no later than seven days*** before the time specified for a hearing, unless the court or court rules state otherwise.

Caution: Super. Ct. Rule 9A provides additional information on this topic which appears to make the seven-day rule ineffective, as described below. In addition, although you have served a motion, it appears that you should not immediately file it in court as we have previously discussed. Therefore, read the following sections very carefully.

A. Objections: Deadline to Serve

According to Super. Ct. Rule 9A(a)(2), a party who receives and opposes a motion must serve an original objection (including all the applicable documents if any) ***and a copy,*** within the deadlines stated below, to the party who served the motion. Any other parties in the case need only a copy. ***Do not*** file anything in court.

1. If the objection is to a *Motion for Summary Judgment,* it (and copy) must be served ***within 21 days*** of receiving the motion. (Don't forget about the additional three days if service was by mail. See Rule 6(d).)
2. If the objection is to any other type of motion, it (and a copy) must be served ***within ten days*** of receiving the motion. (Again, if applicable, don't forget the additional three days.)

B. Serving and Filing Objections

Up until this point, nothing has been filed in court. That's because Super. Ct. Rule 9A(b) directs the party who served the motion to wait to see if there will be an objection as discussed above.

1. *If an Objection Is Served*

   If a party receives an objection to his or her motion, he or she must attach the original motion to the original objection and file them both in court ***within ten days,*** along with a list of all the documents that are being filed.

2. *If No Objection Is Served*

   If no objection is received within ***three business days*** after the expiration of the applicable deadline stated above, the party who served the motion shall then:

   a. File the original motion in court; and

b. Also file in court an affidavit stating that he or she has complied with this Superior Court Rule and no objection has been served; and
c. Serve a Notice of Filing Motion, along with a document list, to all parties in the case.

IV. Calculating Deadlines: Rule 6(d)

Parties must calculate the above-stated deadlines the same way they calculate deadlines for pleadings as described in the state summaries in Chapter 6.

Service is complete upon the following:

1. If the motion is served by hand delivery, service is complete as of the date of such hand delivery.
2. If the motion is served by mail, the party responding to the motion may ***add three days*** to the deadline to respond.

V. Exceptions: Super. Ct. Rule 9A(e)

See this section for the following types of motions:

1. Ex parte motions and other types of emergency motions;
2. Motions for Reconsideration (Super. Ct. Rule 9D.); and
3. Motions Excepted by Administrative Order.

Motion Practice in New Jersey

I. Contents of Motions and Objections: Rule 1:6-2(a)

See Rule 1:4 which confirms that a case caption, attorney's signature and identifying information, etc., are needed. In addition, don't forget the certification of service (referred to as a proof of service in 1:5-3).

A. Motions

A party drafting a motion must take the following steps:

1. Label the document a Notice of Motion.
2. State the grounds for the motion and the relief requested.
3. Include a Notice of Hearing stating the time and place it will be presented in court.
4. Include a proposed form of the order the party is requesting and state whether or not the motion is unopposed.
5. Include affidavits if information outside the record is needed to support the claim.
6. State whether oral argument is requested.

B. Briefs: Rule 1:6-5

Unless a rule of the court otherwise requires, briefs may be filed at the party's option.

If the brief is served with a Notice of Motion, Rule 1:6-5 states that an answering brief must be served and filed at least ***eight days*** before the hearing. This deadline coincides with the eight-day deadline to object found in Rule 1:6-3. See Sections III and IV below.

C. Objections

It appears that objections to motions may come in the form of Opposing Affidavits or Affidavits in Opposition to Motion and include a Brief in Opposition, which provides information opposing the motion and/or affidavits submitted. In addition, be sure to add whether oral argument is requested.

Note: A party who opposes a motion must serve and file the opposing papers within the applicable deadline. Otherwise, the motion is treated as unopposed and will be granted. See Sections III and IV below.

D. Requesting Oral Argument: Rule 1:6-2(d)

We've already discussed items 1 though 4 in this chapter. Here we will explore New Jersey's rules pertaining to oral argument.

A party who wants oral argument must state this in the motion or objection. The request will be granted unless the issue involves pretrial discovery. In these situations, a party who wants oral argument must state the reason in the document. The request is deemed denied unless the court notifies the parties otherwise.

A party may request oral argument, but state that if no objection is filed, oral argument is waived and the matter may be decided by the judge *on the papers.*

E. Oral Argument by Telephone Conference: Rule 1:6-2(e)

The judge assigned to decide a matter may permit the parties to conduct oral argument via a telephone conference rather than appearing in court. If the telephone conference takes place, it must be recorded verbatim, along with the judge's decision on the motion or objection.

F. Affidavits and Certifications: Rules 1:4-4, 1:6-6

These rules address the content and reasons for affidavits and that certifications may be used instead.

II. Deadlines to Serve Motions: Rule 1:6-3

Some motions such as a Motion for Summary Judgment and postjudgment motions have their own deadlines. In addition, the court can order its own deadlines. Rule 1:6-3 applies when a deadline is not already determined and states that a Notice of Motion must be filed in court and served on all parties of record ***no less than 16 days*** before they are scheduled to be decided by the court.

III. Deadlines to Serve Objections to Motions: Rule 1:6-3

Unless otherwise ordered by the court or stated in an applicable court rule, objections, opposing affidavits, certifications, and cross motions must be filed in court and served on all parties of record ***no less than eight days*** before the *return date:* the date the motion is scheduled to be decided by the court, with or without a hearing.

IV. Missed Deadlines to Object: Rule 1:6-2

If a party misses a deadline to file an objection, he or she loses the right to present oral argument. In addition, the motion is treated as unopposed by the court and will be granted.

V. Replies to Objections: Rule 1:6-3

Unless otherwise ordered by the court, if a party wishes to answer or respond to an objection, it should file a reply in court and serve it ***no later than four days*** before the return date.

VI. Notice of Motion and Objections: Service by Mail and Calculating Deadlines

Rule 1:5-4 demonstrates that New Jersey treats calculating deadlines to serve motions and objections differently from serving pleadings. Rule 1:6-3 refers specifically to motions only, as discussed below.

A. Different Types of Service: Rule 1:6-3

Consider the following:

1. **Hand delivery:** either by a person or a courier service, service is complete upon the hand delivery.
2. **Regular mail:** "service of motion papers is complete only on ***receipt*** at the office of adverse counsel or at the address of the pro se party … ***receipt is presumed on the third business day after mailing.***" (Emphasis added.)

Hence, if a party who was served a motion by mail wishes to file an objection, the eight-day deadline begins ***three days after*** the document was postmarked. If there is no postmark, use the date stated in the certification of service.

B. When Computing Less Than a Seven-Day Deadline: Rule 1:3-1

If the deadline at issue is ***less than seven days***, such as a response to an objection, do not count Saturdays, Sundays, and legal holidays.

VII. Motion for Reconsideration: Rules 4:49-2 and 4:50-1 et seq.

Consult Rule 4:50-1 et seq. to ask a court to reconsider an order of judgment that may have arisen out of a decision it made on a motion.

Motion Practice in New York

I. Contents of Motions and Objections

As mentioned in Chapter 4, CPLR 2101 and Unif. Rule 202.5 address the case caption, the attorney's signature, and identifying information. At this point, CPLR 2214 takes over and requires the motion to be labeled a Notice of Motion.

A. Notice of Motion

The Notice of Motion should consist of:

1. the grounds for the motion;
2. the relief requested;
3. a list of supporting papers such as affidavits or affirmations, exhibits, a memorandum of law, etc., that are attached to support the motion;
4. an affirmation: If the motion involves Discovery (called Disclosure in New York, Chapter 10) or a Bill of Particulars, an *affirmation* that the party drafting the motion made a good faith effort to resolve the motion with opposing parties. Include in this affirmation the date, time, nature of the consultation, the issues discussed, any resolution reached, or why no consultation took place. (See Unif. Rule 202.7 and the example on pages 255-257.)
5. a Notice of Hearing that indicates the return date (the date when the motion will be presented to the court); if oral argument is requested, insert the request here; otherwise, oral argument is waived.
6. Optional: Demand that opposing documents be served at least ***seven days*** before the return date. (See Section II B below regarding selecting return dates and deadlines to file objections.)
7. proof of service to all parties of record; and
8. a blue back: While the individual courthouse rules may vary, it appears that this Notice of Motion, with the affirmations, affidavits, and exhibits, should be placed in a blue back, as mentioned in Chapter 4.
9. a *Request for Judicial Intervention form* (*RJI*) and applicable fee: If this is the first motion filed in the case and the case has not yet been assigned a judge, the party filing the motion must include a Request for Judicial Intervention. This request is made by completing a court-issued form and filing it in duplicate with a copy of the receipt obtained when purchasing an index number. If a judge has already been assigned, the form is not needed and the judge's name should be included in the case caption. **Note:** When filing an RJI, the court will require a fee. (See Uniform Rules 202.6 and 202.8 for more information.)

B. Selecting a Return Date

1. If a judge is already assigned to the case, call the clerk's office to determine the next available motion day.
2. If no judge has been assigned at the time the motion is filed, select a return date that gives the clerk's office sufficient time to assign a judge. When assigned, the clerk's office will contact the parties regarding a new return date. (See Uniform Rule 202.8(b).)

C. Memorandums of Law

Memorandums of law (which are optional unless a specific statute, rule, or court order directs otherwise) should be placed in a separate brief cover. (See Uniform Rules 202:8.)

D. Objections and Oral Argument

Objections do not need a Notice of Objection. Instead it appears it is sufficient to simply serve and file opposing affidavits, etc., and opposing memorandums of law. The same rules for blue backs and brief covers apply.

If oral argument was not requested in the Notice of Motion, an opposing party who wants oral argument should include it in the case caption under the heading of the document.

Note: Unif. Rule 202.8(d) seems to suggest that there is a greater chance of being granted oral argument if both parties request it. In any event, if it is granted, the clerk will contact the parties with a new hearing date.

E. The Order: CPLR 309, Unif. Rule 202.48

It appears that an Order is not included in a Notice of Motion. Instead, once the motion is decided by the court, the party who won must draft, serve, and file an Order that reflects the decision. This must be accomplished within ***60 days*** from the date the decision is signed and filed by the judge. See Unif. Rule 202.48 for more details.

II. Deadlines to Serve Motions, Objections, and Replies: CPLR 2214(b)

These deadlines depend upon the return date.

A. Notice of Motion

The Notice of Motion and supporting documents should be served at least ***eight days*** before the return date. (Remember, as stated above, the return date could change if a judge has not yet been assigned the case.)

B. Opposing Documents

Opposing documents should be served at least ***two days*** before the return date. **Note:** This deadline changes if the party serving and filing the motion serves it at least ***12 days*** before the return date. In this instance, the party drafting the Notice of Motion should include a demand that directs the opposing party to serve opposing documents at least ***seven days*** before the return date.

C. Reply Affidavits

Reply affidavits should be served at least ***one day*** before hearing.

D. Extensions of Time: CPLR 2004

In many instances, the court may grant extensions of time whether the motion is made before or after the deadline date.

E. Adjourning Motions: CPLR 2214 and Unif. Rule 202.8(e)(1)

In most instances, without the court's permission, the return date will be postponed if the parties file a written stipulation in court. No more than three written stipulations should be filed within a 60-day time period. In addition, some judges set time limits for motions to be decided.

III. Calculating Deadlines: CPLR 2103

Parties must calculate the above-stated deadlines the same way they calculate deadlines for pleadings as described in the state summaries in Chapter 6. Service is complete upon the following:

1. If the motion is served by hand delivery, service is complete as of the date of such hand delivery.
2. Courier service, if overnight, adds ***one day*** to the deadline to respond.
3. If the motion is served by mail, the party responding to the motion may add ***five days*** to the deadline to respond.

Motion Practice in Rhode Island

I. Contents of Motions snd Objections

Be sure to include the information listed below in motions and objections.

A. Case Captions and Identifying Information

Rule 7(b)(2) states that Rules 10 and 11 regarding the case caption, the attorney's signature, and identifying information apply to motions and objections.

B. Certification of Service: Rule 5(d)

The certification of service applies to motions and objections.

C. Grounds and a Notice of Hearing: Rule 7(b)

A party drafting a motion or objection must include the grounds and a Notice of Hearing.

D. Oral Argument

It appears that oral argument is usually permitted if requested by one of the parties.

E. An Order: Rule 6(g)

When the court rules on a motion, it may direct that a written order be filed. Any party may serve and file the order. After it is filed, if there is no objection within ***four days,*** the clerk will usually enter it. If, however, there is an objection, or if more than one party files its own version of the order, the court will enter it.

F. Memorandums of Law: R.P. 1.6

The format of a Memorandum of Law can be found in this rule.

II. Deadlines to Serve Motions: Rule 6(c)

Motions should be served to opposing parties at least ***ten days*** before the date they are scheduled to be presented to the court, unless the court or applicable court rules determine otherwise.

III. Deadlines to Serve Objections: Rule 6(c)

I did not find a court rule on this issue. Nevertheless, it's probably wise to serve objections no later than 3 days before the hearing. In addition, it seems that opposing affidavits should be served at least ***one day*** before the date the motion is scheduled to be presented to the court, unless the court or applicable court rules determine otherwise.

IV. Motions to Enlarge Deadlines: Rule 6(b)

Consult Rule 6(b) to attempt to postpone a deadline.

V. Calculating Deadlines: Rule 6(d)

Parties must calculate the above-stated deadlines the same way they calculate deadlines for pleadings as described in the state summaries in Chapter 6. Service is complete upon the following:

1. If the motion is served by hand delivery, service is complete as of the date of such hand delivery.
2. If the motion is served by mail, the party responding to the motion may ***add one day*** to the deadline to respond.

VI. Types of Motions That Are Automatically Granted: Rule: 7(b)(3)

The following motions are automatically granted and not placed on the motion calendar unless an objection is served and filed at least ***three days*** before the time specified for a hearing:

Motion to Assign

Motion to Consolidate Cases for Trial

Motion to Enlarge Time pursuant to Rule 6(b)(2), after the expiration of a specified deadline

Motion for Leave to Serve Third-Party Complaint under Rule 14

Motion to Amend Pleadings under Rule 15

Motion for Order for Physical or Mental Exam under Rule 35

Motions under Rules 26 and 37 to obtain Protective Order to Compel Discovery, including the number of days for compliance

8 The Pretrial Stage: Motions in Response to the Plaintiff's Complaint

Terminology

Subject Matter Jurisdiction
Personal Jurisdiction
Insufficiency of Process
Indispensable Party
Insufficiency of Service of Process
Improper Venue
Motion to Strike
More Definite Statement
Failure to State a Claim
Motion to Dismiss

Introduction

When we discussed responsive pleadings in Chapter 6, I mentioned there are three motions a Defendant could file *before* filing an Answer. These motions include a **Motion to Dismiss,** a **Motion for More Definite Statement,** and a **Motion to Strike.** These motions should be filed only if the facts regarding the Complaint make them applicable. Their purpose is to convince the court to throw the Plaintiff's case out of court or to require the Plaintiff to redraft the Complaint, or a part thereof, in a specific manner to make it easier for the Defendant to draft an Answer.

When reviewing this chapter, keep in mind that the majority of the procedural guidelines found in Chapter 7, such as format and deadlines, apply to these motions.

I. Deadlines to File Motions

This section is not applicable to Connecticut. Instead, consult the Connecticut State Summary for this chapter as well as Chapters 6 and 7. Defendants in Massachusetts, New Jersey, New York, and Rhode Island who believe grounds exist to support a Motion to Dismiss, a Motion for More Definite Statement, or a Motion to Strike must serve such motion(s) within the deadline to serve and file an Answer, unless the parties agree or the court orders otherwise. This action will delay the deadline to serve and file an Answer. In addition, if there are grounds for more than one of the motions, they should all be served and filed at the same time. If the Complaint survives the motion(s), specific court rules or a court order will determine when an Answer is due.

II. Motions to Dismiss in Response to Complaint

Again, this section does not apply to Connecticut.

There are two methods regarding serving and filing a Motion to Dismiss: Before the Answer or as part of the Answer.

A. Before the Answer

As stated above, a Motion to Dismiss must be served within the deadline to serve an Answer. For instance, in Massachusetts, a Defendant's Answer is due within 20 days of service of the Plaintiff's original Complaint. Hence, if a Defendant decided to serve a Motion to Dismiss, it must be accomplished within that same 20-day period.

If the motion is granted, there is no need to file an Answer because the case will be dismissed. If, on the other hand, the motion is denied, each state's court rules dictate when the Answer is due. Note that this Answer can still contain other Affirmative Defenses that are not applicable to a Motion to Dismiss, as well as a Counterclaim, Cross Claim, etc.

B. As Part of the Answer, as Affirmative Defenses

Interestingly, it is also permissible for a Defendant to serve and file an Answer (within the Answer deadline) that includes Affirmative Defenses that state the applicable grounds for a Motion to Dismiss. Later, the Defendant will file the actual motion, according to each state's court rules.

If a Defendant elects this method, the Affirmative Defenses must include ***all*** of the applicable grounds to support a Motion to Dismiss, as well as any other types of Affirmative Defenses discussed in Chapter 6 that are applicable to the case.

The deadline to later file the actual motion is determined by each state's court rules.

III. Grounds for a Motion to Dismiss

Keep in mind that this chapter addresses Motions to Dismiss that are filed in response to a Complaint. As you will learn in Chapter 17, other types of Motions to Dismiss may be filed as disciplinary measures if a Plaintiff fails to comply with court rules other than those discussed here.

A. Specific Grounds

All five states permit Defendants to file a Motion to Dismiss on the following grounds:

1. lack of subject matter jurisdiction,
2. lack of personal jurisdiction,
3. improper venue,
4. insufficiency of process, or
5. insufficiency of service of process.

In addition, Massachusetts, New Jersey, New York, and Rhode Island include these additional grounds:

6. failure to state a claim upon which relief can be granted, or
7. failure to join an indispensable party.

B. Specific Grounds That May Be Waived

Remember, Defendants are responsible for recognizing grounds to support a Motion to Dismiss. In addition to asserting all of the grounds for a Motion to Dismiss, note that some of these grounds, however, are mere technical defects that can be corrected. As a result, if they are not raised within a particular time or manner as stated in each state's court rules, the court treats them as waived and the Defendant will not be permitted to raise them later. These defects include:

1. improper venue;
2. lack of personal jurisdiction;
3. insufficiency of process;
4. insufficiency of service of process.

IV. Definitions of Grounds

A. Subject Matter Jurisdiction

A court that lacks **subject matter jurisdiction** does not have authority to hear, decide, and enforce its decision regarding a specific case. Typically, it lacks this authority because the Complaint was filed in the wrong court. For instance, a negligence action involving a motor vehicle accident cannot be decided by a court that is limited to addressing housing cases such as landlord and tenant matters. If the case was accidentally filed in housing court, the Defendant should file a Motion to Dismiss for Lack of Subject Matter Jurisdiction.

1. Lack of Subject Matter Jurisdiction Cannot Be Waived

Unlike some of the other grounds listed for a Motion to Dismiss, subject matter jurisdiction cannot be waived. This means that a Defendant may raise it at any time, even during or after the trial. Hopefully, however, someone, including the Plaintiff, a court clerk, or a judge, will realize the problem before it goes that far. Otherwise, any judgment the Plaintiff obtains against the Defendant will be unenforceable because it is invalid.

2. Avoiding Lack of Subject Matter Jurisdiction Challenges

Plaintiffs can avoid this problem by making sure they file their lawsuits in the appropriate court. Not only must they be concerned with the types of cases a court may handle, they also must address monetary limits. For example, don't file a $50,000 lawsuit in a Small Claims court that only has jurisdiction to award up to $2,500. Even if you win, you will be sadly disappointed in the end.

3. Correcting Subject Matter Jurisdiction

Rather than dismiss a case for lack of subject matter jurisdiction, many states allow a Plaintiff to transfer a case to the appropriate court via a Motion to Transfer. Usually, this can be done even if the Defendant fails to file a Motion to Dismiss. Furthermore, some courts will pick up the mistake first and will authorize the transfer themselves, without requiring a motion.

B. Personal Jurisdiction

A Motion to Dismiss claiming lack of **personal jurisdiction** challenges the court's authority to render and enforce a judgment against a specific Defendant. Under most circumstances, each state has personal jurisdiction over its residents. Questions arise, however, when a case involves a nonresident.

Most states agree that they have personal jurisdiction over nonresidents and foreign partnerships, their executors or administrators who, in person or through an agent, act in the following manner:

1. transact any business in the state;
2. commit a tortious act within the state, except a cause of action for defamation of character arising from the act;
3. commit a tortious act outside the state which causes injury to persons or property within the state if the Defendants regularly do or solicit busi-

ness, or engage in any other persistent course of conduct, or derive substantial revenue from goods used or consumed or services rendered in the state; or expect or should reasonably expect the act to have consequences in the state and derive substantial revenue from interstate or international commerce; or

4. own, use, or possess any real property situated in the state.

A Defendant who challenges the court's jurisdiction is claiming that he or she does not fall within any of the provisions listed above. Therefore, the case must be dismissed for lack of personal jurisdiction.

C. Motion to Dismiss for Improper Venue

Venue is discussed in Chapter 4. Like a Motion to Dismiss for Lack of Subject Matter Jurisdiction, if a Motion to Dismiss claiming **Improper Venue** is filed, the Plaintiff may be permitted to file a Motion to Transfer to correct the mistake.

D. Insufficiency of Process

Insufficiency of process may arise when a Defendant is not served all the appropriate paperwork required, such as a properly completed Summons and Complaint and any other documents that may be required in a particular action. In addition, in some states, a Defendant may claim that too much time lapsed between when the Complaint was filed in court and when the copy was served to the Defendant.

E. Insufficiency of Service of Process

In most cases, **insufficient service of process** means the Defendant was not served in the required manner, according to an applicable statute or rule.

1. Examples of Improper Service of Process

a. The Defendant was not served because he or she did not live at the abode address that was served.

b. The proper officer is mistaken and never left the paperwork at the address stated in the return of service.

c. The officer made service by certified mail, but only abode or in hand service was appropriate.

d. Defendants who live out of state may claim that the Plaintiff or officer failed to take the required steps necessary to perform proper out-of-state service.

2. To Avoid Improper Service of Process

a. Instruct the proper officer to serve the Defendant in hand.

b. If abode process is necessary, double-check the Defendant's address.

Note: A person can have more than one abode. This issue becomes a matter of fact for the court to decide. At a hearing on a Defendant's Motion to Dismiss, the Plaintiff will have the burden of proving that service was left at a location where the Defendant was most likely to find or learn about it. (Parties who fail to pick up their mail cannot claim they were not properly served.)

c. If the officer is unable to locate the Defendant and resorts to certified mail or some other type of service, be sure the return of service states that he or she made a diligent search.

F. Failure to State a Claim upon Which Relief Can Be Granted

An assertion that a Plaintiff **failed to state a claim** upon which relief can be granted can be very tricky. Essentially, it attacks the content of the Plaintiff's Complaint and says something akin to, "Even if you are right, I can't be held liable. Therefore, I do not owe you any damages and your case should be dismissed."

In explaining this defense, the following situation comes to mind:

A group of college students were out one night, intoxicated, and one of them was driving the others in a hatchback car. The driver accidentally slammed the car into a tree, then backed up and tried to get the car back on the road. At the time, the driver was unaware that one of the students had been thrown through the hatchback onto the ground. While backing up, the driver drove over the student and killed him.

The dead student's estate sued the other student passengers in the car. It claimed the students breached their duty to protect the decedent because they permitted him to ride in the rear of the hatchback. It also claimed they breached their duty to protect him because they permitted the driver to drive over him as he was lying helpless on the ground.

The Defendants filed a Motion to Dismiss claiming that the passengers did not owe a duty to protect the decedent or any other fellow passengers in this type of situation. The state's supreme court agreed.

In addition, when relying upon this ground, a Defendant may include information that is outside the pleadings, such as sworn statements, records, physical evidence, etc. If this occurs, the court is permitted (but not required) to treat it as a Motion for Summary Judgment and will allow extra time for the parties (usually the Plaintiff) to submit their own outside information. This is done to save time.

A Motion for Summary Judgment differs from a Motion to Dismiss for Failure to State a Claim upon Which Relief Can Be Granted in that:

1. The court rules provide that a Motion for Summary Judgment should not be filed until after the pleadings are closed (except in Connecticut); and
2. Either party may file a Motion for Summary Judgment.

As stated in Chapter 9, it asserts that there are no issues for a trier of fact to decide because the evidence demonstrates what the truth is. Therefore, there is no need for a trial and the party making the motion is entitled to judgment.

Hence, by permitting this conversion to a Motion for Summary Judgment, the court may be reducing the time the case remains in court if the Defendant's Motion is correct.

Note: In Connecticut, this is called a Motion to Strike. (See the Connecticut State Summary.)

G. Failure to Join an Indispensable Party

Failure to join an indispensable party and ground for a Motion to Dismiss may arise in situations when there is more than one potential Defendant or Plaintiff involved in the case.

V. Drafting a Motion to Dismiss: Grounds Must Be Claimed at the Same Time

When drafting a Motion to Dismiss, keep the following in mind:

1. If a Defendant files a Motion to Dismiss before the Answer, that motion must include ***all of the grounds*** applicable to the motion.
2. If, on the other hand, a Defendant files an Answer first, that Answer must include ***all of the grounds*** to support a later Motion to Dismiss.

If a Defendant fails to include all the applicable grounds in the motion, he or she will probably be prevented from raising any other applicable grounds later. This requirement saves time by preventing more than one Motion to Dismiss to be filed and by not subjecting the Plaintiff to surprise that would justify granting additional time to respond.

For example, a defense attorney who knows a client was not properly served the Complaint and the case is filed in the wrong venue should include both of these grounds in one Motion to Dismiss. If one is left out, it will not be permitted to be raised later.

An exception: It appears that most of the states will allow a Defendant to raise a Failure to State a Claim upon Which Relief Can Be Granted later in the proceedings.

VI. Receiving a Motion to Dismiss for Lack of Personal Jurisdiction, Insufficiency of Process, or Insufficiency of Service of Process

A Plaintiff who receives a Motion to Dismiss on these grounds should:

1. Be sure the motion was filed timely and the Defendant has not filed any other pleadings. Include the existence of either situation in the objection.

2. Contact the officer who served the Summons and Complaint. Verify how service was made. Perhaps the return of service contains an error, or is missing some relevant information. In that case, amend the return of service and attach it to the objection.
3. Be sure to file the objection within the deadline stated in the applicable court rules.

VII. If a Case Is Dismissed

If the statute of limitations has not expired, the Plaintiff may bring the action again by re-serving the Defendant and filing a new case in court.

If the statute of limitations has expired, many states have statutes that permit a Plaintiff to bring a new action within a specific amount of time if the case was dismissed due to a proper officer's mistake in making service.

VIII. Motions for More Definite Statement

In addition to a Motion to Dismiss as described above, Defendants who believe a Complaint is so vague or ambiguous that they cannot reasonably draft an Answer should file a Motion for Definite Statement. (Connecticut calls this a *Request to Revise.*) In this motion they should specify those portions of the Complaint that are at issue, including the defects that should be addressed as well as indicating any additional details they believe are needed.

A. Plaintiff's Response

A Plaintiff who receives this motion may take one of the following actions:

1. File an objection within a specified period of time; or
2. Agree with the Defendant's motion and file an Amended or Revised Complaint that incorporates the corrections.

B. Plaintiff's Obligations When Court Grants Motion

If the Plaintiff objects to the motion and the court overrules it (i.e., the court grants the motion) the Plaintiff will have a specified period of time to file an amended Complaint that complies with the court's order. If the Plaintiff fails to comply, the court may strike the Complaint, which results in dismissing the case.

C. Defendant's Response to Amended Complaint

Presuming the Plaintiff complies with the court order, each state's applicable court rules will determine the Defendant's deadline to file an Answer to a Motion to Dismiss as discussed above.

IX. Motions to Strike

There are times when a Defendant believes that a portion of a Complaint should be removed because it is improper, scandalous, impertinent, or abusive. Some states permit the Defendant to challenge this type of situation using a Motion for More Definite Statement. Others direct the Defendant to file a Motion to Strike. Connecticut has different grounds to support a Motion to Strike. (See the State Summary.)

X. Other Responsive Pleadings and Motions

Although we are focusing on the more common types of cases that involve a single Plaintiff and Defendant who may or may not file defenses with an Answer, don't forget that all the grounds cited for a Motion to Dismiss and a Motion for More Definite Statement apply to all responsive pleadings such as Counterclaims, Cross Claims, Third-Party Complaints, etc.

XI. Conclusion

If no grounds exist for a Motion to Dismiss, a Motion for More Definite Statement, or a Motion to Strike, the Defendant should simply file an Answer, with any applicable defenses, etc. Be sure, however, to read the State Summaries carefully. In them you will find that some states allow other motions or other grounds in addition to those stated in this main chapter. Furthermore, don't forget that these motions may be used by the following:

1. Plaintiffs and other parties to challenge Affirmative Defenses;
2. Plaintiffs and other parties to challenge Counterclaims;
3. Co-defendants and other parties to challenge Cross Claims;
4. Parties subjected to Third-Party actions.

Key Issues in This Chapter

1. In many states, a brief or memorandum of law must be filed with a Motion to Dismiss, Motion for Judgment on the Pleadings, and any corresponding objections.
2. Defendants who want to file a Motion to Dismiss for one or more of the grounds listed in this chapter (other than *subject matter jurisdiction*) must include all the applicable reasons in a single Motion to Dismiss or in the Answer as Affirmative Defenses. Otherwise, the court may rule that they have waived their rights to contest the defect.

3. A Motion to Dismiss claiming lack of subject matter jurisdiction may be filed at any time and cannot be waived. Instead of a dismissal, a *Motion to Transfer* or a *Motion to Amend Process* may correct the defect.
4. Plaintiffs must be sure to file their objections within the deadlines determined by applicable court rules.
5. A Motion for More Definite Statement and a Motion to Strike are applicable when a Defendant believes the content of the Complaint must be modified before he or she can properly draft an Answer. Specific court rules address deadlines to file amended Complaints and responsive pleadings.

STATE SUMMARIES

Connecticut Motions in Response to Plaintiff's Complaint

I. Grounds for a Motion to Dismiss: Pbs 10-30 Et Seq.

According to Pbs 10-30, Connecticut recognizes the following grounds to support a Motion to Dismiss:

1. lack of subject matter jurisdiction;
2. lack of personal jurisdiction;
3. improper venue;
4. insufficiency of process;
5. insufficiency of service of process.

(The remaining grounds cited in the main chapter are raised as part of a Request to Revise or Motion to Strike.)

II. Waiver and Deadline to File Motion to Dismiss

Each of the above-stated grounds, except lack of subject matter jurisdiction, is waived if:

1. the Defendant fails to file the motion within ***30 days*** of filing an Appearance (Pbs 10-31) ; or
2. during that 30-day period, the Defendant first files a Request to Revise, a Motion to Strike, or an Answer prior to filing a Motion to Dismiss (Pbs 10-7 and 10-32).

III. Deadline to Object: Pbs 10-31 and a Hearing: Pbs 11-18

The Plaintiff must file an Objection no later than within ***five days*** of the case being decided at Short Calendar. Remember: The Short Calendar will usually not print a motion until at least two weeks from the date it is filed in court. Therefore, a Plaintiff has plenty of time to file an objection.

The parties are entitled to a hearing at Short Calendar on Motions to Dismiss that are based upon the grounds stated above.

IV. Connecticut's Motion for a More Definite Statement: Request to Revise: Pbs 10-35 et seq.

A. Deadline to File Request to Revise: Pbs 10-7

If a Defendant intends to file a Request to Revise, it must be filed before the Defendant files a Motion to Strike or an Answer. If the Motion to Strike or an Answer is filed first, the Defendant waives the right to file a Request to Revise and may not file one without first obtaining permission from the court.

B. Deadline to Object to Request to Revise: Pbs 10-37

If a Plaintiff decides to object to a Request to Revise, rather than comply with the request and file a Revised Complaint, he or she must object within ***30 days*** from the date the request was filed. Otherwise, the request is treated as granted.

C. No Right to a Hearing: Pbs 11-18

There is no right to a hearing on Objections to Request to Revise. However, the rules do permit a party to ask the court to schedule a hearing.

D. Plaintiff's Obligations if Request Is Granted: Pbs 10-37

If the court overrules the Plaintiff's objection, the Plaintiff must file a Revised Complaint that complies with the court's order or the request (if there was no objection) within ***15 days*** from the date notice of that order was sent.

If the Plaintiff does not file an objection, the matter will not be placed on Short Calendar. Therefore, the Plaintiff must file the Revised Complaint within ***45 days*** of the date the request was filed. Otherwise, the Defendant will file a Motion for Nonsuit, asking the court to dismiss the case. (See Chapter 17.)

E. Defendant's Deadline to File Pleading to Respond to Revised Complaint: Pbs 10-8

Once the Plaintiff's Revised Complaint is filed, the Defendant must file one of the following within ***15 days*** of the date the Revised Complaint was filed:

1. a Motion to Strike; or
2. an Answer

V. Connecticut's Motion to Dismiss for Failure to State a Claim upon Which Relief Can Be Granted: Motion to Strike: Pbs 10-39 et seq.

As stated in the main chapter, Connecticut permits a Defendant to file a Motion to Strike on the grounds that the Plaintiff failed to state a claim upon which relief can be granted.

A. Deadline to File Motion to Strike: Pbs 10-7 and 10-8

If a Defendant intends to file a Motion to Strike, the motion must be accompanied by a Memorandum of Law (Pbs 10-42 and 11-10) and be filed before the Defendant files an Answer. If the Answer is filed first, the Defendant waives the right to file the Motion to Strike, unless the court orders otherwise.

B. Deadline to Object to Motion to Strike: Pbs 10-42

The Plaintiff must file an Objection no later than within *five days* of the case being decided at Short Calendar. Remember: The Short Calendar will usually not print a motion until at least two weeks from the date it is filed in court. Therefore, a Plaintiff has plenty of time to file an objection.

C. Short Calendar Hearing: Pbs 11-18

The parties are entitled to a hearing at Short Calendar on Motions to Strike.

D. Plaintiff's Obligations if Motion Is Granted: Pbs 10-44

If the Motion to Strike is granted, the Plaintiff must file a Substitute Complaint that addresses the issues raised in the motion and/or court order, within *15 days* from notice sent of the court order.

E. Defendant's Response if Plaintiff Fails to File Substitute Complaint: Pbs 10-44

If the Plaintiff fails to file a Substitute Complaint within the deadline stated, the Defendant may file a Motion for Judgment which, if granted, would immediately end the lawsuit in the Defendant's favor.

F. Defendant's Deadline to File Answer to Substitute Complaint: Pbs 10-8

The Defendant must file an Answer to the Substitute Complaint within *15 days* from the date such Complaint was filed.

Example 8-1. Connecticut, Motion to Dismiss, Supporting Affidavit, and Memo of Law; Insufficiency of Service of Process

DOCKET NO. CV 98-0333333 S	:	SUPERIOR COURT
SARAH A. DONAHUE	:	JUDICIAL DISTRICT
	:	OF TOLLAND
VS.	:	AT ROCKVILLE
RICHARD P. ANDREW	:	(date)

MOTION TO DISMISS

Pursuant to Connecticut Practice Book Section 10-30 et seq., the Defendant, Richard P. Andrew, hereby moves the court to dismiss the Plaintiff's Complaint due to insufficiency of service of process.

A memorandum of law and an affidavit are attached hereto in support of this motion.

THE DEFENDANT

BY ____________________________

Neil E. Clifford, Esq.
Michaels, Sabrina and Alexander, P.C.,
his attorneys
259 Sage Road, Suite 200
West Hartford, CT 08080
Tele. # (860) 111-1111
Juris #626262

ORAL ARGUMENT NOT REQUESTED
TESTIMONY NOT REQUIRED

ORDER

The foregoing Motion having been heard and considered by the Court, it is hereby ORDERED: GRANTED/DENIED.

____
BY THE COURT

CERTIFICATION

I hereby certify that a copy of the foregoing Motion and the attached memorandum of law and affidavit were mailed on (date) to all counsel and pro se parties of record, namely: Christine Kulas, Esq., P.O. Box 2005, Ellington, CT 06066.

____
Commissioner of the Superior Court

DOCKET NO. CV 98-0333333 S	:	SUPERIOR COURT
SARAH A. DONAHUE	:	JUDICIAL DISTRICT
	:	OF TOLLAND
VS.	:	AT ROCKVILLE
RICHARD P. ANDREW	:	(date)

MEMORANDUM OF LAW
IN SUPPORT OF MOTION TO DISMISS

FACTS

The Plaintiff brought this action against the Defendant, claiming that she was seriously injured in an automobile accident which he negligently caused. The Defendant was not served a copy of the Summons and Complaint in accordance with Connecticut General Statutes Section 52-57. Therefore, pursuant to Connecticut Practice Book Section 142 et seq. this case must be dismissed due to insufficiency of service of process.

ARGUMENT

The Plaintiff's Complaint should be dismissed due to insufficiency of service of process, pursuant to Connecticut Practice Book Section 142 et seq., due to her noncompliance with Connecticut General Statutes Section 52-57.

> C.G.S. Sec. 52-57 of the Connecticut General Statutes provides: Except as otherwise provided, process in any civil action shall be served by leaving a true and attested copy of it, including the declaration or Complaint, with the Defendant, or at his usual place of abode in this state.

The Defendant is a Connecticut resident in this civil action. Consequently, the Plaintiff was required to serve the Defendant by leaving a true and attested copy of the Summons and Complaint in his hands, or at his usual place of abode.

In this case, however, the officer merely sent a copy of the Summons and Complaint to the Defendant by certified mail. This does not amount to sufficient service of process as required by C.G.S. Sec. 52-57.

Where a particular method of serving a Defendant with a Summons and Complaint is identified by statute, that method must be followed. *Westhelle v. Turner Liedertafel Singing Society, Inc.,* 18 Conn. Sup. 107, 109 (1952). See also *Balkun v. DeAnzona,* 5 Conn. Cir. 580 (1969) where the case was dismissed because the officer left the Summons and Complaint in a mailbox in a hallway outside the Defendant's apartment, rather than in the abode.

CONCLUSION

Accordingly, the Defendant was not properly served pursuant to C.G.S. Sec. 52-57. Therefore, this action should be dismissed.

THE DEFENDANT

BY ___________________________

Neil E. Clifford, Esq.
Michaels, Sabrina and Alexander, P.C.,
his attorneys
259 Sage Road, Suite 200
West Hartford, CT 08080
Tele. # (860) 111-1111
Juris #626262

(Separate Sheet)

DOCKET NO. CV 98-0333333 S	:	SUPERIOR COURT
SARAH A. DONAHUE	:	JUDICIAL DISTRICT
	:	OF TOLLAND
VS.	:	AT ROCKVILLE
RICHARD P. ANDREW	:	(date)

AFFIDAVIT OF RICHARD P. ANDREW

The undersigned, being duly sworn, sayeth:

(1) I am over the age of 18 years and I believe in the obligation of an oath.
(2) I, Richard P. Andrew, am a Defendant in the above-captioned case.
(3) I am a resident of Connecticut.
(4) The Writ, Summons and Complaint were sent to me by certified mail.
(5) A sheriff did not serve me a copy of the Writ, Summons and Complaint in hand.
(6) A sheriff did not leave a copy of the Writ, Summons and Complaint at my usual place of abode.
(7) I have reviewed the above statements and they are true and accurate to the best of my knowledge and belief.

____
Richard P. Andrew

Subscribed and sworn to before me this ____ day of _____, 1998.

____
Commissioner of the Superior Court

Example 8-2. Connecticut, Objection to Motion to Dismiss and Memo of Law

DOCKET NO. CV 98-0333333 S	:	SUPERIOR COURT
SARAH A. DONAHUE	:	JUDICIAL DISTRICT
	:	OF TOLLAND
VS.	:	AT ROCKVILLE
RICHARD P. ANDREW	:	(date)

OBJECTION TO MOTION TO DISMISS

In accordance with Sections 10-30, et seq. of the Connecticut Practice Book, the Plaintiff hereby objects to the Defendant's Motion to Dismiss, dated June 19, 1998, for the following reasons:

(1) Service of process was sufficient, pursuant to Connecticut General Statutes Section 52-63; and

(2) The Defendant's Motion to Dismiss was untimely filed. Therefore, he has waived any defects in the service of process.

A memorandum of law and the Sheriff's Return of Service are attached hereto in support of this objection.

THE PLAINTIFF

BY ___________________________

Christine Kulas, Esq.
Law Offices of Christine Kulas,
her attorney
P.O. Box 2005
Ellington, CT 06066
Tele. #(860) 222-2222
Juris #989898

ORDER

The foregoing Objection having been considered by the Court, it is hereby ORDERED: SUSTAINED/OVERRULED.

____

BY THE COURT

CERTIFICATION

I hereby certify that a copy of the foregoing Objection and the attached memorandum of law and Return of Service were mailed on (date) to all counsel and pro se parties of record, namely: Neil Clifford, Esq., of Michaels, Sabrina and Alexander, P.C., 259 Sage Road, Suite 200, West Hartford, CT 08080.

____

Commissioner of the Superior Court

DOCKET NO. CV 98-0333333 S	:	SUPERIOR COURT
SARAH A. DONAHUE	:	JUDICIAL DISTRICT
	:	OF TOLLAND
VS.	:	AT ROCKVILLE
RICHARD P. ANDREW	:	(date)

MEMORANDUM OF LAW IN SUPPORT
OF
OBJECTION TO MOTION TO DISMISS

FACTS

The Plaintiff brought this action for personal injuries she suffered in an automobile accident allegedly caused by the Defendant's negligence.

The Sheriff's Return of Service, attached hereto, states that after a diligent attempt, he could not make service on the Defendant at his address on file with the Department of Motor Vehicles, or anywhere else in his precincts. As a result, pursuant to C.G.S. Section 52-63, the Sheriff made service upon the Defendant through the Department of Motor Vehicles (hereinafter DMV), and sent copies of said service to the Defendant, by certified mail, postage prepaid, to his last address on file at DMV, at least 12 days before the return date.

The Defendant filed his Appearance on May 21, 1998. Although his Motion to Dismiss is dated June 19, 1998, it was not filed and time stamped in court until June 23, 1998.

ARGUMENT

A. The Defendant's Claim

The Defendant claims this action must be dismissed because the sheriff's service of process was insufficient, pursuant to C.G.S. Sec. 52-57. He fails to realize, however, that C.G.S. Sec. 52-57 does not provide the only method of service of process in cases involving motor vehicles.

B. The Defendant Was Properly Served under C.G.S. Sec. 52-63

The Sheriff's Return of Service clearly states that after diligent attempts, he was unable to make service upon the Defendant at its last address on file with DMV or anywhere else in his precinct. Therefore, he could not make in hand or abode service as stated in C.G.S. Sec. 52-57. Instead, he invoked the provisions found in C.G.S. Sec. 52-63. This statute provides for service upon the Commissioner of the Department of Motor Vehicles and by certified mail to the Defendant when it is alleged that the Defendant caused injuries through the negligent operation of a motor vehicle, and the Defendant cannot be located at its last address on file with DMV. Therefore, the Defendant was properly serviced and its claim of insufficient service of process is without merit.

C. The Defendant Waived All Claims for Insufficient Service of Process

Even if service upon the Defendant was defective, he waived such claim pursuant to Connecticut Practice Sec. 10-32 et seq.

Connecticut Practice Book Sec. 10-30 requires a Defendant's Motion to Dismiss to challenge the court's jurisdiction to be filed within thirty days of filing its Appearance. In addition, Connecticut Practice Book Sec. 10-32 states that:

> Any claim of lack of jurisdiction over the person or improper venue or insufficiency of process or insufficiency of service of process is waived if not raised by a Motion to Dismiss filed in the sequence provided in Sections 10-6 and 10-7, and within the time provided by Section 10-30.

In the instant case, the Defendant filed his Appearance in court on May 21, 1998. Although his Motion to Dismiss is dated June 19, 1998, it was not filed in court until June 22, 1998, which is more than thirty days after he filed his Appearance. Hence, the Defendant has waived this defective process claim and submitted himself to the court's jurisdiction.

CONCLUSION

Based on the foregoing, this instant case should not be dismissed, and the Plaintiff's Objection to the Defendant's Motion to Dismiss should be sustained.

THE PLAINTIFF

BY ______________________

Christine Kulas, Esq.
Law Offices of Christine Kulas,
her attorney
P.O. Box 2005
Ellington, CT 06066
Tele. #(860) 222-2222
Juris #989898

Massachusetts Motions in Response to Plaintiff's Complaint

I. Grounds for a Motion to Dismiss: Rule 12(b)

Massachusetts recognizes the following grounds to support a Motion to Dismiss:

1. lack of subject matter jurisdiction;
2. lack of personal jurisdiction;
3. improper venue;
4. insufficiency of process;
5. insufficiency of service of process;
6. failure to state a Complaint upon which relief can be granted;
7. failure to join a party under Rule 19;
8. misnomer of a party;
9. pendency of a prior action in a court of the Commonwealth.

A. Definitions of Grounds

Grounds one through six have already been addressed in the main chapter. The remaining grounds are discussed below.

7. Failure to Join a Party under Rule 19

This ground applies if there are other individuals who have an interest in the subject matter of the case and should be added as parties because their interest may adversely affect the current parties. (This is similar to a Third-Party Action.)

8. Misnomer of a Party

This ground may be raised if the Plaintiff incorrectly named the Defendant in the case.

9. Pendency of a Prior Action in a Court of the Commonwealth

This ground is self-explanatory: A case addressing the dispute at issue already exists in a Massachusetts court.

B. Waiveable Grounds: Rules 12(g) and (h)

The following grounds are waived if not raised under the circumstances stated below:

a. lack of personal jurisdiction;
b. improper venue;
c. insufficiency of process;
d. insufficiency of service of process;
e. misnomer of a party;
f. pendency of a prior action in a court of the Commonwealth;

1. if the Defendant does not file a Motion to Dismiss and fails to raise these as defenses in the Answer; or

2. if the Defendant omits them in a previous Motion to Dismiss that was served before an Answer.

C. Grounds That May Be Raised Later: Rule 12(h)(2)

In lieu of or in addition to a Motion to Dismiss, the following grounds may be raised as stated below:

1. failure to state a claim upon which relief can be granted;
2. failure to join a party indispensable under Rule 19;
3. objection of failure to state a legal defense.

D. Additional Time to Raise Specific Grounds

The grounds stated in C above may be raised:

1. at the time of trial;
2. in a Motion for Judgment on the Pleadings; or
3. in any pleading permitted or ordered under Rule 7(a).

E. Hearing Granted for Motions to Dismiss: Rule 12(d)

The court will grant the parties a hearing on all nine of the grounds for a Motion to Dismiss as stated above. As a result, Defendants should contact the court to determine when a hearing date is available in the motion as a Notice of Hearing.

F. Plaintiff's Deadline to Object: Rule 9A(a)(2)

A Plaintiff has *ten days* to serve an objection to a Motion to Dismiss.

G. Defendant's New Deadline to File Answer: Rule 12(a)(2)

If the Defendant's Motion to Dismiss is denied or the court decides to delay action upon it until later in the proceedings or at the time of trial, the Defendant must file an Answer within *ten days* after notice of the court's decision.

II. Motion for More Definite Statement: Rule 12(E)

A. The Plaintiff's Objection

As stated in Rule 9A(a)(2), a Plaintiff may object to this motion within *ten days.*

B. Plaintiff's Obligations When Motion Is Granted: Rule 12(a)(2)

If the motion is granted, the Plaintiff must file an Amended Complaint that complies with the court order within *ten days* of notice of the order. If the Plaintiff fails to comply, the Defendant may notify the court. The court may dismiss the case or issue an order that it determines appropriate.

C. Defendant's Response to Amended Complaint: Rule 12 (a)(2)

A Defendant must serve a responsive pleading (an Answer) or a Motion to Dismiss within *ten days* of service of the Plaintiff's Amended Complaint.

III. Motion to Strike: Rule 12(f)

Massachusetts permits a party to file a Motion to Strike if any pleading contains redundant, immaterial, impertinent, or scandalous content. If a party receives this type of motion, the best course of conduct is probably to file an amended pleading that corrects the questionable content.

New Jersey Motions in Response to Plaintiff's Complaint

I. Grounds for a Notice of Motion to Dismiss: Rule 4:6-2

Rule 4:6-2 gives authorization to assert grounds for a Motion to Dismiss as a Notice of Motion or as Affirmative Defenses in an Answer. The grounds to support such a motion include:

1. lack of subject matter jurisdiction;
2. lack of personal jurisdiction;
3. insufficiency of process;
4. insufficiency of service of process;
5. failure to state a Claim upon which relief can be granted;
6. failure to join a party without whom the action cannot proceed.

A. Definitions of Grounds

Grounds one through five have already been addressed in the main chapter.

6. Failure to Join a Party without Whom the Action Cannot Proceed

This ground applies if there are other individuals who have an interest in the subject matter of the case and should be added as parties because their interest may adversely affect the current parties. (This is similar to a Third-Party Action.)

B. Briefs: Rule 4:6-2

Rule 4:6-2 indicates that a brief should be filed with a Notice of Motion to Dismiss. See Rule 1:6-5 regarding details.

C. Waiveable Grounds: Rules 4:6-3 and 4:6-7

The following grounds are waived:

1. lack of personal jurisdiction;
2. insufficiency of process;
3. insufficiency of service of process;

under the following circumstances:

a. if the Defendant does not file a Motion to Dismiss and fails to raise these as defenses in the Answer;
b. if the Defendant omits them in a previous Motion to Dismiss that was served before an Answer; or
c. if the defense is raised in the Answer and the Defendant fails to file a Motion to Dismiss based upon these grounds within ***90 days*** after he or she serves the Answer.

D. Grounds That May Be Raised Later: Rule 4:6-7

This section is an exception to the rule that all grounds must be raised in a motion before serving and filing an Answer or as part of the Answer:

A Defendant may assert a claim that a Complaint fails to state a claim upon which relief can be granted or the failure to join a party as late as in a Notice of Motion for Summary Judgment or at trial. As stated in the main chapter, claim of lack of subject matter jurisdiction can be raised at any time.

E. Hearing Granted for Motions to Dismiss: Rule 4:6-3

The court will grant the parties a hearing on the following claims:

1. lack of subject matter jurisdiction;
2. failure to state a claim upon which relief can be granted; and
3. failure of joinder of party.

As a result, Defendant should contact the court to determine when a hearing date is available and state the date, time, and courtroom location in the motion as a Notice of Hearing.

In addition, remember that a Notice of Hearing is needed anyway to indicate when a motion (without a hearing) will be acted upon by the court. If a party wants a hearing to argue grounds not included above, see Rule 1:6-2(d) and (e).

F. Plaintiff's Deadline to Object: Rule 1:6-3

As stated in Chapter 7, opposing affidavits or certifications and briefs should be served within ***eight days*** prior to the return date (the date the motion is scheduled to be presented to the court, with or without oral argument).

G. Replies to Objections: Rule 1:6-3

A response to opposing affidavits and briefs should be served at least ***four days*** prior to the return date.

H. Defendant's New Deadline to File Answer: Rule 4:6-3

If the Defendant's Motion to Dismiss is denied or the court decides to delay action upon it until later in the proceedings or at the time of trial, the Defendant must file an Answer within ***ten days*** after notice of the court's decision.

II. Motion for More Definite Statement: Rule 4:6-4

Rule 4:6-4 indicates that a party may serve and file a Motion for More Definite Statement, a Motion to Strike, or a Motion to Dismiss for Impropriety of Pleading. Generally, the concepts are substantially similar to what is stated in the main chapter. In addition, the court may strike or even dismiss a Complaint if it finds the content excessively offensive, etc. In such situations, Plaintiffs are usually permitted to refile the Complaint but only under specific conditions. (See Rule 4:37-2.)

A. The Plaintiff's Objection

As stated in Rule 1:6-3, a Plaintiff may serve and file opposing affidavits and objections to this motion at least ***eight days*** before the return date. (The Defendant may respond to the opposition at least ***four days*** prior to the return date.)

B. Plaintiff's Obligations When Motion Is Granted: 4:6-4

If the motion is granted, the Plaintiff must serve and file an Amended Complaint that complies with the court order within ***ten days*** of notice of the order.

C. Defendant's Response to Amended Complaint: Rule 4:6-1(b)

A Defendant must serve and file a responsive pleading (an Answer) or a Motion to Dismiss within ***ten days*** of service of the Plaintiff's Amended Complaint.

III. Motion to Strike Defenses: Rule 4:6-5

If a defense is insufficient in law, a party may serve and file a Notice of Motion to Strike such defense within ***20 days*** of their service.

New York Motions in Response to Plaintiff's Complaint

I. Grounds for a Motion to Dismiss: CPLR 3211

Some of the grounds to support a Motion to Dismiss in New York differ from those cited in the main chapter and the other states' summaries. In fact, some grounds resemble Affirmative Defenses. According to CPLR 3211 they include:

1. A defense is available through documentary evidence.
2. The court lacks subject matter jurisdiction over the case.
3. The party asserting the cause of action lacks the legal capacity to sue.
4. There is another action pending between the parties for the same cause of action in another court.
5. The cause of action may not be maintained due to arbitration and award, collateral estoppel, discharge in bankruptcy, infancy or other malady of the moving party, payment, release, res judicata, statute of limitations, or statute of frauds.
6. If the pleading being attacked is a counterclaim, a party (usually the Plaintiff) may assert that the counterclaim is improperly asserted in the action.
7. The pleading does not state a cause of action.
8. The court lacks personal jurisdiction over the Defendant.
9. The court does not have jurisdiction in an action where service is made pursuant to CPLR 314 or 315.
10. The court should not proceed in an action where an absent person should be made a party.
11. The party is immune from liability in that it is a not-for-profit corporation, etc.

In addition, if the pleading being attacked is an affirmative defense, a party (usually the Plaintiff) may assert that the defense is not stated or has no merit.

Note: Only one Motion to Dismiss, asserting all the available grounds mentioned above, should be served and filed.

II. Waiver, Deadline, and Evidence: Motion to Dismiss

The deadline to file a Motion to Dismiss is no later than the deadline to serve a responsive pleading, hence, ***20 days*** from such service.

A. Grounds 1, 3, 4, 5, and 6

A party must assert the grounds stated in 1, 3, 4, 5, and 6 above either in a responsive pleading or as a Motion to Dismiss during the 20-day deadline. Otherwise, they have waived their right to assert these grounds.

B. Improper or Insufficiency of Service

As stated in the main chapter, the grounds stated above may be asserted as Affirmative Defenses or in a Motion to Dismiss. Parties who choose to allege, as an Affirmative Defense, that they were not properly served a Summons, must serve and file their Motion to Dismiss within ***60 days*** of such service. Otherwise, they will have waived this claim.

C. Lack of Jurisdiction: Grounds 8 and 9

An objection based on lack of jurisdiction over the Defendant or that the court lacks jurisdiction because the Defendant was served under CPLR 314 or 315 must be alleged as an Affirmative Defense or a Motion to Dismiss. Otherwise, it is waived.

D. Grounds 2, 7, and 10

A party may allege the grounds cited in 2, 7, or 10 above in the responsive pleading, in a Motion to Dismiss, or at a later time, if permitted by the court. It appears that this may be done through a Motion for Summary Judgment.

E. Evidence Submitted to Support and Object to Motion to Dismiss

The parties may submit the same type of evidence permitted to support or object to a Motion for Summary Judgment, i.e., evidence outside the pleadings. In addition, the court may treat the Motion to Dismiss as a Motion for Summary Judgment, even if all the responsive pleadings have not yet been served and filed.

F. Amending Pleadings

A party faced with the grounds cited in 1 or 7 may decide to serve and file an amended pleading to correct the problem. If so, state this in the objection to the motion and ask the court's permission. It's also possible that the opposing party will agree to the correction and the motion will not need to be ruled on by the court.

III. When Motion to Dismiss Is Denied

If a Motion to Dismiss is denied, the next responsive pleading (usually from the Defendant) is due within ***ten days*** of notice of the court's decision.

IV. Motions to Correct Pleadings: CPLR 3024

The deadline to serve either a Motion for More Definite Statement or a Motion to Strike is within ***20 days*** of service of the challenged pleading.

A. Motion for More Definite Statement

This motion should be served and filed if a pleading is vague or ambiguous, making it difficult to frame a responsive pleading.

B. Motion to Strike

This motion should be served and filed if a pleading is scandalous or prejudicial.

C. The Court's Ruling and Deadlines to Respond

If the motion is granted, the party who drafted the challenged pleading must serve and file a corrected pleading that complies with the court's order within ***ten days*** of notice of that order.

If the motion is denied, the party who challenged the pleading must serve and file a responsive pleading within ***ten days*** of notice of that order.

RHODE ISLAND MOTIONS IN RESPONSE TO PLAINTIFF'S COMPLAINT

I. Grounds for a Motion to Dismiss: Rule 12

Rhode Island recognizes the following grounds to support a Motion to Dismiss:

1. lack of subject matter jurisdiction;
2. lack of personal jurisdiction;
3. improper venue;
4. insufficiency of process;
5. insufficiency of service of process;
6. failure to state a Complaint upon which relief can be granted;
7. failure to join an indispensable party.

A. Definitions of Grounds

Grounds one through six have already been addressed in the main chapter.

7. Failure to Join an Indispensable Party

This ground applies if there are other individuals who have an interest in the subject matter of the case and should be added as parties because their interest may adversely affect the current parties. (This is similar to a Third-Party Action.)

B. Waiveable Grounds

The following grounds are waived if not raised under the circumstances stated below:

a. lack of personal jurisdiction;
b. improper venue;
c. insufficiency of process;
d. insufficiency of service of process;

if:

1. the Defendant does not file a Motion to Dismiss and fails to raise these as defenses in the Answer; or
2. the Defendant omits them in a previous Motion to Dismiss that was served before an Answer.

C. Grounds That May Be Raised Later: Rule 12(h)(2)

In lieu of or in addition to a Motion to Dismiss,

1. failure to state a claim upon which relief can be granted;
2. failure to join an indispensable party;
3. objection of failure to state a legal defense;

may be raised:

a. at the time of trial;
b. in a Motion for Judgment on the Pleadings; or
c. in any pleading permitted or court ordered.

D. Hearing Granted for Motions to Dismiss: Rule 12(d)

If a hearing is requested, the court will grant the parties a hearing on all nine of the grounds for a Motion to Strike as stated above. As a result, Defendants should contact the court to determine when a hearing date is available and include that date in the motion as a Notice of Hearing.

E. Plaintiff's Deadline to Object: Rule 6(c)

Opposing affidavits are due no later than *one day* before the motion is scheduled to be presented to the court.

F. Defendant's New Deadline to File Answer: Rule 12(a)(3)(B)

If the Defendant's Motion to Dismiss is denied or the court decides to delay action upon it until later in the proceedings or at the time of trial, the Defendant must file an Answer within *ten days* after notice of the court's decision.

II. Motion for More Definite Statement: Rule 12(E)

A. The Plaintiff's Objection

As stated in Rule 6(c), a Plaintiff may serve an objection to this motion no later than *the day before* it is scheduled to be presented to the court.

B. Plaintiff's Obligations When Motion Is Granted: Rule 12(e)

If the motion is granted, the Plaintiff must file an Amended Complaint that complies with the court order within *ten days* of notice of the order.

C. Defendant's Response to Amended Complaint: Rule 12 (a)(3)(B)

A Defendant must serve a responsive pleading (an Answer) or a Motion to Dismiss within *ten days* of service of the Plaintiff's Amended Complaint.

III. Motion to Strike: Rule 12(f)

Rhode Island permits a party to file a Motion to Strike within ***20 days*** of service of a pleading that contains redundant, immaterial, impertinent, or scandalous content. If a party receives this type of motion, the best course of conduct is probably to file an amended pleading that corrects the questionable content.

Example 8-3. Motion to Dismiss, Failure to State a Cause of Action, and Memorandum of Law (unrelated case)

(date)

SAMSON SHELTI	:	SUPERIOR COURT
	:	
vs.	:	CA 98-0000
	:	
HERMAN SHEPPERD, ET AL.	:	

MOTION TO DISMISS

Pursuant to Rule ____, the Defendant, Oakmont Terrace Condominium Association, hereby moves to dismiss the Sixth and Seventh Counts of the Plaintiff's Complaint dated October 19, 19__ on the grounds that said counts fail to state a claim upon which relief can be granted and are insufficient as a matter of law.

A memorandum of law in support of this motion is attached hereto.

THE DEFENDANT,
OAKMONT TERRACE
CONDOMINIUM ASSOCIATION

BY ______________________________

Heidi Zimmerman, Esq.
Law Office of Heidi Zimmerman,
its attorney
P.O. Box 256
Anytown, RI
Tele. #(123) 334-1212
Bar #123789

CERTIFICATION

I hereby certify that a copy of the above was mailed on ____________ 1999 to all counsel and pro se parties of record as follows: Joshua A. Graham, Esq., of Mahoney & Taylor, P.C., P.O. Box 145, Anytown, RI 09870.

____

(date)

SAMSON SHELTI	:	SUPERIOR COURT
	:	
vs.	:	CA 98-0000
	:	
HERMAN SHEPPERD, ET AL.	:	

MEMORANDUM OF LAW
IN SUPPORT OF MOTION TO DISMISS

FACTS

The Plaintiff, Samson Zanewchio, claims he was injured when he was allegedly bitten by a dog on October 24, 1997. The Plaintiff has sued five separate Defendants.

The Defendant, Herman Shepperd, owns the dog in question. The Defendant, Oakmont Terrace Condominium Association (hereinafter referred to as "Oakmont") is the location in which the Defendant, Herman Shepperd, resides with the dog in question.

The Plaintiff's Complaint contains seven counts. The first two counts are directed against Herman Shepperd. The third through fifth counts are directed at Defendant, New Haven Savings Bank. The remaining sixth and seventh counts are directed at the Defendant, Oakmont, alleging negligence, presumably pursuant to G.L. __________, known as the Dog Bite Statute.

The Defendant, Oakmont, files this instant Motion to Dismiss on the ground that the allegations set forth in the sixth and seventh counts against it fail to state a cause of action.

In his Complaint, the Plaintiff alleges that the Defendant, Oakmont, owned and controlled the area where the alleged attack took place. In paragraph two of the sixth count, the Plaintiff alleges that the Defendant, Oakmont, knew or should have known of the dog's dangerous propensities. It appears that the Plaintiff believes these two allegations are sufficient to hold the Defendant, Oakmont, liable for the Plaintiff's injuries. The Defendant, Oakmont, disagrees.

ARGUMENT

Paragraph two of the Sixth Count of the Plaintiff's Amended Complaint claims the Defendant, Oakmont, was negligent, and therefore liable for the Plaintiff's injuries. This allegation, however, does not justify holding the Defendant, Oakmont, liable under G.L. _____, the dog bite statute, which states:

> If any dog does any damage to either the body or property of any person, the *owner or keeper,* or if the owner or keeper is a minor, the parent or guardian of such minor, shall be liable for such damage, except when such damage has been occasioned to the body or property of the person who, at the time such damage was sustained, was committing a trespass or other tort, or was teasing, tormenting or abusing such dog.

The Statute defines keeper as: "any person, other than the owner, harboring or having in his possession any dog."

In addition, in order for a duty to arise under G.L.____ some degree of control over the dog must be exercised. *Buturla v. St. Onge, Et Al.,* _____________, (1987).

There is no dispute that the Defendant, Oakmont, is not the owner or keeper of the dog. Nor did the Plaintiff claim that the Defendant, Oakmont, had any degree of control over the dog at any time of the alleged attack. Therefore, the Defendant, Oakmont, cannot be found liable for the Plaintiff's injuries.

Pursuant to Rule____, a Motion to Dismiss tests the legal sufficiency of a cause of action or defense. In this case, there is no authority to hold the Defendant, Oakmont, liable for the Plaintiff's claims.

CONCLUSION

Accordingly, the allegations in the sixth and seventh counts of the Plaintiff's Amended Complaint fail to state a cause of action against the Defendant, Oakmont, under G.L.____ or any case law, and should be stricken.

THE DEFENDANT,
OAKMONT TERRACE
CONDOMINIUM ASSOCIATION

BY ______________________________

Heidi Zimmerman, Esq.
Law Office of Heidi Zimmerman,
its attorney
P.O. Box 256
Anytown, RI 09870
Tele. # (123) 334-1212
Bar #123789

Example 8-4. Objection to Motion to Dismiss and Memorandum of Law (unrelated case)

(date)

SAMSON SHELTI	:	SUPERIOR COURT
	:	
vs.	:	CA 98-0000
	:	
HERMAN SHEPPERD, ET AL.	:	

OBJECTION TO MOTION TO DISMISS

In accordance with Rule ___ the Plaintiff hereby objects to the Motion to Dismiss filed by the Defendant, Oakmont Terrace Condominium Association, dated January 7, 1999. The Plaintiff makes this objection on the grounds that he has stated a cause of action upon which relief can be granted, against the Defendant, Oakmont Terrace Condominium Association. Therefore, this Objection to the Defendant's Motion to Dismiss should be sustained.

THE PLAINTIFF

BY ______________________

Joshua A. Graham, Esq.
Mahoney & Taylor, P.C.,
his attorneys
P.O. Box 145
Anytown, RI 09870
Tele. #(123) 344-5151
Bar # 70598

CERTIFICATION

I hereby certify that a copy of the foregoing objection and attached memorandum of law was mailed on ______________ to all counsel and pro se parties of record, namely: Heidi Zimmerman, Esq., P.O. Box 256, Anytown, RI 09870.

____

(date)

SAMSON SHELTI	:	SUPERIOR COURT
	:	
	:	CA 98-0000
vs.	:	
	:	
HERMAN SHEPPERD, ET AL.	:	

MEMORANDUM OF LAW IN SUPPORT OF OBJECTION TO MOTION TO DISMISS

FACTS

The Plaintiff in the above-captioned case brought suit for injuries he sustained as a result of being viciously attacked by a dog owned by the Defendant, Herman Shepperd.

The Plaintiff was a resident of the Defendant, Oakmont Terrace Condominiums, at the time of the incident at issue. The Defendant, Herman Shepperd, was also a resident of the Defendant condominium complex at the time of the incident.

On or about October 24, 1997, the Plaintiff was jogging in the jogging path located on the common areas of the condominium complex. While the Plaintiff was jogging, a large German Shepherd mix dog chased and viciously attacked the Plaintiff. The Plaintiff was then rushed to the hospital where he was subsequently treated for his injuries.

In October 1998, the Plaintiff instituted this action against the owner of the dog and the condominium association. In his Complaint, the Plaintiff asserts that the condominium association was negligent in that it owned and controlled the condominium complex where the Defendant dog owner resided and:

(a) it knew or should have known the dog lived with the Defendant owner at the condominium complex;
(b) the Defendant condominium association permitted the Defendant dog owner to have the animal, although the condominium association charter clearly states no dogs are allowed and several residents have filed written Complaints about the dog with the Defendant condominium association;
(c) the Defendant condominium association knew or should have known of the animal's dangerous propensities because it attacked other residents, including children, before attacking the Plaintiff.

As a result of the attack, the Plaintiff was knocked to the ground by the dog, received several sutures as a result of bite marks, broke his tibia, and tore several ligaments which required surgery and will require additional surgery in the future, all of which has resulted in permanent injury.

LAW AND ARGUMENT

In its Motion to Dismiss, the Defendant condominium association incorrectly asserts that the Plaintiff's action against it is based on the Dog Bite statute, G.L. ____. It is not. The Plaintiff's cause of action against the Defendant condominium association rests solely on negligence.

A claim for negligence is based on a breach of duty by the Defendant to the Plaintiff and the causal connection between the Defendant's breach of duty and the resulting harm to the Plaintiff. *Catz v. Rubenstein,* ____________________ (1986).

In this instant case, the Defendant condominium association breached its duty to the Plaintiff by permitting the dog to live at the condominium complex although it knew the dog's presence was a violation of the condominium association charter and that the dog had dangerous propensities. Hence, the Plaintiff has stated a cause of action in which relief can be granted against the Defendant condominium association.

CONCLUSION

Based on the foregoing, the Plaintiff's Objection to Motion to Dismiss should be sustained.

THE PLAINTIFF

BY _________________________
Joshua A. Graham, Esq.
Mahoney & Taylor, P.C.,
his attorneys
P.O. Box 145
Anytown, RI 09870
Tele. #(123) 344-5151
Bar # 70598

9 THE PRETRIAL STAGE: MOTIONS FOR JUDGMENT AFTER PLEADINGS ARE CLOSED

TERMINOLOGY

Summary Judgment
Judgment on the Pleadings
Material Fact
Affidavits

INTRODUCTION

Motions for Summary Judgment and Motions for Judgment are attempts to end a lawsuit before it goes to trial. There are, however, several differences between them and the motions discussed in Chapter 8. Specifically, Motions for Summary Judgment and Motions for Judgment are directed specifically at the dispute between the parties rather than at technicalities. Other differences are discussed below.

I. GROUNDS FOR MOTIONS FOR JUDGMENT ON THE PLEADINGS AND MOTIONS FOR SUMMARY JUDGMENT

A. The Purpose of These Motions

The purpose of both of these motions is to convince a judge, through pleadings, other documents, and oral argument during a hearing (rather than at a trial), that there are no genuine issues of **material fact** in the case. Without such issues, there is nothing for a trier of fact to determine at trial. Therefore, there is no need for a trial and the party who brought the motion is entitled to judgment in his or her favor, now.

B. Time to Bring These Motions

Except in Connecticut, both motions may be brought at any time after the pleadings are closed as long as they do not delay the trial. (Connecticut does not have a Motion for Judgment on the Pleadings.)

II. Any Party May Bring Motions for Judgment on the Pleadings and Motions for Summary Judgment

Presume once again we are addressing cases with one Plaintiff and one Defendant. There are no Counterclaims, no Cross Claims, and no Third-Party actions. Unlike a Motion to Dismiss, a Motion for a More Definite Statement, etc., a Motion for Judgment on the Pleadings and a Motion for Summary Judgment may be brought by either party, not just by the Defendant against the Plaintiff.

Furthermore, both parties may bring either motion if they believe their version of the facts can be supported by the pleadings, etc. **Note:** In this situation, they will probably be denied because each party's motion will contain the exact opposite information and conclusions, thereby creating the existence of one or more genuine issues of material fact that a trier of fact should determine, rather than one judge during a motions hearing.

III. Differences between Motions for Judgment on the Pleadings and Motions for Summary Judgment

Though these motions are brought to accomplish the same goal, they differ procedurally.

A. Motions for Judgment on the Pleadings

Technically, a **Motion for Judgment on the Pleadings** should be based solely upon the pleadings filed in the case. They are most effective in those extremely rare cases in which a Defendant admits every allegation in the Plaintiff's Complaint and as a result, there is nothing to argue about, i.e., there is no genuine issue of material fact.

B. Motions for Summary Judgment

Motions for Summary Judgment are more common than Motions for Judgment on the Pleadings because a party who brings a Motion for Summary Judgment is permitted to include and rely upon other documentary evidence in the motion to support the claim that there is no genuine issue of material fact. This permits the party to make a much stronger argument than simply relying upon the pleadings.

Motions for Summary Judgment are typically filed later than Motions for Judgment on the Pleadings, usually after the party has conducted discovery. The documentary evidence permitted includes but is not limited to:

1. the pleadings;
2. affidavits and certified copies of relevant documents that are not part of the court file;
3. certified transcripts of testimony given under oath, such as deposition testimony;
4. relevant responses to Interrogatories and Requests for Production; and
5. written admissions, etc. (Requests for Admissions).

The purpose of this documentation is to convince the court that it is quite clear what the truth is and what really happened during the dispute in question. As a result, there is no need for a trier of fact to waste time determining the facts during a trial.

C. Motions for Judgment on the Pleadings May Be Treated As Motions for Summary Judgment

In some situations, a Motion for Judgment on the Pleadings may turn into a Motion for Summary Judgment because a party may introduce evidence outside the pleadings to support his or her motion or objection. In this situation, the court has the discretion to permit this additional information or end the hearing and require the parties to file a Motion and Objection for Summary Judgment. If the court permits this additional information, it will treat the motion as a Motion for Summary Judgment and postpone the hearing to another date in order to give both parties the opportunity to present such information.

IV. Objecting to a Motion for Summary Judgment

In their objection, parties opposing a Motion for Summary Judgment must convince the court that some real (genuine) issue of material fact still exists, which questions liability or damages. As a result of the unresolved issue(s), the moving party is not entitled to judgment as a matter of law. Instead, there must be a trial to determine the facts.

V. Briefs or Memorandums of Law

Briefs or memorandums of law are typically required to be filed with a Motion for Judgment on the Pleadings and a Motion for Summary Judgment.

VI. Hearings Are Permitted

Each state addressed in this text permits the parties to present their arguments at a hearing.

VII. The Plaintiff and Motions for Summary Judgment

As mentioned in Chapter 3, a civil lawsuit consists of two issues:

1. the Defendant's **liability** to the Plaintiff, if any; and
2. the amount of **damages** due to the Plaintiff from the Defendant, if any.

These issues are determined by the facts of each lawsuit. At trial, a Plaintiff who intends to win on the Complaint must be able to prove both liability and damages. As a result, the same is true if a Plaintiff intends to prevail on a Motion for Summary Judgment. This is possible in certain types of cases; in others it is not.

A. Contract or Debt Collection Cases

Contract or debt collection cases such as *Skillman, Et Al. v. Auto Service Center, Inc.* in this text, are fairly simplistic:

The Defendant promised to pay a certain sum of money to the Plaintiff, by a certain date.

The Defendant's *liability* to the Plaintiff is established by the Defendant's signature on a written contract: the promissory note. The *damages* owed to the Plaintiff are established by how much, if anything, the Defendant has already paid to the Plaintiff. This amount can be proven by written receipts, canceled checks, bank statements, etc. Likewise, any interest and attorney's fees allowed under the terms of the note can also be established by documentation.

Accordingly, the Plaintiff may file a Motion for Summary Judgment, along with a memorandum of law, and attach the appropriate documents to prove the Defendant's liability and damages due to the Plaintiff. Based upon this information, he or she will claim that there is no genuine issue as to any material fact. Therefore, the court should enter Summary Judgment now, as a matter of law.

In response, the Defendant may assert defenses that are stated in his or her Answer, to demonstrate that liability is not absolute. In addition, he or she should attach contrary documentation to an objection and provide proof to support the claim that genuine issues of material fact still exist. As a result, a trial is necessary to determine these issues.

B. Negligence Cases, Intentional Torts, Breach of Contract without a Specified Sum, etc.

It is difficult to prove liability and damages in negligence cases without a trial. Both depend very much upon the credibility of witnesses and the content of their testimony, rather than just on documents.

1. Proving Liability Only: Interlocutory in Character

Liability is a bit easier to prove than damages because witness statements can be reduced to writing, such as affidavits, depositions, etc. As a result, many Plaintiffs who file Motions for Summary Judgment will ask the court to enter Summary Judgment only as to liability. This type of motion is often referred to as a *Motion for Summary Judgment Interlocutory in Character with Respect to Liability.* If the Plaintiff wins the motion, the trial will consist only of a Hearing in Damages.

Through documentation, the Plaintiff will attempt to establish the Defendant's liability. In response, a Defendant will claim that even liability cannot be proven by documents. Instead, a trier of fact needs to observe each witness and determine his or her credibility in order to determine the facts necessary to prove whether or not the Defendant is liable. The court often agrees.

If the Plaintiff is successful, the court will do the following:

- **a.** Grant Summary Judgment in favor of the Plaintiff, as to liability; and
- **b.** Order a hearing before a judge or a jury in which the sole issue will be to determine the amount of damages the Plaintiff is entitled to from the Defendant.

2. Damages

Damages in personal injury cases, specifically, are extremely difficult to prove through documentation because someone who is qualified must place a dollar amount on a Plaintiff's pain and suffering. But who? The Plaintiff? No. At least at trial, the trier of fact will have the opportunity to listen to the entire story, from both the Plaintiff and the Defendant, their witnesses, and their experts, before it decides on a dollar amount that is appropriate to address the Plaintiff's losses.

VIII. The Defendant and Motions for Summary Judgment

A. Contract or Debt Collection Cases, Sum Specific Cases: Liability

Defendants who attempt Summary Judgment must only prove that they are not liable to the Plaintiff. If there is no liability, there can be no damages. As a result, Defendants may rely upon the defenses (even if they have not yet filed an Answer) in order to prove that they are not liable. For instance, they can present documentation that proves one or more of the following:

1. They are not liable, because they did not sign the contract or promissory note or enter into the agreement the Plaintiff claims.
2. They are not liable because they paid the Plaintiff the entire amount due.
3. The Plaintiff released them from the obligation.
4. The agreement was illegal.

5. The agreement was made while the Defendant was an infant (under legal age).
6. The agreement was made at a time in which the Defendant lacked sufficient mental capacity or legal capacity.
7. This dispute was resolved during arbitration or another proceeding (res judicata).
8. The agreement was created as a result of the Plaintiff's fraud or duress.
9. The statute of limitations expired before the case commenced.
10. In addition to the above, any other defense the Defendant raised in the Answer that was not addressed by a Motion to Dismiss may be included.

B. Contract or Debt Collection Cases, Sum Specific Cases: Damages

If a Defendant is in fact liable, he or she may still contest the amount of damages the Plaintiff claims due. Again, this can be accomplished through documentation to support any applicable defenses as stated above, or through documentation that proves he or she owes an amount that is less than what the Plaintiff claims.

It is possible for the Defendant's defense to apply to only a part of the Plaintiff's claim. In that situation, Summary Judgment may be granted in favor of the Plaintiff for issues not applicable to the Defendant's defenses.

C. Negligence Cases, Intentional Torts, Breach of Contract without a Specified Sum, Etc.

For the same reasons stated above, it is difficult for a Defendant to demonstrate through a Motion for Summary Judgment that he or she is not liable in these types of cases. As a result, it is often difficult to prevail on such a motion.

IX. Affidavits and Other Documents Must Be Made in Good Faith

Any affidavits and other documents filed to support or object to a Motion for Summary Judgment must be made in good faith. If not, or if they were created to purposely delay the case, the court may order the offending party to pay the opposing party's reasonable expenses, including attorney's fees, incurred due to such bad faith. In addition, the offending party may be found in contempt and, if appropriate, the attorney involved may be disciplined by the court.

X. When There Is More Than One Plaintiff or Defendant

When there is more than one Plaintiff or Defendant, one or more of either party may seek Summary Judgment for those counts in the Complaint that apply to them.

XI. Counterclaims and Cross Complaints

In addition to the Complaint, any party may file a Motion for Summary Judgment with respect to Counterclaims and Cross Complaints filed in an action.

XII. Conclusion

Key Issues in This Chapter

Motions for Judgment on the Pleadings and Motions for Summary Judgment prevent a party from having his or her day in court at trial. As a result, courts are often reluctant to grant them in cases in which the Defendant has appeared and actively participated in the litigation process. Instead, the courts prefer the case to go to trial and be decided by a trier of fact who has heard all the evidence. Nevertheless, these motions are commonly filed and occasionally granted.

STATE SUMMARIES

Summary Judgment in Connecticut: PBs 17-44 et seq.

Filing and Objecting to Motions for Summary Judgment

Plaintiffs and Defendants of any type may bring a Motion for Summary Judgment, along with a supporting memorandum of law and any applicable pleadings, affidavits, answers to Interrogatories, deposition transcripts, and admissions at any time without the court's permission unless the case has been assigned for trial. In that situation, the party should first obtain the court's permission.

Objections, with the applicable papers mentioned above, must be filed no later than ***the day before*** the hearing scheduled for the motion. Typically, this is the Friday before a Monday Short Calendar.

Example 9-1. Connecticut, Motion for Summary Judgment Interlocutory in Character and Memo of Law

DOCKET NO. CV 98 0333333 S	:	SUPERIOR COURT
SARAH A. DONAHUE	:	JUDICIAL DISTRICT OF TOLLAND
VS.	:	AT ROCKVILLE
RICHARD P. ANDREW	:	(date)

MOTION FOR SUMMARY JUDGMENT INTERLOCUTORY IN CHARACTER, WITH RESPECT TO LIABILITY

Pursuant to Connecticut Practice Book Section 17-50, the Plaintiff, Sarah A. Donahue, hereby respectfully submits that there is no genuine issue as to any material fact with respect to the Defendant's liability. Therefore, the Plaintiff respectfully moves for Summary Judgment in its favor on the issue of liability.

Furthermore, the Plaintiff respectfully moves for an Order for an Immediate Hearing before a jury, pursuant to Connecticut Practice Book Section 17-50, to determine the amount of damages suffered by the Plaintiff.

The Plaintiff submits the following documents in support of her Motion for Summary Judgment: an affidavit of the Plaintiff, Sarah A. Donahue, the police accident report and a memorandum of law.

THE PLAINTIFF,
SARAH A. DONAHUE

BY ___________________________

Christine Kulas, Esq.
Law Offices of Christine Kulas,
her attorney
P.O. Box 2005
Ellington, CT 06066
Tele. #(860) 222-2222
Juris #989898

ORAL ARGUMENT REQUESTED
TESTIMONY NOT REQUIRED

ORDER

The foregoing Motion having been duly presented and heard by the Court, it is hereby ORDERED: GRANTED/DENIED

____

BY THE COURT

CERTIFICATION

I hereby certify that a copy of the above was mailed on (date) to all counsel and pro se parties of record as follows: Neil E. Clifford, Esq., of Michaels, Sabrina and Alexander, P.C., 259 Sage Road, Suite 200, West Hartford, CT 06080.

____

Commissioner of the Superior Court

Note to readers: A memorandum of law in support of this motion is not included here but would be needed if this motion were to be filed in court.

Example 9-2. Connecticut, Objection to Motion for Summary Judgment Interlocutory in Character and Memo of Law

DOCKET NO. CV 98 0333333 S	:	SUPERIOR COURT
SARAH A. DONAHUE	:	JUDICIAL DISTRICT OF TOLLAND
VS.	:	AT ROCKVILLE
RICHARD P. ANDREW	:	(date)

OBJECTION TO MOTION FOR SUMMARY JUDGMENT

The Defendant, in the above-captioned action, hereby objects to the Plaintiff's Motion for Summary Judgment Interlocutory in Character with Respect to Liability dated February 16, 1999. The Defendant respectfully submits that there are genuine issues as to material facts with regard to liability and the Plaintiff is not entitled to judgment as a matter of law. A memorandum of law and an affidavit are attached hereto, in support of this objection.

THE DEFENDANT,
RICHARD P. ANDREW

BY ______________________________

Neil E. Clifford, Esq.
Michaels, Sabrina and Alexander, P.C.,
his attorneys
259 Sage Road, Suite 200
West Hartford, CT 06080
Tele. # (860) 111-1111
Juris #626262

ORAL ARGUMENT REQUESTED
TESTIMONY NOT REQUIRED

ORDER

The foregoing Objection having been duly presented and heard by the Court, it is hereby ORDERED: SUSTAINED/OVERRULED.

____

BY THE COURT

CERTIFICATION

I hereby certify that a copy of the above objection, a memorandum of law and an affidavit were mailed on (date) to all counsel and pro se parties of record as follows: Attorney Christine Kulas, P.O. Box 2005, Ellington, CT 06066.

____

Commissioner of the Superior Court

Note to readers: A memorandum of law in support of this objection is not included here but would be needed if this motion were to be filed in court.

Summary Judgment in Massachusetts Rule 56

I. Time to Bring Motions for Summary Judgment

A. Plaintiffs

Plaintiffs, Third-Party Plaintiffs, and parties who bring Cross Claims may bring a Motion for Summary Judgment:

1. any time after the expiration of *20 days* from the commencement of the action; or
2. any time after the adverse party brings a Motion for Summary Judgment.

B. Defendants

Defendants may bring a Motion for Summary Judgment at any time.

Note: The Tracking Sheet may require Motions for Summary Judgment to be filed at an earlier time.

II. Serving Motions and Objections

A. Motions

The motion, along with a supporting memorandum of law and copies of applicable pleadings, original affidavits, answers to Interrogatories, deposition transcripts, and admissions, if applicable, must be served on the opposing party at least *ten days* from the date scheduled for a hearing.

B. Objections

If a party intends to object to a Motion for Summary Judgment, Rule 56(c) states that "opposing affidavits" must be served "prior to the date of the hearing." **Note:** It is probably advisable to include a memorandum of law in opposition to the motion, as well as any applicable pleadings, deposition transcripts, answers to Interrogatories, admissions, etc.

Summary Judgment in New Jersey: Rule 4:46

I. Time to Bring Motions for Summary Judgment

A. Plaintiffs

Plaintiffs, Third-Party Plaintiffs, and parties who bring Cross Claims may bring a Motion for Summary Judgment:

1. any time after the expiration of *35 days* from the commencement of the action; or
2. any time after the adverse party brings a Motion for Summary Judgment.

B. Defendants

Defendants may bring a Motion for Summary Judgment at any time.

II. Serving Motions and Objections

A. Motions

The motion, along with a supporting brief, copies of applicable pleadings, original affidavit, answers to Interrogatories, deposition transcripts, admissions, etc., must be served on the opposing party at least ***28 days*** before the date scheduled for a hearing.

B. Objections

A party who intends to object to a Motion for Summary Judgment must serve an opposing brief, along with applicable opposing affidavits, answers to Interrogatories, deposition transcripts, admissions, etc., no less than ***ten days*** before the date scheduled for the hearing.

C. Replies to Objections

A party who initiated a Motion for Summary Judgment may serve a written response to an opposing party's objection no less than ***four days*** before the date of the hearing.

Summary Judgment in New York: CPLR 3212

Time to Bring Motions for Summary Judgment

In New York, a Motion for Summary Judgment may be served no later than ***120 days*** after filing the Note of Issue (see page 358) unless the court orders otherwise.

Summary Judgment in Rhode Island: Rule 56

I. Time to Bring Motions for Summary Judgment

A. Plaintiffs

Plaintiffs, Third-Party Plaintiffs, and parties who bring Cross Claims may serve a Motion for Summary Judgment:

1. any time after the expiration of ***20 days*** from the commencement of the action; or
2. any time after the adverse party brings a Motion for Summary Judgment.

B. Defendants

Defendants may bring a Motion for Summary Judgment at any time.

II. Serving Motions and Objections

A. Motions

The motion, along with a supporting memorandum of law and copies of any applicable pleadings, original affidavits, answers to Interrogatories, deposition transcripts, and admissions must be served on the opposing party at least ***ten days*** before the date scheduled for a hearing.

B. Objections

If a party intends to object to a Motion for Summary Judgment, Rule 56(c) states that "opposing affidavits" must be served "***prior to the day*** of hearing." **Note:** It is advisable to include a memorandum of law in opposition to the motion, as well as any applicable pleadings, deposition transcripts, answers to Interrogatories, admissions, etc.

10 THE PRETRIAL STAGE: OVERVIEW OF DISCOVERY

TERMINOLOGY

- Interrogatories
- Requests for Admission
- Protective Order
- Stipulation
- Request for Mental or Physical Exam
- Requests for Production
- Deposition
- Disclosure of Expert Witnesses
- Request to Inspect Property

INTRODUCTION

The purpose of **discovery** is to assist the parties in preparing their cases and to prevent any surprises at trial. Discovery permits each party in a lawsuit to formally investigate allegations and defenses, strengths and weaknesses. Armed with this information, they formulate strategies for trial.

Unlike in courtroom dramas and comedies on television, once a civil trial starts, there should be no last-minute surprise witnesses running into the courtroom, excitedly waving a piece of paper containing new information vital to the case. Instead, each party should have the names of all witnesses both sides expect to testify, and should have a pretty good idea what these witnesses will say. In addition, the parties should examine, prior to trial, any incriminating photographs, documents, test results, etc., their opponent possesses.

Having said that, it's important to understand that discovery is optional and expensive. No one can force a party to prepare a case for trial. Most often, a client's financial resources, along with the strengths and value of the case, will determine how much and what type of discovery will be pursued. The risk, of course, is that the case will go to trial and both the unprepared attorney and the client will look like fools. To avoid that, many cases settle the evening before, or on the actual day the trial is scheduled to begin.

As you read this and the other discovery chapters, keep the following in mind: Both parties usually conduct discovery at the same time. As a result, it is sometimes difficult to keep track of who's who when reading the applicable court rules. One way is to remember that the *requesting party* serves discovery requests to be complied with. The opposing party receives these discovery requests and is expected to respond. Therefore, he or she is called the *responding party.*

I. Forms of Discovery

As I stated above, discovery permits each party in a lawsuit to formally investigate allegations and defenses, strengths and weaknesses. This is done by asking the right questions of the right persons, according to the applicable court rules.

All the states addressed in this text recognize the following types of discovery:

1. **Interrogatories:** written questions to an opposing party to answer in writing, under oath.
2. **Requests for Production of Documents:** written requests to an opposing party seeking to be permitted to inspect or copy documents, statements, photographs, or other tangible items in the party's control. This type may be combined with a Request for Inspection or Examination, described below.
3. **Request for Inspection or Examination:** a written request to an opposing party seeking to enter onto land to inspect, take measurements, take photographs, etc., or requesting an opposing party to produce a tangible object to be tested, inspected, examined, etc. In either situation, the land or the object must be relevant to the case and in the possession or control of the opposing party. (Otherwise, a party can simply ask permission or pay a nonparty owner or controller to inspect or examine, etc.)
4. **Requests for Admissions:** written statements an opposing party is requested to admit or deny in writing, under oath.
5. **Request for Mental and/or Physical Exam:** a written request to allow a qualified physician to perform a mental or physical examination of an opposing party.
6. **Deposition:** an oral examination of an opposing party, witnesses, and expert witnesses, under oath and recorded by a court reporter (also called a stenographer), video, etc.
7. **Experts:** Each party is eventually required to disclose the name and proposed testimony of any expert witnesses he or she intends to call to testify at trial.

All these types of discovery are discussed in the next several chapters.

II. Insurance Information

Each state mentioned in this text requires Defendants to disclose applicable insurance policy agreements.

III. Discovery Limitations

A. Discovery Cannot Be Used As a Fishing Expedition or to Harass

The states substantially agree that information sought through discovery:

a. must relate to the subject matter of the pending action; and
b. must assist requesting parties to prove their case or defend themselves; and
c. must not be considered privileged between the attorney and his or her client, or the attorney's work product, prepared in anticipation of litigation or trial.

The party asked to produce information through discovery must be able to obtain that information with "greater facility than the requesting party." In other words, the information must be available and/or easier for the responding party to provide than it would be for the requesting party to obtain the information.

Furthermore, discovery cannot be used as a fishing expedition to seek answers to irrelevant questions or to harass someone. Any party who believes a question is inappropriate may file an objection or a **protective order.** If necessary, the court will decide whether the question must be answered.

B. Protective Order

1. Purpose of a Protective Order

Any party may serve and file a Motion for Protective Order. Generally, the purpose of this motion is:

a. to ask the court to relieve a party of his or her obligation to comply with specific discovery requests because they are inappropriate; or
b. to ask the court to establish specific parameters for compliance.

2. Grounds for a Protective Order

A protective order protects a party from annoyance, embarrassment, oppression, or undue burden or expense.

3. Relief Requested in a Motion for Protective Order

A party may request the court to:

a. not permit the discovery;
b. specify the terms and conditions, including time and place to provide discovery;
c. allow the discovery, but in a different form;
d. limit the scope of discovery;
e. limit the persons present at the time the discovery is disclosed;
f. allow a deposition, after being sealed by the court reporter, to be opened only by the court;
g. rule that trade secrets or other confidential research, development, or other commercial information not be disclosed or be disclosed only in a specified manner;
h. rule that the parties both file specific discovery, in sealed envelopes, to be opened only upon court order.

IV. To Whom Discovery Is Directed

A. Parties and Nonparties

A party can request discoverable information from three sources:

1. *An opposing party* that is:
   a. a pro se;
   b. a client, in the presence of his or her attorney;
   c. an agent, employee, officer, or director of a public or private corporation, partnership, association, or governmental agency;
2. *Witnesses:* individuals who are not parties but who observed the incident at issue, or have special knowledge of the incident. Note, however, that because the parties will testify as witnesses at the trial, the term *nonparty* may be used to distinguish the two.
3. *Expert witnesses:* individuals who are not parties and who provide expert opinions based upon their expertise and the facts of the case. (Experts are included as nonparties in this text.)

B. Depositions Apply to Parties and Nonparties

The following types of discovery apply only to parties:

Interrogatories
Requests for Production
Depositions
Requests for Inspection of Property

Requests for Admission
Requests for Mental or Physical Exam
Disclosure of Expert Witnesses

In most states, a *deposition* is the only type of discovery that applies to all parties, as well as nonparties. Thus, either party can depose the other party and any nonparties who may potentially testify at trial.

V. Continuing Duty to Disclose

Each type of discovery must be conducted and responded to according to specific parameters and deadlines. In addition, most states indicate that there is a "continuing duty to disclose" new or additional information that may come to light, after a party has responded to an opposing party's discovery requests. Hence, neither party can later claim, "I told you the truth when you asked me the question. I didn't know until later that my answer was wrong," or, "I didn't know about this new witness when you asked me. She came out of the woodwork just a few days ago."

VI. Court Conferences: Preliminary, Scheduling, or Status Conferences

Although discovery deadlines are included in the court rules, many courts place a deadline in which both parties are expected to complete all of their requesting and responding. The purpose of this deadline is probably to ensure that a case will be ready for trial within a specific time frame.

In some states, the deadline to complete discovery can be found in the court rules. In other states, the parties are summoned to court shortly after the case is filed and are expected to agree upon such deadline with the help and approval of a judge. These court appearances are usually called preliminary conferences, scheduling conferences, or status conferences. Often this deadline is made a court order which cannot be extended unless the court agrees.

VII. Stipulations

Many states permit the parties to reach agreements to modify discovery procedures and deadlines set forth in the court rules so long as the court does not order otherwise (for example, if the deadline was determined at a conference described above). These agreements are called **stipulations.** In most cases, it's best to confirm stipulations in writing and file them in court, to prevent a future misunderstanding.

Stipulations are not limited to discovery issues. The parties can agree to almost anything—deadlines to serve and file pleadings and motions, whether specific photographs and documents will be introduced at trial, etc.—so long as the purpose of the stipulation is not to intentionally and unduly delay a proceeding or otherwise interfere with courthouse procedures.

An agreement to settle a lawsuit is often referred to as a stipulation. Either side can put the agreement in writing for the clients or the attorneys or both to sign. It is then filed in court.

VIII. Serving and Filing Requirements

Although all pleadings, motions, objections, and other similar types of documents must be filed in court as well as served on all parties in a case, some states or individual courthouses do not require all discovery requests and responses to be filed in court. Instead, simply serving the parties is sufficient. Therefore, be sure to check applicable court rules pertaining to each type of discovery. If you're still not sure, call the court and ask.

IX. When a Party Fails to Comply with Discovery Requests

Each states has rules that permit a party seeking discovery to ask the court to penalize an opposing party who fails to timely comply with discovery requests. Typically, they may file a Motion to compel discovery, Motion for Sanctions, Motion for Nonsuit, Motion for Default, or even a Motion for Dismissal. Penalties requested can include legal fees and costs for bringing the motion or for causing delays, prohibiting certain evidence from being introduced at trial, or even throwing the case out of court. An example of a Motion for Order of Compliance appears on pages 214–216. Chapter 17 will address the remaining motions.

Note: Connecticut, Massachusetts, New York, and Rhode Island require the parties to attempt to resolve many of their discovery disputes before requesting the court to rule on them.

X. Conclusion

Key Issues in This Chapter

As you explore the various types of discovery described in the next several chapters, remember the following:

Discovery is a large and essential part of adequately preparing a case for trial. Nevertheless, you will encounter many clients who are unwilling to spend the thousands of dollars necessary to adequately prepare their cases. They may not have the money, or the actual damages involved may be small in comparison to the costs of proper discovery.

For example, if a case is worth $10,000, many clients (both Plaintiffs and Defendants) will not want to pay even $1,000 for discovery and court costs. It's just not worth it to them. In addition to the money, there are the aggravations of waiting years for a trial date and missing time from work to attend depositions and the trial. Plaintiffs face the additional possibility that the Defendant will not or cannot pay a $10,000 judgment. Defendant clients are worse off: Whether they win or lose at trial, they're stuck with a legal bill for the cost of their defense.

What's the moral of this story? Keep discovery in perspective.

STATE SUMMARIES

Overview of Discovery in Connecticut

I. Discovery Generally: Pbs 13-1 Et Seq.

Connecticut's scope of discovery is substantially similar to what is stated in the main chapter. In addition, the court rules regarding most types of discovery include deadlines for compliance.

II. Stipulations

Pbs 13-32 permits the parties to reach stipulations regarding discovery procedures and deadlines. If, however, the deadline was established at a status or scheduling conference (sometimes called a *joint trial management order*), be sure to file a motion asking for an extension to time. Include any agreements with opposing parties in the motion.

III. Discovery Conferences with Opposing Parties to Resolve Disputes

The parties must first attempt to resolve their objections to the following types of discovery:

1. Nonstandard Interrogatories;
2. Requests for Production;
3. Requests for Admission;

before requesting the court to rule on these disputes. Proof of this attempt must be in the form of an affidavit of one party (the attorney) that is filed in court. See applicable court rules for details.

IV. Failure to Comply with Discovery Requests

Pbs 13-14 permits a party to file a Motion for Order of Compliance if an opposing party fails to properly respond to discovery requests.

V. Filing Requirements

All discovery must be served to other parties in the case. The rules vary, however, regarding what types of discovery must also be filed in court. This summary may be used for a quick reference.

A. Interrogatories: Pbs 13-6(c) and 13-7

Neither interrogatories nor the answers should be filed in court. Unresolved objections should be described in an affidavit which should be filed in court.

B. Requests for Production: Pbs 13-9

Do not file requests for answers in court. Follow the same procedure applicable to interrogatories.

C. Requests for Inspection or Examination: Pbs 13-9 and 13-10

Do not file requests or answers in court. Follow the same procedure applicable to interrogatories.

D. Request for Mental or Physical Exam: Pbs 13-11

Serve the request and any objection in court.

E. Requests for Admission: Pbs 13-22 through 13-25

1. Notice of Serving Requests for Admission

Do not file the actual requests in court. Instead, file only a Notice of Serving Requests for Admission that states the name of the party expected to respond and the date the requests were served.

2. Objections: Pbs 13-23

File answers and objections in court and include a cover sheet.

F. Notice of Deposition: Pbs 13-27

Do not file a Notice of Deposition in court.

G. Disclosure of Experts: Pbs 13-4

This type of disclosure is usually filed in court.

Overview of Discovery in Massachusetts

I. Discovery Generally: Rule 26 et seq.

Massachusetts' scope of discovery is substantially similar to what is stated in the main chapter. In addition, the court rules regarding most types of discovery include deadlines for compliance.

II. The Tracking Sheet

Don't forget, however, that the Tracking Sheet issued by the clerk's office when the case is filed in court will determine when all discovery must be completed by both parties.

III. Stipulations: Rule 29

The parties may stipulate (reach agreements) to modifying discovery procedures.

IV. Failure to Comply with Discovery and Discovery Conferences: Rule 37 and Super. Ct. Rules 9C, 30, and 30A

If a party fails to comply with a discovery request, the requesting party may serve and file a Motion for Order Compelling Discovery. Before serving and filing such motion, however, the party drafting it must attempt to resolve the dispute with opposing counsel. In addition, if the conference is not successful, he or she must include a certification in the motion that indicates the date, the time, and the names of the parties who participated in the conference. If the certification is not included, the motion will be denied without prejudice. It may be renewed when the certification is served and filed.

V. Briefs Must Accompany Motions for Discovery Orders: Super. Ct. Rule 30A.

A brief must be served and filed with any motion that challenges:

a. responses to interrogatories;
b. responses to requests for admission;
c. responses or a failure to comply with a request for production of documents.

VI. Obtaining Hospital Records: Super. Ct. Rule 13

In personal injury cases, the hospital records of any party may be obtained pursuant to filing (and serving) an application for an order for copies of any hospital records of a party and include:

a. a copy of the proposed order;
b. an affidavit stating that the requesting party notified the other party at least *seven days* before filing the application in court and that no written objection has been received.

VII. Filing Requirements

All discovery must be served to other parties in the case. The rules vary, however, regarding what types of discovery must also be filed in court. This summary may be used for a quick reference.

A. Interrogatories: Rule 33(a)

The party who serves interrogatories should not file them in court unless the Plaintiff wishes to serve them within *60 days* of the Defendant being served with the Summons and Complaint.

The party responding to the interrogatories must file answers and objections, along with the interrogatories, in court.

B. Requests for Production of Documents, Things, Entry upon Land for Inspection, etc.: Rule 5(d)(2)

Do not file the requests or the responses in court.

C. Request for Physical or Mental Examination: Rule 35

In Massachusetts, this request is actually a motion and it, as well as any objection, must be filed in court.

D. Requests for Admissions

It appears that both the requests and the answers are filed in court.

E. Notice of Deposition: Rule 5(d)(2)

Do not file a Notice of Deposition in court.

OVERVIEW OF DISCOVERY IN NEW JERSEY

I. Discovery Generally: Rule 4:10 Et Seq.

New Jersey's scope of discovery is substantially similar to what is stated in the main chapter. In addition:

II. Stipulations: Rule 4:13(b)

The parties may stipulate (reach agreements) to modify discovery procedures except that they cannot extend the deadline to respond to Interrogatories without the court's permission.

III. Deadline to Complete Discovery: Rule 4:24-1

The majority of discovery, such as Interrogatories, requests for production of documents, inspections, etc., conducted by parties in New Jersey must be completed within ***150 days*** of the date the Defendant is served a Summons and Complaint, unless the court grants additional time.

IV. Failure to Comply with Discovery Requests

If a party fails to comply with a discovery request, the requesting party may serve and file a motion that asks the court to order compliance. There are specific provisions for each type of discovery.

V. Filing Requirements

All discovery must be served to other parties in the case. The rules vary, however, regarding what types of discovery must also be filed in court. This summary may be used for a quick reference.

A. Interrogatories: Rule 4:17-8(b)

Do not file interrogatories or answers in court. Objections are handled through a motion. See Rule 4:17-5 et seq.

B. Requests for Production of Documents, Things, Entry Upon Land for Inspection, etc.

Check with the court. Unless I missed something, the rule does not appear to address this issue.

C. Request for Physical or Mental Examination: Rule 4:19

In New Jersey, this can be a two-step process:

1. Serve a Request first, and do not file it in court.
2. If the party objects to the Request, then serve and file a motion in court.

D. Requests for Admissions: Rule 4:22

Do not file the requests or the answers in court.

Example 10-1. New Jersey, Notice of Motion to Compel Discovery with Certification and Order

Marsh & Marsh
2719 Bergen Street
Wayne, New Jersey, 17470
(201) 696-9523
Attorney for Plaintiff

SUPERIOR COURT OF NEW JERSEY
LAW DIVISION: BERGEN COUNTY

Plaintiff BIRCH REALTY CO. vs.	DOCKET NO.: BER-L-11111-98
Defendant/Third-Party Plaintiff SAFETY INSURANCE CO.,	Civil Action
vs. *Third-Party Defendant* JOSEPH DEXTER	NOTICE OF MOTION TO COMPEL DISCOVERY

TO: Walter Madison, Esq.
Gravy, Madison & Paul, P.C.
190 Court Street
Newark, New Jersey 07102-5497

COUNSEL:

Please take notice that on Friday, (date) at 9:00 in the forenoon or as soon thereafter as counsel may be heard, the undersigned attorneys for Plaintiff shall apply to the Superior Court of New Jersey, Law Division, Bergen County at the Court house in Hackensack, New Jersey, for an order directing Defendant, to herein answer Plaintiff's Interrogatories and requests of admission herein on or before (date).

In supporting of this application, the undersigned will rely upon the annexed certification of Robert A. Hathaway, and the form of order likewise annexed.

Oral argument of this motion is waived.

MARSH & MARSH

Attorneys for Plaintiff

Dated_______

By:_______________
Robert A. Hathaway

Marsh & Marsh
2719 Bergen Street
Wayne, New Jersey, 07470
(201) 696-9523
Attorney for Plaintiff

SUPERIOR COURT OF NEW JERSEY
LAW DIVISION: BERGEN COUNTY

Plaintiff	
BIRCH REALTY CO.	
vs.	DOCKET NO.: BER-L-11111-98
Defendant/Third-Party Plaintiff	
SAFTEY INSURANCE CO.,	Civil Action
vs.	
Third-Party Defendant	SUPPORTING CERTIFICATION
JOSEPH DEXTER	

I, Robert A. Hathaway, hereby certify under penalty of perjury to the following facts being aware in doing so that I am liable to punishment in the event of any willfully false statement.

(1) I am a member of the firm of Marsh & Marsh, Esqs. and I am entrusted with the conduct and management of this action.

(2) On (date) I sent to the attorneys for the Defendant herein an original and two copies of Interrogatories and on (date) I sent requests for admissions pursuant to the rules.

(3) Notwithstanding expiration of the rule period, Defendant has not responded to either our Interrogatories or our requests for admissions.

(4) I have conferred with Defendant's attorney by telephone on at least two occasions and have also written him twice on this subject and on each occasion I have been promised the necessary discovery, yet it has not been forthcoming.

(5) Neither Plaintiff nor third-party Defendant who I represent are in default as to any discovery requests made by Defendant. To the contrary, Plaintiff and third-party Defendant have been deposed at length in this matter and further have answered voluminous Interrogatories and have provided in total 360 pages of documents in response to Defendant's requests for documents.

(6) I made this certification in support of Plaintiff's Motion to Compel Defendant to provide discovery.

Dated: ________________

____
Robert A. Hathaway

Marsh & Marsh
2719 Bergen Street
Wayne, New Jersey, 07470
(201) 696-9523
Attorney for Plaintiff

	SUPERIOR COURT OF NEW JERSEY LAW DIVISION: BERGEN COUNTY
Plaintiff	
BIRCH REALTY CO. vs.	DOCKET NO.: BER-L-11111-98
Defendant/Third-Party Plaintiff	
SAFTEY INSURANCE CO.,	Civil Action
vs.	
Third-Party Defendant	ORDER
JOSEPH DEXTER	

THIS MATTER, having been opened to the Court on the application of Robert A. Hathaway of MARSH & MARSH, attorneys for Plaintiff for an Order directing Defendant, Safety Insurance Company to answer Plaintiff's Interrogatories and Plaintiff's Requests for Admissions on (date) , and the Court having considered the Papers of the Plaintiff and the Defendants and for good cause show,

IT IS on this _____ day of _______, 19__

ORDERED that the Defendant Answer Plaintiff's Interrogatories and Requests for Admissions by (date), and it is further

ORDERED that a copy of the Order be served upon all parties or their counsel within ___ days from the date hereof.

____
J.S.C.

CERTIFICATION OF SERVICE

I hereby certify that on (date) I have caused an original and one copy of the within Notice of Motion, Supporting Certification and a proposed form of Order to be filed via hand delivery with the Clerk, Bergen County, Superior Court of New Jersey, 10 Main Street, Justice Center, Hackensack, New Jersey and one copy was hand-delivered to:

Walter M. Madison, Esq.,
Gravy, Madison & Paul, P.C.
190 Court Street
Newark, New Jersey 07102

Dated: _______________

____
Robert A. Hathaway

Overview of Discovery in New York

I. Discovery Generally: CPLR 3010 et seq.

New York uses the term ***disclosure*** when referring to discovery.

Generally, the scope of disclosure is substantially similar to what is stated in the main chapter. **Caution:** Be sure to check applicable Uniform Rules for additional requirements. Some of the rules are mentioned in the New York summaries; however, there may be others that also apply.

A. Other Types of Disclosure: CPLR 3118

In addition to the types of discovery addressed in the main chapter, New York adds "Demand for Address" which is discussed in CPLR 3118. As the title states, this is a written demand from one party to another, requesting him or her to disclose his or her address within ***ten days*** of service.

B. Protective Orders: CPLR 3101

Protective Orders are addressed in CPLR 3101 to prevent undue burden, embarrassment, harassment, etc. **Note:** The parties use a Motion for Protective Order for objections to various discovery requests. See CPLR 3122: Objection to discovery, inspection, or examination.

C. Affirmations and Motions Regarding Disclosure: Unif. Rule 202.7

Any party who makes a motion regarding disclosure (or a Demand for Bill of Particulars) must include an Affirmation that he or she has made a good faith effort to resolve the issue raised in the motion with the opposing party, without success.

An affirmation is similar to an affidavit except that it does not need to be acknowledged by anyone. In addition, affirmations are used by attorneys whereas affidavits are more commonly used for clients, witnesses, etc.

Examples of when an affirmation is needed include when making a Motion for Protective Order or a motion that seeks a court order requiring a party to comply with disclosure requests.

D. Preliminary Conferences: Unif. Rules 202.8 and 202.12

Pursuant to Unif. Rule 202.12, either party may request or the court may order a *preliminary conference* after the issue has been joined (i.e., the pleadings are closed) and the deadline for a Bill of Particulars has passed but disclosure is still ongoing. The purpose of this conference is to determine a disclosure schedule, resolve disclosure and bill of particular disputes, attempt settlement, etc.

Prior to the conference, the parties are expected to attempt to enter into a written stipulation. If the stipulation is reached there may be no need for a conference. Last, disclosure is commonly expected to be completed ***within 12 months.*** More complex cases may take ***up to 15 months.***

E. Time for Disclosure: CPLR 3102(d)

Disclosure should not take place during trial or afterward unless the court orders otherwise. In addition, disclosure should be completed when or before the Note of Issue and Certificate of Readiness has been filed. See page 358.

F. Stipulations: CPLR 3102(b)

The parties may stipulate (reach agreements) to modify discovery procedures. See CPLR 3102(b).

G. Court Supervision: CPLR: 3104

CPLR 3104 specifically permits a party to make a motion to the court asking the court to supervise one or more types of disclosure proceedings. If the motion is granted, a judge or a referee will be assigned to handle the issue. The parties, however, may be required to pay such referee's fees.

H. Failing to Comply with Disclosure Requests: CPLR 3124-3126

A party may make a Motion to Compel Disclosure under CPLR 3124 if any other party in the action fails to comply with his or her notice for any type of discovery or production. (Don't forget to attach an affirmation as stated in C. above. In addition, see CPLR 3125 regarding where to file the motion if it involves a deposition or an inspection of property that is in another county, and CPLR 3126 for sanctions.)

I. Staying Disclosure: CPLR 3214(b)

Unless the court orders otherwise, all disclosure is automatically stayed (meaning that it does not have to be complied with) if a Motion to Dismiss or a Motion for Summary Judgment is served. (**Note:** An exception is if the Motion to Dismiss alleges that the Summons and Complaint were not served properly. In that situation, disclosure is not stayed unless the court orders otherwise.)

J. Interrogatories and Bill of Particulars

A party who served a Demand for a Bill of Particulars may not also serve interrogatories without first obtaining the court's permission. See page 232-233 for more details.

K. Interrogatories and Depositions in Negligence Actions

It appears that a party in a negligence action must chose between serving interrogatories and deposing the opposing party unless the court orders otherwise. See page 233 for more details.

Overview of Discovery in Rhode Island

I. Discovery Generally: Rule 26 Et Seq.

Rhode Island's scope of discovery is substantially similar to what is stated in the main chapter. Pursuant to R.P. 2.4, the court may order the parties to report for a status conference to develop a discovery schedule and discuss settling the case.

II. Stipulations

The parties may stipulate (reach agreements) to modifying discovery procedures. **Caution:** If deadlines were determined at a status conference, the court's permission may be needed. See Rule 49 for depositions. Also see R.P. 1.4. which states that all such agreements must be in writing. Otherwise, the court will not recognize them.

III. Failure to Comply with Discovery: Rule 37

If a party fails to comply with a discovery request, the requesting party may serve and file a motion that asks the court to order compliance.

IV. Parties Must Attempt to Resolve Objections and Noncompliance

When bringing a Motion to Compel Discovery, the party drafting the motion must include a ***certification*** that he or she made a good faith attempt to resolve the issues in dispute with the opposing party, if the dispute involves:

1. interrogatories;
2. requests for production and inspection;
3. written and oral depositions;
4. failure to serve a corporate designation.

V. Motion for Protective Order: Certification: Rule 26

A Motion for Protective Order under Rule 26 requires the same ***certification*** that is required in Section IV above.

VI. Filing Requirements

All discovery must be served to other parties in the case. The rules vary, however, regarding what types of discovery must also be filed in court. This summary may be used for a quick reference.

According to Rule 5(d), the court may order, on its own or pursuant to a motion brought by one of the parties, that the following types of discovery and responses do not have to be filed in court:

Interrogatories
Requests for Production of Documents
Requests for Admissions

11

The Pretrial Stage: Discovery—Interrogatories

Introduction

Interrogatories are the most common, and often the least costly, form of discovery. They are written questions from one party to his or her opponent, who must provide written answers under oath.

I. Drafting Interrogatories

Most states require the following format:

1. Each interrogatory must be numbered.
2. Each interrogatory must be followed by sufficient space for the responding party to insert an answer. If more space is needed, the responding party may attach a separate sheet of paper.
3. A certification of service must be inserted at the end of the document, stating when the documents were mailed or hand delivered to the opponent's attorney.
4. In addition to serving opposing parties, check applicable court rules to determine if the Interrogatories (and/or their answers) must also be filed in court.

A. Limiting Interrogatories

Some states limit Interrogatories by requiring the parties to use a court-approved set in certain kinds of cases. For instance, Connecticut provides a standard set created to address most personal injury cases that do not involve death or product liability. In addition, there is another set designed to address premises liability (fall down) cases. Requesting parties who want to expand on these standardized sets may file a Motion for Additional Discovery on the ground that the applicable set is inappropriate or inadequate to address a particular case. (**Note:** Responding party may not object to answering any of the Interrogatories that exist in these standardized sets.)

In other types of cases, there is no limit to the type or number of Interrogatories a party may ask his or her opponent. In fact, in some cases it's common to send out one set of Interrogatories, followed by one or more additional sets. The only criteria are that the Interrogatories must relate to the subject matter of the case and assist the requesting party in proving or defending the case.

As with motions, I strongly suggest that you avoid reinventing the wheel when it comes to drafting Interrogatories. Your firm's forms files are bound to contain several types of Interrogatories you will want to ask your opponent. In addition, the law libraries contain numerous texts on discovery you will find helpful.

B. Responding to Interrogatories

Many states require Interrogatories to be:

1. answered under oath;
2. answered by the party they are directed to, meaning the client;
3. signed by the answering client and witnessed by a Notary Public or other official recognized by the court;
4. answered and served to the requesting party within a specific time, usually ***20 to 60 days*** after the date stated in the requesting party's certification of service, unless an extension of time is permitted.

C. Stipulations and Motions for Extension of Time

If a party is unable to respond to the Interrogatories within the time required, each state allows the party to file a Motion for Extension of Time (or to Enlarge Time, etc.). In addition, the court rules often (but not in New Jersey) allow the parties to enter into a stipulation (if the parties can agree on a new deadline) regarding the deadline to respond.

II. Objections to Interrogatories

As stated above, the courts do not usually permit parties to object to standard Interrogatories. Objections to nonstandard Interrogatories, however, are quite common. **Caution:** Any Interrogatories that are not objected to must be answered within the deadline stated in the court rule.

A. Deadline to Object

Parties who wish to object to one or more nonstandard Interrogatories must do one of the following:

1. Serve the objection(s) on the requesting party within the initial time period to answer; or
2. Specify in the Motion for Extension of Time that more time is needed to answer and/or object to the Interrogatories; or
3. Obtain a stipulation from the requesting party on this issue.

Otherwise, the court may require the party to answer Interrogatories that could have been successfully objected to.

B. Reasons to Object to Nonstandard Interrogatories

The following are reasons why a party may object to Interrogatories:

1. It is beyond the permissible scope of discovery.
2. It is not material to the subject matter of the instant action.
3. It would not be of assistance in the prosecution of this action.
4. The answer is neither admissible nor reasonably calculated to lead to the discovery of admissible evidence.
5. It is designed to annoy, embarrass, or oppress the respondent, or have the effect thereof.
6. It is unduly burdensome to answer.
7. The requesting party has not demonstrated a substantial need for said information in the preparation of its case.
8. The responding party does not have access to the information sought and that information can be obtained with substantially greater facility by the requesting party.
9. It is unclear and unduly vague.
10. It seeks information that is the responding party's opinion, rather than fact.
11. It seeks information that has been prepared in anticipation of litigation for trail.
12. It seeks information that consists of mental impressions, conclusions, or legal theories of the responding party's attorney, which is the attorney's work product.
13. It seeks information that is privileged.
14. It is beyond the scope permitted under the applicable court rules.

In addition, be sure to check in the law library for examples of other types of objections that may apply to your case.

C. Drafting Objections

There are two general ways a party may object to Interrogatories:

1. Simply state "Objection" and the grounds for the objection, rather than an answer, in the space provided under each interrogatory; or
2. Serve and file a separate document that restates each interrogatory objected to and the grounds for the objection.

Each state's court rules determine when these objections may be decided by the court. For instance, in Connecticut and New York, the rules require the parties to attempt to resolve the dispute before the court will address any objections.

D. Discovery Conferences

Some states, as mentioned above, require the parties to make a bona fide attempt to resolve the objections themselves. In essence, this means the attorneys should hold some type of conference, often referred to as a **discovery conference,** usually by telephone, to discuss the objections and try to reach an agreement concerning what information, if any, the responding party should provide.

Often, the attorneys will settle most if not all of their disputes during the discovery conference. As a result, there is no need for the court to rule on the objections. If, however, the parties still have unresolved objections, either attorney may notify the court by filing the appropriate document that informs the court that outstanding objections exist and asks for a decision.

E. Overruled Objections

If the court overrules any of the responding party's objections, the responding party must provide the answers to those Interrogatories within a specific time period.

III. Conclusion

Key Issues in This Chapter

1. The Interrogatories discussed in this chapter are directed to parties.
2. Check the applicable court rules to determine if there are limits on the number and type of Interrogatories a party can file in a specific type of

case. If so, file a motion asking the court for permission to file additional Interrogatories if the standard set is inappropriate or inadequate.

3. The deadline to respond to Interrogatories is usually within ***30 to 45 days*** of service, unless the responding party obtains an extension of time from the court or enters into a stipulation (except in New Jersey) with the opposing party regarding the deadline to comply. Motions for Extension of Time should be served and filed before the time to respond expires.
4. If timely objections are not made, the court will order a party to answer the objectionable Interrogatories.
5. If the court overrules an objection, the interrogatory must be responded to within a specific time after the court's ruling.
6. A Motion for Order of Compliance, Motion for Dismissal, Motion for Nonsuit, or Motion for Default is usually appropriate if a party fails to properly respond to Interrogatories.
7. In many cases, Interrogatories are served along with Requests for Production. (See Chapter 12.)

STATE SUMMARIES

CONNECTICUT INTERROGATORIES: PBS 13-6 THROUGH 13-8

In Connecticut, neither Interrogatories nor their answers are filed in court unless there is a dispute regarding an answer that requires the court's attention.

A. Time to Serve Interrogatories

Interrogatories may be served at any time after the return date and by any party.

B. Standard Set in Personal Injury Cases

Parties in most personal injury cases are limited to the Interrogatories contained in the standard sets found in Form 106.10A, B, and C of the Connecticut Practice Book. Parties may file a motion asking the court for permission to file additional Interrogatories if they believe the forms are inappropriate or inadequate. Last, parties who are served with standard Interrogatories cannot object to them. They must be answered.

C. Deadline to Respond and Extensions of Time

Answers to Interrogatories and all objections shall be served to the requesting party within ***30 days*** of service. They should not be filed in court.

1. Cover Sheet

A cover sheet that is very similar to the cover sheet mentioned when responding to a Request to Revise should be attached to the responses. If there are no objections, the cover sheet should state that all the Interrogatories have been answered. Any objections should be listed on the sheet.

2. Motion for Extension for Time

A Motion for Extension of Time for an additional ***30 days*** should be granted automatically, as long as the case is not yet assigned for trial and no objection is filed within ***10 days.*** Note, however, for nonstandard Interrogatories, you may want to use the following terminology in the motion:

"The Plaintiff hereby requests an additional 30 days to *answer and/or object* …." Otherwise, the party will still be required to serve all objections within the initial 30 days.

D. Objections: Discovery Conference and Discovery Affidavit

1. Attempt to Resolve Disputes

Connecticut courts will not address objections to Interrogatories unless the parties have first made a good faith attempt to resolve their differences. Usually this can be accomplished over the phone. When an agreement cannot be reached, either party may file a Discovery Affidavit which states that such attempt was made and sets forth those Interrogatories and the answers or objections that are still in dispute.

2. Court Intervention

If timely objections are not made, the court will order a party to answer the objectionable Interrogatories. In addition, if the court overrules an objection, the interrogatory must be responded to within ***20 days*** after the court's ruling.

E. Failure to Comply

A Motion for Order of Compliance under Pbs 13-14 is appropriate if a party fails to properly respond to Interrogatories.

F. Service with Requests for Production

In many cases, Interrogatories are served along with Requests for Production.

Example 11-1. Connecticut, Notice of Serving Interrogatories and Requests for Production (which are commonly served together)

DOCKET NO. CV 98-0333333 S	:	SUPERIOR COURT
SARAH A. DONAHUE	:	J.D. OF TOLLAND
VS.	:	AT ROCKVILLE
RICHARD P. ANDREW	:	(date)

NOTICE OF SERVING
INTERROGATORIES AND REQUESTS FOR PRODUCTION

The Plaintiff, Sarah A. Donahue, hereby gives notice that she has served, this date, upon the Defendant, Richard P. Andrew, Interrogatories and Requests for Production by mailing a copy of the same to: Attorney Neil E. Clifford, of Michaels, Sabrina and Alexander, P.C., 259 Sage Road, Suite 200, West Hartford, CT 08080.

THE PLAINTIFF

BY ______________________
Christine Kulas, Esq.
Her attorney
Law Offices of Christine Kulas
P.O. Box 2005
Ellington, CT 06066
Tele. #(860) 222-2222
Juris #989898

CERTIFICATION

I hereby certify that a copy of the foregoing and attached Interrogatories and Requests for Production were mailed on __________ to all counsel and pro se parties of record, namely: Attorney Neil E. Clifford, of Michaels, Sabrina and Alexander, P.C., 259 Sage Road, Suite 200, West Hartford, CT 08080.

____
Commissioner of the Superior Court

Example 11-2. Connecticut, Heading for Interrogatories

DOCKET NO. CV 98-0333333 S	:	SUPERIOR COURT
SARAH A. DONAHUE	:	J.D. OF TOLLAND
VS.	:	AT ROCKVILLE
RICHARD P. ANDREW	:	(date)

INTERROGATORIES

Pursuant to Connecticut Practice Book Section 13-6 et seq., the Plaintiff, Sarah A. Donahue, hereby propounds the following Interrogatories to be answered by the Defendant, Richard P. Andrew, under oath, within 30 days of August 5, 1998. The disclosure sought will be of assistance in the prosecution of this action and can be provided by the Defendant with substantially greater facility than it could otherwise be obtained.

Insert interrogatories and space for answers below.

Example 11-3. Connecticut, Motion for Extension of Time (30-Day Extension)

DOCKET NO. CV 96-0333333 S	:	SUPERIOR COURT
SARAH A. DONAHUE	:	J.D. OF TOLLAND
VS.	:	AT ROCKVILLE
RICHARD P. ANDREW	:	(date)

REQUEST FOR EXTENSION OF TIME

Pursuant to Connecticut Practice Book Sections 13-7(a)2 and 13-10(a)2, the Defendant hereby respectfully requests an extension of time of 30 days to and including _______________ within which to answer and/or object to the Plaintiff's first set of Interrogatories and Requests for Production dated _______________.

The Defendant seeks this additional time in order to properly comply with the Plaintiff's requests.

This is the Defendant's first request for extension of time. The undersigned hereby certifies that this case has not been assigned for trial as of the date of this request.

THE DEFENDANT

BY ___________________________

Neil E. Clifford, Esq.
Michaels, Sabrina and Alexander, P.C.
His attorneys
259 Sage Road, Suite 200
West Hartford, CT 08080
Tel. (860) 111-1111
Juris #626262

ORAL ARGUMENT NOT REQUESTED
TESTIMONY NOT REQUIRED

ORDER

The foregoing Motion having been considered by the Court, it is hereby ORDERED: GRANTED/DENIED.

____

BY THE COURT

CERTIFICATION

I hereby certify that the above was mailed on _____________ to all attorneys and pro se parties of record, namely: Attorney Christine Kulas, P.O. Box 2005, Ellington, CT 06066.

____

Commissioner of the Superior Court

Example 11-4. Connecticut, Cover Sheet, Discovery Responses

DOCKET NO. CV 98-0333333 S	:	SUPERIOR COURT
SARAH A. DONAHUE	:	J.D. OF TOLLAND
VS.	:	AT ROCKVILLE
RICHARD P. ANDREW	:	(date)

COVER SHEET RE: DISCOVERY RESPONSES

Pursuant to Connecticut Practice Book Sections 13-7 and 13-10, the Defendant, Richard P. Andrew, hereby states that he has answered all the Interrogatories and permitted all copying, inspections, etc., as requested by the Plaintiff in her Interrogatories and Requests for Production dated August 5, 1998.

THE DEFENDANT

BY ______________________

Neil E. Clifford, Esq.
Michaels, Sabrina and Alexander, P.C.
His attorneys
259 Sage Road, Suite 200
West Hartford, CT 08080
Tel. (860) 111-1111
Juris #626262

CERTIFICATION

I hereby certify that the above Cover Sheet and attached responses were mailed on _______ to all attorneys and pro se parties of record, namely: Attorney Christine Kulas, P.O. Box 2005, Ellington, CT 06066.

____
Commissioner of the Superior Court

Massachusetts Interrogatories: Rule 33 et seq. and Super. Ct. Rule 30

A. Interrogatories Are Not Filed in Court and Exceptions

Interrogatories are only served on the parties. They are not filed in court unless a Plaintiff wishes to serve them within ***60 days*** of the Defendant being served the Summons and Complaint. Note, however, that the original responses should be filed in court and copies served to the parties of record. See Rule 33(a).

B. No Standard Set

Massachusetts does not require parties to use a standard set of Interrogatories in specific types of cases.

C. A Limited Number of Interrogatories Are Permitted: Rule 33(a)

Although Massachusetts does not have a standard set of Interrogatories, parties are limited to serving a total of 30 Interrogatories on each other. A party who wishes to serve more than 30 Interrogatories must first obtain the court's permission.

D. Time to Serve Interrogatories: Rule 33(a)

Interrogatories may be served upon the parties as follows:

To Defendants: along with the Summons and Complaint or after the action has commenced.

To Plaintiffs: after the action has commenced.

E. Deadline to Answer Interrogatories: Rule 33(a)

Answers to Interrogatories that are not objected to must be served within ***45 days*** after such Interrogatories were served. In addition, as stated above, serve a copy of the answers (including the objections) and file the original answers in court.

F. Deadline to Object to Interrogatories: Rule 33(a)

Objections to Interrogatories must be served within the same ***45 days*** stated in E. above to serve answers. Be sure to state the reason for each objection. Failure to object during this time will act as a waiver and the court will compel the party to provide an answer.

G. Response to Objections: Rule 37(a)

A party who disagrees with an objection to an Interrogatory may bring a Motion for Order Compelling Discovery.

H. Response When Party Misses Deadlines to Answer Discovery: Rule 33(a)

If a party fails to comply with discovery requests or a court's order regarding such requests, the party who served the requests may file an applicable motion asking the court to dismiss the case or enter judgment in his or her favor, whichever is appropriate.

I. Amending Answers: Rule 26(e)

Massachusetts sets forth specific grounds for providing supplemental answers to discovery, including Interrogatories.

New Jersey Interrogatories: Rule 4:17 et seq. and 4:23 et seq.

A. Interrogatories and Answer Are Not Filed in Court: Rule 4:17-8(b)

The parties should not file Interrogatories or the answers thereto in court. Instead, only serve them to each other. (See Rule 4:17-8(b) and also Section H below when objections to Interrogatories arise.)

B. Standard Set for Certain Cases: Rule 4:17-1

In certain types of cases listed below, parties in New Jersey are limited to serving a standard set of Interrogatories, called Uniform Interrogatories. These types of cases include:

1. property damage to automobiles; and
2. all personal injury cases except:
   a. product liability;
   b. toxic torts;
   c. professional malpractice other than medical malpractice or wrongful death.

Parties involved in types of cases other than those mentioned above may serve an unlimited number and type of Interrogatories on each other. (See Rule 4:17-6.)

C. Location of Uniform Interrogatories

These Uniform Interrogatories can be found in Forms A, B, and C of Appendix II of the court rules.

D. Additional Interrogatories Permitted

Along with these Uniform Interrogatories, the parties in these types of case may serve ten additional Interrogatories. If they wish to exceed ten, they must file a motion asking the court's permission.

E. Serving Uniform Interrogatories

Rather than reprint the Interrogatories listed in the above-stated forms, a party may serve a Letter of Demand, indicating that they are requesting the opposing party to respond to the applicable set.

F. Time to Serve All Types of Interrogatories: Rule 4:17-2

New Jersey has a definite timeline for serving Interrogatories (or a Letter of Demand), as follows:

1. Served to Plaintiffs: after the action starts.
2. Served to Defendants and any other party: with the Summons and Complaint or after such service.

In addition, "initial Interrogatories shall be served … within ***40 days*** after the expiration of the time allowed for service of the last permissible responsive pleading as to each Defendant."

G. Deadline to Serve Answers: Rule 4:17-4

Answers must be served within ***60 days*** of the date the Interrogatories or Letter of Demand was served. A party who needs more time must file a Motion for Enlargement of Time during that 60-day period.

Note: The original answers must be served to the party who requested them. The requesting party will then make copies of the answer and serve these copies to any other parties in the case.

H. Objections to Interrogatories: Rule 4:17-5 et seq.

A party who objects to an Interrogatory may take the following course of action:

1. Answer the Interrogatory by stating that "The question is improper"; or
2. Bring a Motion to Strike Interrogatories within ***20 days*** of being served the Interrogatory. In this motion, include the Interrogatories at issue, the reasons for the objections, and a Notice of Hearing for the matter to be presented to the court.

If the Motion to Strike is denied, the party who made the motion must answer the Interrogatories in question within the time remaining of the original 60 days (as of the date the Notice of Motion was served) or at a time determined by the court.

I. Insufficient Answers

A party who is dissatisfied with an answer to an Interrogatory may file a Motion to Compel Answers within ***20 days*** of being served with the answer at issue. In this motion, be sure to state the reason the answer is inadequate. If the motion is granted, the court will determine the deadline for the party to serve a new answer. See also Rule 4:23 et seq.

J. Costs and Legal Fees: Rule 4:17-5(d)

The court may order a party who loses a Motion to Strike or Motion to Compel to pay costs and attorney's fees to the other party. See also Rule 4:23 et seq.

K. Amending Answers to Interrogatories: Rule 4:17-7

Although there is always a continuing duty to disclose new information that has been previously requested, a party who has such new information must serve it no later than ***20 days*** before the first date set for trial. Otherwise, the party wishing to amend an answer must ask the court's permission. In these situations, the court will grant the motion only for "extraordinary or compelling reasons and to prevent manifest injustice...."

New York Interrogatories: CPLR 3130-3133

Though any party may serve Interrogatories to any other party at any time after the action starts, the use of Interrogatories in New York is much more restricted than in the remaining four states. For instance:

1. Except in matrimonial cases, a party may not serve Interrogatories and also serve a Bill of Particulars upon the same party. Instead, he or she

must choose one or the other. (**Note:** The opposing party is not controlled by this decision. He or she may select either tool, regardless of what the other party selected.)

2. In personal injury, wrongful death, and injury to property actions, a party is again limited in that he or she must choose between serving Interrogatories and conducting a deposition of the same party. (Again, the opposing party is not controlled by this decision.) If both are desired, the party must first obtain the court's permission unless the parties agree otherwise by a stipulation. See page 294 for an example of a Notice of Motion for Permission to Take Deposition after Service of Written Interrogatories. (**Note:** It appears that this restriction may be limited to those cases in which only negligence is alleged.)
3. Pursuant to CPLR 3102(f), in cases in which the State of New York is a party, the state should not be served Interrogatories.

A. No Standard Set or Limits

New York does not require the parties to use a standard set of Interrogatories, nor does it limit the number of Interrogatories that may be served.

B. Deadline to Answer and Object to Interrogatories: CPLR 3133

Answers to Interrogatories are due within ***20 days*** after service. If a party objects to an Interrogatory, the objection and the grounds should be stated in the space provided for the response.

C. Responding to Objections: Compelling Compliance: CPLR 3124-3126

If objections cannot be resolved after a good faith effort, the party requesting the information objected to should file a Motion to Compel Disclosure with an affirmation. (Unif. Rule 202.7.)

Rhode Island Interrogatories: Rules 33 and 37

A. Interrogatories Are Not Filed in Court and Exceptions

Interrogatories are only served on the parties; they are not filed in court unless a Plaintiff wishes to serve them within ***60 days*** of the Defendant being served the Summons and Complaint. (See Rule 33(a-b).)

B. No Standard Set

Rhode Island does not require parties to use a standard set of Interrogatories in specific types of cases.

C. A Limited Number of Interrogatories Are Permitted: Rule 33(b)

Although Rhode Island does not have a standard set of Interrogatories, parties are limited to serving a total of 30 Interrogatories on each other. A party who wishes to serve more than 30 Interrogatories must first obtain the court's permission.

D. Deadline to Answer Interrogatories: Rule 33(b)

Answers to Interrogatories that are not objected to must be served within ***40 days*** after such Interrogatories were served.

E. Deadline to Object to Interrogatories: Rule 33(b)

Objections to Interrogatories must be served within the same ***40 days*** stated in D. above to serve answers. Be sure to state the reason for each interrogatory objected to. Failure to object during this time will act as a waiver and the court will compel the party to provide an answer.

F. Motion to Enlarge Time: Rules 6(b)(2) and 7(b)(3)

If a party needs more time to respond to Interrogatories, he or she should serve and file a Motion to Enlarge Time to Respond to Interrogatories. In that motion, include a date by which to serve such answers.

G. Motion to Compel Answers to Interrogatories: Rules 37 and 7(b)(3)

If a party fails to respond to Interrogatories or provides inadequate responses or objections, the serving party may file this Motion to Compel. In this motion, the party should state a final date for such answers.

1. Discovery Conference

As stated in the main chapter, Rhode Island is one of the states that requires a party who files a Motion for Order Compelling Discovery to certify that he or she attempted to resolve the situation with the objecting party, but was unsuccessful.

2. Costs and Legal Fees

If an objection is filed, the court may order a party who loses a motion or objection pertaining to an order compelling discovery to pay costs and attorney's fees to the other party.

Note: The motion will be granted if an objection is not served and filed within *three days* of the date it is scheduled to be decided by the court.

H. Failing to Comply with Court Order

In addition to costs and legal fees, if a party fails to comply with an order to answer Interrogatories, the court may enter judgment against that party.

I. Amending Answers: Rule 33(c)

Although there is always a continuing duty to disclose new information or correct inaccurate information that has been previously provided, a party who has such new information must serve it no later than ***ten days*** before the first date set for trial. Otherwise, the party wishing to amend an answer must ask the court's permission.

Example 11-5. Rhode Island, Interrogatories

STATE OF RHODE ISLAND SUPERIOR COURT
PROVIDENCE, SC

JOHN MARTIN	:	
	:	C.A. NO. PC 98-0000
V.	:	
	:	
JAMES TYLER,	:	DEFENDANT JAMES TYLER'S
PETER SMITH and	:	INTERROGATORIES PROPOUNDED
LUCY SMITH	:	TO JOHN MARTIN

TO: Charlene M. Murphy, Esq.
Murphy & Sable
333 Landing Ave.
Providence, RI 02910

Request is hereby made that the above-named party answer the following Interrogatories pursuant to Rule 33 of the Rhode Island Rules of Civil Procedure. These Interrogatories shall be deemed continuing so as to require supplemental answers if said party obtains further information between the time answers are served and the time of trial.

(1) Please state your full name, other names by which you have been known date and place of birth, marital status, residence address, employer and employer's address, occupation, and social security number.

(2) Please state when and where the accident occurred, including the year, month, day, time and exact place and its surroundings.

(3) Please describe the weather and scene conditions at the time of the accident.

(4) In your own words, please state fully how the accident occurred, including any observations you may have made prior to, during, and after the accident.

Defendant James Tyler
By his attorneys,

____

Lucus Moore, Esq., #7777
Law Offices of Lucus Moore,
89 Willow Street
Pawtucket, RI 02860
(401) 555-6666

Dated: ________________

CERTIFICATION

I hereby certify that on the ___ day of ___, 19__, I mailed a true copy of the within Interrogatories to Attorney Charlene M. Murphy, Esq., 333 Landing Avenue, Providence, RI 02910 and Ronald Jacobs, Esq., 67 Market Street, Providence, RI 02910.

____

Lucus Moore, Esq., #7777

Note to readers: Typically, there are several more Interrogatories included. This is just a sample.

Example 11-6. Rhode Island, Motion to Strike Interrogatory Answers

STATE OF RHODE ISLAND SUPERIOR COURT
PROVIDENCE, SC

JOHN MARTIN	:	
	:	C.A. NO. PC 98-0000
V.	:	
	:	
JAMES TYLER,	:	
PETER SMITH and	:	
LUCY SMITH	:	

MOTION TO STRIKE

Now come the Defendants, Peter and Lucy Smith, and move to strike Plaintiff's answers to interrogatories.

As grounds therefore, the Defendants state that said answers to interrogatories were not executed by a party.

Accordingly, the Defendants move to compel interrogatory answers that are signed under oath by the Plaintiff within 30 days from the granting of this motion.

Defendants,
By their Attorneys,

____

Lucus Moore, Esq., #7777
Law Offices of Lucus Moore,
89 Willow Street
Pawtucket, RI 02860
(401) 555-6666

Dated: ________________

NOTICE OF HEARING

Please take notice that this motion will be called for hearing before a Justice of this honorable court on ________.

CERTIFICATION

I hereby certify that on the ___ day of ___, 19___, I mailed a true copy of the within Interrogatories to all counsel of record: Attorney Charlene M. Murphy, Esq., 333 Landing Avenue, Providence, RI 02910 and Attorney Ronald Jacobs, 67 Market Street, Providence RI 02910.

____

Lucus Moore, Esq., #7777

12 The Pretrial Stage: Discovery—Requests for Production, Inspection, and Examination

Introduction

Requests for Production and Requests for Inspection and Examination are similar to Interrogatories in that they seek information. Such information, however, comes in the form of documents, photographs, tangible objects, etc., rather than written answers to written questions. It is common to include one or both of these requests with a set of Interrogatories.

I. Requests for Production vs. Requests for Inspection and Examination

A. Requests for Production of Documents

Requests for Production ask the responding party to provide actual tangible objects. These objects include:

1. photographs;
2. copies of specific documents; these documents include but are not limited to writings, reports, statements, drawings, graphs, charts, photographs, etc.

B. Requests for Inspection and Examination

Requests for Inspection and Examination pertain to:

1. other objects in the possession, custody, or control of the responding party that the requesting party wishes to *inspect, copy, test, or sample,* for instance, a request to inspect and test the brakes of an automobile involved in a collision; or
2. permission to enter a parcel of land that is in the possession, custody, or control of the responding party for the purpose of inspecting, measuring, surveying, photographing, testing, or sampling, or to perform these tasks on a specific object or operation that is located on the land.

II. Drafting Requests for Production and Requests for Inspection and Examination

Both requests are quite similar in format to Interrogatories.

1. In addition to serving these requests to the opposing party, check the applicable court rules to see if they should be filed in court.
2. They are directed to a specific party, rather than to anyone who is not a party.
3. They are drafted in the same manner: numbered and with sufficient space after each one for a response (usually used for an objection or to state how production will be conducted); and are followed by a certification of service.
4. They can be mailed or hand delivered to the party and in some states served with the Summons and Complaint.
5. Check the applicable court rules to determine any limitations relating to Requests for Production such as a standard set of requests. (Connecticut has such a set.) If standard sets are inappropriate or inadequate, file a Motion for Additional Discovery.
6. The same time period to respond usually applies.
7. The objection process is usually the same.

   Furthermore, each request must:

   a. specifically designate the items to be provided and/or inspected; and
   b. state a reasonable time, place, and manner of making the inspection.

III. Methods of Production or Inspection and Examination

In requests that seek only copies of documents, it is customary for the responding party to provide these copies within a specific time period, by mail or hand delivery, unless he or she objects or files a Stipulation or Motion for Extension of Time.

Items that need to be inspected or tested are a bit more complicated to actually produce. The same concerns exist for arranging an entry upon land. As a result, the requesting party should state how and when he or she wishes the production or inspection to occur. Sometimes, it's easier to make the request by telephone to coordinate schedules, then confirm it in a stipulation.

IV. Grounds for Objections

The same reasons used to object to nonstandard Interrogatories apply to nonstandard Requests for Production, as well as Requests for Inspection and Examination.

V. Overruled Objections

Objections are handled in the same manner as Interrogatories. If the court overrules an objection, it will also determine the time and method by which the responding party must comply with the request.

VI. Conclusion

For the most part, the rules for Interrogatories and Requests for Production, Inspection, and Examination are quite similar. Clearly, it is a very important discovery tool for both parties to utilize.

STATE SUMMARIES

Connecticut: Requests for Production, Inspection, and Examination: PBs 13-9 and 13-10

I. Drafting Requests for Production and Requests for Inspection and Examination

Both types of requests are quite similar in format to Interrogatories:

1. They should not be filed in court.

2. They are directed to a specific party, rather than to anyone who is not a party.
3. They are drafted in the same manner: numbered and with sufficient space after each one for a response; and are followed by a certification of service. Be sure each request:
   a. specifically designates the items to be provided and/or inspected; and
   b. states a reasonable time, place, and manner of production or conducting the inspection.
4. They can be mailed or hand delivered to the party at any time after the return date.
5. Personal injury and fall down cases are often limited to a standard set of requests for production. See Forms 106.11A, B, and C in the *Connecticut Practice Book.* If they are inappropriate or inadequate, file a Motion for Additional Discovery.
6. The same ***30-day*** time limit for compliance applies when producing documents. Don't forget the cover sheet.
7. The objection process is the same, including the discovery conference and discovery affidavit.

   Furthermore, each request must:

   a. specifically designate the items to be provided and/or inspected; and
   b. state a reasonable time, place, and manner of making the inspection.

II. Methods of Production or Inspection and Examination

In requests that seek only copies of documents, it is customary for the responding party to provide these copies within the ***30-day*** time period, by mail or hand delivery, unless he or she objects or files a Stipulation or Motion for Extension of Time.

Items that need to be inspected or tested are a bit more complicated to actually produce. The same concerns exist for arranging an entry upon land. As a result, the requesting party should state how and when he or she wishes the production or inspection to occur. Sometimes, it's easier to make the request by telephone to coordinate schedules, then confirm it in a stipulation.

MASSACHUSETTS: PRODUCTION OF DOCUMENTS, THINGS, AND ENTRY UPON LAND FOR INSPECTION AND OTHER PURPOSES: RULE 34

Massachusetts follows substantially the same procedures as described in the main chapter. Minor differences are mentioned below.

I. Do Not File Requests or Responses in Court: Rule 5(d)(2)

Requests and responses should not be filed in court unless it becomes necessary for a court to make a ruling on them.

II. Time to Serve Requests for Production of Documents, Inspection, Etc.

Plaintiffs may be served a Request to Produce Documents, etc. after a suit has been commenced. Defendants may be served a request along with a copy of the Summons and Complaint or afterward.

III. Drafting the Request

A party making this request must be sure to state specifically what he or she is asking for. In addition, include the date, time, and manner for such production or inspection.

IV. Responding to the Request

The party served with the request should respond (by agreeing or objecting) in writing within ***30 days.*** **Note:** For a Defendant who is served with a request at the same time he or she was served the Summons and Complaint, the deadline is within ***45 days*** of such service.

Objections or no responses to such requests are handled in the same way an objection for failure to respond to Interrogatories is handled. See Rule 37.

New Jersey: Production of Documents, Things, and Entry upon Land for Inspection and Other Purposes: 4:18 et seq. and 4:23 et seq.

New Jersey follows substantially the same procedures as described in the main chapter. Minor differences are mentioned below. (See also Rule 4:18 et seq.)

I. Time to Serve Requests for Production of Documents, Inspection, Etc.

Plaintiffs may be served a Request to Produce Documents, etc. after a suit has been commenced. Defendants may be served a request along with the copy of the Summons and Complaint or afterward.

II. Drafting the Request

A party making this request must be sure to specifically state what he or she is asking for. In addition, include the date, time, and manner for such production or inspection.

III. Responding to the Request

The party served with the request should respond (by agreeing or objecting) in writing within ***30 days.*** **Note:** A Defendant who was served with a request at the same time he or she was served the Summons and Complaint must respond within ***45 days*** of such service. See Rule 4:23 et seq. for objections or lack of compliance.

IV. Obtaining Copies of Documents Referred to in Pleadings: Rule 4:18-2

At times, a party will refer to a document in a responsive pleading but fail to attach a copy of that document to the pleading when serving it to the opposing party. In this situation, the opposing party may make a written demand for the copy. This demand should be complied with within ***five days*** after it is served.

New York: Discovery and Production of Documents and Things for Inspection, Testing, Copying, or Photographing: CPLR 3120 et Seq.

New York follows substantially the same procedures as described in the main chapter except that the title differs. Rather than a Request, it is known as a "Notice to Produce." **Note:** This rule includes producing documents as well as testing, entering upon land or other property, obtaining samples for testing, etc.

I. Time to Serve Notice to Produce Documents, Etc.

Any time after the case has started a party may serve a notice requesting the other party to produce documents or to allow a party to enter land or other property to inspect, test, etc.

II. Drafting the Notice

Be sure to include the time, which cannot be less than ***20 days*** after service of the notice, and the place and manner of inspection, copying, testing, entering upon land, etc.

III. Objecting: CPLR 3122

A party who objects to a Notice of Disclosure and Production should serve and file an objection within ***20 days*** of service of the notice. If the deadline is missed, the objection may be waived unless it alleges privileged matter, attorney's work product, material prepared in anticipation of litigation, etc.

Don't forget to include an Affirmation with the motion stating that a good faith effort was made to resolve the issue raised in the motion as required by Uniform Rule sec. 202.7. See CPLR 3124 regarding compelling disclosure.

IV. Serving Notice upon Nonparties

CPLR 3120(a)(2) allows a party who wants disclosure and/or production by a nonparty to make a motion and obtain a court order. All parties in the case must receive a copy of the notice of the motion, which must be served on the nonparty like a summons, i.e., hand delivered or served abode by a person who is 18 years old or older, etc. In addition, the motion must address how any costs incurred by the nonparty will be reimbursed.

Example 12-1. New York, Notice to Permit Entry upon Real Property for Certain Purposes

SUPREME COURT OF THE STATE OF NEW YORK
COUNTY OF NEW YORK

--X
SHEILA WILKENSON,)
Plaintiff,)
)
-against-)
)
)
RYAN KEEGAN,)
Defendant.)
--X

NOTICE TO PERMIT ENTRY UPON REAL PROPERTY

Index No. _______
[name of assigned Judge]

Sirs:

PLEASE TAKE NOTICE, that pursuant to CPLR 3120, you are hereby required to permit the Plaintiff, Sheila Wilkenson and/or her attorney or someone else on her behalf to enter upon 43 East Center Street, New York, New York for the purpose of inspecting, measuring, surveying, photographing, recording etc. the scene of the incident that led to the cause of action in this instant lawsuit.

It is anticipated that this entry will occur on ________, at ___ p.m.

PETERS, McROY & SILVER
Attorney for Plaintiff
2700 E. Broad Street
New York, NY 66666
(212) 232-2323

Dated: ________________
New York, New York

To:
Herman S. Marks, Esq.
Marks, Jerome & Penny
206 Salem Street
New York, NY 10007

Rhode Island: Production of Documents, Things, and Entry upon Land for Inspection and Other Purposes: Rules 34 and 37

Rhode Island follows substantially the same procedures as described in the main chapter. Minor differences are mentioned below. (See also Rule 34.)

I. Time to Serve Requests for Production of Documents, Inspection, Etc.

Plaintiffs may be served a Request to Produce Documents, etc. after a suit has commenced. Defendants may be served with such request at any time after they have been served a Summons and Complaint. The request is not filed in court unless there is an objection.

II. Drafting the Request

A party making this request must be sure to state specifically what he or she is asking for. In addition, include the date, time, and manner for such production or inspection.

III. Responding to the Request

The party served with the request should respond (by agreeing or objecting) in writing within ***40 days,*** unless he or she is the Defendant. In that situation, he or she may respond within ***60 days*** of being served a copy of the Summons and Complaint.

Objections or no responses to such requests are handled in the same way an objection for failure to respond to Interrogatories is handled. See Rule 37(a).

Example 12-2. Rhode Island, Defendant's Request for Production

STATE OF RHODE ISLAND
PROVIDENCE, SC.

SUPERIOR COURT

JOHN MARTIN	:	
	:	C.A. NO. PC 98-0000
vs.	:	
	:	DEFENDANT JAMES TYLER'S REQUESTS FOR PRODUCTION TO JOHN MARTIN
JAMES TYLER, PETER SMITH and LUCY SMITH	:	

TO: Charlene M. Murphy, Esq.
Murphy & Sable
333 Landing Ave.
Providence, RI 02910

Pursuant to Rule 34 of the Rhode Island Rules of Civil Procedure, as amended, request is hereby made that the following items be produced within thirty days of service.

(1) Copies of any and all medical reports and itemized bills relating to you and this action from Rhode Island Hospital.
(2) Copies of any and all medical reports and itemized bills relating to you and this action from Garden City Physical Therapy.

It is understood that we will pay any reasonable copying costs.

Defendant James Tyler
By his attorneys,

____
Lucus Moore, Esq., BC #7777
Law Offices of Lucus Moore,
89 Willow Street
Pawtucket, RI 02860
(401) 555-6666

Dated: ________________

CERTIFICATION

I hereby certify that on the ___ day of ___, 19__, I mailed a true copy of the within Request for Production to Attorney Charlene M. Murphy, Esq., 333 Landing Avenue, Providence, RI 02910.

____
Lucus Moore

Example 12-3. Rhode Island, Motion to Dismiss for Failure to Comply with Court Orders

STATE OF RHODE ISLAND
PROVIDENCE, SC.

SUPERIOR COURT

JOHN MARTIN :
vs. : C.A. NO: 98-6666
JAMES TYYLER, :
PETER SMITH and :
LUCY SMITH :

RULE 37 MOTION TO DISMISS BASED ON PLAINTIFF'S FAILURE TO COMPLY WITH COURT ORDER COMPELLING PRODUCTION

Defendant, James Tyler, pursuant to Rule 37(b)(2), hereby moves this Honorable Court to enter a five-day conditional order dismissing Plaintiff's Complaint against him based upon the Plaintiff's failure to produce documents which, by prior Court Order, should have been produced on or before _____. The documents sought, pursuant to the Defendant's Request for Production of Documents, are of significant importance to enable Defendant to prepare his case before the date certain for trial of November 24, 1998.

Plaintiff has failed to file any response to the document request, the Motion to Compel or the Court Order compelling production.

Defendant, James Tyler
By his Attorneys

____
Lucus Moore, Esq., BC #7777
Law Offices of Lucus Moore,
89 Willow Street
Pawtucket, RI 02860
(401) 555-6666

Dated: _______________

PLEASE TAKE NOTICE that the within motion will be called for hearing before this Honorable Court on the _____ of _____, 19__ at 9:30 a.m.

____

CERTIFICATION OF SERVICE

I hereby certify that on the ___ day of ___, 19__, I mailed a true copy of the within Rule 37 Motion to Dismiss Based upon Plaintiff's Failure to Comply with Court Order Compelling Production to be sent to Attorney Charlene M. Murphy, 333 Landing Avenue, Providence, RI 02910 and Attorney Ronald Jacob, 67 Market Street, Providence, RI 02910.

____
Lucus Moore

Note to readers: See also Chapter 17, Defaults, Nonsuits, and Dismissals, page 322 for a Motion to Default Defendants pertaining to who failed to comply with discovery orders.

13 The Pretrial Stage: Discovery—Requests for Physical or Mental Examination

Terminology

Independent Medical Examination (IME)

Introduction

A request for a physical or medical examination is common in cases in which a party's physical or mental condition is at issue. Personal injury cases are good examples. There, the Plaintiff is usually seeking to recover damages for his or her physical injuries.

I. Purpose of a Request for Physical or Mental Examination

In most states, a Defendant may request that a Plaintiff submit to an examination by a physician selected by the Defendant. This type of examination is often called an **IME: independent medical examination**. The Defendant, as the requesting party, is responsible for the IME's expense.

The purpose of an IME is similar to the reason people often get second opinions regarding their own medical conditions: to provide (the Defendant with) an impartial medical opinion from a physician who has not treated the Plaintiff for his or her alleged injuries.

After the examination, the Defendant will usually compare the IME physician's report to the report produced by the Plaintiff's own physician(s). Specifically, the Defendant will look for inconsistencies in the two reports and for indications that the Plaintiff's injuries are not really as significant as the Plaintiff claims.

II. Drafting a Request for a Physical or Mental Examination

A. Personal Injury Cases

IMEs are often automatically permitted in personal injury cases. All that is needed is a written request or notice that is filed in court and includes a certification of service.

B. All Other Cases

In other types of cases, the Defendant usually files a motion asking permission from the court to authorize such exam. The motion will be granted only if the Defendant can convince the court he or she has "good cause" for such an examination.

C. Content

The request or motion should include the following:

1. time and date of proposed exam;
2. location of proposed exam;
3. name(s) of the physician(s) conducting the exam;
4. manner, conditions, and scope of the exam, including blood tests or x-rays, etc.;
5. "good cause" (for motions).

III. Objecting to a Request for a Physical Examination

In many personal injury cases, though the IME will probably take place, a Plaintiff will not be compelled to undergo a physical examination by any physician to whom he or she objects in writing. The same is not usually said for mental examinations. Nevertheless, a Plaintiff's objection must be served and filed in court within a specific period of time and should specify:

1. which portion(s) of the request the Plaintiff objects to; and
2. the reasons for the objection(s).

A common reason to object to a physician is because the Plaintiff believes the physician is defense-oriented or a "Defendant's doctor." Therefore, he or she will produce a report that is inaccurate and will tend to minimize the Plaintiff's injuries.

Another reason to object may have nothing to do with the named physician. Instead, Plaintiffs may object to the scheduled date because of a conflict with work or vacation, or because the location of the exam is too far from their home or work.

IV. Objecting to a Request for a Mental Examination

The time and content of an objection to a mental examination are often the same as for a physical examination. Check the applicable court rules.

V. The IME Report

After the examination, the Plaintiff may request a copy of the examining physician's written report. That report should include the physician's finding, including all tests results, any diagnosis and conclusions, along with any reports from all earlier examinations relating to the same condition.

If necessary, either party can make a motion to the court to receive a copy of these reports. In addition, if a physician fails to provide such a report, the court may not permit him or her to testify at the trial.

VI. Conclusion

Key Issues in This Chapter

1. Requests for physical and mental medical exams are quite straightforward. If agreements cannot be reached, the requesting party will usually file a motion that asks the court to order such an exam.
2. Don't forget: Unlike Interrogatories and Requests for Production and Inspection, a request or motion for a physical or mental examination is usually filed in court as well as served on all parties of record.

STATE SUMMARIES

Connecticut: Request for Mental or Physical Exam: Pbs 13-11

I. Physical Exams

A Request for Physical Exam should be filed in court as well as served on all parties of record in a case. In addition, Pbs 13-11 specifically states that "no Plaintiff will be compelled to undergo a physical examination by any physician to whom he objects in writing." This part of the rule appears to apply only to personal injury cases. In other types of cases, the Defendant must make a motion and demonstrate good cause.

The Plaintiff's objection to a request must be filed in court within ***ten days*** after the request is filed and will appear on the Short Calendar. The rule does not appear to state a deadline to object to a motion. Nevertheless, I would hesitate to file an objection later than ***ten days*** after the date of the motion.

II. Mental Examinations

Pbs 13-11 permits a mental examination in personal injury cases pursuant to a request. In all other types of cases, the party seeking the exam should file a motion.

The content of a request or motion and objection to a mental examination is the same as for a physical examination. Note, however, that Pbs 13-11 does not appear to give a Plaintiff the right to base an objection solely upon the physician selected to perform the examination. If an agreement cannot be reached, the party requesting the exam should file a Motion to Compel Examination.

Example 13-1. Connecticut, Objection to Physical Exam

DOCKET NO. CV 98 0333333 S	:	SUPERIOR COURT
SARAH A. DONAHUE	:	J. D. OF TOLLAND
VS.	:	AT ROCKVILLE
RICHARD P. ANDREW	:	AUGUST 5, 1998

OBJECTION TO MOTION FOR ORDER OF COMPLIANCE

Pursuant to Connecticut General Statutes Section 52-178a and Practice Book Section 13-11, the Plaintiff, Sarah A. Donahue, hereby objects to the Defendant's Motion to Compel dated August 3, 1998 in which the Defendant seeks to have the court order the Plaintiff to submit to a medical examination by Dr. Daffy Duck.

The Plaintiff will submit herself for an independent medical examination for the purpose of obtaining an unbiased opinion of her injuries, but requests that the physician selected be one who actively treats patients, rather than one who is retired and/or makes a substantial living performing IMEs for insurance companies. The Plaintiff objects to Dr. Duck because he makes a substantial amount of his living working for insurance companies and therefore may not be objective. Furthermore, the Plaintiff objects to any doctors who are in Old England Orthopedic or any related groups such as IME, Inc., for the same reasons stated above.

Connecticut General Statutes section 52-178a provides:

> "In any action to recover damages for personal injuries, the court or judge may order the Plaintiff to submit to a physical examination by one or more physicians or surgeons. No party may be compelled to undergo a physical examination by any physician to whom he objects in writing submitted to the court or judge."

Connecticut Practice Book Section 13-11 essentially provides for the same requirements in actions to recover damages for personal injuries.

The Defendant claims, in its Motion to Compel, that "[t]he instant action is not a negligence personal injury claim. It is a claim for contract benefits." Therefore, the Defendant argues that the Plaintiff must comply with the language of the insurance contract which requires her to submit to a medical examination by a physician chosen by the Defendant.

Neither C.G.S. Sec. 52-178a nor Conn. Prac. Book Sec. 13-11 requires that the action be a "negligent personal injury claim." Nor can there be any dispute that the amount of contract benefits in this case will be based upon damages for the personal injuries the Plaintiff sustained in the automobile accident due to the negligent driving of another individual. Therefore, both the statute and the practice book apply to this instant action and permit the Plaintiff to object to the physician selected by the Defendant.

To require a Plaintiff to submit herself to a physical examination by a physician she objects to certainly flies in the face of public policy as well as C.G.S. Sec. 52-178a, Conn. Prac. Book Sec. 13-11 and case law. "It is not unreasonable to object because the physician designated by the Defendant devotes a large portion of his or her practice to examining Plaintiffs for insurance companies." *Rosenfield v. Milner's Cafe, et al.,* 10 Conn. L.R., vol. 14, 454, 456 (1994). Moreover, policies must follow regulations and statutes. *Loika v. Aetna Casualty & Surety, Co.,* 44 Conn. Sup., 59, 66 (1995). "Where certain terms of a contract have been, in effect, leg-

ORAL ARGUMENT REQUESTED
TESTIMONY NOT REQUIRED

islatively dictated, it is appropriate to consider legislative intent in interpreting those terms." *Gaudet v. Safeco Ins. Co.,* 219 Conn. 391, 397 (1991).

Clearly, the legislature was concerned about forcing Plaintiffs to undergo the highly intrusive act of a physical examination by a doctor they object to, and our courts have recognized that certain doctors who obtain a significant amount of their income performing IMEs may not be objective. See *Rosenfield v. Milner's Cafe, et al.,* supra, and *LeBlanc v. Cambo,* 26 Conn. Sup. 338 (1966). Accordingly, the specific provision of the policy which the Defendant relies upon, to wit, that the Plaintiff is required to submit to a physical examination by a physician of its choosing, is contrary to Connecticut law and therefore should be interpreted to comply with C.G.S. Sec. 52-178a and Conn. Prac. Book. Sec. 229.

Based on the foregoing, the Plaintiff respectfully requests the court to deny the Defendant's Motion to Compel her to be examined by Dr. Daffy Duck, or anyone in Old England Orthopedic or any related groups such as IME, Inc., or who is retired and makes his or her living performing IMEs for insurance companies.

THE PLAINTIFF

BY __________________________

Ann Lambert, Esq.
Lambert and Smith, P.C.
her attorney
529 Corporate Place
Fairfield, CT 04540
Tele. #(203) 777-7777
Juris #545454

ORDER

The foregoing Objection having been considered by the Court, it is hereby ORDERED: SUSTAINED/DENIED

____

Judge/Clerk

CERTIFICATION

I hereby certify that a copy of the foregoing was mailed on August 5, 1998 to all counsel and pro se parties of record, namely: Attorney Glen Lutley, of Lutley & Associates, 906 Park Plaza, Bridgeport, CT 04530.

____

Commissioner of the Superior Court

MASSACHUSETS: REQUESTS FOR MENTAL OR PHYSICAL EXAM: RULE 35

In Massachusetts, the Defendant must serve and file a Motion for Mental or Physical Exam in court. It will be granted upon "good cause." See the rule for more information regarding the physician's report of this exam and reports regarding other exams performed on the Plaintiff.

NEW JERSEY: REQUESTS FOR MENTAL OR PHYSICAL EXAM: RULE 4:19

In New Jersey, Defendants must first serve a request for the type of exam they want. This request should not be filed in court. If the request is denied, Defendants should then serve and file a motion asking the court to order the exam. In the motion, include the following:

1. circumstances that demonstrate good cause for the exam;
2. an affidavit that states the Plaintiff's refusal; and
3. an Order that states the time, place, manner, and scope of the exam and the name of the person who will perform the exam.

NEW YORK: REQUESTS FOR MENTAL OR PHYSICAL EXAM: CPLR 3121

In New York, Defendants must serve a notice (rather than a motion or a request) that indicates the type of exam they wish the Plaintiff to undergo. In addition to a mental or physical exam, the Defendant may request a blood test when a blood relationship is in controversy. The notice must be served at least ***20 days*** (but see Uniform Rules sec. 202.17) before the date of the proposed exam. In addition, it appears that the Plaintiff client, in addition to the Plaintiff's attorney, must be served with a copy of the notice.

A. Uniform Rules Impose Different Requirements: Unif. Rule 202.17

CPLR 3121 appears broad in scope. The Uniform Rules provide additional details and requirements that are more stringent and may be different than CPLR 3121. For instance, in personal injury, disability, or death cases, Unif. Rule. 202.17 states that a notice for an exam may be served:

1. after joinder of issue; and
2. service of a Bill of Particulars.

In addition, the time for serving the motion is different. Unless the parties stipulate otherwise, Unif. Rule. 202.17(a) requires that the exam be held at least ***30 days*** after service of the notice but not more than ***60 days*** after the service of the notice.

B. Individuals Present at an Exam

New York cases on this topic address the issue of whether the Plaintiff's counsel, a court reporter, and/or a medical representative may be present during the exam. Though CPLR 3121 does not address this, it appears it is not an uncommon situation. The basis for their presence is to ensure that the examining physician's report portrays an accurate picture of what took place during the exam, what was said between the physician and the Plaintiff, etc.

C. Objections: CPLR 3122

A party who objects to a Notice of Physical or Mental Examination should simply serve and file an objection within ***20 days*** after service of the notice. This is the same procedure as objecting to production of documents, etc.

If the deadline is missed, the objection will probably be waived. Don't forget to include an Affirmation with the motion, stating that a good faith effort was made to resolve the issue raised in the motion, as required by Unif. Rule 202.7.

Example 13-2. New York, Notice to Submit to Physical Examination

SUPREME COURT OF THE STATE OF NEW YORK
COUNTY OF NEW YORK

---X	
SHEILA WILKENSON,)	
Plaintiff,)	NOTICE TO SUBMIT TO
)	PHYSICAL EXAMINATION
-against-)	
)	Index No. _______
)	[name of assigned Judge]
RYAN KEEGAN,)	
Defendant.)	
---X	

Sirs:

PLEASE TAKE NOTICE that, pursuant to CPLR 3121, the Defendant demands that the Plaintiff, Sheila Wilkenson, submit to a physical examination by _____, M.D., at ________, County of _____, State of New York, on the _____ day of ____, 199 at .

The examination shall include x-rays, etc. (fill in)

The Plaintiff is further required to duly execute and acknowledge written authorizations permitting the Defendant to inspect and made copies of the records of ____ hospital relating to the physical condition of the Plaintiff and to serve those authorizations on or before the __ day of ____, 19______

Yours, etc.

Dated: _______________
New York, New York

HERMAN S. MARKS, ESQ.,
MARKS, JEROME & PENNY
Attorneys for Defendant
206 Salem Street
New York, NY 10007
Tele. #(212) 888-0101

To:
Alan F. Peters, Esq.,
Peters, McRoy & Silver
2700 E. Broad Street
New York, NY 14540

Example 13-3. New York, Notice of Motion to Require Plaintiff to Submit to Physical Examination and Affirmation

SUPREME COURT OF THE STATE OF NEW YORK
COUNTY OF NEW YORK

--X	
SHEILA WILKENSON,)	
Plaintiff,)	NOTICE OF MOTION TO
)	SUBMIT TO PHYSICAL
)	EXAMINATION
-against-)	
)	Index No. _______
)	[name of assigned Judge]
RYAN KEEGAN,)	
Defendant.)	
--X	

Sirs:

PLEASE TAKE NOTICE, that upon the affirmation of HERMAN MARKS, ESQ., a motion will be made at _________, of this Court (room ____) to be held in the County of New York, at the Courthouse thereof, located at (address) on _______ at ____ a.m./p.m. or as soon thereafter as counsel can come on to be heard, for an order, pursuant of CPLR 3121, requiring the Plaintiff to submit to a physical examination.

The above-entitled case is an action for personal injuries that resulted when the Plaintiff fell down a flight of stairs at the Defendant's premises which the Plaintiff alleges were unsafe.

An affirmation that a good faith effort has been made to resolve the issues raised in this motion is attached hereto.

Pursuant to CPLR 2214(b), answering affidavits, if any, are required to be served upon the undersigned at least seven days before the return date of this motion.

Dated: _______________
New York, New York

HERMAN S. MARKS, ESQ.,
MARKS, JEROME & PENNY
Attorneys for Defendant
206 Salem Street
New York, NY 10007
Tele. #(212) 888-0101

To:
Alan F. Peters, Esq.
Peters, McRoy & Silver
2700 E. Broad Street,
New York, NY 14540

SUPREME COURT OF THE STATE OF NEW YORK
COUNTY OF NEW YORK

SHEILA WILKENSON, Plaintiff, -against- RYAN KEEGAN, Defendant.	AFFIRMATION IN SUPPORT OF MOTION TO SUBMIT TO PHYSICAL EXAMINATION Index No. _______ [name of assigned Judge]

I, HERMAN S. MARKS, an attorney admitted to practice before the Courts of this state, and associated with the firm of MARKS, JEROME & PENNY, attorneys of record for the Defendant, states that he is familiar with the facts and circumstances heretofore had herein by virtue of the file maintained in this matter in his office and affirms that the following statement is true under penalties of perjury and pursuant to CPLR 2106.

(1) This affirmation is submitted in support of the accompanying motion.
(2) This is an action by the Plaintiff for personal injuries allegedly sustained as the result of falling down a flight of stairs on the Defendant's property.
(3) As a result, it is essential to the defense that the Plaintiff submit to a physical examination of the injuries she claims.
(4) The affirmant telephoned the office of the Plaintiff's counsel on ___, reasonably requesting that a time and place, mutually acceptable, be set down for a physical examination. This reasonable request was effectively refused in that he never returned the call, hereby mandating this motion to this Honorable Court for relief hereinafter requested.

WHEREFORE, it is respectfully requested that this motion be granted and that this court set down a time and place mutually acceptable for a physical examination by Dr. ____ to examine the Plaintiff.

Dated: _______________

____
HERMAN S. MARKS

Rhode Island: Requests for Mental or Physical Exam: Rule 35

In Rhode Island, the Defendant must serve and file a Motion for Mental or Physical Exam in court. It will be granted upon "good cause." See the rule for more information regarding the physician's report of this exam and reports regarding other exams performed on the Plaintiff.

14 The Pretrial Stage: Discovery—Requests for Admission

Introduction

Although Requests for Admission may be used in any type of civil case, they are my personal favorites to use in contract and debt collection cases. These requests require a party to either *admit* or *deny* certain statements in writing. Their purpose is to streamline contested issues and compel a Defendant to admit his or her liability.

I. Requests for Admission vs. the Answer

Don't confuse Requests for Admissions with the Answer. Remember, all types of discovery are optional and either party may elect to use them. An Answer, on the other hand, is a required pleading that must be filed in response to a Complaint, Counterclaim, or Cross Complaint. You will notice other important differences throughout this chapter.

A. Unlimited Requests

There does not appear to be any limit regarding how many Requests for Admission a party may serve on another. The scope of the requests, however, must fall within the general scope of the applicable discovery rules.

B. Response Time: Unanswered Requests Are Treated As True

A party usually has ***30 days*** from the date a Notice of Request for Admission is filed in court to respond to all the requests. Every request that is not answered or objected to within 30 days is treated as true, unless the responding party files a stipulation or a motion to extend the deadline.

C. Admitted Requests

All admissions are treated as true and therefore do not have to be proven at trial. Furthermore, a party can use such admissions to attempt to obtain judgment now, through Summary Judgment (see Example 14-2) rather than wait for a trial.

In most states, admissions by a responding party may only be used in the instant action. They cannot be used in any other proceedings.

II. The Scope of Requests for Admission

Like all other types of discovery, the purpose of Requests for Admission must be to assist a party in proving or defending his or her case. Specifically, they must be:

1. relevant to the subject matter of the pending action; and
2. related to statements or opinions of fact, or application of law to fact, including the existence, due execution, and genuineness of any documents described in the request.

Turn to page 260 and review the Requests for Admission in *Skillman Et Al. vs. Auto Service Center, Inc.* Then turn to the Motion for Summary Judgment found on pages 265-269. As you can see, these requests force Joseph Kelly, the Defendant corporation's president, to admit or deny that Exhibit A is the contract he entered into and to acknowledge his signature. If the Defendant admits all of the requests, he will not be permitted to deny the allegations of the Complaint in his Answer or later at trial. Nor can he claim that the signature on the contract is a forgery.

What if the Defendant denies a request? Then the Plaintiff knows he or she is in for a lot of work to prepare for trial.

III. How to Draft Requests for Admission

Unlike Interrogatories, Requests for Admission are not questions. Instead, they are actual statements. However, like Interrogatories, Requests for Production, and Requests to Revise, there should be sufficient space after each request for the responding party to insert his or her response. Also, be sure to attach copies (not originals) of any documents that are mentioned in the requests.

IV. How to Serve Requests for Admission

In addition to serving requests to the opposing party, check the applicable court rules to determine if they must be filed in court.

V. Responding to Requests for Admission

A. Answers to Requests for Admission

1. Directly under Each Request

Like Interrogatories, the responding party must insert the response: an admission, a denial, or an objection, directly after each request.

2. Types of Responses

a. If an objection is made, the reasons must be stated.

b. A denial must address the substance of the request. For example, the responding party must admit and specify which portion of a request is true, if any, and which portion he or she denies.

c. If the responding party cannot admit or deny a request, he or she must state why. Unlike Answers, parties may not fail to admit or deny a request by claiming they lack sufficient information or knowledge. Instead, they must state that they made a reasonable inquiry but have insufficient knowledge to admit or deny the request.

d. Parties may not object or fail to admit or deny a request on the ground that the request involves a genuine issue to be decided at trial. Instead, they must deny the request or state the reasons why they can't admit or deny.

If more room is needed, an additional sheet must be attached.

B. Filing Requirements

The responding party must serve (and possibly file) his or her responses within the time permitted. Otherwise, the requests will be deemed admitted.

VI. Challenging Objections and Other Responses

The requesting party may challenge the sufficiency of a response or an objection in court.

VII. The Court's Ruling on Objections and Answers

A. Objections

If the court overrules an objection, it will order the party to respond within a specified time period.

B. Insufficient Answers

If the court determines that a response does not comply with specific requirements, it may order:

1. that the matter is admitted, or
2. that an amended answer be served, or
3. that the matter will be resolved at a later time, prior to trial.

VIII. Withdrawing or Amending Admissions

In most states, admissions by a responding party may only be used in the instant action. They cannot be used in any other proceedings. In addition, a party may file a motion to withdraw or amend an admission.

IX. Penalties for Failing to Admit

A responding party's failure to admit a document or request must be reasonable. Otherwise, a requesting party who later proves the document or request should have been admitted may ask the court to order the responding party to pay reasonable expenses, including attorney's fees, incurred to make this proof.

X. Conclusion

Key Issues in This Chapter

1. The purpose of Requests for Admission is to narrow down the contested issues in a case and if appropriate, file a Motion for Summary Judgment, based upon the Respondent's answers.
2. A party must respond to Requests for Admission within ***20 to 45 days*** of being served or the requests are deemed admitted.
3. The Connecticut Summary provides an example of a Motion for Summary Judgment as a result of Requests for Admission. In that case, the Defendant did not file objections or seek an extension of time to respond to the Requests for Admission. Instead, he simply failed to respond to the requests. As a result, the requests are deemed admitted and enable the Plaintiffs to claim that there are no contested issues in the case. Therefore, they are entitled to Summary Judgment.

STATE SUMMARIES

Connecticut: Requests for Admission: PBs 13-22 et seq.

Like other types of discovery in Connecticut, either party may serve the other with Requests for Admission at any time after the return date.

I. How to Serve Requests for Admission

Pursuant to Pbs 13-22(b), the Requests for Admission are not filed in court. Instead, a **Notice of Serving Requests for Admission** must be served and filed in court. The Notice must include:

1. that Requests for Admission have been served on another party;
2. the name of the party served;
3. the date service was made;
4. the signature of the serving party's attorney or pro se;
5. a certification of service, which states that the Notice and the Requests for Admission were mailed or hand delivered on a certain date to all counsel and pro se parties of record.

II. Responding to Requests for Admission

A. Deadline to Respond

All admissions, denials, and objections must be filed in court no later than ***30 days*** after the Notice of Serving Requests for Admission was filed in court. A responding party who needs additional time should file a Motion for Extension of Time before the expiration of the ***30-day*** deadline.

B. The Cover Sheet

As stated in the main chapter, admissions, denials, or objections should be inserted directly under each request. In addition, Pbs 13-23 requires the responding party to draft and attach a cover sheet that follows the same format as the one used for responses to Interrogatories, Requests for Production, and Requests to Revise: Specify which requests were answered and which were objected to.

C. Filing Requirements

Pursuant to Pbs 13-23, the responding party must file his or her cover sheet and responses in court by the ***30-day*** deadline and serve a copy to all other counsel and pro se parties of record.

III. Challenging Objections and Other Responses: Discovery Conference and Affidavit

Pbs 13-23 permits the requesting party to challenge the sufficiency of a party's answer and objection(s) in court. Unlike Interrogatories, etc., this challenge must come in the form of a motion, probably a Motion for Order of Compliance pursuant to Pbs 13-14. The motion, however, will not be placed on the Short Calendar until either party files an affidavit certifying that "bona fide attempts have been made to resolve the differences … and that counsel have been unable to reach an accord." Hence, they are handled similarly to objections to Interrogatories, Requests for Production, etc.

Example 14-1. Connecticut, Notice and Requests for Admission (unrelated case)

DOCKET NO. CV 98 0444444 S	:	SUPERIOR COURT
GEORGE SKILLMAN, ET AL.	:	JUDICIAL DISTRICT OF
	:	HARTFORD/NEW BRITAIN
VS.	:	AT HARTFORD
AUTO SERVICE CENTER, INC.	:	(date)

NOTICE OF PLAINTIFF'S SERVICE OF REQUESTS FOR ADMISSION

Pursuant to Connecticut Practice Book Section 13-22 et seq., the Plaintiff in the above-captioned case has served Requests for Admission upon Mr. Joseph Kelly, President and sole shareholder and director of the Defendant, Auto Service Center, Inc.

Service was made by mail to the Defendant's attorney of record, Mark Peters, Esq., 1001 Sanberg Street, Manchester, CT 06660 on __________, in accordance with Connecticut Practice Book Section 10-12 et seq.

THE PLAINTIFF

BY ___________________________

Kenneth I. Marcus, Esq.
Friedman & Marcus, P.C.,
his attorney
27 Main Street
Bristol, CT 00000
Tele. #(860) 955-9595
Juris #424242

CERTIFICATION

I hereby certify that a copy of the above was mailed on ___________ to all counsel and pro se parties of record, namely: Mark Peters, Esq., 1001 Sanberg Street, Manchester, CT 06660.

____

Commissioner of Superior Court

DOCKET NO. CV 98 0444444 S	:	SUPERIOR COURT
GEORGE SKILLMAN, ET AL.	:	JUDICIAL DISTRICT OF
	:	HARTFORD/NEW BRITAIN
VS.	:	AT HARTFORD
AUTO SERVICE CENTER, INC.	:	(date)

PLAINTIFF'S REQUESTS FOR ADMISSION TO DEFENDANT

Pursuant to Connecticut Practice Book Section 13-22 et seq., the Defendant through its President, Mr. Joseph Kelly, is hereby requested to either admit or deny the truth of each matter asserted below, within thirty days of the filing of the Notice of Plaintiff's Service of Requests for Admission, dated __________ .

(1) The Defendant, through its President, Mr. Joseph Kelly, agreed to purchase Auto Service Center, Inc., located at 126 Maple Street, Hartford, CT from the Plaintiffs, George Skillman and Barbara Skillman, for the sum of One Hundred Thousand Dollars ($100,000.00).

RESPONSE: (Mr. Kelly would insert his response in this space.)

(2) On behalf of the Defendant, Mr. Joseph Kelly signed a promissory note, dated September 1, 1995 in the amount of One Hundred Thousand Dollars ($100,000.00), plus interest, in favor of the Plaintiffs, George Skillman and Barbara Skillman, which specifies the terms in which the Defendant would pay for Auto Service Center, Inc..

RESPONSE:

(3) A copy of the same promissory note Mr. Kelly signed pertaining to Request for Admission #2 above is attached hereto as Exhibit A.

RESPONSE:

(4) Mr. Kelly acknowledges that a copy of his signature appears on the copy of the promissory note which is attached hereto as Exhibit A.

RESPONSE:

(5) Pursuant to the terms of the promissory note, attached hereto as Exhibit A, in the event the Defendant fails to make any of the payments stated therein, the Defendant is responsible to pay the Plaintiff for all of its costs and reasonable attorney's fees incurred in the collection of said $100,000.00 or any part thereof.

RESPONSE:

(6) Pursuant to the terms of said promissory note, the Defendant promised to pay the Plaintiff the sum of Ten Thousand ($10,000.00) Dollars on the first of the month commencing January 15, 1998 and Ten Thousand ($10,000.00) Dollars each month thereafter with a final payment being made on October 15, 1998.

RESPONSE:

(7) Pursuant to the terms of said promissory note, should the Defendant fail to pay any one or more of the payments specified therein, the entire balance of the promissory notice remaining, plus interest, would become immediately due and owing to the Plaintiff.

RESPONSE:

(8) The Defendant has failed, refused, and/or neglected to make any payments whatsoever specified in said promissory note to the Plaintiff, as of the date of these instant Requests for Admission.

RESPONSE:

Personally appeared, Joseph Kelly, being duly sworn, deposes and says:

that the answers to the preceding Requests for Admission are true and accurate to the best of his/her knowledge and belief.

Subscribed and sworn to before me this ____ day of _______, 199__.

____

Notary Public (or)
Commissioner of Superior Court

Example 14-2. Connecticut, Motion for Summary Judgment and Memo of Law Based on Failing to Respond to Requests for Admission

DOCKET NO. CV 98-04444444 S	:	SUPERIOR COURT
GEORGE SKILLMAN, ET AL.	:	JUDICIAL DISTRICT OF
	:	HARTFORD/NEW BRITAIN
VS.	:	AT HARTFORD
AUTO SERVICE CENTER, INC.	:	(date)

MOTION FOR SUMMARY JUDGMENT

The Plaintiffs in the above-captioned action hereby respectfully move that the Court grant Summary Judgment in their favor in the amount of ONE HUNDRED THOUSAND DOLLARS ($100,000.00), plus interest, costs and attorney's fees.

The Plaintiffs make this motion on the ground that no genuine issues of material fact exist and therefore, they are entitled to judgment as a matter of law.

The Plaintiffs have attached a memorandum of law, Requests for Admission, George Skillman's affidavit, and an Affidavit of Debt in support of this motion.

THE PLAINTIFFS

BY ____________________________

Kenneth I. Marcus, Esq.
Friedman & Marcus, P.C.,
their attorneys
27 Main Street
Bristol, CT 00000
Tele. #(860) 955-9595
Juris #424242

ORAL ARGUMENT REQUESTED
TESTIMONY NOT REQUIRED

ORDER

The foregoing Motion having been presented and heard by the court, it is hereby ORDERED: GRANTED/DENIED.

____

BY THE COURT

CERTIFICATION

I hereby certify that a copy of the foregoing motion, memorandum of law, **Requests for Admission, and Affidavit of Debt were mailed on _________ to all counsel and pro se parties of record, namely: Mark Peters, Esq., 1001 Sanberg Street, Manchester, CT 06660.

____

Commissioner of the Superior Court

**Rather than object to this motion, the Defendant in this case settled with the Plaintiffs.

DOCKET NO. CV 98-0444444 S	:	SUPERIOR COURT
GEORGE SKILLMAN, ET AL.	:	JUDICIAL DISTRICT OF
	:	HARTFORD/NEW BRITAIN
VS.	:	AT HARTFORD
AUTO SERVICE CENTER, INC.	:	(date)

MEMORANDUM OF LAW IN SUPPORT OF MOTION SUMMARY JUDGMENT

FACTS

On or about September 1, 1997, the Plaintiffs, George Skillman and Barbara Skillman, entered into a Purchase and Sale Agreement to sell all of their interest in Auto Service Center, Inc. to Joseph Kelly. According to said Agreement, the Defendant agreed to purchase from the Plaintiffs a business known as Auto Service Center, located at 126 Main Street, Hartford, CT, for the sum of One Hundred Thousand Dollars ($100,000.00).

On September 1, 1997, the Defendant signed a promissory note in the amount of One Hundred Thousand Dollars ($100,000.00) payable to the Plaintiffs, representing the agreed-upon price for Auto Service Center, Inc. Pursuant to the terms of the promissory note, the Defendant was to pay said sum in ten monthly installments, commencing January 15, 1998. A copy of the promissory note is attached hereto and incorporated herein as Exhibit A.

Contrary to the terms of said promissory note, as of the date of this instant motion, the Defendant has failed to make any payments at all to the Plaintiffs. As a result, according to said terms, the entire amount of One Hundred Thousand Dollars ($100,000.00), plus interest, costs and attorney's fees, is now due and owing to the Plaintiffs from the Defendant.

On May 18, 1998, the Plaintiffs served a set of Requests for Admission upon the Defendant, through its attorney of record. A copy of the required Notice and the Requests for Admission are attached hereto and incorporated herein as Exhibit B.

Pursuant to Connecticut Practice Book Section 13-23, the Defendant was required to answer said Requests within thirty (30) days of the filing of the Plaintiff's Notice of Service of Requests for Admissions. As of the date of this motion, more than sixty days have passed, and still, the Defendant has failed to respond to said Requests.

The Plaintiff, George Skillman, has attached his affidavit hereto as Exhibit C. In that affidavit he affirms that in spite of the terms of the Purchase and Sale agreement, the promissory note and the Defendant's oral promises, the Defendant has failed to pay any of the money due.

ARGUMENT

A party is entitled to Summary Judgment "if the pleadings, affidavits and other proof submitted show that there is no genuine issue as to any material fact and that the moving party is entitled to Judgment as a matter of law." Connecticut Practice Book section 17-49; *Strada v. Connecticut Newspaper, Inc.*, 193 Conn. 313, 316-317 (1984).

In this instant case, the Plaintiffs have the burden of showing that there was no genuine issue of material fact. See *Amendola v. Geremia,* 21 Conn. App. 35, 37 (1990).

The court defines the material fact as a fact which will make a difference in the result of a case. *Yanow v. Teal Industry, Inc.,* 178 Conn. 262, 268 (1979). Hence, the Plaintiffs must satisfy this burden by showing that "it is quite clear what the truth is, and that excludes any real doubt as to the existence of any genuine issue of material fact." *Dougherty v. Grapheme,* 161 Conn. 248, 250 (1971); *Fogarty v. Rashaw,* 193 Conn. 442 (1984).

Pursuant to Connecticut Practice Book Section 13-23, each Request for Admission the Defendant failed to respond to within thirty (30) days of the filing of the Plaintiffs' Notice, is deemed admitted, unless the Defendant obtained an extension of time to respond or has an objection pending.

In this case, the Defendant neither requested an extension of time or objected to any of the Requests. Therefore, each admission is now deemed truth.

Accordingly, the Defendant has admitted the following:

(1) Through its president, and sole director and shareholder, Joseph Kelly, it agreed to purchase a business known as Auto Service Center, Inc. from the Defendant.
(2) Pursuant to that agreement, Joseph Kelly signed a promissory note agreeing to pay the Plaintiffs the sum of One Hundred Thousand Dollars ($100,000.00) representing the purchase price of Auto Service Center, Inc.
(3) Pursuant to the terms of the promissory note, the Defendant was to make ten monthly installments of Ten Thousand Dollars ($10,000.00) to the Plaintiffs, commencing January 15, 1998.
(4) The Defendant has failed to make any payments at all to the Plaintiffs, although said payments are past due.
(5) Pursuant to the terms of the promissory note, in the event the Defendant fails to make any payments when due, the entire remaining balance of the note becomes due and owing.
(6) In addition, pursuant to the terms of the promissory note, the Defendant must pay the Plaintiffs all of their costs and reasonable attorney's fees incurred in the collection of the sum due.

"In a summary judgment motion, the parties are entitled to consideration, not only of the facts presented by their affidavits, but of the inferences which could reasonably and logically be drawn from them as well." *DeDominicis v. American Fire Insurance Co.,* 2 Conn. App. 686, 687 (1984).

In the present case, the facts, the unanswered Requests for Admissions, the promissory note and the Plaintiff's affidavit leave no doubt what the facts are in this case. Hence, the Plaintiffs have met their burden of proof.

CONCLUSION

Accordingly, the Plaintiffs are entitled to Summary Judgment against the Defendant in the amount of $113,179.00, representing the principal, interest, attorney's fees and costs due, as demonstrated by the attached Affidavit of Debt.

THE PLAINTIFF

BY ________________________

Kenneth I. Marcus, Esq.
Friedman & Marcus, P.C.,
their attorneys
27 Main Street
Bristol, CT 00000
Tele. #(860) 955-9595
Juris #424242

MASSACHUSETTS: REQUESTS FOR ADMISSION: RULE 36

Like other types of discovery in Massachusetts, Requests for Admission may be served upon Defendants at the time they are served a copy of the Summons and Complaint, or afterward. They may be served to Plaintiffs at any time after the lawsuit begins.

The deadline to serve answers and any objections is ***30 days*** from the date of service. Defendants who are served such requests with a copy of the Summons and Complaint have ***45 days*** to serve their answers and objections.

NEW JERSEY: REQUESTS FOR ADMISSION: RULE 4:22

Requests for Admission may be served upon Defendants at the time they are served a copy of the Summons and Complaint, or afterward. They may be served to Plaintiffs at any time after the lawsuit begins.

The deadline to serve answers and any objections is ***30 days*** from the date of service. Defendants who are served such requests with a copy of the Summons and Complaint have ***45 days*** to serve their answers and objections.

Note: Requests for Admission and the answers should not be filed in court unless the court orders otherwise.

NEW YORK: NOTICE TO ADMIT: CPLR 3123

New York calls a Request for Admission a "Notice to Admit." In addition, it appears that this type of document should only be used when the party believes that the requested admission will not be an issue at trial. For instance, a Notice to Admit can be properly used to ask a Defendant to admit and authenticate the genuineness of his or her signature on a specific promissory note in a debt collection case or that a collision involving the Defendant's and Plaintiff's vehicle occurred on a certain date and at a specific location. To ask the Defendant to admit that he or she was negligent in causing the collision may be improper.

Any party may serve a Notice to Admit to any other party except the State of New York. Pursuant to CPLR 3102(f) the State of New York is exempt from responding to a Notice to Admit or to Interrogatories.

A Notice to Admit may be served under the following conditions:

1. at any time after the answer has been served; or
2. no sooner than ***20 days*** from the date the summons was served, whichever is sooner; but
3. no later than ***20 days*** before trial is scheduled to begin. (**Caution:** This appears contrary to the rule that all discovery must be completed before or at the time the Note of Issue and Certificate of Readiness is filed.)

CPLR 3123 divides the types of admissions sought into the following categories, which request a party to admit:

1. the truth of any matters of fact that are set forth in the Notice;
2. that the documents attached to the Notice are genuine;
3. that the photographs attached to the Notice are correct or are a fair presentation of what the Notice states they represent.

The deadline to serve answers to a Notice to Admit is within ***20 days*** of its service unless the court orders otherwise. Any objections must be served within this time by stating the objection in the space provided for an answer. In addition, it appears that a party seeking to object to any of the requests should do so by filing a Motion for Protective Order with an affirmation within this ***20-day*** period. Note that the party who served the Notice to Admit may also serve a Notice of Motion to Compel.

Example 14-3. New York, Notice to Admit Correctness or Fairness of Representation of Photograph

SUPREME COURT OF THE STATE OF NEW YORK
COUNTY OF NEW YORK

---X		
SHEILA WILKENSON, Plaintiff,	)	Notice to Admit Correctness or Fairness of Representation of Photograph
-against-	)	
RYAN KEEGAN, Defendant.	)	Index No. _______ [name of assigned Judge]
---X		

Sirs:

PLEASE TAKE NOTICE that pursuant to CPLR 3123 you are requested to serve the undersigned, within twenty (20) days after the service of this notice a written admission that the photographs, a print of which is annexed hereto, is a fair and/or correct representation of __________ as it appeared on the _____ day of ____, 19 __ at ____ o'clock in the p.m.

Your etc.,

Dated: _______________
New York, NY

Alan F. Peters, Esq.
Peters, McRoy & Silver
2700 E. Broad Street
New York, NY 14540
Tele. #(212) 232-2323

To
HERMAN S. MARKS, ESQ.
MARKS, JEROME & PENNY
Attorneys for Defendant
206 Salem Street
New York, NY 10007

Rhode Island: Requests for Admission: Rule 36

Requests for Admission may be served upon Defendants at the time they are served a copy of the Summons and Complaint or afterward. They may be served to Plaintiffs at any time after the lawsuit begins.

The deadline to serve answers and any objections is ***30 days*** from the date of service. Defendants who are served simultaneously with a Summons and Complaint have ***45 days*** to serve their answers and objections.

15 The Pretrial Stage: Discovery—Depositions

Terminology

Deponent	Notice of Deposition	Court Reporter
Transcript	Subpoena	Nonparty
Indifferent Person	Subpoena Duces Tecum	Motion to Quash

Introduction

As briefly mentioned in Chapter 10, any party in a lawsuit may take the deposition of any other *party* as well as any other *person* who is not a party in the lawsuit but who has information relevant to the case. These persons are called witnesses or nonparties. (I prefer the term nonparties because the parties become witnesses when they testify at their depositions and at trial.)

I. What Is a Deposition?

A deposition involves obtaining testimony of a party through an **oral examination,** i.e., orally asking questions and receiving oral responses. The party being deposed is known as the **deponent** (usually reserved for nonparties) or **party deponent.**

Deposition procedures are quite similar to those procedures used during a trial. The difference is that depositions usually take place at an attorney's office, rather than in a courtroom, and there is usually no judge present. Like a trial, however:

1. All the attorneys and pro ses in an action may attend and participate. Clients are also welcome.
2. The deponent is placed under oath by an appropriate individual, i.e., a notary public, a judge, a clerk of any court, or a Commissioner of Superior Court (who is often an attorney).
3. During the deposition, a **court reporter** is present and records every word uttered by everyone present at the deposition. In addition, the deposition may be videotaped.
4. The party (pro se or attorney) taking the deposition begins by asking questions which the deponent must answer truthfully. (See the discussion in Chapter 20 regarding direct and cross examination during trial, which also applies to depositions.)
5. The deponent's attorney may object to certain questions, when appropriate.
6. When the party taking the deposition is finished, the deponent's attorney has the opportunity to ask questions that relate to the questions and answers just discussed, to clarify the deponent's previous answers, and to ask his or her own related questions. (This is termed *direct examination* and *cross examination.*)
7. In cases involving more than one Plaintiff and Defendant who have their own attorneys or represent themselves pro se, these attorneys and pro ses may also ask the deponent questions.
8. After the deposition, the court reporter will produce a written document of the proceeding. This document is called a **transcript.** Every party in the case is entitled to receive a copy of the transcript. The expense is paid by the party who initiated taking the deposition.
9. In some cases, a party may decide to serve the deponent written questions in a sealed envelope, rather than meet face to face. The deponent will give the sealed envelope to an officer (usually a court reporter) who will ask the questions and record the answers. (This might be done for an out-of-state party to save everyone the expense of traveling, etc.)

II. Purpose of Depositions

As stated earlier, the purpose of discovery is to prevent surprises at trial. Depositions are one of the best ways to prevent such surprises because they permit a party to ask the deponent questions, including those questions that will be asked at trial. The parties then have the opportunity to not only hear the answers, but observe the demeanor of the deponent. This enables the parties to determine what type of witness the deponent will make at trial. Will he or she be strong and convincing, or weak and timid or unbelievable? All parties who attend the deposition will use the information obtained and their observations to prepare their cases for trial or to convince their clients to settle the case.

If the deponent who becomes a witness at the trial changes his or her testimony at trial, the deposition transcript can be used to inform the trier of fact of this change. This can cause the trier of fact to question the witness's credibility and possibly choose to disbelieve everything the person says. Hence, depositions can be extremely useful discovery tools.

III. When a Deposition May Take Place

A. The Time of Day

Depositions usually take place during regular business hours. If all the parties agree, however, a deposition can take place during the evening and on weekends. This request is made when a party has difficulty taking time off from work or does not have day care for children, etc.

IV. Where a Deposition May Take Place

Typically, depositions take place in the attorney's office of one of the parties. Some states have distance requirements that protect parties and witnesses from having to travel long distances if they are being deposed.

V. Authority Who Must Be Present during a Deposition

In addition to the parties (meaning the deponent, other clients, attorneys, and any pro ses,) a deposition must be taken before one of the following:

1. a judge (not usually necessary);
2. a clerk of any court;
3. a notary public; or
4. in some states, an attorney licensed in the state but not involved in the case.

Note: The individuals stated above must not be related to or employed by any of the parties or the attorneys in the case, nor may they have a financial interest in the case.

As I said earlier, in most cases depositions take place in an office rather than a courthouse. Therefore, since the court reporter is a notary public, he or she may administer the oath.

Be aware, however, that some deponents may choose to be difficult and refuse to answer one or more of the questions asked. Or, a deponent may claim that the attorney or pro se conducting the deposition is acting in bad faith, to harass or annoy him or her, etc.

In these situations, a deposition may end up taking place in a conference room in the courthouse, or in a courtroom with a judge or clerk present, in order to ensure that the deponent and party or attorney conducting the deposition conduct themselves properly.

VI. Recording a Deposition: Court Reporter or Videotape and Fees

A. Purpose of a Court Reporter

As stated above, most depositions are recorded by a court reporter who is present. These men and women are specially trained and certified to record testimony in court and at depositions, by typing into a specialized computer or stenographic machine to provide an accurate transcript of every word said during the proceeding.

B. The Transcripts

When the transcript is complete, a copy should be given to the deponent to review for errors, unless the parties stipulate otherwise. In most cases, the deponent must notify the court reporter of any necessary changes or inaccuracies within a specific time after receiving the transcript. Otherwise, the transcript may be presumed to be accurate.

C. How to Find a Court Reporter

Court reporters can be found in the yellow pages of the telephone book, in legal publications, at courthouses, etc. In addition, most offices that handle a lot of litigation usually have a list of court reporters they use frequently.

When scheduling a deposition, be sure to contact a court reporter and make sure he or she is available. In addition to regular business hours, most court reporters will agree to work during evenings and on weekends, if requested. Be sure to remember to promptly notify the court reporter if a deposition is postponed or canceled.

D. Fees

The party taking the deposition is responsible to pay the court reporter's fee. This fee includes the time at the proceeding and the cost of producing a transcript. In addition, the party is responsible for paying for sufficient copies of the transcript to be given to all pro ses or attorneys in the action.

E. Videotaping a Deposition

A party may wish to have a deponent's deposition videotaped. In many states, the party must first file a motion in court. If granted, the court will order how the deposition shall take place, to assure that the recorded testimony will be accurate and trustworthy. Any party attending the deposition may also make arrangements for a court reporter to record the testimony and produce a transcript at his or her own expense.

Note: Videotaped depositions are helpful if a nonparty will not be available to testify at trial, or if a party's health is failing and there is a concern that he or she will not be alive at the time of trial.

F. Written Depositions and Telephone Depositions

Some states will permit depositions to be conducted in writing or by telephone. See applicable court rules for more details.

VII. Notice of Deposition

Each state requires any party who wishes to take the deposition of any other party to send written notice of the pending deposition to all parties in the action.

This **Notice of Deposition** must provide each party with reasonable time in which to make arrangements to attend and participate and should include the following:

1. case caption and title;
2. name of the party taking the deposition;
3. name and address of the party (or nonparty) to be deposed;
4. the date and time of the deposition;
5. the address where the deposition will take place;
6. that the deposition will be taken under oath before an authorized officer and possibly the method of the deposition such as by court reporter, videotape, etc.;
7. signature of the deposing party's attorney or pro se;
8. certification of service to all counsel and pro se parties of record.

VIII. Production of Materials at a Deposition

In addition to testimony, the party seeking to take a deposition may request that the deponent bring certain materials to the deposition. These materials may include designated books, papers, documents, or tangible things to be inspected or copied that fall within the scope of permissible discovery. Often, these materials include originals or copies of specific bank or telephone records, medical records, photographs, contracts, etc.

IX. When a Party Fails to Cooperate

A. Stipulations and Postponements

As with all discovery, court rules often allow the parties to reach agreements (stipulations) as to scheduling and conducting depositions. If the date originally selected is inconvenient for the deponent party or attorney, a prompt telephone call to reschedule will often resolve the situation.

In addition, a party may disappear or perhaps go on a long vacation. Although the attorney received the Notice of Deposition, he or she may be unable to reach the client in time to inform him or her of the pending deposition. In this situation, the attorney will eventually have to inform the other attorneys and reach some sort of agreement. Otherwise, a Motion for Order of Compliance or other motion may be needed.

B. When a Party Does Not Appear to Be Deposed

Furthermore, there are situations when a party or his or her attorney (or both) will simply fail to appear for a deposition. The reasons vary. Sometimes, it's a mistake. Other times, an attorney may be detained in court, or either the attorney or deponent is ill, a car broke down, or a party refuses, for whatever reason, to attend.

In any of the above situations, the attorney who arranged the deposition ends up sitting at a conference table, usually with his or her annoyed client who took time off from work and a court reporter who still expects to be paid for the time spent. The situation worsens if other attorneys and parties (except the deponent) are also in attendance.

If the failed deposition is due to sudden illness, accident, etc., the attorney involved will usually call the opposing attorney to reschedule and agree to pay the costs of the court reporter. If, on the other hand, a party simply refuses to be deposed, a court order compelling the party (or his or her officers, agents, or employees in cases involving corporations) to testify may be necessary.

C. Attorney's Fees and Costs

In addition to the above, in some states, if a deposition fails to take place because the party who initiated the deposition (by sending notice, etc.) fails to appear at the deposition or if that party failed to subpoena the deponent and the deponent fails to appear at the deposition, he or she may be ordered by the court to pay the other parties' attorneys' fees and related costs, etc. for the waste of their time.

X. Deposing Nonparties

Unlike parties who must appear to be deposed, nonparties are under no obligation until they are served with a subpoena. In addition, nonparties may move to stop the deposition from taking place. **Note:** All the provisions stated in this chapter relating to depositions of parties also apply to depositions of nonparties.

A. Purpose of Deposing a Nonparty

Nonparties often have new or additional information pertaining to a case that a party may be unaware of. Rather than wait for trial and the inevitable surprises that are sure to follow, deposing a witness enables the parties to better evaluate and prepare their cases. In addition, the parties will have the opportunity to determine how believable an individual will be as a witness at trial.

B. Subpoenas

Parties in a lawsuit are subject to the court's jurisdiction and must permit themselves to be deposed by opposing parties. Nonparty deponents, unless they are agents of the party, are not under the court's jurisdiction. As a result, they must be served a **subpoena** which commands them to appear at the deposition. Once served, these nonparty deponents are subject to the court's jurisdiction, including fines and possible incarceration if they fail to comply with the terms of the subpoena.

A subpoena is a written document and may be used for two types of proceedings:

1. to command a person to appear at court, on a specific date and time, to testify at a hearing or trial; or
2. to command a person to appear at court or at a specific location, on a specific date and time, to testify at a deposition.

In most states, subpoenas may be issued (drafted and signed) by any of the following:

1. a judge; or
2. a clerk of any court; or
3. a notary public; or
4. an attorney.

The attorney for the party who wishes to depose a nonparty will issue (or obtain from the court) the subpoena.

1. Subpoena Duces Tecum: Production of Materials

A **subpoena duces tecum** is a type of subpoena that commands a person to appear and testify at a deposition or at trial *and* commands him or her to produce specific documents or materials at the deposition or at trial. The specific documents or materials are listed in the subpoena duces tecum.

As you can see from the samples at the end of this chapter, the two types of subpoenas look quite similar. In addition, they command the same compliance and are served in the same manner.

Types of materials requested in a subpoena duces tecum include but are not limited to specific books, papers, documents, or tangible things to be inspected or copied that fall within the scope of permissible discovery. Often, these materials include originals or copies of specific bank or telephone records, medical records, photographs, contracts, etc.

2. Drafting Subpoenas

Some states require the parties to use a court-issued subpoena. In many others, legal supply stores provide subpoena and subpoena duces tecum forms that contain the required information with appropriate blanks to fill in the names, date, time, and location of the deposition. In addition, many firms have this basic format on their computer systems.

The contents of a subpoena and subpoena duces tecum usually include:

- **a.** the name of the party seeking to take the deposition;
- **b.** the name and address of the person to be deposed; if the name is not known, include a general description sufficient to identify the individual person, or a particular group or class to which he or she belongs;
- **c.** the date and time of the deposition; and
- **d.** the address where the deposition will take place.

In addition, the subpoena or subpoena duces tecum should state:

- **a.** that the deposition will take place before an officer authorized to administer oaths within this state; and
- **b.** that the deponent will give testimony concerning what he or she knows about a case between the Plaintiff and the Defendant; and
- **c.** that the deponent is commanded to appear at the designated time and at the designated place;
- **d.** if it is a subpoena duces tecum, list the materials requested;
- **e.** words similar to HEREOF FAIL NOT, UNDER PENALTY OF THE LAW IN THAT CASE PROVIDED.

Note: Even if a deposition is postponed, the deponent who is served is still under the court's authority for a specific number of days. Hence, as long as it is rescheduled to take place within that time period, the deponent named in the subpoena or subpoena duces tecum is still compelled to attend.

3. Serving Subpoenas

a. Notice to Other Parties

In addition to serving a deponent with a subpoena or subpoena duces tecum, the party seeking to take the deposition must send a Notice of Deposition to all other parties in the action. In addition, attach a copy of the subpoena or subpoena duces tecum to the Notice of Deposition.

b. Serving the Subpoena or Subpoena Duces Tecum

i. Who May Serve Subpoenas

All types of subpoenas must be served by a proper officer or anyone else the state authorizes to conduct such service. Mailing the subpoena is not sufficient service. Each of the five states herein permits a person who is 18 years or older and unrelated to the case or to the parties or attorneys to serve subpoenas. These individuals are called **indifferent persons**.

ii. Method of Service

Most states require subpoenas to be served ***in hand,*** to the person named in the document. In addition, they may require the subpoena to be read out loud to the party being served.

iii. Time to Serve

Each state has deadlines to serve subpoenas. For instance, in Connecticut, most nonparties must be served at least 18 hours before the time they are scheduled to appear for the deposition (or to testify in court). The time may be longer to subpoena hospital or bank records, etc.

iv. Witness Fees

In addition to serving the subpoena, the officer must give the nonparty **witness fees** to cover travel expenses. It is a nominal amount.

v. Return of Service

After service, the officer must provide a Return of Service, similar to a Return of Service used for a Complaint. This return will be needed as proof of service if the deponent witness fails to attend the deposition.

C. Motions to Quash or Modify and Objections

A nonparty who is served any type of subpoena may take action to prevent a deposition from taking place, or object to producing or copying requested materials, or to modify the terms of the subpoena by serving and filing a Motion to Quash or Modify Subpoena or an Objection to Subpoena.

1. Purpose of a Motion to Quash, a Motion to Modify, or an Objection

A Motion to Quash may be used to challenge a subpoena or a subpoena duces tecum and prevent a nonparty from being compelled to testify at a deposition (or at trial) or to produce documents, etc. A Motion to Modify or an Objection to Subpoena is an attempt to modify the terms of the subpoena to meet the nonparty's concerns.

2. Grounds for Motion to Quash or Modify or Objection

a. The subpoena is unreasonable or oppressive; and/or

b. The subpoena duces tecum seeks the production of materials that are not subject to production under applicable rules; and/or

c. The nonparty will agree to comply on the condition that the party taking the deposition pay the reasonable costs of producing the requested materials.

3. Serving and Filing a Motion to Quash, Motion to Modify, or Objection

Motions challenging a subpoena should be filed promptly after it is served. Connecticut has a ***15-day*** deadline, Rhode Island has a ***14-day*** deadline, and New Jersey has a ***10-day*** deadline. If, however, the deponent is given less notice than these deadlines, he or she may serve the motion at any time prior to the time the deposition is scheduled to occur.

4. Who May Draft and File a Motion to Quash, Motion to Modify, or Objection

The nonparty is not a party in the action. He or she may not even have an attorney. In some cases, the opposing party who considers the nonparty his or her witness will draft and serve the objection on behalf of the deponent. In other cases, the nonparty will retain an attorney to handle the matter. If the nonparty retains an attorney, that attorney should file an Appearance in court, strictly for the purpose of addressing the motion or objection.

D. When a Deposition of a Nonparty May Take Place

A deposition of a nonparty deponent may take place under the same circumstances and times as a deposition of a party.

E. When a Nonparty Deponent Fails to Cooperate

If subpoenaed nonparties fail to obey the subpoenas and appear at their deposition, the court may hold them in contempt of court. The punishment could be jail time but usually it is no more than a fine that includes the costs of all damages relating to the lack of compliance. If the nonparty cannot be located, the court may issue a **capias** or find the person in contempt and order his or her arrest.

A capias is similar to an arrest warrant. It is a court order that directs the police to take the subpoenaed person into custody to appear before the court. With a capias or a contempt charge, once the individual is brought before the court, the court could order that he or she spend time in jail until he or she is willing to comply with the subpoena.

Proper service is satisfied by the Return of Service on the subpoena and possibly by testimony of the officer who made the service.

XI. Conclusion

Key Issues in This Chapter

1. One significant difference between deposing parties and nonparties is that nonparties should be subpoenaed to attend their depositions. This

way, if they change their mind about attending, they are already under the court's jurisdiction and may be compelled to cooperate.

2. A nonparty who does not want to be deposed, but who has been served with a subpoena, may file a Motion to Quash or a Motion to Modify Subpoena.
3. Not every witness who testifies at a trial is deposed. Sometimes statements made to a private investigator are enough to inform a party what the witness will say. Experts, however, are another story. Due to the often technical nature and the importance of their testimony, it's good practice to know ahead of time what they will say.

   Note also that some witnesses who are deposed are not called to testify at trial. They may not be needed or they may know less about the case than anticipated. It's also possible that their testimony isn't reliable or credible.
4. In most instances, a deponent must be served with a subpoena within a specific time before the scheduled court appearance or deposition.
5. The rules and statutes pertaining to subpoenaing nonparty deponents to attend a deposition are often the same as or similar to those for subpoenaing witnesses to testify at trial.
6. Be sure to arrange for a qualified *court reporter* to record the deposition and remember to notify the court reporter as soon as possible if the deposition is postponed or rescheduled.
7. Conducting depositions of parties can be costly, but they are great discovery tools because they force the parties to meet face to face and answer questions they often prefer to avoid. In addition, depositions allow the parties to size one another up and determine what kind of witnesses they will make at trial.

STATE SUMMARIES

DEPOSITIONS IN CONNECTICUT: PBS 13-26 ET SEQ.

I. When Court Permission Is Needed: Pbs. 13-27

In most instances, a party does not need the court's permission to conduct a deposition. See Pbs 13-27, however, if a party wishes to take a deposition before the expiration of ***20 days*** after the return date, etc. See Pbs 13-26 if the deponent is in jail or prison.

II. Notice of Deposition and Service: Pbs 13-27(a)

A Notice of Deposition should not be filed in court. Instead it must be served on all attorneys (and pro se parties) of record by certified or registered mail or by hand delivery. The content of a Notice of Deposition is substantially similar to the information stated in the main chapter.

III. Depositions and Requests for Production of Documents: Pbs 13-27(f)

The Notice of Deposition directed to deposing a party may include a Request for Production of Documents under Pbs 13-9. Note, however, that the party must be provided with at least ***30 days*** notice in accordance with that rule.

IV. Subpoenas: Pbs 13-28

The rules concerning subpoenas, including objecting and Motions to Quash, are substantially similar to what is stated in the main chapter. See Pbs 13-28 for more details.

V. Audiovisual Depositions: Pbs 13-27(e)

See Pbs 13-27(e) for details.

VI. Depositions upon Written Questions: Pbs 13-27(e)

If requested, the court may order this type of deposition.

Example 15-1. Connecticut, Notice of Deposition (of a Party)

DOCKET NO. CV 96-0333333 S	:	SUPERIOR COURT
SARAH A. DONAHUE	:	JUDICIAL DISTRICT TOLLAND
VS.	:	AT ROCKVILLE
RICHARD P. ANDREW	:	(date)

NOTICE OF DEPOSITION

Pursuant to Connecticut Practice Book Section 13-26 et seq., the Plaintiff, Sarah A. Donahue, hereby gives notice that her counsel intends to take the deposition of the Defendant, Richard P. Andrew, regarding his knowledge of the above-captioned case, on December 18, 19__ at 10:00 a.m., before Rogers and Associates, court reporters or other competent authority, at the law offices of the Plaintiff's counsel located at 21 North Street, Ellington, CT..

THE PLAINTIFF

BY ______________________

Christine Kulas, Esq.
Law Offices of Christine Kulas,
her attorney
P.O. Box 2005
Ellington, CT 06066
Tele. #(860) 222-2222
Juris #989898

CERTIFICATION

I hereby certify that a copy of the above was mailed, certified, return receipt requested, on ________ to all counsel and pro se parties of record namely: Neil E. Clifford, Esq., Michaels, Sabrina and Alexander, P.C., 259 Sage Road, Suite 200, West Hartford, CT 08080.

____

Commissioner of Superior Court

Example 15-2. Connecticut, Notice of Deposition (of a Nonparty)

DOCKET NO. CV 98-0333333 S	:	SUPERIOR COURT
SARAH A. DONAHUE	:	JUDICIAL DISTRICT
	:	OF TOLLAND
VS.	:	AT ROCKVILLE
RICHARD P. ANDREW	:	(date)

NOTICE OF DEPOSITION

Pursuant to Connecticut Practice Book Section 13-26, the Defendant, Richard P. Andrew, hereby gives notice that his counsel intends to take the deposition of Mr. Thomas O'Neill regarding his knowledge of the above-captioned case, on November 19, 19__ at 10:00 a.m., before Matthews and Associates Reporting Service or other competent authority, at the law offices of the Defendant's counsel located at 259 Sage Road, Suite 200, West Hartford, CT 08080.

Mr. O'Neill was served a (*subpoena or subpoena duces tecum, whichever is applicable*), a copy of which is attached hereto.

THE DEFENDANT

BY ____________________________

Neil E. Clifford, Esq.
Michaels, Sabrina and Alexander, P.C.,
his attorneys
259 Sage Road, Suite 200
West Hartford, CT 08080
Tele. # (860) 111-1111
Juris #626262

CERTIFICATION

I hereby certify that a copy of the Notice of Deposition and the attached (subpoena or subpoena duces tecum) were mailed certified, return receipt requested, on ________ to all counsel and pro se parties of record namely: Attorney Christine Kulas, P.O. Box 2005, Ellington, CT 06066.

____

Commissioner of the Superior Court

Example 15-3. Connecticut, Subpoena to Compel Testimony Only, No Documents Required

SUBPOENA

JUDICIAL DISTRICT OF TOLLAND
DOCKET NO. CV 98-0333333 S

TO: Mr. Thomas O'Neill, 251 Pepperbush Court, South Windsor, CT 06074

BY THE AUTHORITY OF THE STATE OF CONNECTICUT, you are hereby commanded to appear at a deposition taken by a Commissioner of the Superior Court, before a proper officer from Matthews & Associates Reporting Service who is authorized to administer oaths within this state, to be held at the law firm of Michaels, Sabrina and Alexander, P.C., 259 Sage Road, Suite 200, West Hartford, CT 08080 on November 19, 1998 at 10:00 a.m., then and there to testify what you know in a certain cause therein pending, wherein

Sarah A. Donahue is the Plaintiff and
Richard P. Andrew is the Defendant

or to such day thereafter and within 60 days thereof on which said action is legally to be tried.

HEREOF FAIL NOT, UNDER PENALTY OF THE LAW IN THAT CASE PROVIDED.

Dated at Ellington, this ____ of _____ 19__.

To any proper officer or indifferent person to serve and return.

____
Commissioner of the Superior Court

Example 15-4. Connecticut, Subpoena Duces Tecum, Documents Required in Addition to Testimony

SUBPOENA DUCES TECUM

JUDICIAL DISTRICT OF TOLLAND
DOCKET NO. CV 98-0333333 S

TO: Mr. Thomas O'Neill, 251 Pepperbush Court, South Windsor, CT 06074

BY THE AUTHORITY OF THE STATE OF CONNECTICUT, you are hereby commanded to appear at a deposition taken by a Commissioner of the Superior Court, before a proper officer from Matthews & Associates Reporting Service who is authorized to administer oaths within this state, to be held at the law firm of Michaels, Sabrina and Alexander, P.C., 259 Sage Road, Suite 200, West Hartford, CT 08080 on __________ at 10:00 a.m., then and there to testify what you know in a certain cause therein pending, wherein

Sarah A. Donahue is the Plaintiff and
Richard P. Andrew is the Defendant

or to such day thereafter and within 60 days thereof on which said action is legally to be tried, **AND YOU ARE FURTHER COMMANDED TO BRING WITH YOU AND PRODUCE AT THE SAME TIME AND PLACE:**

(1) Legible copies of all invoices, bills, etc., indicating any type of repairs and/or maintenance made or provided by you or your employees at Tommy's Auto Repair Service, to a 1995 Honda Civic, owned by Sarah A. Donahue, during the years 1996, 1997 and 1998.

HEREOF FAIL NOT, UNDER PENALTY OF THE LAW IN THAT CASE PROVIDED.

Dated at Ellington, this 2nd day of November, 19__.

To any proper officer or indifferent person to serve and return.

____
Commissioner of the Superior Court

Depositions in Massachusetts: Rules 27-32 and 45

I. When Court Permission Is Needed: Rules 27 and 30

In most instances, a party does not need the court's permission to conduct a deposition and the Notice of Deposition does not need to be filed in court. See Rules 27 and 30, however, if a party wishes to take a deposition before the case starts, or pending an appeal, or a deponent is in jail or prison, or if a Plaintiff wants to depose a Defendant within ***30 days*** of service of the Summons and Complaint, etc.

II. Notice of Deposition: Rule 30(b)(1)

A Notice of Deposition should not be filed in court. A party who wishes to take the deposition of a party or of a nonparty must serve all parties in the case with such written notice at least ***seven days*** before the date of the deposition. If a nonparty is served a subpoena or subpoena duces tecum, a copy of it should be attached to the notice of deposition.

The content of a Notice of Deposition is substantially similar to the information stated in the main chapter.

III. Depositions and Requests for Production of Documents: Rule 30(b)(4)

The Notice of Deposition directed to deposing a party may include a Request for Production of Documents under Rule 34. Note, however, that the party must be provided with at least ***30 days*** notice in accordance with that rule.

IV. Subpoenas: Rule 45

The rules concerning subpoenas, including objecting and Motions to Quash, are substantially similar to what is stated in the main chapter. See Rule 45 for more details.

V. Audiovisual Depositions: Rule 30A

See Rule 30A for details.

VI. Depositions upon Written Questions: Rule 31

See Rule 31 for details.

Depositions in New Jersey: Rules 4:11-4:16 and 1:9

I. When Court Permission Is Needed: Rules 4:11-4:14

In most instances, a party does not need the court's permission to conduct a deposition. See Rules 4:11–4:14, however, if a party wishes to take a deposition before the case starts, or pending an appeal, or if a deponent is in prison or jail, or if a Plaintiff wants to depose a Defendant within ***30 days*** of service of the Summons and Complaint, etc.

II. Notice of Deposition: Rule 4:14-2

A party who wishes to take the deposition of a party or of a nonparty must serve all parties in the case with a written notice at least ***ten days*** before the date of the deposition. If a nonparty is served a subpoena or subpoena duces tecum, a copy of it should be attached to the notice of deposition. Neither the notice nor the subpoena should be filed in court.

The content of a Notice of Deposition is substantially similar to the information stated in the main chapter.

III. Depositions and Requests for Production of Documents: Rule 4:14-2(d)

The Notice of Deposition that names a party as the deponent may include a Request for Production of Documents under Rule 4:18-1. Note, however, that the party must be provided with at least ***30 days*** notice in accordance with that rule.

IV. Subpoenas: Rules 4:14-7 and 1:9

The rules concerning subpoenas, including objections and Motions to Quash, are substantially similar to what is stated in the main chapter. See Rule 4:14-7 for more details. (**Note:** A subpoena that commands a person to produce documents must be served at least ***ten days*** before the date designated for the deposition. In addition, it appears it must be served simultaneously on the nonparty deponent and all parties.)

V. Audiovisual Depositions: Rule 4:14-9

See Rule 4:14-9 for details.

VI. Depositions upon Written Questions: Rules 4:14-3(e) and 4:15

See Rules 4:14-3 and 4:15 for details.

Depositions in New York: CPLR 3106-3117

I. When Court Permission Is Needed: CPLR 3106

Permission from the court is needed in the following circumstances: the deposition takes place before the deadline to file responsive pleadings expires, or the deponent is incarcerated.

II. Notice of Deposition: CPLR 3107

A Notice of Deposition must be served at least ***20 days*** before the scheduled deposition unless the court orders otherwise. In addition, if one party serves a notice to depose another party in the case, the deponent party may serve a notice to depose the first party at the same time and location. Such notice, however, must be served at least ***ten days*** before the scheduled deposition.

Note: Any errors in the Notice of Deposition are treated as waived unless a written objection is served and filed at least ***three days*** before the deposition is scheduled to take place.

III. Depositions and Requests for Documents: CPLR 3111

Be sure to include the documents requested in the Notice of Deposition and if applicable, the subpoena duces tecum.

IV. Subpoenas: CPLR 2301-2308

The information concerning a subpoena and a subpoena duces tecum, including a Motion to Quash, is substantially similar to what is stated in the main chapter. See CPLR 2301-2308 for more details. In addition:

1. It appears that if a party wants a nonparty to testify and produce documents at the deposition, the nonparty must be served with both a subpoena and a subpoena duces tecum.
2. As with a Notice of Deposition, the deadline to serve either type of subpoena is at least ***20 days*** before the scheduled deposition.

V. Depositions upon Written Questions: CPLR 3108-3109

See CPLR 3108-3109 regarding written depositions.

VI. Videotaping a Deposition: Unif. Rule 202.15

See Unif. Rule 202.15 regarding videotaping a deposition.

Example 15-5. New York, Notice of Motion for Permission to Take Deposition

SUPREME COURT OF THE STATE OF NEW YORK
COUNTY OF NEW YORK

---X	
SHEILA WILKENSON,)	Notice of Motion for Permission to Take Deposition
)	
Plaintiff,)	
)	
-against-)	
)	Index No. 2222
)	[name of assigned Judge]
RYAN KEEGAN,)	
Defendant.)	
---X	

SIRS:

PLEASE TAKE NOTICE that upon the annexed affidavit of Alan F. Peters, Esq., sworn to on (date), and upon the interrogatories served on the Defendant, Ryan Keegan, on (date) and the answers thereto, a motion pursuant to CPLR 3130 will be made at this court, in courtroom ______, located at ________ New York, NY, on (date) at ___ a.m./p.m. or as soon thereafter as counsel can be heard, for an order allowing the Plaintiff to take the deposition of the Defendant, Ryan Keegan, upon the grounds that the Defendant's answers to said interrogatories do not provide an adequate portrayal of what the Defendant believes took place during the evening in question.

The above-entitled case is a personal injury action in which the Plaintiff was severely injured as a result of the Defendant's negligence when she fell down a flight of stairs at the Defendant's home.

An affirmation that a good faith effort has been made to resolve the issues stated in this motion is annexed hereto.

Pursuant to CPLR 2214(b) answering affidavits, if any, must be served upon the Plaintiff 's counsel at least seven (7) days before the return date of this motion.

Your etc.,

Dated: _______________
New York, NY

Alan F. Peters, Esq.
Peters, McRoy & Silver
2700 E. Broad Street
New York, NY 14540
Tele. #(212) 232-2323

To
HERMAN S. MARKS, ESQ.
MARKS, JEROME & PENNY
Attorneys for Defendant
206 Salem Street
New York, NY 10007

Note to readers: Be sure to attach an affirmation or affidavit.

Depositions in Rhode Island: Rules 27-32

I. When Court Permission Is Needed: Rule 27

In most instances, a party does not need the court's permission to conduct a deposition. See Rules 27, 29, and 30(a) if a party wishes to take a deposition before the case starts, or pending an appeal, or if a Plaintiff wants to depose a Defendant within ***30 days*** after service of the Summons and Complaint, or if a deponent is confined to jail or prison, etc.

II. Notice of Deposition: Rule 30(b)

A party who wishes to take the deposition of a party or of a nonparty must give all parties reasonable notice in writing of the deposition. If a nonparty is served a subpoena duces tecum, a copy of it should be attached to the Notice of Deposition.

The content of the Notice of Deposition is substantially similar to the information stated in the main chapter, including the method of recording that will be used. If other parties wish to use another method to record the deposition they will do so at their own expense and should give prior notice to the party taking the deposition.

III. Deposition and Requests for Production of Documents: Rule 30(b)(5)

The Notice of Deposition used to depose a party may include a Request for Production of Documents as authorized by Rule 34. The procedures and time periods stated in Rule 34 apply.

IV. Subpoenas: Rule 45

The rules concerning subpoenas, including objections and Motions to Quash, are substantially similar to what is stated in the main chapter. The deadline to object or serve a Motion to Quash is within ***14 days*** after the subpoena is served, or before the time of the deposition, if the subpoena was served within a shorter period of time.

V. Audiovisual and Telephone Depositions: Rules 30(b)(2) and 30(b)(7)

See Rule 30(b)(2) for details. In addition, Rhode Island permits deposition by telephone. See Rule 30(b)(7).

VI. Depositions upon Written Questions: Rule 31

See Rule 31 for details.

VII. Use of Depositions at Trial: Rule 32

See Rule 32 for details.

Example 15-6. Rhode Island, Subpoena

SUBPOENA

SUPERIOR COURT

[ ] PROVIDENCE/BRISTOL [ ] KENT [ ] WASHINGTON [ ] NEWPORT

____________________ vs. ____________________	CASE NO.

[ ] YOU ARE HEREBY COMMANDED to appear in the Superior Court for the above County on ______ to testify in the above entitled action [and bring with you:

____]

LOCATION OF COURT COURTROOM #

DATE TIME

[ ] **YOU ARE HEREBY COMMANDED** to appear at the place, date and time specified below to testify at the taking of a deposition in the above entitled action.

LOCATION OF DEPOSITION DATE AND TIME

[ ] **YOU ARE HEREBY COMMANDED** to produce and permit inspection and copy of the following documents or objects at the place, date and time specified below (*list the documents or objections*)

DOCUMENTS/OBJECTS

LOCATION ROOM #

DATE TIME

[ ] **YOU ARE COMMANDED** to permit inspection of the following premises at the date and time specified below.

LOCATION ROOM #

DATE TIME

(ON BACK OF SUBPOENA)

Any organization not a party to this suit that is subpoenaed for the taking of a deposition shall designate one or more officers, directors or managing agents, or other persons who consent to testify on its behalf and may set for each person designated, the matters on which the person will testify. [Superior Court Rule of Civil Procedure 30 (b)(6).]

______________________________ ______________

ISSUING OFFICER SIGNATURE DATE

ATTORNEY FOR [ ] Plaintiff [ ]Defendant

____

ISSUING OFFICER'S NAME REGISTRATION #

____

STREET CITY/TOWN STATE ZIP

PROOF OF SERVICE

____

DATE PLACE

SERVED

____

SERVED ON (PRINT NAME) MANNER OF SERVICE

____

SERVED BY (PRINT NAME) TITLE

DECLARATION OF SERVER

I declare under penalty of perjury that the foregoing information contained in the Proof of Service is true and correct.

Executed on _________ _________________________

SIGNATURE OF SERVER

____

ADDRESS OF SERVER

Example 15-7. Rhode Island, Objection to Subpoena Duces Tecum

STATE OF RHODE ISLAND SUPERIOR COURT
PROVIDENCE, SC

JOHN MARTIN :
: C.A. NO. PC 98-0000
v. :
:
JAMES TYLER, :
PETER SMITH and :
LUCY SMITH :

OBJECTION TO SUBPOENA DUCES TECUM

Now comes Defendant, Lucy Smith, and thereby objects, pursuant to Rule 45 (c)(2)(B) of the Superior Court Rules of Civil Procedure, to the subpoena duces tecum served upon said, Defendant Lucy Smith, on ____, commanding her to appear at a deposition on ________ and to bring certain records relating to her motor vehicle which is involved in this civil action. For a number of reasons, Defendant Lucy Smith, objects to the subpoena.

First, the Plaintiff is attempting to use a Rule 45 subpoena to circumvent the forty (40) day time period provided to all parties to produce documents. The Plaintiff could have requested the documents sought either pursuant to Rule 34 or through a deposition notice accompanied by a Request for Production of Documents, pursuant to Rule 30(b)(5). Either of these methods of discovery would have given Defendant Lucy Smith forty (40) days in which to respond. Instead, the Plaintiff has given said Defendant two weeks to product the requested documents.

Second, it is not appropriate or necessary to serve a subpoena upon a party. "Though the rules do not say so expressly, a subpoena is not necessary if the person to be examined is a party." *Pinkham v. Paul,* 91 F.R.D. 613, 614 (D.Me. 1981), quoting ***Wright & Miller,*** Federal Practice and Procedure: Civil, Section 2107.

Accordingly, Defendant Lucy Smith's objection to the subpoena should be sustained.

DEFENDANT
LUCY SMITH,
By her Attorney,

____

Ronald Jacobs, Esq., #31313
67 Market Street
Providence, RI 02910
(401) 666-5555

NOTICE OF HEARING

Please take notice that the within matter shall be called for hearing before this Honorable Court on the __ day of ____, ___ or such other time as counsel may be heard.

CERTIFICATION

I hereby certify that on the ____ day of _________, I mailed a true and accurate copy of the within objection to: Charlene M. Murphy, Esq., Murphy & Sable, 333 Landing Ave., Providence, RI 02910 and Lucus Moore, Esq., 89 Willow Street, Pawtucket, RI 02860.

____

Ronald Jacobs, Esq., #31313

16 The Pretrial Stage: Discovery—Disclosure of Experts

Terminology

Expert Witness

Introduction

Expert witnesses are perfect examples of nonparty deponents. Both parties may obtain their own experts to support their case and testify at trial. In addition, deposing an opposing party's expert is the best way to determine what he or she will say at trial in order to prepare accordingly.

The purpose of hiring an expert is threefold: to assist parties in preparing their case by reviewing or examining evidence (including a physical or mental condition) and drawing conclusions that support causes of action, damages, or defense; to explain to the trier of fact technical issues that are relevant to the specific facts in a case; and to provide the trier of fact with an opinion, based upon the expert's knowledge and experience.

I. Why Experts?

Experts are usually necessary in any case that involves technical or specialized issues that are not commonly known to the average person. For instance, in personal injury cases, it is doubtful that the judge or all six members of a jury are also physicians. How then can they, as the triers of fact, understand the full scope and impact of the Plaintiff's injuries?

To address this predicament, each side usually obtains an expert physician who specializes in the Plaintiff's condition to testify at trial. This testimony is very important. If the jury believes the expert, the entire case could rise or fall on his or her testimony. Now you can see why independent medical exams are permitted. In most situations, the physician who performs the IME will testify at trial as the Defendant's expert witness.

Other cases in which experts are common include product liability, medical and legal malpractice, and situations involving a dangerous condition such as the construction of a stairwell, faulty elevator installation, etc. An expert will explain what went wrong to the trier of fact.

II. Who May Be an Expert?

An expert may be any objective individual who does not know either the Plaintiff (client) or the Defendant (client) and has sufficient knowledge, education, and experience in the subject he or she will testify to. Before an expert witness is permitted to testify, the court must *qualify the witness as an expert.* This entails a party providing the court with the witness' qualifications. The opposing party may object to a witness being qualified as an expert at that time. If the objection is sustained, the witness is usually permitted to testify, but his or her testimony will not include providing an "expert opinion" concerning the issue in dispute. Therefore, the witness' testimony has the same weight as that of any other "non-expert" witness.

III. How to Find an Expert

Individuals who wish to testify in court often advertise their services in various trade magazines relating to their field of expertise and in legal publications. In addition, many experts are well recognized in their field and can be contacted directly from area hospitals and universities.

A. Issues to Keep in Mind

When obtaining an expert, keep two issues in mind:

1. Experts cost money. A doctor who is accustomed to earning over a thousand dollars a day will expect to be paid that same amount to spend a day in court. In addition, they often charge hundreds of dollars for the time they take to examine the Plaintiff, prepare their written reports, and comply with discovery requests described below.
2. Each party wants an expert who will testify in his or her favor. Why would any party pay an expert thousands of dollars to ruin the case? At the same time, each party must be careful to find an expert who is con-

sidered impartial or unbiased. For example, physicians who often testify in court, rather than practice medicine full-time, and testify only for Plaintiffs or only for Defendants, quickly develop a questionable reputation for themselves in the legal community. This reputation may lead to being labeled an "expert for hire," or a "Plaintiff's expert," or a "Defendant's expert." In many instances, the opposing side will inform the trier of fact of this reputation, in hopes of persuading it to discount or totally ignore the opposing expert's opinion.

B. Criteria to Consider

The best experts:

1. are well respected in their field;
2. actually work in their occupation on a full-time basis;
3. review all the facts and make all the necessary examinations and inspections;
4. objectively formulate their opinions;
5. clearly explain their opinions and reasoning to the trier of fact in a way it can understand; and
6. form an impartial and unbiased opinion in one party's favor.

As a result, when each party obtains an expert, the expression, "It's a war between the experts," often comes to mind. This means that the trier is faced with opposite or contrary expert opinions and must decide which expert to believe. It can be a tough decision.

IV. Disclosing an Expert

Parties obtain information about their opponent's experts through discovery. An opposing party's expert's opinions and the facts relied upon to form these opinions are discoverable through Interrogatories and documents entitled "Disclosure of Expert Witnesses."

A. Interrogatories

A party may use Interrogatories addressed to the opposing party to obtain the following information:

1. to identify each person who is expected to be called as an expert witness at trial;
2. to state the subject matter to which the expert is expected to testify;

3. to state the substance of the facts and opinions to which the expert is to testify;
4. to provide a summary of the grounds for each opinion.

It's possible that the responding party may not have obtained an expert(s) within the time frame required by the Interrogatories. In addition to filing a stipulation or Motion for Extension of Time, it is appropriate for the responding party to state something like:

"No expert has been obtained at this time. The requested information will be timely disclosed when it is determined."

This response is appropriate; however, the information must be disclosed once it becomes available.

B. Disclosure of Expert Witnesses: Required Information and Time Limits

1. Disclosure of Expert Witnesses

In addition to or in lieu of Interrogatories, a state may require the parties to serve and file a Disclosure of Expert Witnesses. The information contained in this document is very similar to what is requested in the Interrogatories. It should include:

a. the name of the expert;
b. the subject matter on which the expert is expected to testify;
c. the substance of the facts and opinions to which the expert is expected to testify;
d. a summary of the grounds for each opinion.

2. Motion to Preclude Expert Testimony

If a party fails to disclose his or her experts within a specified time, the opposing party may ask the court to prohibit such experts from testifying at trial for the following reasons:

1. The testimony will cause undue prejudice to the party filing the motion; or
2. The testimony will cause undue interference with the orderly progress of the trial; or
3. The delay in disclosing the expert was caused by bad faith on the part of the disclosing party.

V. Depositions

As stated in Chapter 15, either party may take the deposition of the opposing party and any nonparty who has information that is relevant to the lawsuit. As with other depositions, the purpose is to learn firsthand what an expert will say and determine what type of a witness he or she will make at trial.

VI. Conclusion

Key Issues in This Chapter

1. If you intend to depose the opposing party's experts, be sure to serve them with a subpoena or subpoena duces tecum. Otherwise, they are usually under no obligation to be deposed.
2. Remember that most states require the names and addresses of expert witnesses to be disclosed "within a reasonable time" prior to trial. Otherwise, the court may not permit them to testify at trial.

STATE SUMMARIES

Connecticut Experts: PBs 13-4

In Connecticut, the parties must serve and file a Notice of Disclosure of Experts within a reasonable time before trial. In addition, parties may serve their opposition with Interrogatories inquiring about experts and conduct depositions.

Massachusetts Experts: Rule 26(b)(4) et seq.

Massachusetts does not appear to require a specific document resembling a Disclosure of Experts. See Rule 26(b)(4) et seq. for specific details.

New Jersey Experts: Rules 4:10 and 4:17, Rules of Evidence 702-705

New Jersey does not appear to require a specific document resembling a Disclosure of Experts. Rule 4:10-2(d) addresses experts generally. In addition, Rule 4:17-4(e) addresses Interrogatories and experts and Rule 4:14-7(b)(2) addresses depositions and experts.

In addition to the above, be sure to consult Rules 702–705 of the Rules of Evidence concerning experts testifying at trial.

New York Experts

I. Disclosing Experts: CPLR 3101(d)

Generally, New York's procedure for disclosing experts is substantially the same as stated in the main chapter. In addition, some interesting differences are mentioned below.

A. Medical, Dental, and Pediatric Malpractice Cases

Disclosing experts in these types of malpractice actions is a bit different in New York. While the subject matter of their testimony must be disclosed upon request, their names may be withheld to protect their identities. The parties then make each other a written offer to disclose their expert's names and to make them available for a deposition. Each party receiving such an offer must accept it within ***20 days*** of service. Otherwise, the offer is treated as rejected. A party who makes the offer or accepts an offer but fails to produce its own expert at a deposition will be prevented from having that expert testify at trial.

B. Accident Reports: CPLR 3101(g)

CPLR 3101(g) makes specific mention that each party must disclose any type of accident report that is created by "any person, firm, corporation, association, or other public or private entity" in its regular course of business operations, except if such report is created by law enforcement for a criminal investigation or prosecution and its disclosure would interfere with these purposes. The persons who create such reports are often reconstruction experts or other types of experts.

Rhode Island Experts: Rules 26(b)(4) and 701-706

Rhode Island does not appear to require a specific document resembling a Disclosure of Experts. Instead, Rule 26(b)(4) addresses experts generally. In addition, see Rules 701 through 706 of the Rules of Evidence regarding experts testifying at trial.

17

Defaults, Nonsuits, and Dismissals: When Parties Do Not Comply with Court Rules

Terminology

Nonsuit	Dormancy	Dismissal
Default	Military Affidavit	Stay

Introduction

This chapter addresses penalties Plaintiffs and Defendants face when they fail to follow court rules. Why would this happen? There are lots of reasons, many of which involve law office errors and uncooperative clients. Take, for example, a Defendant. Understandably, people who are being sued are not always cooperative, especially if they believe they've done nothing wrong or have no money to finance a defense. Some wait until the last minute to hire an attorney or to forward the Complaint to their insurance company. Others totally ignore the action against them, hoping it will go away. Unfortunately, in most instances, it does not and such Defendants risk having a judgment entered against them.

Plaintiffs, on the other hand, have their own share of problems. Clients disappear or stop paying their legal bills or lose interest in prosecuting a case, etc. In addition, Plaintiff's attorneys (as well as Defense attorneys) sometimes get bogged down with too many cases and aren't always able to keep on top of them. As a result, they may miss deadlines or court appearances and risk having the court dismiss their cases.

In addition to the penalties parties face for failing to comply with court rules, this chapter discusses some remedies that are available. Note, however, that no law office should become accustomed to relying upon these remedies. None of them are guaranteed and the courts do not look kindly upon firms that constantly flirt with this type of potential malpractice.

I. Defaults vs. Nonsuits and Dismissals

At times, it may appear that the courts use the terms **default, nonsuit,** and **dismissal** interchangeably. In practice, however, it has been my experience that defaults are used against Defendants and nonsuits and dismissals are used against Plaintiffs when either fail to comply with court rules. Some states use the terms nonsuit and dismissal interchangeably. Others use one or the other or apply their own definitions.

II. Defaults against Defendants

After being served with a Summons and Complaint, Defendants are faced with a number of responsibilities, none of them pleasant. These responsibilities include but are not limited to:

1. serving applicable responsive pleadings or motions that challenge the Complaint within specific deadlines;
2. serving sufficient discovery requests on opposing parties within specific deadlines;
3. serving responses to discovery that is requested by opposing parties within specific deadlines;
4. appearing in court to argue motions, attend status or pretrial conferences, etc.;
5. attending the trial, testifying, etc.;
6. complying with any other court rules or orders.

Defendants (and Plaintiffs who have Counterclaims asserted against them) who fail to comply with the above risk having the court penalize them. This penalty comes in two forms:

1. convincing the court to enter a default against the Defendant as to *liability;* and
2. obtaining a default judgment (damages) against the same Defendant.

A. Defaults and Liability

Plaintiffs like defaults because they prevent Defendants from presenting a defense at trial. Instead, the Defendant's liability is established by the default: The

Defendant gave up the right to present a defense when he or she failed to comply with a court rule. As a result, the only issue left to be decided by the trier of fact is the amount of the Plaintiff's damages. Yikes! This seems awfully harsh for missing a simple deadline. Nevertheless, it happens.

1. Default for Failure to Appear

A Defendant who fails to serve and file an Answer or any of the motions that challenge a Complaint will be *defaulted for failure to appear.* Those who serve and file their Answer or applicable motion but fail to comply with other court rules or orders are simply defaulted.

2. Serving Subsequent Papers

If a Defendant is defaulted, the other parties in the action do not need to continue to serve them copies of papers that are filed in court. There are two exceptions to this rule:

a. if an opposing party wants to add or change the cause of action and/or relief sought that is stated in the original Complaint; or

b. if an opposing party wants to file a motion to determine damages against the defaulted party.

In either of these two situations, the court may require that service be made in the same manner as serving a Summons and Complaint.

B. Default Judgments and Damages

As you should recall, a judgment means a case is over. In this situation, it means that the Defendant has lost.

The two types of default judgments are described below.

1. Immediate Judgments in Certain Types of Contract Cases

This type of judgment adds salt to a Defendant's wounds by permitting a court to enter judgment against the Defendant without permitting him or her to challenge the amount of damages the Plaintiff claims at a trial. In most instances, these are debt collection cases.

Providing a Defendant is not in the military (see subsection C. 3 below), it is quite simple to obtain a default and immediate judgment in most debt collection cases. The Plaintiff merely presents a written contract or promissory note or similar type of document that demonstrates the Defendant's indebtedness. This document must be the original (unless the court accepts a copy) and must contain all the terms of the agreement, including the sum the Defendant had promised to pay, attorney's fees, late charges, and interest. Under oath, either by testimony or by an affidavit, the Plaintiff testifies regarding the amount of the Defendant's debt and asks the court to enter judgment in that amount, along with attorney's fees, etc. If attorney's fees, late charges, or interest are not specified in the document, the court will usually not award them.

2. Judgment after a Hearing

In most other types of cases, although a Defendant's liability is already determined by the default, the Plaintiff's damages cannot be found in a contract. Instead, he or she must prove them to a trier of fact at a hearing (a mini trial) in which the Defendant may participate.

For instance, in a personal injury case, a Plaintiff must convince the trier of fact that he or she experienced physical injuries, pain and suffering, lost wages, and medical bills and faced other types of future damages. Though the Defendant cannot present a defense, he or she can challenge the Plaintiff's claimed damages and attempt to convince the trier of fact that they are not as high as the Plaintiff claims.

C. Motion for Default or Motion for Default and Judgment

A Plaintiff must file a Motion for Default (or Default and Judgment) which includes:

1. the grounds for the motion; see the list of Defendants' responsibilities in this section above;
2. proof that the Defendant was properly served a copy of the Summons and Complaint:
    a. If the Defendant has failed to appear, as mentioned above, proof that he or she was properly served the Summons and Complaint can come in the form of the proper officer's Return of Service (but see Military Affidavits and Order of Notice below).
    b. If the Defendant has failed to comply with a court order regarding other pleadings, discovery, other court rules or orders, etc., proof of service is already established by the Defendant's pleadings in the court file.
3. **Military Affidavits:** In most states, a court will not enter a default judgment unless the Plaintiff provides an affidavit that states the Defendant is not in the military. This avoids the possibility that a Defendant failed to comply with court rules or orders because he or she was serving active duty and was unaware of the lawsuit or was summoned to report to duty during the lawsuit.
4. **Orders of Notice:** In addition to a military affidavit, if a Defendant has failed to acknowledge the lawsuit, the court may require the Plaintiff to provide a Defendant with additional notice of the lawsuit through an Order of Notice. An Order of Notice directs a proper officer to re-serve a Summons and Complaint, along with a Motion for Default, to a Defendant by certified mail to his or her last known address. If the Defendant's

whereabouts are unknown, the court may order the Plaintiff to publish notice of the lawsuit in certain newspapers.

D. Vacating or Opening a Default

Clearly, disallowing defenses or granting judgment against a Defendant for missing a deadline to serve and file a responsive pleading or motion seems a bit extreme. What if the Defendant was ill at the time of service, or became ill shortly thereafter and didn't have time to hire an attorney? What if he or she did hire an attorney but the attorney neglected to serve and file a responsive pleading or motion before the deadline expired?

Fortunately for Defendants, if they act quickly after a default is granted and the case has not gone to judgment, the court or the clerk will often vacate or open it and permit them to proceed with the case. All that is needed is to serve and file the responsive pleading. Failing to comply with discovery requests or missing a court appearance could take a bit more of a song and dance to explain. However, if the Defendant can convince the court that it was unavoidable or accidental, the default could still be vacated. (See Section VIII for more details on this topic.)

III. Nonsuits and Dismissals against Plaintiffs

In addition to bearing the burden of proof at trial, Plaintiffs must respond to counterclaims and discovery requests, serve and file new Complaints if a Motion for More Definite Statement or Motion to Strike is granted, etc. They must also be sure to attend court appearances and the trial. If they fail to do so, the Defendant may file a Motion for Nonsuit or the court can order a nonsuit on its own.

When a Motion for Nonsuit or a Motion for Dismissal (depending upon a state's terminology) is granted, the Plaintiff's case is over and the Defendant essentially wins without having to present a case at trial. The Plaintiff is out of luck. The only hope is to ask the court to vacate the nonsuit and allow the case to proceed. If this doesn't work, some states permit the Plaintiff to refile the action and start all over.

IV. Dismissal for Failure to Prosecute

In addition to nonsuits and dismissals as described above, many states have an internal program to dismiss cases when they believe a Plaintiff has failed to prosecute it with due diligence. For instance, every six months, each Superior Court in Connecticut generates a list of pending cases that have remained dormant or are not yet placed on the waiting list for trial. Plaintiffs involved in these cases have approximately six to eight weeks to remedy the situation. If they don't and the court refuses to grant them an extension, the case could be dismissed. In Rhode Island, if the case is older than five years and not yet ready for trial, it can be dismissed. See more examples in the State Summaries.

As with defaults and nonsuits, many states have remedies available to Plaintiffs faced with such a dismissal; however, they involve more time and money and there is no guarantee that the court will be receptive.

V. Diarying Important Dates

Now you can see why is it so important for each party to diary (or calendar) their own deadlines as well as their opponent's. Not only do they want to meet their deadlines, they also want to keep track of their opponent's in order to seize the opportunity to end the case in their favor before trial. Plaintiffs especially want to keep apprised of the status of the case at all times. Otherwise, the court may dismiss it due to the Plaintiff's failure to prosecute.

VI. Defaults, Nonsuits, Dismissals, and Motions to Compel Discovery

In some states, a Motion or Order to Compel Discovery may include a request to enter a default, nonsuit, or dismissal against the noncomplying party. Check the applicable court rules for more details.

VII. Staying Judgments

Some states have rules that do not permit a Plaintiff to collect a judgment until a specific period of time has passed. This delay gives defaulted parties the opportunity to attempt to **stay**, set aside or open the judgment.

VIII. Vacating Defaults, Nonsuits, and Dismissals

Parties who are faced with these dilemmas must consult the applicable court rules to be sure they do not miss additional deadlines to remedy their predicament. In many states, they must file a motion that asks the court to undo the default judgment. This motion often comes in the form of the following, all of which are intended to accomplish the same goal:

1. Motion to Open Default Judgment;
2. Motion to Vacate Default Judgment;
3. Motion to Set Aside Default Judgment;
4. Motion to Open Nonsuit;
5. Motion to Vacate Nonsuit;
6. Motion to Set Aside Nonsuit;

7. Motion to Open Dismissal;
8. Motion to Vacate Dismissal;
9. Motion to Set Aside Dismissal.

Whichever way it is entitled, each state requires this type of motion to be served and filed within a specific amount of time and will usually require a filing fee. Otherwise, the default judgment will remain in effect, possibly for good.

In the motion, defaulted parties must state the reasons for their noncompliance and probably include at least one affidavit to support their claims. They may also be required to comply with whatever rule they had violated before the motion is granted. If possible, attempt to convince the opposing party to stipulate to open the case. Sometimes, they will. If this occurs, be sure to put it in the motion.

To its horror, a defaulted party may be faced with an objection to open or vacate from the opposing party. Often such objections are not pleasant and tend to cite other instances of noncompliance that have occurred in the case in the past. Nevertheless, if satisfied with the party's excuse or satisfied that the problem has been remedied, the courts will often open or vacate defaults, nonsuits, and dismissals, or allow a new action. If not, the noncomplying party could appeal the trial court's decision. (See Chapter 22.)

Note: When drafting a Motion to Open (or Set Aside, etc.) Default Judgment, it's a good idea to ask the court to stay any attempt the Plaintiff may intend to make to collect the judgment while the Motion to Open is pending.

IX. Conclusion

Key Issues in This Chapter

1. Defaults are against Defendants. Nonsuits and dismissals are against Plaintiffs.
2. Both parties must diary their own deadlines as well as their opponent's to keep abreast of the status of the case and to bring any motions for default, nonsuit, or dismissal that are appropriate.
3. Most states have specific remedies to vacate or open a default, nonsuit, or dismissal. If they don't, they may permit the Plaintiff (in a nonsuit or dismissal situation) to refile the case. If the court refuses to grant such a remedy, the party may appeal that decision to the applicable appellate court.

Caution: Do not get into the habit of relying on the available remedies in order to justify missing deadlines and other sloppy habits. There are no guarantees that these remedies will always work and you will be flirting with malpractice.

STATE SUMMARIES

Defaults, Nonsuits, and Dismissals in Connecticut

I. Two Types of Defaults

Defaults in Connecticut are handled in a substantially similar manner to that stated in the main chapter. Remember, however, that Connecticut has specific procedures for Defendants to appear and then to file pleadings. As a result, there are two types of defaults and each has its own requirements: A Motion for Default for Failure to Appear and a Motion for Default for Failure to Plead.

A. Motion for Default for Failure to Appear (without Judgment): Pbs 17-20

If a Defendant fails to file an Appearance within ***two days*** after the Return Date, the Plaintiff may file a Motion for Default for Failure to Appear. The clerk will automatically grant the motion as of the date it was filed if an Appearance has not been filed.

1. Opening or Setting Aside the Default for Failure to Appear (without Judgment): Pbs 17-20(c)

It is very easy to open or set aside a Default for Failure to Appear. All the Defendant has to do is file an Appearance before the Plaintiff obtains judgment. No specific motion is needed.

2. Opening or Setting Aside a Default Judgment

This procedure is much more complicated. See Section C below.

B. Motion for Default to Plead: Pbs 10-18, 17-31, and 17-32

If a Defendant fails to file an Answer or any of the other responsive pleadings within the deadlines stated in Pbs 10-6 through 10-8, the Plaintiff may file a Motion for Default for Failure to Plead.

1. Opening or Setting Aside a Default for Failure to Plead (without Judgment)

Pursuant to Pbs 17-32, this is also a very simple procedure. All the Defendant has to do is file an Answer before the Plaintiff claims the case to the Hearing in Damages List. Once an Answer is filed, the default is opened or set aside and the Plaintiff may claim the case to the **trial list.**

Note: Pursuant to Pbs 17-31, if, instead of an Answer, a Defendant wants to file a Motion to Dismiss, a Request to Revise, or a Motion to Strike, he or she must first file a **Motion to Open (or Set Aside) Default.** Why? Requiring an Answer is a way of penalizing a Defendant by preventing him or her from further delaying the case by filing a Request to Revise or a Motion to Strike. As stated above, once an Answer is filed, the case may be placed on the trial list.

C. Judgment: Pbs 17-20(c), 17-33

Except in cases that involve a specific sum (when the default and the judgment may occur at the same time) as stated in the main chapter, a Plaintiff must wait ***15 days*** after a Default for Failure to Appear or a Default for Failure to Plead is granted before filing a Motion for Judgment (used in foreclosure cases) or claiming the case for a Hearing in Damages. During this time, the Defendant may open the default by filing an Appearance or an Answer. Otherwise, the Defendant is still defaulted unless the court grants his or her Motion to Open (or Set Aside Default) under Pbs 17-31.

1. When Damages Must Be Determined: Hearing in Damages: Pbs 17-34 et seq.

A Plaintiff may claim a case to the **Hearing in Damages** list by filing a *Certificate of Closed Pleadings* and marking the appropriate box on the form. Like a trial, the trier of fact may be a judge or a jury, at the Plaintiff's option. See Pbs 17-34 et seq. pertaining to the role of a Plaintiff and a defaulted Defendant during a Hearing in Damages.

2. When a Default Judgment Is Granted

After judgment is granted, the Plaintiff and the court will send notice of the judgment to the Defendant.

3. Opening a Default Judgment: Pbs 17-43

Pbs 17-43 requires a Motion to Open Default Judgment (or Set Aside Default Judgment) and an affidavit that addresses the situation. Both must be served and filed within *four months* from the date notice of default was sent.

II. Nonsuits and Dismissals against Plaintiffs: Pbs 14-3, 17-19, 17-31

It is not uncommon for the terms nonsuit and dismissal to be used interchangeably. Typically, however, nonsuits are entered against Plaintiffs who fail to comply with court ordered discovery or a required pleading. Dismissals often occur when Plaintiffs fail to appear at a scheduled court appearance or otherwise diligently prosecute their cases.

A. The Dormancy Program: Pbs 17-19

Failing to comply with a court order or missing a court appearance is self-explanatory. In addition, Connecticut has a specific program, called the Dormancy Program, that requires Plaintiffs in most cases to claim their cases to the trial list within a specific amount of time. If a Plaintiff misses this deadline, the case will be dismissed.

Fortunately, Plaintiffs are usually given plenty of notice that their case has been targeted for a dismissal. During this time, they are often able to successfully address the situation. In addition, many courts will grant Plaintiffs an extension to meet the applicable deadline as long as they act quickly.

B. Setting Aside a Nonsuit: Pbs 17-43

Setting aside a nonsuit is treated the same way as setting aside a default judgment. Essentially, a motion and an affidavit are needed. See Pbs 17-43 for details.

C. Setting Aside a Dismissal: Pbs 17-4

Pbs 17-4 provides instructions pertaining to setting aside a dismissal. Note that a memorandum of law must accompany the motion. Both must be filed within *four months.*

Example 17-1. Connecticut, Motion to Open Judgment of Default for Failure to Appear and Affidavit (unrelated case)

DOCKET NO. CV 98-0444444 S	:	SUPERIOR COURT
GEORGE SKILLMAN, ET AL.	:	JUDICIAL DISTRICT OF
	:	HARTFORD/N.B.
VS.	:	AT HARTFORD
AUTO SERVICE CENTER, INC.	:	May 1, 1998

MOTION TO OPEN JUDGMENT OF DEFAULT FOR FAILURE TO APPEAR

Pursuant to Connecticut Practice Book Section 17-43, the Defendant in the above-captioned case hereby respectfully requests the court to open the judgment entered against it on March 13, 1998, on the following grounds:

I. FACTS: A Mistake

Joseph Kelly, president of the Defendant corporation, contacted an attorney almost immediately after being served the Writ, Summons and Complaint in this action. An appointment to meet with the attorney was scheduled for February 18, 1998.

On February 17, 1998, Mr. Kelly received an emergency telephone call from family in Scotland. His father had suffered a serious heart attack. Mr. Kelly left immediately for Scotland, forgetting about the meeting with the attorney. Mr. Kelly did not return from Scotland until March 27, 1998.

Mr. Kelly is the sole director and the president of the corporation. The corporation's secretary is his wife, who accompanied him to Scotland. The corporation has only one part-time office assistant who was unaware of this lawsuit. As a result of Mr. Kelly's mistake and his and his wife's absence, judgment entered against the Defendant corporation.

II. ARGUMENT: A Good Defense Exists

The Defendant respectfully asserts that a good defense exists in that the Defendant believes it was misled by the Plaintiff when it agreed to purchase Auto Service Center, Inc. and signed the promissory note at issue. In any event, since April 2, 1998, Mr. Kelly and the Plaintiffs, Mr. and Mrs. Skillman, have been working diligently to reach a settlement.

Based on the foregoing, although the Defendant feels confident a settlement will be reached shortly, finalizing such agreement could exceed the four months permitted under Connecticut Practice Book Sec. 17-43 to open a judgment. Furthermore, if there is no settlement, the Defendant wishes to be heard on the merits of the case and to be given the opportunity to present its defenses.

Attached hereto is an affidavit from Mr. Kelly in support of this Motion to Open and an Appearance from the undersigned counsel.

ORAL ARGUMENT NOT REQUESTED
TESTIMONY NOT REQUIRED

III. CONCLUSION

WHEREFORE, the Defendant respectfully requests the following:

(1) That the Plaintiff be enjoined from enforcing said Judgment until the court renders its decision on this instant motion;
(2) That said Default Judgment be opened in accordance with Connecticut Practice Book Section 17-43;
(3) That the attached Appearance from the undersigned counsel be filed in this case.

RESPECTFULLY,
THE DEFENDANT

BY ______________________________

Mark Peters, Esq.
Mark Peters & Associates, P.C.,
its attorneys
1001 Sanberg Street
Manchester, CT 06666
Tele. # (860) 648-0000
Juris #246135

ORDER

The foregoing Motion having been considered by the Court, it is hereby ORDERED: GRANTED/DENIED

____

BY THE COURT

CERTIFICATION

I hereby certify that a copy of the foregoing Motion and attached Affidavit and Appearance were mailed on ________ to all counsel and pro se parties of record, namely: Kenneth I. Marcus, Esq., Friedman & Marcus, P.C., 27 Main Street, Bristol, CT 00000.

____

Commissioner of Superior Court

DOCKET NO. CV 98-0444444 S	:	SUPERIOR COURT
GEORGE SKILLMAN, ET AL.	:	JUDICIAL DISTRICT OF
	:	HARTFORD/N.B.
VS.	:	AT HARTFORD
AUTO SERVICE CENTER, INC.	:	May 1, 1998

AFFIDAVIT

I, the undersigned, being duly sworn, do hereby depose and say:

(1) I am over the age of eighteen years and understand the obligation of an oath and have personal knowledge of the above-captained case in that I am the President of Defendant, Auto Service Center, Inc., a Connecticut corporation.

(2) On February 17, 1998, my wife and I were notified that my father had suffered a serious heart attack in Scotland. We left immediately to be with him and did not return until March 27, 1998. Unfortunately, before I left, I forgot to contact the attorney I spoke with who I intended to hire to represent the corporation in this instant lawsuit. As a result, judgment had already entered against the corporation by the time I returned.

(3) I believe that the Defendant corporation has a good defense to this action. Specifically, on behalf of the corporation I had several meetings and discussions with the Plaintiffs within a month of buying the corporation because I began to suspect that the value placed on the company at the time of the purchase was significantly higher than what it was worth. There are not nearly as many credit card holders as represented, nor have the Plaintiffs made improvements to the building or assisted in its operating for the first six months as they had promised.

(4) Since April 2, 19__, the Plaintiffs and I have made great efforts to resolve this matter. I feel confident that we will resolve this issue soon, however I am not certain we can finalize everything before the four-month period to open the judgment expires. Furthermore, if we cannot settle this matter, I wish to have the opportunity to have the case tried on its merits and for me to present my good defenses.

(5) Based on my mistake and the fact I believe the Defendant corporation has a good defense, I respectfully request the court to open the judgment against the Defendant and enjoin the Plaintiff from enforcing the judgment until the court renders its decision on this instant motion.

____

Joseph Kelly

Subscribed and sworn to before me this 1st day of May, 1998.

____

Commissioner of the Superior Court

Defaults, Nonsuits, and Dismissals in Massachusetts

I. Defaults: Rule 55

Defaults in Massachusetts are handled in a substantially similar manner to that stated in the main chapter. See Rule 55 for more details.

II. Nonsuits and Dismissals

See Sup. Ct. Rules 30 and 30A regarding dismissals for failing to answer interrogatories.

Example 17-2. Massachusetts, Request for Default

HAMPDEN, ss

SUPERIOR COURT DEPARTMENT
OF THE TRIAL COURT

CIVIL ACTION

No. 98-0000

PLAINTIFFS: George Jones, Jr.
by his Father and Next Friend,
George Jones, Sr.

VS.

DEFENDANT: City in Massachusetts

REQUEST FOR DEFAULT

I, Ann Lambert, Esq., attorney for the Plaintiffs, George Jones, Jr., by his Father and Next Friend, George Jones, Sr., state the Complaint and Summons have been served on the Defendant, City in Massachusetts, on ______, as appears from the officer's return and the time in which the Defendant may serve an answer or responsive pleading upon me has expired and that the Defendant has not served an answer or responsive pleading upon me nor has it filed any pleading in court.

Wherefore, the Plaintiffs, George Jones, Jr., by his Father and Next Friend, George Jones, Sr., make this application that the Defendant be defaulted.

Signed under the penalties of perjury,

____

Ann Lambert, Esq.
Lambert & Smith, P.C.
529 Corporate Place
Agawam, MA 04540
Tele. (413) 777-7777
BBO #45454

Dated: ______________

Note to readers: No hearing is needed. Don't forget a certification of service.

Example 17-3. Massachusetts, Default (ordered by court)

HAMPDEN, ss

SUPERIOR COURT DEPARTMENT
OF THE TRIAL COURT

CIVIL ACTION

No. 98-0000

PLAINTIFFS: George Jones, Jr.
by his Father and Next Friend,
George Jones, Sr.

vs.

DEFENDANT: City in Massachusetts

DEFAULT

This action came on to be heard upon an application of the Plaintiff, George Jones, Jr. by his Father and Next Friend, George Jones, Sr., for a Default against the Defendant, City in Massachusetts, for failure to serve an Answer within twenty (20) days after the service of the Complaint and Summons upon said Defendant, and thereupon, upon consideration thereof, it is ORDERED and ADJUDGED that the said Defendant be defaulted.

____
Assistant Clerk

Note to readers: The date of the default will usually be court stamped somewhere on this document.

Defaults, Nonsuits, and Dismissals in New Jersey

I. Defaults: Rule 4:43 et seq.

Defaults in New Jersey are handled in a substantially similar manner to that stated in the main chapter. Check Rule 4:43 et seq. for details. Rule 4:50-1 et seq may also help.

II. Dismissals: Rule 1:2-4

Rule 1:2-4 grants the court authority to dismiss a Complaint, Cross Claim, Counterclaim, etc., if a party fails to appear at court for a calendar call, a pretrial conference, or for trial, without permission. In addition, or in lieu of this, the court could order the delinquent party to pay costs to the court or the adverse party. Consult Rule 1:2-4 for other action the court may take and Rule 4:50-1 et seq. to help parties in this predicament.

Defaults, Nonsuits, and Dismissals in New York

I. Defaults: CPLR 3215, 2005, and 5015

Defaults in New York are handled in a substantially similar manner to that stated in the main chapter. See CPLR 3215 for more details. In addition, New York recognizes that errors sometimes occur in law firms. Therefore, a party who wishes to have a default vacated may file an application under CPLR 2005 and claim that the error was due to "law office failure." In addition, a default may be vacated under CPLR 5015.

II. Nonsuits and Dismissals: CPLR 3404

If a Plaintiff fails to respond at a calendar call or the case is marked off the trial calendar, etc., the Plaintiff should serve and file a Motion to Restore to Calendar no later than within ***one year.*** Otherwise, the court will automatically dismiss the case due to the Plaintiff's failure to prosecute.

If the one-year period to restore a case to the calendar expires, the Plaintiff should serve and file the motion and attach affidavits regarding the merits of the case and explain how he or she has actively worked on the case during that year and has not failed to prosecute it.

Defaults and Dismissals in Rhode Island

I. Defaults: Rule 55

Defaults in Rhode Island are handled in a substantially similar manner to that stated in the main chapter. See Rule 55 for more details.

II. Nonsuits and Dismissals: Rules 41 and 60

In Rhode Island, the court may dismiss a case on its own for the following reasons:

1. The case has been pending for more than five years;

2. At any time the Plaintiff failed to comply with a court rule;
3. Plaintiff failed to proceed when the case was assigned for a trial.

In addition, the court may dismiss a case pursuant to the Defendant's Motion for Dismissal for failing to comply with court rules or orders, etc. See Rule 60 for vacating a dismissal.

Example 17-4. Rhode Island, Motion for Default Judgment for Failing to Comply with Court Order

STATE OF RHODE ISLAND SUPERIOR COURT
PROVIDENCE, SC.

JOHN MARTIN :
: C.A. NO. PC 98-0000
V. :
:
JAMES TYLER, :
PETER SMITH and :
LUCY SMITH :

PLAINTIFF'S MOTION TO DEFAULT

Now comes the Plaintiff in the above-entitled matter and moves this Honorable Court for a default judgment against Defendants, Peter Smith and Lucy Smith, for their failure to answer Plaintiff's interrogatories on or before____ as per the Court's Order entered on _________, pursuant to Plaintiff's Motion to Compel Discovery. A copy of said Order is attached hereto.

WHEREFORE, Plaintiff requests this Honorable Court to grant this Motion to Default against Defendants Peter Smith and Lucy Smith.

JOHN MARTIN,
By his Attorneys,

____
CHARLENE M. MURPHY, ESQ.
Bar # 1111
MURPHY & SABLE
333 Landing Ave.
Providence, RI 02910
(401) 946-1111

NOTICE OF HEARING

Please take notice that the within motion will be heard in this Honorable Court on the ___ day of ______, ______.

CERTIFICATION BY ATTORNEY

I, Charlene M. Murphy, Registration #1111, counsel for the Plaintiff, certify that before filing the within Motion, I made a good faith effort by attempting to confer with Attorney Ronald Jacobs, Defendants' counsel, by telephone on several occasions including ________, to resolve the pending discovery issue that raised a Motion to Compel dated ______ and ruled on by the Court.

____
CHARLENE M. MURPHY, ESQ.

CERTIFICATION

I hereby certify that on ____________, I mailed a true and accurate copy of the within motion by regular mail, postage prepaid to all counsel of record: Ronald Jacobs, Esq., 67 Market Street, Providence, RI 02910.

____
CHARLENE M. MURPHY, ESQ.

STATE OF RHODE ISLAND
PROVIDENCE, SC.

SUPERIOR COURT

JOHN MARTIN :
: C.A. NO. PC 98-0000
V. :
:
JAMES TYLER, :
PETER SMITH and :
LUCY SMITH :

ORDER

This matter was to be heard before this Honorable Court on the __ day of ____, on Plaintiff's Motion to Compel Answers to Interrogatories of Defendants, Peter Smith and Lucy Smith, dated _____. No objection having been timely filed, it is hereby:

ORDRED, ADJUDGED AND DECREED

(1) Plaintiff's Motion to Compel Answers to Interrogatories of Defendants, Peter Smith and Lucy Smith is granted by Rule of Court. Defendants Peter Smith and Lucy Smith shall have twenty (20) days up to and including _____, within which to answer.

PER ORDER,

____

ENTER:

____

Presented by:

____

CHARLENE M. MURPHY, ESQ.
Bar # 1111
MURPHY & SABLE
333 Landing Ave.
Providence, RI 02910
(401) 946-1111

18 Prejudgment Remedies

Terminology

Prejudgment Remedy	Garnishee
Fraudulent Conveyances	Mechanic's Lien
Attachment	Lis Pendens
Judgment Proof	Ex Parte PJR

Introduction

What can Plaintiffs do if they win a million-dollar judgment against a Defendant, but the Defendant does not have any assets, cash, or insurance to pay the judgment? The answer is, not much. A judgment is usually valid for 20 or more years. However, if the Defendant is unemployed during that time, or out of business and has no other assets, such as a house, car, expensive equipment, money in the bank, etc., the Plaintiff may be out of luck. These Defendants are labeled **judgment proof.**

No Plaintiff's attorney (especially those working for a contingency fee) wants to take a case if the Defendant is or will be judgment proof. Why bother? After all the time and money spent on litigation, the judgment will be worthless. **Prejudgment Remedies** (known as **PJR**s) help Plaintiffs avoid this situation. If a Defendant has any assets at the time the suit is brought, a PJR allows a Plaintiff to **attach** (also known as freeze or lien) a Defendant's assets either *before* or *during* a lawsuit. Hence, the name: *prejudgment.*

If a Plaintiff obtains a Prejudgment Remedy against a Defendant, that Defendant will not be able to spend, sell, transfer, give away, destroy, and sometimes use any assets listed in the Prejudgment Remedy while the lawsuit is ongoing. At the end of the lawsuit, if the Plaintiff wins, the court will direct the attached assets to be turned over directly to the Plaintiff to pay the judgment. If the Defendant wins, he or she will get the assets back.

Prejudgment Remedies are serious business. In many situations, there's no better way to bring Defendants to their knees than to attach all of their assets. Settlements tend to occur much more quickly when Defendants need the thousands of dollars in a bank account to operate a business or meet other financial obligations. They won't have time to toss the dice and hope to win in court several years later. If they don't resolve the dispute now, they could be ruined forever.

I. Definition of a PJR Remedy

A Prejudgment Remedy enables a Plaintiff to obtain an attachment on a Defendant's assets that prevents the Defendant from using, possessing, or enjoying such assets during the litigation process.

II. Types of PJRs

A. Four Types of PJRs

Typically, there are four types of PJRs:

1. A *regular PJR* brought *prior* to suit, which requires a hearing and a court order *before* any assets may be frozen.
2. A *regular PJR* brought *after* suit has already started. It still requires a hearing and a court order before any assets may be frozen. This usually occurs if the Plaintiff learns after the suit has started that the Defendant does not have enough insurance or other assets to satisfy the damages claimed.
3. A *commercial waiver PJR*. Some states recognize this type of PJR that is applicable in commercial cases involving contracts and promissory notes. The waiver is stated in these documents, which the Defendant has previously signed, and the PJR is agreed to in the event the Defendant breaches the contract or note. This is highly effective because it does not require notice to the Defendant or a court order. The assets are frozen as soon as the PJR documents are served. (See Garnishees, below.)
4. An ***ex parte PJR***. This type is effective because it may be granted by the court, either before or during the suit, without first notifying the opposing party. **Note:** Courts are reluctant to grant this type of PJR unless a Plaintiff can demonstrate that the Defendant is in the process of committing fraud to hide himself or his assets from creditors such as the Plaintiff.

B. Garnishees

A **garnishee** is a person or entity who owes or may owe a Defendant money or who has possession of a Defendant's assets. For example, a garnishee can be a bank in which a Defendant's accounts are located, a company in which a Defendant owns stock, or even an insurance company that may owe a Defendant insurance proceeds from another matter. In addition, if a Defendant is a contractor, the people who owe the contractor money can be garnishees.

When a PJR is granted, a proper officer will serve all the garnishees in the case with a court order that prevents them from paying the Defendant the amount owed or from returning any funds or assets to a Defendant, until the court orders otherwise. This is called garnishing or attaching or liening the funds or assets. In most instances, the court will order the funds or assets to be held in escrow pending the resolution of the case. If the garnishee disregards the court order to withhold a Defendant's funds or assets, the garnishee will be responsible to the Plaintiff for the amount of value of the funds or assets not garnished and up to the amount of the judgment if the Plaintiff wins his or her case, and may face other consequences determined by the court.

When preparing the necessary PJR documents, the Plaintiff will need to bring two sets of original documents to court and make enough copies for his or her own file and for each Defendant and the garnishees.

III. Who May Obtain a PJR and Defendants' Rights

PJRs are most commonly sought by Plaintiffs and we will refer to this scenario throughout the remainder of this chapter. Defendants, however, may seek a PJR if they file a Counterclaim in an action. Any other party (such as a Third-Party Plaintiff) who is seeking damages from another party in the action may also seek a PJR.

If a PJR is granted, a Defendant may ask the court to order the Plaintiff to post a bond to protect the Defendant's interest in the attached property.

IV. PJR Requirements

Due to the serious nature of PJRs, the courts will usually strictly enforce all applicable rules and statutes. This means that Plaintiffs must specifically follow each requirement. Otherwise, the court will deny a PJR and the Defendant may go off and spend or give away all of the assets to prevent the Plaintiff from trying again. Though there is a remedy for such **fraudulent conveyances,** it is usually extremely time-consuming and expensive to prove. As a result, it's best to follow all the requirements the first time and get the PJR granted.

V. What Can Be Attached with a PJR

It's up to the Plaintiff to somehow identify all of the Defendant's attachable assets and include them in the PJR. Almost anything the Defendant has a right in can be attached.

A. What Can Be Attached

The following assets may be attached:

1. bank accounts, joint or in the Defendant's name exclusively;
2. stocks and bonds in the Defendant's name, in part or joint;
3. cars, boats, planes, motorcycles, etc., in the Defendant's name in part or joint;
4. equipment, in the Defendant's name in part or joint;
5. real estate: Although the Defendant will be allowed to live or work in the attached real estate, a lien is placed on the land records to prevent someone from purchasing the property without knowledge of the lien. If someone purchases it anyway, and a judgment is rendered, the purchaser will be compelled to turn the property over to the Plaintiff. (See also **Notice of Lis Pendens.**)

B. Substitute Assets

If a PJR is granted, the Defendant may be permitted to post a bond or provide any other type of security that is sufficient to meet the purposes of the PJR, as a substitute for the attached assets.

C. Motion to Disclose Assets

Most states permit Plaintiffs to file a **Motion to Disclose Assets** when seeking a PJR. If the PJR is granted, the court will order the Defendant to disclose his or her assets at a specific date and time. The Plaintiff will then move to obtain a PJR against those assets.

VI. The Ex Parte PJR

Most states allow an ex parte PJR if a Plaintiff can convince the court that there is a reasonable likelihood that the Defendant is engaged in one or more of the following:

1. Has hidden or will hide so that process cannot be served;
2. Is about to leave the state or remove attachable property from the state;
3. Is about to fraudulently dispose of or has fraudulently disposed of attachable property with intent to hinder, delay, or defraud creditors;
4. Has fraudulently hidden or withheld money, property, or effects that should be liable to satisfy debts.

VII. Other Types of Liens

In addition to Prejudgment Remedies, most states allow Plaintiffs to protect their interests by placing a lien against real estate that is in some way involved in the dispute with an opponent. The purpose of the lien is to prevent the opponent from selling or transferring the real estate until the dispute has been resolved. Two types of liens, a Mechanic's Lien and a Notice of Lis Pendens, are described below.

A. Mechanic's Liens

The purpose of a **Mechanic's Lien** is to protect Plaintiffs who are owed money for work performed on a building or piece of real estate. In general terms, it may be utilized by those Plaintiffs who are in construction or a similar type of profession that involves, but is not limited to, building, improving, removing, and repairing real estate or any type of structure on the real estate.

Plaintiffs who have claims against owners of a building or real estate for services or materials relating thereto may protect their interests by filing a Mechanic's Lien at the town or city hall where the real estate is located. As a result, one of two scenarios may occur:

1. If the owner sells the property, he or she must first pay the Plaintiff the amount of money claimed due in the Mechanic's Lien. Otherwise, the new owner will become liable to the Plaintiff; or
2. If the owner of the real estate still fails to pay the sum due, the Plaintiff may bring a lawsuit to attempt to foreclose on the real estate, just like a bank or other lender may foreclose on a mortgage, to collect the money that is owed.

B. Notice of Lis Pendens

A **Notice of Lis Pendens** is permitted in those cases that are "intended to affect real property…." In many instances, these are foreclosure and dissolution of marriage cases.

In a foreclosure action, the real estate is at issue because the Defendant allegedly defaulted on the mortgage that is secured by the real estate. The Plaintiff sues to receive the property and sell it in order to pay off the Defendant's mortgage.

In dissolution of marriage actions, real property such as the marital home and other real property often make up the majority of the parties' assets. Therefore, their value is a major component in an equitable distribution of the marital estate.

The purpose of a Notice of Lis Pendens is to prevent one party from selling or transferring the property to a third party in order to defeat a judgment. A Notice of Lis Pendens places all potential purchasers of the property on notice that they will be bound by the court's decision regarding the property as if they were a party to the action. This can include being ordered to transfer the property back to one or more of the parties and not receiving a refund for the purchase price, unless they later bring their own separate lawsuit.

VIII. Conclusion

Key Issues in This Chapter

1. Prejudgment Remedies

Prejudgment Remedies are great when they work. They are also quite time-consuming to prepare. Be sure to carefully read and comply with each applicable rule and statute. In addition, some courts handle the scheduling or the hearing process differently from others. Therefore, it never hurts to call the court at issue beforehand and speak with the clerk who handles PJRs to verify the procedures.

2. Mechanic's Liens

Mechanic's Liens are applicable when the Plaintiff has performed some type of work upon a piece of land, or a building thereon, or has supplied materials for such work, and has not been paid by the owner for such services or materials.

3. Notice of Lis Pendens

A Notice of Lis Pendens protects a party's interest in real property. It is commonly used in foreclosure and dissolution of marriage actions.

STATE SUMMARIES

When drafting documents for any type of PJR, be sure to read and follow each applicable statute and court rule very carefully.

Prejudgment Remedies in Connecticut

I. Mechanic's Liens: C.G.S. sec. 49-33 et seq.

See these statutes for more information and page 331 for an example.

II. Notice of Lis Pendens: C.G.S. sec. 46b-80 and 52-325 et seq

See these statutes for more information and page 332 for an example.

III. Regular, Ex Parte, Waiver PJRs: C.G.S. sec. 52-278a-n

See each provision of this statute for more information.

Example18-1. Connecticut, Mechanic's Lien (unrelated case)

MECHANIC'S LIEN

THIS IS TO CERTIFY THAT ABC Buildings, Inc., of the City of New Britain, County of Hartford and State of Connecticut, its heirs, successors and assigns, in accordance with a certain contract between ABC Buildings, Inc., the Contractor, and Jack Mason, of the City of New Britain, County of Hartford and State of Connecticut has a lien under the Connecticut General Statutes in such cases made and provided, on the premises, owned by said Jack Mason, and described in Exhibit "A" attached hereto and to other buildings standing thereon, to the amount of Six Thousand ($6,000.00) Dollars as nearly as the same can be ascertained.

THE LIEN is for services rendered and materials furnished in the construction, erecting, raising and removal of said building and for repairs thereon, commencing the July 15, 1997 and ending on March 14, 1998.

THE SAID PREMISES are situated in the City of New Britain, County of Hartford and State of Connecticut, recorded in the name of Jack Mason, of the City of New Britain, in Vol. 27, Page 458, and are bounded and described in Exhibit "A" attached hereto.

The name and names against whom this lien is being filed is: Jack Mason.

THIS CERTIFICATE is made and filed within ninety days from the time of ceasing to render services and furnish material, as aforesaid.

IN WITNESS WHEREOF, I have hereunto set my hand this 30th day of April, 1998.

____________________ BY ____________________

Mary Steward

Walter Martin,
President and duly authorized
agent of ABC Buildings, Inc.

____

George Murry

STATE OF CONNECTICUT)
) ss. NEW BRITAIN
COUNTY OF HARTFORD)

PERSONALLY APPEARED, Walter Martin, Signer and Sealer of the foregoing Certificate, and made solemn oath to the truth of the same and that the amount above named is justly due to the said ABC Buildings, Inc., as nearly as the same can be ascertained. Before me.

____

Commissioner of the Superior Court

Notary Public, Justice of the Peace

Received:
Town Clerk

Note to readers: Be sure to include or attach the property description.

Example 18-2. Connecticut, Notice of Lis Pendens (unrelated case)

RETURN DATE: MARCH 4, 1998	:	SUPERIOR COURT
DELILAH FARRARA	:	J.D. OF HARTFORD/
	:	NEW BRITAIN
VS.	:	
	:	AT HARTFORD
MAXWELL FARRARA	:	(date)

NOTICE OF LIS PENDENS

Notice is hereby given of the pendency of a civil action between the above-named parties by a Complaint made returnable to the Superior Court at Hartford, Connecticut, within and for the Judicial District of Hartford/New Britain, at Hartford, on _______, which action is brought claiming a dissolution of marriage and an equitable distribution of the parties' marital assets. Such marital assets include real property known as 506 South Logan Way, Bloomfield, Connecticut and is bounded and described as set forth in Exhibit A, attached hereto.

Dated in Hartford, this ___day of _________, 19___.

THE DEFENDANT

BY ___________________________

Felicia Sullivan, Esq.
his attorney
P.O. Box 105
Rocky Hill, CT 06067
Tele. No. (860) 333-9999
Juris No. 888888

Note to readers: Be sure to attach the property description.

Prejudgment Remedies in Massachusetts

I. Notice of Lis Pendens

See Chapter 184, section 15 et seq. of the *Massachusetts General Laws* for more information.

II. Mechanic's Liens

See Chapter 254, section 1 et seq. of the *Massachusetts General Laws* for more information.

III. Regular and Ex Parte PJRs: Rule 4.1

A party may obtain a court-issued form entitled Writ of Attachment that directs the sheriff to attach property. See Rule 4.1 for more information.

Example 18-3. Massachusetts, Writ of Attachment

COMMONWEALTH OF MASSACHUSETTS

HAMPDEN, ss

SUPERIOR COURT
DEPARTMENT OF THE TRIAL COURT
CIVIL ACTION
NO.

______________________________, Plaintiff

v.

______________________________, Defendant

WRIT OF ATTACHMENT

To the sheriffs of our several counties or their deputies:

We command you to attach the goods or estate of defendant, ________, of _________, to the value of $_____ (the amount authorized), as prayed for by plaintiff ______, of _______, whose attorney is _____, of ______, in an action brought by said Plaintiff, ________, against said defendant, ________, in the Superior Court for Hampden County, and make due return of this writ with your doings thereon.

The complaint in this case was filed on _________ 19___. This attachment was approved on ____, 19__ by _______J., in the amount of $_____________.

Witness, _______ at Springfield the ______day of ______19.

CLERK/MAGISTRATE

Note to readers: This form must contain the court seal and the clerk/magistrate's signature.

Prejudgment Remedies in New Jersey

I. Mechanic's Liens

Under Construction Liens, see 2A:44A-2 et seq. for more information.

II. Notice of Lis Pendens

See Rules 4:63A and 2A:15-6 et seq. of the New Jersey Statutes for more information.

III. Regular and Ex Parte PJRs: Rule 4:60 et seq.

A party may obtain a court-issued form entitled Writ of Attachment that directs the sheriff to attach property. See Rule 4.60 et seq. for more information.

Prejudgment Remedies in New York

I. Mechanic's Liens

See CPLR 6501for more information.

II. Notice of Lis Pendens

See CPLR 6501 et seq. for more information.

III. Regular and Ex Parte PJRs

A party may obtain a court-issued form entitled Writ of Attachment that directs the sheriff to attach property. See CPLR 6201 et seq. for more information.

Prejudgment Remedies in Rhode Island

I. Mechanic's Liens

See Chapter 28 of the *General Laws of Rhode Island,* Sec. 34-28-1 et seq. for more information.

II. Notice of Lis Pendens

See Sec. 9-4-4 and 34-28-11 et seq. of the *General Laws of Rhode Island* for more information.

III. Regular and Ex Parte PJRs: Rule 4(m)

A party may obtain a court-issued form entitled Writ of Attachment that directs the sheriff to attach property. See Rule 4(m) for more information.

19 THE TRIAL STAGE: PREPARATIONS FOR TRIAL

TERMINOLOGY

Motion in Limine | Offer of Judgment | Pretrial Conference

INTRODUCTION

The parties have served and filed all of their responsive pleadings and discovery is well underway or completed. A trial date may soon be hovering over the horizon. Be on your toes. Bench trials are usually scheduled for a specific date and come up years earlier than jury trials. Some courts place their jury cases on an alert list and inform the attorneys to be prepared to start sometime during a specific month or week, because many cases on the list will settle as late as the day before, the morning of, or even in the middle of trial. As a result, your case could be next!

In this chapter we will address preparing for trial. The topics include **pretrial conferences, stipulated judgments, offers of judgment, and Motions in Limine.**

I. CLOSING THE PLEADINGS

Unlike the remaining states, Connecticut and New York have their own specific procedures for "closing the pleadings" and placing a case on the waiting list for trial. This procedure requires filing specific documents in court and indicating whether or not a jury trial is requested.

As you may recall, such specific procedures are not necessary in Massachusetts, New Jersey, and Rhode Island because the parties decide early on in the case whether or not they want a jury and the court has its own deadlines for scheduling cases for trial. See the Connecticut and New York summaries for details.

II. Pretrial Conferences

A **pretrial conference** is a required court appearance that permits the parties to discuss the case face to face, in front of a judge or a qualified attorney. The judge or attorney will listen to the parties' arguments in an informal settling such as a conference room or judge's chambers. He or she will then point out each side's weaknesses and place a proposed settlement figure on the case.

A. Purpose of a Pretrial Conference: Settlement or Scheduling

Many cases settle during the pretrial process or shortly thereafter when the parties have had opportunities to discuss the case seriously with their clients. The time and expense of going to trial, along with an impending trial date quickly approaching, often help clients view their cases in a more realistic light. If a case cannot be settled during the pretrial, the parties will attempt to narrow down the contested issues that will be presented at trial and address potential problems.

B. Scheduling Pretrial Conferences

Rather than wait to the end of the Pretrial Stage, some courts order the parties to attend a pretrial conference (sometimes called a status conference) early on in the litigation process in hopes of reducing the number of cases on their docket. In these situations, if the case cannot be settled, the parties will determine deadlines to respond to pleadings, hearing dates on motions, and discovery schedules. As the case approaches trial, the court will often order another pretrial conference. In addition, the parties may request a pretrial conference at any time prior to trial.

C. Pretrial Memos

Most states order the parties to complete a pretrial memo that explains the facts of the case, the contested issues, and special damages such as medical bills or property damages a party (usually the Plaintiff) expects to be compensated for. This memo is utilized by the judge or attorney assigned to preside over the pretrial.

Connecticut has a court-issued form to meet this pretrial memo requirement. Other states require a written statement, similar to the form of a motion or brief. New Jersey requires the parties to present a joint pretrial memo.

III. Motions in Limine

A **Motion in Limine** is decided before a trial begins, by the judge who is assigned as the trial judge for a specific case that will be decided by a jury. If the case will be decided by a judge rather than a jury, a party may file the Motion in Limine and ask that it be decided by a judge who will not decide the case. Go on to the next section to learn why.

A. Purpose of a Motion in Limine

The purpose of a Motion in Limine is to prevent an opposing party from introducing specific evidence at trial, or to limit its introduction to definite boundaries. In such cases, the party drafting the motion should claim that the evidence in question is irrelevant to the case and highly prejudicial. Therefore, it is not needed to support or to prove any issues and will unfairly affect the trier of fact's decision.

For instance, if the Plaintiff in a civil case served a short prison sentence after the motor vehicle accident at issue in the case, the Plaintiff may not want the jury to know about this criminal record or incarceration at the trial. Therefore, he or she may file a Motion in Limine, asking the court to prevent the Defendant from disclosing that information to the jury because it is irrelevant to the instant lawsuit and it may unfairly prejudice the jury against the Plaintiff.

As with all motions, the opposing party may object. In this situation, the Defendant may claim that the Plaintiff's incarceration aggravated the injuries claimed, due to riots in the prison and inadequate medical care the Plaintiff received during that time. As a result, the Defendant will argue that this information must be disclosed to the jury so that it may fairly determine what percentage, if any, of the Plaintiff's injuries the Defendant should be held liable for.

B. The Court's Ruling

The court may grant the Motion in Limine and order the relief the party requests or order some other kind of relief to address the situation. On the other hand, the court may grant or deny the motion, with or without prejudice. Furthermore, the court may simply decide not to rule on the motion until later in the proceedings, after it has had the opportunity to hear a portion of the case and is better able to determine what prejudicial effect, if any, the questionable evidence may have.

IV. Offer of Judgment

An **Offer of Judgment** is a written offer, submitted before trial by one party to another, suggesting to settle the case for a specific sum stated therein. In Connecticut and New Jersey, either the Plaintiff or Defendant or both may submit an

Offer of Judgment to each other. In the remaining states, it appears that only the Defendant (or a NY Plaintiff faced with a Counterclaim, etc.) may submit an Offer of Judgment.

A. Accepting an Offer of Judgment

Once a party is presented with an Offer of Judgment, it must be accepted within a specific amount of time. Otherwise, it is treated as rejected. In each state addressed, if an Offer of Judgment is rejected, a party may submit another offer at any time in the future within the deadlines that are established prior to trial.

B. Consequences of Rejecting an Offer of Judgment

If an Offer of Judgment is rejected and the verdict is more than the offer, the party who rejected the offer will not suffer any consequences. However, if the damages awarded are equal to or less than the Offer of Judgment, the party who rejected the offer may be required to pay all of the offering party's costs for the trial and face other consequences as well. This becomes a critical issue if the party making the offer has one or more expensive experts testify at the trial.

V. Privileged Cases

Privileged cases are entitled to be scheduled for trial earlier than others, for example, if one of the parties is elderly or terminally ill, or if the trial court already ruled in favor of the Plaintiff as to liability and only damages need to be tried. These cases are often designated as privileged and it is up to the parties, usually the Plaintiff, to notify the court of the situation in order to obtain an early trial date.

VI. Bifurcated Cases

If a case is unusually complicated, such as a product liability case with several Defendants, the parties may ask the court to **bifurcate** the case for trial. This means that the case will be tried in two separate parts: liability first, and then damages.

During the first half of a bifurcated case, the parties will introduce evidence that is exclusively related to whether or not the Defendant(s) is liable. At the end of the evidence, the trier of fact will determine which Defendants, if any, are liable. Moreover:

1. If no Defendants are found to be liable, the trial is over.
2. If all the Defendants are found to be liable, the trial will continue (or a new trial will begin, depending upon the state) to determine damages involving all those Defendants.

3. If only some Defendants are found liable, the remainder are removed from the case with judgments in their favor.

Note: If more than one Plaintiff is involved, some may be dismissed if the finder of fact determines the Defendants are not liable for their injuries, etc.

VII. Postponing a Trial Date

Each court attempts to provide all parties in a case with as much advance notice as possible regarding a trial date. If a continuance is needed, it should be requested as soon as a party realizes it is necessary.

A. Reasons to Seek a Continuance

All clients and their attorneys on both sides of a lawsuit must be present and ready to begin trial on the day and time it is scheduled. What happens, however, if an important witness cannot be available to testify on the date of trial? Or, if an important document or other evidence cannot be made available on that date? Or, if one of the attorneys is already *on trial*, or a vacation is already scheduled, etc.?

Each state's court rules should indicate the steps any party should take to ask the court to continue the trial to another date. In addition, if all the parties in the case agree to the continuance, some courts will grant this request over the telephone or pursuant to a letter from the requesting party. To be safe, the requesting party should call the court and ask which procedure the presiding judge requires.

On the other hand, a court may not grant the motion for a continuance if: it believes the requesting party did not have a good reason for not properly preparing to have the witness or evidence available; or if the opposing party is willing to stipulate to the affidavit regarding evidence of what the material witness would say if he or she were to testify at trial or to the content of the evidence, if either were available. In these situations, the affidavit or a written stipulation would be introduced to the trier of fact at trial, instead of the actual witness or evidence.

In addition to the above, keep in mind that a witness's deposition testimony may be read to the trier of fact by an individual agreed to by all parties, if the witness is unavailable to testify at trial.

B. Failure to Appear at Trial

Any party who fails to appear at trial without a proper excuse may face a court order dismissing the case or entering judgment against the absent party.

VIII. Conclusion

Key Issues in This Chapter

1. Promptly notify all clients and witnesses of trial dates. If a continuance is needed, try to obtain an agreement from the opposing party and include it in your request to the court.
2. Be sure to review your case thoroughly to determine if a Motion in Limine is appropriate.
3. An Offer of Judgment can create great inducement to settle a case.
4. As the trial date approaches, timely serve all necessary subpoenas.

STATE SUMMARIES

Connecticut: Trial Preparation

I. Closing the Pleadings, Claiming the Case to the Trial List, and Electing a Jury Trial: Pbs 14-8, 14-9, 14-10

Unlike Massachusetts, New Jersey, and Rhode Island, Connecticut (and New York) have specific procedures for closing the pleadings, claiming the case to the trial list, and electing a jury trial, as follows:

A. Certificate of Closed Pleadings

1. When all of the responsive pleadings are filed, the pleadings are deemed closed and either party must file a court-issued form entitled a Certificate of Closed Pleadings. Usually the Plaintiff takes this action.
2. In this certificate, the party must check the applicable box to indicate whether he or she wants a jury trial or bench trial.
3. If the party elects a jury trial, he or she must include the court fee of $350. No money is needed for a bench trial.
4. If a party or the case fits the privileged criteria, be sure to mark the privileged box.

Once filed, this form places the case on the court or jury trial list. (The case will not be placed on either trial list without this form being filed.)

B. Jury Claim Slip

If the party who filed the Certificate of Closed Pleadings elected a bench trial, the opposing party may file a court-issued form entitled a Jury Claim, along with the $350 fee. This form and fee will move the case over to the jury trial list.

Caution: This form must be filed no later than ***ten days*** after the Certificate of Closed Pleadings was filed. Otherwise, the party waives his or her right to a jury trial. If the ***ten-day*** deadline is missed, all the parties in the case may enter into a stipulation to place the case on the jury trial list, or the party who missed the deadline may file a motion asking the court to order the case to be placed on the jury trial list.

II. Pretrial Conferences: Pbs 14-11, 14-12, 14-14

Plaintiffs and any other parties who are claiming relief pursuant to a Counterclaim, Third-Party claim, or Cross Claim are required to complete the court-issued pretrial form and bring it to the pretrial conference. In addition, they should bring a copy for all opposing parties. **Note:** In many instances, the court may require all the parties to complete this form. Be sure to carefully read and follow the instructions that accompany the notice to appear for the pretrial.

III. Motions in Limine: Pbs 15-3

Motions in Limine are addressed as discussed in the main chapter.

IV. Offers of Judgment: Pbs 17-11 et seq.

Connecticut permits both Plaintiffs and Defendants to file Offers of Judgment.

A. Defendant's Offer of Judgment to Plaintiff

1. Time to File Notice of Offer of Judgment

A Defendant may file a Notice of Offer of Judgment at any time ***before*** evidence is offered during trial. Hence, the Defendant may make this offer early on in the case, or during the Pleadings Stage, or even as late as during jury selection.

2. The Plaintiff's Response: Accepted

The Plaintiff has ***ten days*** after receiving the Defendant's Notice of the Offer to accept the offer in writing, by filing an Acceptance of Offer of Judgment. In many cases, however, if evidence is scheduled to start during the ten-day period, the Plaintiff must accept before evidence begins, unless the court is willing to delay the trial or permit the Plaintiff to accept after evidence begins.

If the Plaintiff accepts the Offer of Judgment, the case is over. The judgment against the Defendant is treated as a default in the amount offered, plus the Plaintiff's costs that had been incurred up until the time the Offer of Judgment was made.

3. The Plaintiff's Response: Rejected

If the Plaintiff does not accept the Offer of Judgment as stated above, the offer is deemed withdrawn.

4. Consequences for a Plaintiff Who Rejects an Offer of Judgment

If the verdict is in favor of the Plaintiff and the damages awarded are more than the Offer of Judgment, the Plaintiff suffers no consequences. However, if the damages awarded are equal to or less than the Offer of Judgment, the Plaintiff:

- **a.** shall not recover any costs from the Defendant which the Plaintiff incurred after receiving the Defendant's Notice of Offer of Judgment; and
- **b.** shall pay all the Defendant's costs which were incurred after the Plaintiff received the Defendant's Notice of Offer of Judgment. These costs may include up to as much as $350 for reasonable attorney's fees.

As a result of these consequences, a Plaintiff who receives a small damage award could end up having to pay several hundred or even thousands of dollars in costs for both sides. **Note:** The rules regarding costs and an Offer of Judgment usually do not override any contract the parties may have entered into regarding attorney's fees.

B. Plaintiff's Offer of Judgment to Defendant

1. Time to File

A Plaintiff may file his or her Notice of Offer of Judgment at any time before trial.

2. Defendant's Response: Accepted

The Defendant has ***30 days*** after the Plaintiff's Notice of Offer of Judgment is filed (and before a jury or court reaches a verdict) to file a written Acceptance of Offer of Judgment. In this Acceptance, the Defendant agrees to stipulate to the amount stated in the Plaintiff's offer.

If the Plaintiff's Offer of Judgment is accepted, the case is over and judgment will be in the amount stated in the Plaintiff's offer.

3. Defendant's Response: Rejected

If the Plaintiff's Offer of Judgment is not accepted by the Defendant within the time stated above, the offer is considered rejected.

4. Consequences for a Defendant Who Rejects an Offer of Judgment

If the damages awarded are equal to or greater than the Plaintiff's Offer of Judgment, the court will increase the judgment against the Defendant by adding interest and attorney's fees.

V. Postponing Trial Dates: Pbs 14-23

The rules stated above address requesting the court to continue (postpone) a trial date.

Example 19-1. Connecticut, Plaintiff's Offer of Judgment

DOCKET NO. CV 98-0333333 S	:	SUPERIOR COURT
SARAH A. DONAHUE	:	JUDICIAL DISTRICT OF
	:	TOLLAND
VS.	:	AT ROCKVILLE
RICHARD P. ANDREW	:	(date)

NOTICE OF PLAINTIFF'S OFFER OF JUDGMENT

Pursuant to Connecticut Practice Book Section 17-14, the Plaintiff hereby offers to take judgment against the Defendant in the amount of One Hundred Thousand Dollars ($100,000.00).

THE PLAINTIFF

BY ______________________________

Christine Kulas, Esq.
Law Office of Christine Kulas
her attorney
P.O. Box 2005
Ellington, CT 06060
Tele. #(860) 222-2222
Juris # 989898

CERTIFICATION

I hereby certify that a copy of the foregoing was mailed on ________ to all counsel and pro se parties of record, namely: Attorney Neil E. Clifford, Esq., Michaels, Sabrina and Alexander, PC, 259 Sage Road, Suite 200, West Hartford, CT 08080.

____

Commissioner of the Superior Court

Example 19-2. Connecticut, Defendant's Acceptance of Plaintiff's Offer of Judgment

DOCKET NO. CV 98-0333333 S	:	SUPERIOR COURT
SARAH A. DONAHUE	:	JUDICIAL DISTRICT OF
	:	TOLLAND
VS.	:	AT ROCKVILLE
RICHARD P. ANDREW	:	(date)

ACCEPTANCE OF OFFER OF JUDGMENT

The Defendant, Ryan Keegan, hereby accepts the Plaintiff's Offer of Judgment dated October 9, 1998, and agrees to stipulate to a judgment in the amount of One Hundred Thousand Dollars ($100,000.00), pursuant to Connecticut Practice Book Section 17-15.

THE DEFENDANT

BY ______________________________

Neil E. Clifford, Esq.
Michaels, Sabrina and Alexander, PC
259 Sage Road, Suite 200
906 Park Plaza
West Hartford, CT 08080
Tele. #(860) 111-1111
Juris #626262

CERTIFICATION

I hereby certify that a copy of the foregoing was mailed on __________ to all counsel and pro se parties of record, namely: Attorney Christine Kulas, P.O. Box 2005, Ellington, CT 06066.

____
Commissioner of the Superior Court

MASSACHUSETTS: TRIAL PREPARATION

I. Certificate of Readiness and the Trial List: Super. Ct. Rules 33 and 35

See these rules to determine how to place a case on the waiting list for trial.

II. Electing a Jury Trial: Rule 38 et seq.

A party in Massachusetts who wants a jury trial must serve and file written notice early in the litigation process, specifically, any time after the action begins but not later than ***ten days*** after service of the Defendant's Answer (or other pleading that responds to issues that a party wants a jury to resolve).

Note: Written notice may be included in a pleading. As a result, many Plaintiffs include it in the Complaint. Many Defendants include it in their Answer (and if applicable, their Counterclaim or Cross Claim).

III. Pretrial Conferences: Super. Ct. Rule 27, Rule 16 and Standing Order 1-88

Pretrial conferences are mentioned in Super. Ct. Rule 27 which refers readers to Rule 16 for more details. See also Standing Order 1-88 which mentions a *Joint Pretrial Memorandum.*

IV. Offers of Judgment: Rule 68

In Massachusetts, it appears that only the party who is defending against a claim may file an Offer of Judgment. These parties include Defendants, Plaintiffs defending a Counterclaim, Third-Party Defendants, and parties who have had a Cross Claim filed against them.

An Offer of Judgment may be served (but not filed) at any time, but no less than ***ten days*** before the trial is scheduled to start.

If an Offer of Judgment is accepted, the party must serve written notice of the acceptance within ***ten days*** of the date the offer was served. Next, one of the parties must file both the offer and the acceptance in court. The clerk will then enter judgment according to the documents. On the other hand, if the offer is not accepted during this time, it is treated as withdrawn.

V. Postponing Trial Dates: Rule 40 and Super. Ct. Rule 4

The rules stated above address requesting the court to continue (postpone) a trial date.

Example 19-3. Massachusetts, Format for Joint Pretrial Memo

COMMONWEATH OF MASSACHUSETTS

HAMPDEN, ss.

SUPERIOR COURT
DEPARTMENT OF
THE TRIAL COURT
CIVIL ACTION
NO. 98-0000

GEORGE JONES, JR., by his father and next friend, GEORGE JONES, SR. Plaintiff vs. CITY IN MASSACHUSETTS, Defendant	JOINT PRETRIAL MEMORANDUM

In accordance with Standing Order 1-88, the parties agree to file the following memorandum.

(1) AGREED-UPON FACTS

(2) BRIEF STATEMENT

(A) PLAINTIFF'S STATEMENT

(B) DEFENDANT'S STATEMENT

(3) AGREED UPON DESCRIPTION FOR THE JURY

(4) UNUSUAL LEGAL ISSUES

(A) PLAINTIFF

(B) DEFENDANT

(5) WITNESS LIST

(A) PLAINTIFF'S LIST

(B) DEFENDANT'S LIST

(6) EXPERT LIST

(A) PLAINTIFF'S LIST

(B) DEFENDANT'S LIST

(7) ESTIMATED LENGTH OF TRIAL

(8) NEGOTIATIONS

THE PLAINTIFFS	***THE DEFENDANT***
BY: ____________________	BY: ____________________
(attorney's identifying info.)	(attorney's identifying info.)

Example 19-4. Massachusetts, Motion in Limine

COMMONWEATH OF MASSACHUSETTS

HAMPDEN, ss.	SUPERIOR COURT DEPARTMENT OF THE TRIAL COURT CIVIL ACTION NO. 98-0000
GEORGE JONES, JR., by his father and next friend, GEORGE JONES, SR. Plaintiff vs. CITY IN MASSACHUSETTS, Defendant	DEFENDANT, CITY IN MASSACHUSETTS, MOTION IN LIMINE

Now comes the Defendant, City in Massachusetts, and hereby moves **IN LIMINE** for an order prohibiting the Plaintiff from introducing evidence of subsequent repairs to the radiator involved in this case.

This case involves an injury allegedly suffered by the Plaintiff on ____ at the _____ School in _____ Massachusetts. The Plaintiff alleges that the Defendant negligently maintained a radiator by not covering it, on which radiator the Plaintiff was burned. Subsequent to the date of the alleged injury, the Defendant placed a cover over the radiator. The Defendant anticipates that the Plaintiff may try to introduce evidence of that repair to support his negligence claim.

Evidence of subsequent repairs is not admissible to prove negligence. Evidence of post accident repairs or improvement "is not admissible as an admission of negligence or of the existence of the defect." Liacos, *Handbook of Massachusetts Evidence,* 5th edition, p. 285. Evidence of this type may be admissible on issues such as control, feasibility of precautionary measure or ownership. Whether or not to admit such evidence is in the judge's discretion and it is properly excluded when he or she concludes that "the jury would be likely to infer negligence therefrom." *Black v. Springfield, St. Ry.,* 6 Mass. App. Ct. 553, 557 (1978).

Control, feasibility and ownership are not in dispute. The Defendant admits that the radiator was under its custody and control. Nor is the Defendant raising the defense that the remedial work done on the radiator was not feasible prior to the incident at issue. As a result, the only way in which the jury could interpret such evidence of subsequent repair is as some admission of negligence by the Defendant. For that reason, the Defendant requests that the evidence not be admitted at trial.

THE DEFENDANT,

Dated: _______________

By: ____________________________

Martha Pierson, Esq.
City Solicitor
Law Department
City in Massachusetts
932 Center Street
Citytown, MA 04444
(413) 787-9090
BBO #898980

CERTIFICATION

I hereby certify that a copy of the foregoing was mailed, postage pre-paid to all counsel of record, namely: Ann Lambert, Esq., 60 Main Street, E. Longmeadow, MA 04340 on _______.

____

Martha Pierson

New Jersey: Trial Preparation

I. Electing a Jury Trial: Rule 4:35-1

A party in New Jersey who wants a jury trial must serve and file written notice early in the litigation process, specifically, any time after the action begins but not later than ***ten days*** after service of the Defendant's Answer or other pleading that responds to issues that a party wants a jury to resolve.

Note: Written notice may be included in a pleading. As a result, many Plaintiffs include it in the Complaint. Many Defendants include it in their Answer and if applicable, their Counterclaim or Cross Claim.

II. Pretrial Conferences: Rule 4:25

Pretrial conferences are mentioned in Rule 4:25. Specifically, the parties are required to draft a Pretrial Memo and serve it to each other at least ***three days*** prior to the pretrial conference. The content of the memo is stated in Rule 4:25-1(b) and 4:25-3. After the conference, if the case has not settled, the judge who pretried the case will issue orders that will determine the progression of the lawsuit unless they are later modified by the court.

III. Motions in Limine

See pages 352–357 for an example of a Motion in Limine.

IV. Offers of Judgment: Rule 4:58

In New Jersey, any party may serve and file an Offer of Judgment at any time but no less than ***20 days*** before the first scheduled trial date or daily or weekly trial calendar call.

If an Offer of Judgment is accepted, the party must serve and file written notice of the acceptance within ***ten days*** before the first trial date, or as stated above.

If the Offer of Judgment is not accepted within the 10 days stated above, or within 90 days of service if it was served much earlier in the case, the offer is withdrawn.

Example 19-5. New Jersey, Motion in Limine and Supporting Brief

GRAVEY, MADISON AND PAUL, P.C.
190 Court Street
Newark, New Jersey 07102-5497
(201) 623-0000
Attorneys for Defendant/Third-Party Plaintiff,
Safety Insurance Co.

		SUPERIOR COURT OF NEW JERSEY LAW DIVISION: BERGEN COUNTY
Plaintiff	:	
	:	
BIRCH REALTY CO.	:	
vs.	:	DOCKET NO.: BER-L-11111-98
	:	
Defendant/Third-Party Plaintiff	:	
	:	
SAFTEY INSURANCE CO.	:	Civil Action
	:	
vs.	:	NOTICE OF
Third-Party Defendant	:	MOTION IN LIMINE
	:	
JOSEPH DEXTER	:	
	:	

TO: Robert A. Hathaway,
Marsh & Marsh
2719 Bergen Street
Wayne, New Jersey, 17470

COUNSEL:

PLEASE TAKE NOTICE that Defendant/Third-Party Plaintiff, Safety Insurance Company, through its undersigned attorneys, will move before the Superior Court of New Jersey, Law Division, Bergen County, at the Bergen County Court House, 119 Justice Center, 10 Main Street, Hackensack, New Jersey on _____ or as soon thereafter as counsel may be heard, for an Order granting its Motion in Limine precluding Plaintiff and Third-Party Defendant and their respective counsel from offering evidence, making any argument or referencing at the time of trial that fact that the Bergen County Prosecutor's Office has failed to file criminal charges against the Third-Party Defendant.

In support of the within motion, Safety Insurance Company will rely upon the Certification of _____ and the brief submitted herein.

Gravey, Madison & Paul, P.C.
Attorneys for Defendant/Third-Party
Plaintiff, Safety Insurance Company

By: ______________________
Walter M. Madison

Dated:

CERTIFICATION OF SERVICE

I hereby certify that on _____ I have caused an original and one copy of the within Notice of Motion, Brief of Defendant/Third-Party Plaintiff Safety Insurance Company and a proposed form of Order to be filed via hand delivery with the Clerk, Bergen County, Superior Court of New Jersey, 10 Main Street, Justice Center, Hackensack, New Jersey and one copy was hand-delivered to:

Robert A. Hathaway, Esq.
Marsh & Marsh
2719 Bergen Street
Wayne, New Jersey, 07470

Dated: ______________________________

Walter M. Madison

		SUPERIOR COURT OF NEW JERSEY LAW DIVISION: BERGEN COUNTY
Plaintiff	:	
	:	
BIRCH REALTY CO.	:	
vs.	:	DOCKET NO.: BER-L-11111-98
	:	
Defendant/Third-Party Plaintiff	:	
	:	
SAFTEY INSURANCE CO.	:	Civil Action
	:	
vs.	:	BRIEF IN SUPPORT OF
	:	MOTION IN LIMINE
Third-Party Defendant	:	
	:	
JOSEPH DEXTER	:	

DEFENDANT/THIRD-PARTY PLAINTIFF
SAFETY INSURANCE COMPANY'S MOTION IN LIMINE

GRAVEY, MADISON AND PAUL, P.C.
190 Court Street
Newark, New Jersey 07102-5497
(201) 623-0000
Attorneys for Defendant/
Third-Party Plaintiff,
Safety Insurance Co.

On the Brief:
Walter M. Madison, Esq.

PRELIMINARY STATEMENT

This is a civil arson case in which the Plaintiff seeks to recover under a fire insurance policy issued by Defendant, Safety Insurance Company ("Safety"). Safety has claimed the defense of arson and named the Plaintiff's partner, Joseph Dexter, a Third-Party Defendant.

The arson Squad of the Bergen County Prosecutor's Office previously determined that the fire was intentionally set and that the Third-Party Defendant was a suspect in the case. Nevertheless, criminal charges have not been filed and the investigation has been closed.

Safety seeks an order barring Plaintiff and Third-Party Defendant from offering any evidence, making any argument nor referencing the fact that the prosecutor's office has closed the case and has failed to file charges against the Third-Party Defendant.

STATEMENT OF FACTS

On October 1, 1997, Safety issued a certain insurance policy to Plaintiff covering a certain premises located at 34 Lake Road, Newark, NJ. The premises consisted of a bar and restaurant on the first floor, several studio apartments on the second floor and a vacant third floor. The effective dates of the policy were October 1, 1997 through October 1, 1998.

Sometime between approximately 11:00 p.m. on January 15, 1998 and 1:20 a.m. on January 16, 1998, a fire occurred at the premises. Following an extensive investigation by the Arson Squad it was determined that:

(1) the fire was intentionally set in five separate areas in the first floor area.
(2) petroleum distillants such as kerosene, diesel fuel or charcoal lighter fluid were found at the scene.
(3) a door leading into the restaurant are was unlocked.

See exhibit A, fire report by Bergen County Arson task Force.

ARGUMENT

POINT ONE

EVIDENCE THAT ARSON CHARGES HAVE NOT BEEN FILED AGAINST THIRD-PARTY DEFENDANT IS INADMISSIBLE IN THE PRESENT ACTION

Plaintiff and Third-Party Defendant should be precluded from offering any evidence, making any argument or referencing the fact that the Bergen County Prosecutor's Office has not brought any criminal charges against the Third-Party Defendant and has closed the case. This proposition is fully supported by the New Jersey Rules of Evidence, case law and common sense.

One needs to look no further than the Third Circuit decision in *Galbraith v. Hartford Fire Insurance Company*, 464 F.2d 225 (3rd Cir. (1972) applying New Jersey law) to reach the inescapable conclusion that this type of evidence may not be introduced. In Galbraith, the insureds sought to recover under a fire insurance policy for damage to their home. The insurer, The Hartford Fire Insurance Company, defended the grounds that the insured was responsible for the fire and therefore was precluded from recovery pursuant to the terms of the policy. Id. at 226.

During direct examination of the insured, the trial court permitted, over objection, questions regarding whether the insured was ever charged with any crime relative to the fire. In addition, the summation for insured's counsel again mentioned the fact that no criminal charges had been filed.

On appeal, the Hartford asserted that it was prejudicial error to allow Plaintiff's counsel to pursue this line of question and introduce evidence on non-prosecution. The Third Circuit court agreed.

The Third Circuit Court stated that although there were no cases directly on point, "New Jersey law indicates clearly that evidence of an accused's acquittal in a criminal proceeding is not admissible in a civil suit arising out of the event which formed the basis of the criminal charge. Id. at 227, citing *Mean v. Wiley Methodist Episcopal Church,* 23 N.J. Super. 342 (App. Div. 1952).

The Court also concluded that the reason behind this exclusion stemmed from a realization that an acquittal in a criminal context "is not necessarily a judgment of innocence, but merely a negative statement that the quantum of proof necessary for conviction has not been presented." Id. (Footnote omitted.) Moreover, the Court reasoned that the failure of the Prosecutor's Office to charge the insured could have been based on a number of reasons including that definitive proof "beyond a reasonable doubt" was lacking, or investigative procedures were inconclusive. The Court noted that all these reasons may be beyond the comprehension of the average laymen and therefore could result in prejudice.

Accordingly, the Court ruled that evidence of non-prosecution "would only have been an opinion, which, moreover would not have been based on personal knowledge." Id. at 227-228.

CONCLUSION

The Defendant/Third-Party Plaintiff respectively moves that the court grant its Motion in Limine and issue an Order precluding the Plaintiff and Third-Party Defendant from submitting evidence of this issue to the jury in any manner.

GRAVEY, MADISON AND PAUL, P.C.
190 Court Street
Newark, New Jersey 07102-5497
(201) 623-0000
Attorneys for Defendant/Third-Party Plaintiff, Safety Insurance Co.

Dated:______________ By: ______________________
Walter M. Madison

GRAVEY, MADISON AND PAUL, P.C.
190 Court Street
Newark, New Jersey 07102-5497
(201) 623-0000
Attorneys for Defendant/Third-Party Plaintiff,
Safety Insurance Co.

	SUPERIOR COURT OF NEW JERSEY LAW DIVISION: BERGEN COUNTY
Plaintiff BIRCH REALTY CO. vs.	DOCKET NO.: BER-L-11111-98
Defendant/Third-Party Plaintiff SAFTEY INSURANCE CO.	Civil Action
vs.	***ORDER***
Third-Party Defendant JOSEPH DEXTER	

THIS MATTER, having been opened to the Court on the application of Walter M. Madison of Gravey, Madison & Paul, P.C., attorneys for Defendant/Third-Party Plaintiff, having considered the papers submitted and having heard oral arguments of counsel and good cause being shown;

IT IS on this _____ day of _______, 19__

ORDERED that the Defendant/Third-Party Plaintiff's Motion in Limine is hereby granted in all respects and it is further

ORDERED that Plaintiff, and Third-Party Defendant, and their respective counsel are barred from offering any evidence, making any argument or referencing at the time of trial the fact that the Bergen County Prosecutor's Office has not filed criminal charges against the Third-Party Defendant and that the case is closed.

____

New York: Trial Preparations

Like Connecticut, New York has a specific procedure for placing a case on the trial list. Instead of filing a Certificate of Closed Pleadings, either party may file a *Note of Issue* with a *Certificate of Readiness.*

I. Note of Issue: CPLR 3402 and Unif. Rule 202.21

A Note of Issue is simply a court-issued form that must be served and filed after "issue is joined." This means that the Defendant has filed the Answer and all other requisite responsive pleadings have been served and filed, i.e., the pleadings are closed.

Note: Local court rules require that the Note of Issue should not be filed until all pretrial procedures such as disclosure (New York's discovery) and the Bill of Particulars have been completed, and the case is ready for trial. If the Note of Issue is filed before this time, a party must ask the court's permission to conduct further disclosure.

II. Certificate of Readiness: Unif. Rule 202.21

In addition to the Note of Issue, Unif. Rule 202.21 requires a Certificate of Readiness to accompany the Note of Issue. In fact, many Note of Issue forms contain a Certificate of Readiness on the reverse side.

Specifically, the Certificate of Readiness states that:

1. All disclosure proceedings and Bill of Particular steps are concluded (or that there has been sufficient time to conduct these procedures and the parties do not intend to do so); and
2. Settlement attempts have not been successful; and
3. The case is ready for trial.

III. Serving and Filing the Note of Issue and Certificate of Readiness: CPLR 3403

Two copies of each document should be filed within ***ten days*** of serving them on the remaining parties in the action. As always, be sure to include a proof of service for the court.

IV. Preference Cases: CPLR 3403, Unif. Rules. 202.24 and 202.25

New York refers to its privileged cases as preference cases, which are discussed in the main chapter. If a party believes his or her case is entitled to a quick trial date, it must be stated in the Note of Issue or a Notice of Motion for Preference should be attached. **Note:** A party may object to treating a case as a preference case. See Unif. Rule 202.25.

V. Jury Demand: CPLR 4102 and Unif. Rule 202.21 (c)

Like in Connecticut, now is the time to notify the court that a party wants a jury trial. This demand must be included in the Note of Issue.

If no jury demand is made in the Note of Issue, any of the remaining parties in the case who want a jury trial may serve a Demand for Jury within ***15 days*** after the Note of Issue was served. Otherwise, both parties are deemed to have waived their right to a jury trial.

VI. Pretrial Conferences: Unif. Rule 202.26

According to Rule 202.26, after the Notice of Issue and Certificate of Readiness have been filed, the court will schedule a pretrial conference in order to attempt settlement and/or to discuss the impending trial.

VII. Offers of Compromise: CPLR 3221

New York uses the term "Offer of Compromise" instead of Offer of Judgment. A Defendant may serve an Offer of Compromise no later than ***ten days*** before trial is scheduled to begin.

The Plaintiff has ***ten days*** to accept the Defendant's offer. If the Plaintiff wins the case but the verdict is less than the Defendant's Offer of Compromise, he or she will not be entitled to obtain costs from the Defendant that arose after the date the offer was made. In addition, the Plaintiff must reimburse the Defendant for costs incurred after the date the offer was made. If the Plaintiff loses the case, he or she must reimburse the Defendant all his or her costs. (This is true with or without an Offer of Compromise.)

VIII. Bifurcated Trials: Unif. Rule 202.42

See Unif. Rule 202.42 regarding bifurcated trials.

IX. Readiness for Trial: Unif. Rule 202.22(d)

If a case is ready for trial but there is a short delay in obtaining an available courtroom or the judge is occupied, the parties and the judge or clerk may agree that the parties will remain available to be contacted by telephone to appear in court with approximately one hour (or more) notice.

Rhode Island: Trial Preparation

I. Electing a Jury Trial: Rule 38 et seq.

A party in Rhode Island who wants a jury trial must serve and file written notice early in the litigation process, specifically, any time after the action begins but not later than ***ten days*** after service of the Defendant's Answer (or other pleading that responds to issues that a party wants a jury to resolve).

Note: Written notice may be included in a pleading. As a result, many Plaintiffs include it in the Complaint. Many Defendants include it in the Answer (and if applicable, the Counterclaim or Cross Claim).

II. Pretrial Conferences and Status Conferences: Rules 16 and R.P. 2.4

Pretrial conferences are addressed in Rule 16. Status conferences are addressed in Rules of Practice 2.4. **Note:** Parties in bench trials must file a pretrial memorandum no later than Tuesday preceding the Friday on which the case is scheduled for a trial calendar call. See R.P. 2.8 for more details.

III. Motions in Limine

Motions in Limine are recognized in Rhode Island, however, I did not find a court rule to address them.

IV. Offers of Judgment: Rule 68

In Rhode Island, it appears that only the party who is defending against a claim may file an Offer of Judgment. These parties include Defendants, Plaintiffs defending a Counterclaim, Third-Party Defendants, and parties who have had a Cross Claim filed against them.

Rhode Island permits two different types of Offer of Judgment:

1. A Written Offer

An Offer of Judgment may be served (but not filed) at any time, but no less than ***ten days*** before the trial is scheduled to start.

If an Offer of Judgment is accepted, the party must serve written notice of the acceptance within ***ten days*** of the date the offer was served. Next, one of the parties must file both the offer and the acceptance in court. The clerk will then enter judgment according to the documents. On the other hand, if the offer is not accepted during this time, it is treated as withdrawn.

2. Payment in Court

A Defendant or other party as described above may deposit a specific sum of money with the court clerk and plead that he or she does not owe any additional money to the Plaintiff, etc.

The Plaintiff has three options:

- **a.** Accept the sum and have judgment enter in his or her favor in that amount; or
- **b.** Reject the sum outright; or
- **c.** Accept the amount as a partial payment and continue the lawsuit but focus exclusively on the amount of damages (because by making the payment to the court, the Defendant has agreed that he or she is liable).

Note: Pursuant to Rule 408 of the Rules of Evidence, any offer to settle will not be admitted into evidence at trial.

V. Postponing Trial Dates: Rule 40

The rules stated above address requesting the court to continue (postpone) a trial date.

VI. Nonjury Trials: R.P. 2.8

According to R.P. 2.8, a bench trial will not take place until a specific type of pretrial memo is filed. In this memo, include the following:

1. the facts agreed upon;
2. agreed upon exhibits and objections;
3. qualification of experts;
4. issues for the court to decide, etc.

20 The Trial Stage: The Trial

Terminology

Voir Dire	Sequester	Exception	Jury Instructions
Challenges	Verdict	Evidence	Requests to Charge
Jury Selection	Testimony	Exhibits	Opening Statements
Cross Examination	Veniremen	Judge's Charge	Closing Arguments
Direct Examination	Interrogatories	Rebuttal	Charge Conference
Preponderance of Evidence		Witnesses	

Introduction

Typically, the following individuals are present during a trial: the trial judge, the jury if it's a jury trial, all the attorneys involved in the case, all the clients involved in the case, at least one court sheriff to assist the witnesses and jurors, the court reporter, and the courtroom clerk.

I. Stages of a Trial

The stages of a trial are described below. They include:

1. jury selection;
2. Plaintiff's opening argument;
3. Plaintiff's case in chief, during which evidence is presented through witnesses and exhibits;

4. Defendant's case, during which evidence is presented through witnesses and exhibits;
5. Plaintiff's Rebuttal;
6. Plaintiff's and Defendant's Closing Arguments;
7. judge's decision, if it is a bench trial;
8. judge's charge to the jury, if there is a jury;
9. jury deliberations;
10. jury's verdict.

II. Jury Selection

In cases tried to a jury, members of the jury must be selected before the trial actually begins. In addition, it is customary to select at least two additional jurors to act as alternates, to replace any juror who is not able to complete the entire trial. The jury selection process is known as **Voir Dire**.

A. Jury Duty and Voir Dire

Each day court is in session, several individuals are present at various courthouses throughout the state to serve jury duty. After a brief orientation, they are instructed to remain in one specific location in their respective courthouses, usually designated as the *jury room,* until they are called for a case.

When a new case is ready to start trial, the clerk will select a *panel* of potential jurors (also known as **veniremen**) and bring them to the courtroom. The trial judge will swear in the panel and briefly explain the nature of the case. The attorneys then introduce themselves and their clients and read off the names of the witnesses they intend to call during the trial. A venireman who knows any of the attorneys, clients, or witnesses or who is familiar with the case may be excused **for cause** from serving on the jury for that case.

In Connecticut, the parties are permitted to examine each member of the panel individually, outside the presence of the other members. This examination is similar to an interview. In most other states, the jurors stay together and are expected to answer the attorney's questions in front of each other and the judge.

Members of the panel who are *accepted* by both sides become jurors. Members of the panel who are *excused* are sent back to the original jury room to wait to be called for another case.

Each individual Plaintiff and Defendant in a case is given a certain number of peremptory **challenges** to use to excuse an individual for any reason. When a party runs out of challenges, he or she will be stuck accepting a potential juror, unless the other parties exercise one of their challenges or the judge agrees to excuse the individual **for cause.**

Excused for cause usually means that the parties agree or the court determines that a potential juror should be disqualified to sit on a particular case.

Therefore, neither party is required to use a challenge. The reasons can include a situation in which the individual's bias or prejudice toward or against one party is obvious, or perhaps the individual is ill, or will be going into the hospital for major surgery during the trial. In some situations, a judge may completely excuse a person from the remainder of his or her jury duty.

Jury selection can take an hour, or a day, or in the state of Connecticut, several weeks. It depends upon the type of case, the number of parties, and the number of available challenges.

B. No Communications during Trial

Once the entire jury is selected, the trial judge will swear the panel in again and warn everyone to avoid and ignore all news reports of the case. In addition they must not discuss the case with anyone else until the judge tells them to begin deliberations. Then, they may discuss it only among themselves.

In addition, neither the parties, their attorneys, employees, representatives, nor agents shall contact, communicate with, or interview any juror or alternate or any relative, friend, or associate of any juror or alternate juror regarding the deliberations or verdict, until the case is over and the jurors are discharged. Any individual who violates this section could be charged and found in contempt of court. An attorney could be disbarred.

C. Sequestering the Jury

To **sequester** a jury means that the jurors will not be permitted to go home or anywhere else until the trial is over. Instead, they will be required to attend the trial each day and reside at a specific motel or hotel under the watchful eyes of sheriffs each evening and weekend. The purpose of sequestering a jury is to prevent the jurors from being contacted by the press or the public and to reduce their exposure to vast media coverage. Juries are rarely sequestered in civil cases. A party who wants the jury sequestered must bring the request to the trial judge's attention at the earliest possible time before jury selection begins.

III. Opening Statements

Each state allows each party to make an **opening statement** to the jury (or the trial judge in a bench trial) regarding the nature of the case. This opening statement should not take longer than one hour, unless otherwise ordered by the judge.

IV. Plaintiff's Burden of Proof and Case-in-Chief

A. Preponderance of Evidence

In order to win any case at trial, the Plaintiff must meet the required **burden of proof.** In most civil cases, this burden of proof is by **preponderance of the evi-**

dence. By contrast, in criminal cases, the Plaintiff (being the State or the People, etc.) must prove the case *beyond a reasonable doubt.* A small minority of civil cases require the Plaintiff to prove the case by *clear and convincing evidence.*

Over the years, I have heard these terms interpreted as follows:

1. Preponderance of the evidence: The Plaintiff must prove that the evidence weighs in his or her favor 51% or more, compared to the Defendant.
2. Clear and convincing evidence: The Plaintiff must prove that the evidence weighs in his or her favor 85% or more, compared to the Defendant.
3. Beyond a reasonable doubt: The Plaintiff must prove that the evidence weighs in his or her favor 95% or more, compared to the Defendant.

B. Plaintiff's Case in Chief

In every trial, the Plaintiff has the opportunity to present his or her case first. This is called the **Plaintiff's case-in-chief.** After the Plaintiff presents an opening argument, he or she must then present the evidence necessary to prove the case to the trier of fact.

The term **evidence** encompasses everything the parties introduce to the trier of fact during trial. Generally speaking, there are two types of evidence: testimony and exhibits.

1. Testimony

A witness's statements, made under oath, to the trier of fact during a trial are called **testimony.** Witnesses include clients and are individuals who have knowledge pertaining to a case. (Don't forget to subpoena nonparty witnesses. Otherwise, they are not subject to the court's jurisdiction if they fail to appear. The rules for subpoenaing nonparty witnesses to testify at trial are the same as for subpoenaing a nonparty witness to appear and testify at a deposition.)

Some witnesses are permitted to wait in the courtroom to be called to testify. Other witnesses are sequestered. Unlike sequestered juries who are confined until the end of trial, sequestered witnesses are merely required to wait outside the courtroom until it is their turn to testify, unless they are under some type of protective custody. As a result, they are prevented from hearing the testimony of any other witnesses. The question of whether to sequester or not sequester witnesses should be addressed prior to the beginning of trial.

The Plaintiff calls witnesses, one at a time, to take the witness stand and asks them a series of questions through **direct examination,** in front of the trier of fact. The witness's responses are called **testimony.**

Direct examination involves questions that require an open-ended response, rather than a simple yes or no answer.

For instance:

Question 1: When did you first meet the Plaintiff? versus

Question 2: You met the Plaintiff the same day the Defendant collided into her car. Isn't that correct?

Question 1 is an open-ended question, appropriate to ask during direct examination. Question 2 is called a **leading question:** It requires merely a yes or no response, and is usually appropriate only during **cross examination.**

When the Plaintiff is finished with direct examination, the Defendant may then ask the witness questions about his or her testimony. This is called **cross examination.** Unlike direct examination, cross examination often involves a series of questions that require only a yes or no response.

When the Defendant is finished cross examining, the Plaintiff may again question the witness. This is called **re-direct examination.** Its purpose is to allow the witness to explain any issues raised or clouded during the cross examination. In many instances, the court will permit the Defendant to re-cross examine the Plaintiff's witness also.

Note: If a Plaintiff calls the Defendant (or a corporate Defendant's agent) to testify, the Plaintiff may exercise what has been called statutory cross examination. In essence, the Plaintiff is permitted to treat the witness as a hostile witness and ask questions in the form of cross examination. The Defendant's cross examination is in the form of a direct examination.

In many situations, an attorney will have another attorney, either from his or her law firm or from another firm, assist during the trial. Usually, however, only one attorney for each client may examine a witness.

2. Exhibits

Exhibits are tangible items that pertain to the case that a party introduces to the trier of fact through the witnesses, for instance, documents, photographs, medical reports, medical bills, etc. The clerk marks each exhibit that is introduced by each side, by number or letter, and keeps a list. The parties can stipulate, prior to trial, that specific documents or items will be entered as exhibits, or they can wait until trial.

When both parties have finished their examinations of a witness, the witness will be permitted to *step down,* meaning he or she is excused. The Plaintiff will then call the next witness and the process will begin again.

V. The Defendant's Case

When all of the Plaintiff's witnesses have been examined, the Plaintiff will rest. At that point, the Defendant will have the opportunity to present an opening argument and call his or her witnesses to the stand. Now, the Defendant will perform direct examination and the Plaintiff will perform cross examination, followed by re-direct and re-cross as described above. The Defendant may call the Plaintiff or his or her corporate agent and exercise statutory cross examination.

VI. Plaintiff's Rebuttal

When the Defendant is finished presenting his or her case and rests, the Plaintiff will have the last word through rebuttal. **Rebuttal** is the Plaintiff's response to the evidence the Defendant presented. Witnesses called to testify during this time are called rebuttal witnesses.

VII. Objecting to Evidence

There are numerous rules that dictate if and in what matter testimony and exhibits should be introduced to the trier of fact. As with motions, a party who wishes to challenge specific evidence must object to it at the time the evidence is being introduced. After hearing both sides, the trial judge may make a decision or require the parties to brief the issue. In this scenario, it will make a decision later, after reviewing the briefs and any other relevant law. In some instances, if the party disagrees with the judge's ruling, the party must take an **exception in order to possibly appeal that ruling later.** The purpose of an exception is to advise the judge that the party believes it made a mistake that is appealable to an appellate court.

VIII. Rules regarding Juries

A. Note Taking

Some states such as Connecticut permit a trial judge to allow jurors to take notes and submit questions to be asked of witnesses during a civil trial.

B. Insurance Coverage

In most states, a party's insurance coverage, or lack thereof, is not generally admissible at trial unless the dispute at issue specifically involves a contract for insurance. This matter depends upon the facts of each case and should be addressed prior to trial.

C. Viewing

If appropriate, during the trial and before closing arguments, the trial judge may permit the jury to be brought to a specific location to view a scene or object, to assist the jury in determining a material factual issue in the case.

IX. Closing Arguments

After all the evidence is introduced and the parties have rested, each party may present a closing argument to the trier of fact. Each argument should not exceed one hour, unless the court orders otherwise. After the Defendant has completed his or her closing argument, the court often permits the Plaintiff to have one last opportunity to address the trier of fact.

Some states do not permit the Plaintiff to disclose to the jury the sum of damages the Plaintiff demanded in the Complaint or any other specific amount of damages. Instead, any party may, during closing arguments, mention a lump sum or mathematical formula regarding damages claimed, subject to cautionary instructions made by the trial judge. Other states permit Plaintiffs to specifically state the sum of money they are seeking.

X. Bench Trial Decisions

If the case is tried to the court, the trial judge may do one of the following:

1. Rule from the bench; or
2. Adjourn court and mail a memorandum of decision to the parties; or
3. Ask the parties to submit briefs pertaining to the issues presented at trial. After the briefs are received the judge will then write a memorandum of decision and mail it to the parties.

XI. Jury Trials: Interrogatories, Requests to Charge, and Jury Instructions

As stated in the previous chapter, in a jury trial, the judge's functions involve deciding issues and questions of law. When both parties have finished presenting their evidence and their closing arguments, the judge will then instruct the jurors on their role in the deliberations room and explain the principles of law that apply to the case. These instructions or the explanation are often referred to as **Jury Instructions** or the **Judge's Charge.** At this time, at the parties' request, the court will also submit **Interrogatories** (not related to any Interrogatories served during the Discovery Stage) to the jury. During the Judge's Charge, the courtroom is usually locked, to prevent any interruptions or distractions.

A. Interrogatories

The purpose of Interrogatories (these are different from the Interrogatories used as a discovery tool) is to ask the jurors to clarify their verdict by stating the *facts* (not the law) they determined to reach the verdict. As a result, Interrogatories may prevent the Plaintiff from unjustly receiving a **general verdict** in his or her favor on all of the counts or causes of action in the Complaint, if the facts determined by the jury only support a verdict for one count or cause of action.

Parties who want Interrogatories submitted to the jury must make this request in their **Requests to Charge,** to be discussed during the **charge confer-**

ence. (Both are described below.) If possible, the parties will work together to draft Interrogatories that are acceptable to everyone, and stipulate to them. The decision to submit Interrogatories is within the trial judge's discretion, although it appears that if there is more than one count or cause of action in the Plaintiff's Complaint, the Defendant's request should be granted.

B. Requests to Charge

Requests to Charge are a party's own written version of the **jury instructions** he or she wants the trial judge to use to explain the applicable law to the jury. Many judges already have their own jury instructions prepared, which they routinely use in civil cases. Other judges rely upon the parties to prepare this information. They will then review the information and make adjustments as they deem proper. Parties who draft a Request to Charge will find several texts in the law library that provide various versions of Requests to Charge that apply in civil cases.

C. Drafting a Request to Charge

Requests to Charge should follow the criteria stated below:

1. There is usually a limited number of specific requests, unless the trial judge permits more for good cause shown.
2. Each request should be in paragraph form and numbered separately.
3. Each request should state the specific "proposition of law," clearly and concisely, *in only one way,* and include the authority (case law) to support the proposition and the evidence presented at trial that the proposition applies to.

Usually, the parties may amend their Requests to Charge in writing at any time before the beginning of the charge conference.

D. Charge Conference

Either party may request a **charge conference.** During this conference, the trial judge will address the parties' Requests to Charge, if any, and disclose the general content of jury instructions (also known as the judge's charge) the jury will receive. This conference takes place out of the presence of the jury and before closing arguments. Any objections to the judge's proposed jury instructions should be made at this time and possibly resolved.

E. The Charge and Objections

After the trial judge charges the jury, the jury will be sent to a specific room to wait for further instructions. During this time, the judge will permit the attorneys to place their specific objections to the charge, and the grounds they rely upon, on the record. Sometimes the judge will call the jury back and amend a portion of the charge. If not, the objecting attorney must be sure to properly preserve his or objection as an issue for appeal.

XII. Deliberations

Jurors usually deliberate in a room adjacent to the courtroom that they have been using each day while waiting for court to begin, during recesses, and when the trial judge excuses them to listen to arguments from the attorneys that are not appropriate for them to hear. A court officer (often a deputy sheriff) is posted outside this room when the jury is inside, and especially during deliberations.

A. Beginning of Deliberations

At the start of deliberations, the jury will receive all the exhibits accepted into evidence. In addition, at the court's discretion, the jury will receive:

1. the Complaint, Counterclaim, and Cross Claim and responsive pleadings thereto (i.e., the Answer to each); and possibly
2. a copy or tape recording of the jury instructions (judge's charge); or
3. upon the jury's request, a copy or tape recording of an appropriate portion of the jury instructions.

B. During Deliberations: Review of Testimony and Request for Additional Instructions

During deliberations, the jury is permitted to request to review testimony of the trial. In addition, the jury may request that the judge reread a portion of the jury instructions or provide additional jury instructions to help them reach a verdict. If this occurs, the judge will provide each party with the opportunity to make suggestions regarding this request for additional instructions.

XIII. The Verdict

A. Unanimous Verdict

In most states, all six jurors must agree on the verdict. When the verdict is reached, the jury will contact the court officer guarding the room, who will notify the clerk, the judge, and the parties. If the jury is unable to agree, the judge may require it to continue deliberating, but will not threaten or require it to deliberate for unreasonable intervals or lengths of time. The judge may also provide instruction regarding disagreements.

B. Reconsideration

A judge may send a jury back to deliberate further if it believes the jury has mistaken the evidence or arrived at a verdict that is contrary to the evidence, or contrary to the court's direction on a matter of law.

C. Reading the Verdict

Once a verdict is reached, a member of the jury (usually the foreperson) will write the verdict on a form and give the form to the court officer. The officer will give the form to the courtroom clerk who will hand it to the judge. After reviewing the verdict, the judge will give back the form to the clerk who will read the verdict aloud.

D. Polling the Jury

To be certain a jury verdict is unanimous, either party may request that the jury be polled. This request must be made before the jury is discharged. In addition, the judge may proceed without a request.

To **poll the jury** means that the clerk will ask each individual juror, out loud, if the verdict announced was in fact his or her verdict. If the verdict was not unanimous, the jury will be sent back to continue deliberations or may be discharged.

E. Accepting the Verdict

If everything is in order, the judge will **accept the verdict** "without comment." Note, however, that Chapter 21 discusses motions that either party may make to challenge the verdict.

F. Discharging the Jury

After a verdict or a *mistrial,* the judge will discharge the jury.

XIV. Conclusion

Key Issues in This Chapter

1. Two types of evidence are often introduced at trial: *exhibits* and *testimony* from witnesses.
2. Plaintiffs begin each case with their *case in chief.* When the Plaintiff *rests,* the Defendant presents his or her case, which is followed by the Plaintiff's *rebuttal.*

3. During the trial, if a party disagrees with the judge's ruling on an issue, the applicable court rules and laws of evidence may require him or her to take an exception in order to preserve that issue for appeal.
4. The Plaintiff's burden of proof is *preponderance of evidence.*
5. *Direct examination* takes place when a party questions his or her own witnesses. After direct examination, the opposing party will ask the witness questions through *cross examination. Re-direct, re-cross,* and *rebuttal* follow.
6. When submitting a *Request to Charge,* timely present it to the trial judge. Include *Interrogatories,* if applicable. In addition, ask the judge for a *charge conference.* During the conference, inform the judge of any objections you may have to the proposed jury instructions.
7. After the jury instructions are given, an attorney who objects to a portion of the judge's charge must be sure to properly preserve the issue for appeal, outside the presence of the jury.
8. If necessary, after the verdict is announced, a party may ask the court to poll each juror to make sure the verdict was unanimous.

STATE SUMMARIES

Trials in Connecticut

Details of trial procedures addressed in the main chapter can be found in Chapter 5 and Chapter 16 of the *Connecticut Practice Book.*

Trials in Massachusetts

Details of trial procedures addressed in the main chapter can be found in Rules 47, 48, 49, and 51 of the *Massachusetts Rules of Civil Procedure.* See also Super. Ct. Rules 5-8A, 13, 14, 24, and 25.

Note: According to Rule 48, civil cases in Massachusetts may have up to 12 jurors. In this situation, the verdict does not have to be unanimous.

Trials in New Jersey

Details of trial procedures addressed in the main chapter can be found in Rules 1:7 and 1:8 and 4:39.

Trials in New York

Details of trial procedures addressed in the main chapter can be found in CPLR 4001 et seq. Unif. Rule 202.33 discusses jury selection. In addition, Unif. Rule 202.35 discusses submitting the pleadings and Bill of Particulars and any relevant statutory provisions by the party who filed the Note of Issue. At the parties' option or by court order, they may also serve and file a trial memorandum.

Note: Although a civil jury trial is typically tried to six jurors, the verdict does not have to be unanimous. Instead, a vote of five out of six is sufficient. See CPLR 4104-416 and 4113.

Trials in Rhode Island

Details of trial procedures in Rhode Island can be found in Rules 38-40, 43-46, 48-49, and 51-52.

Example 20-1. Massachusetts, Plaintiff's Jury Instructions

COMMONWEALTH OF MASSACHUSETTS

HAMPDEN, SS.

SUPERIOR COURT
DEPARTMENT OF
THE TRIAL COURT
CIVIL ACTION
NO. 98-0000

GEORGE JONES, JR., by his father and next friend, GEORGE JONES, SR.
Plaintiff

v.

CITY IN MASSACHUSETTS,
Defendant

PLAINTIFF'S REQUEST FOR JURY INSTRUCTIONS

Now comes the Plaintiff and hereby requests that in addition to the normal instructions that the Court instruct the jury as follows:

(1) In a civil case, the party having the burden of persuading you need only prove that a fact exists by a "preponderance of the evidence." To establish a fact by a preponderance of the evidence means to prove that it is more likely to be so than not to be so. You must weigh the evidence that supports a fact in issue and compare it with the evidence opposed to that fact. A fact is proved by a preponderance of the evidence if, in weighing the evidence, that fact appears even slightly more likely or probable, notwithstanding any doubts that may still linger in your minds. *Sargent v. Massachusetts Accident Co.,* 307 Mass. 246, 250 (1940).

(2) The Commonwealth and its counties, municipalities, and districts may be liable for personal injuries, death or property damages caused by the negligent or wrongful conduct of its public employees acting within the scope of their employment. *Whitney v. City of Worcester,* 373 Mass. 208 (1977); M.G.S. C. 258, sec. 1.

Note to readers: In a real request, more instructions would be included. Also, don't forget the certification of service.

Example 20-2. Massachusetts, Defendant's Jury Instructions

COMMONWEALTH OF MASSACHUSETTS

HAMPDEN, SS.

SUPERIOR COURT
DEPARTMENT OF
THE TRIAL COURT
CIVIL ACTION
NO. 98-0000

GEORGE JONES, JR., by his father
and next friend, GEORGE JONES, SR.
Plaintiff

v.

CITY IN MASSACHUSETTS,
Defendant

DEFENDANT'S REQUEST FOR
JURY INSTRUCTIONS

Now comes the Defendant and hereby requests that in addition to the normal instructions that the Court instruct the jury as follows:

(1) The mere occurrence of an accident is not evidence of negligence. *Linergan v. American Railway Express Co.,* 250 Mass. 30, 36 (1924).

(2) The Plaintiff has the burden of proving by a preponderance of the evidence not only that the Defendant was negligent, but that he incurred damages or injury as a direct and proximate result of the Defendant's negligence and unless you find both of these elements, you must find for the Defendant. *Coburn v. Moore,* 320 Mass. 116 (1949); *Williams v. Fontes,* 9 Mass. App. Ct. 883 (1980).

Note to readers: In a real request, more instructions would be included. Also, don't forget the certification of service.

Example 20-3. Rhode Island, Interrogatories to Jury

STATE OF RHODE ISLAND
PROVIDENCE, SC.

SUPERIOR COURT

JOHN MARTIN	:	C.A. NO. PC 98-0000
v.	:	
JAMES TYLER, PETER SMITH and LUCY SMITH	:	

PLAINTIFF, JOHN MARTIN'S INTERROGATORIES ADDRESSED TO THE JURY

(1) Was Defendant, James Tyler, negligent and was that negligence the proximate cause of the accident?

Answer: Yes: ___________ No: ___________

If your answer to Question No. 1 is "yes," state what percentage of responsibility James Tyler bears. The total negligence of any or all of the defendants would be 100%. If you find James Tyler is the sole cause of the accident, than you should answer the following question with "100%." If you find James Tyler was not the sole cause, you should answer the following question with that percentage which is less than 100%.

James Tyler's percentage of negligence: _______________%

If you have answered the above question by stating James Tyler was 100% responsible for this accident, skip Question No. 2 and go directly to Question No. 3. If you found James Tyler to only be partially at fault for the accident or not at fault at all, answer Question No 2. Then answer Question No. 3.

(2) Was Defendant, Peter Smith, negligent and was that negligence the proximate cause of the accident?

Answer: Yes: ___________ No: ___________

If your answer to Question No. 2 is "yes," state what percentage of liability Peter Smith bears as follows:

Peter Smith's percentage of negligence: _______________%

(3) What is the total amount of damages recoverable by the Plaintiff, John Martin?

TOTAL DAMAGES: $_______________

21 The Trial Stage: Motions Filed during and after Trial

Terminology

Bank Execution	Set Aside Verdict	Reduce Verdict	Mistrial
Remittitur	Prima Facie	Additur	Judgment Lien
Wage Execution	Collateral Source	Postjudgment	
Property Execution	Stay of Execution	Taxation of Costs	

Introduction

Under certain circumstances, the court may call a **mistrial** at any time during a trial and essentially end the case. In addition, the Defendant may ask the court to end the trial and direct the verdict in his or her favor because the Plaintiff did not meet the burden of proof during the case in chief. Finally, after the jury reaches a verdict, the parties may file one or more of several motions that challenge the verdict within ten days of the judge's acceptance of the verdict.

I. Motions Made during Trial

A. Mistrials

A mistrial is appropriate at any time if it appears that the trial cannot or should not continue. Either party may make a motion, orally or in writing, for a mistrial, or the judge may call a mistrial on its own. A mistrial can be appropriate in bench trials and in jury trials. If a party is making a motion for a mistrial in a jury trial, the motion should be made outside the presence of the jury.

Examples of reasons for mistrials include: If the trial judge becomes ill in the middle of a long and complicated case and cannot complete the trial; if one of the parties violates a rule or statute, such as inappropriately mentioning the availability of insurance to the jury, and the judge believes this reference will substantially interfere with and prejudice the jury's deliberations; if a jury cannot reach a unanimous verdict, regardless of its diligent efforts. When a mistrial occurs, the case will be rescheduled to begin a new trial at another time.

B. Motion for Dismissal: Bench Trials

At the conclusion of the Plaintiff's case in chief, a Defendant may make a motion to the court to dismiss the case, on the grounds that the Plaintiff failed to establish a **prima facie** case against the Defendant. In other words, the Defendant claims that the Plaintiff's evidence, if fully believed, would not permit the court to find in favor of the Plaintiff on the Complaint.

When deciding the motion, the court must treat the Plaintiff's evidence as true and draw every reasonable inference in the Plaintiff's favor. If the Motion for Dismissal is granted, the case is finished. If it is denied, the trial continues and the Defendant will present his or her case.

C. Motion for Directed Verdict: Cases Tried to a Jury

A Motion for Directed Verdict is appropriate in cases tried to a jury, not to the court. It is typically brought by the Defendant at the conclusion of the Plaintiff's case in chief and should be made outside the presence of the jury.

The purpose of a Motion for Directed Verdict is to ask the court to stop the trial, remove the case from the jury (discharge the jury), and render a verdict in the Defendant's favor. If the motion is denied, the trial will continue.

A Defendant making a Motion for a Directed Verdict must convince the court that the evidence presented by the Plaintiff, even if viewed in the Plaintiff's favor, will still cause the jury to reasonably and legally find in favor of the Defendant. Note that our courts do not grant a Motion for a Directed Verdict often. Instead, they prefer the jury to have the opportunity to hear the entire case and reach a verdict.

II. Motions Made after Verdict Is Accepted

After the verdict is accepted, a party who disagrees with the verdict has a specific amount of time to file one or more of the following:

1. **Motion to Set Aside Verdict** or Motion for New Trial: usually filed by the party who lost the case or who is dissatisfied with the outcome of the trial;

2. **Motion for Remittitur:** filed by the Defendant to reduce the verdict;
3. **Motion for Additur:** filed by a prevailing Plaintiff who wants the court to increase the verdict;
4. **Motion for Reduction of Verdict:** filed by the Defendant to reduce the verdict in the amount the Plaintiff has already received from **collateral sources.**

A. Motion to Set Aside Verdict or Motion for New Trial

The grounds for a Motion to Set Aside Verdict must assert that the evidence presented at trial does not support or justify the verdict. Therefore, the verdict must be set aside and a new trial must occur.

This motion is commonly filed by Plaintiffs in cases where the jury found in favor of the Defendant and did not award any damages to the Plaintiff or vice versa. In addition, it is often filed if no damages are awarded on a Counterclaim or Cross Claim or by both parties, if they are both dissatisfied with the verdict.

B. Motion for Additur and Motion for Remittitur

These motions are appropriate if the jury awards damages on a Complaint, Counterclaim, or Cross Claim. They may also be filed in conjunction with a Motion to Set Aside Verdict or Motion for New Trial.

1. A Motion for Additur permits the Plaintiff to ask the court to increase the amount of the jury's verdict, based upon the law and the evidence presented at trial.
2. A Motion for a Remittitur permits the Defendant to ask the court to reduce the jury's verdict, on the grounds of a mistake, a clerical error, or that the verdict is excessive, based upon the law and the evidence presented at trial.

C. Motion to Reduce Verdict: Collateral Source Payments

In many states, a Motion to Reduce Verdict is appropriate if the jury awards damages to the Plaintiff and some or all of the Plaintiff's medical bills claimed in the lawsuit have already been paid by another source. This source is called a **collateral source** and usually involves payments made pursuant to medical insurance. In this situation, a Defendant is permitted to ask the court to reduce the jury's verdict by the amount of money the Plaintiff already received, either directly or on his or her behalf, from such collateral sources. Note that verdicts in favor of Counterclaims and Cross Claims may also be reduced by the amount paid from a collateral source.

III. Rendering Judgment

A. When No Motions Challenging the Verdict Are Filed

If no motions challenging the jury's verdict are filed within a specific time period, the trial judge who accepted will render judgment on the verdict and include, if applicable, any adjustments required by statutes, with costs. The date of the judgment shall be the date the verdict was accepted.

B. When Motions That Challenge the Verdict Are Filed

After the court rules on one or more of these post-trial motions, it will render judgment according to its decision(s). The date of the judgment shall be the date the court decided the last motion.

IV. Taxation of Costs

In most states, parties who win their cases at trial (not at settlement) are entitled to be reimbursed by the opposing party for certain costs they expended in order to prosecute or defend the lawsuit. This is known as **taxation of costs.** Each case is addressed individually. In addition, such tax action could be directly affected by an Offer of Judgment that is rejected. See pages 339-340.

V. Postjudgment Procedures: Collecting Judgments

Once a party (presume it's a Plaintiff) obtains a verdict in his or her favor, the next hurdles involve whether the Defendant will appeal, and if not, when and how the verdict (now called the judgment) will be paid. As stated in Chapter 18, if a Plaintiff obtained a Prejudgment Remedy, the attached assets may be sufficient to pay the judgment, or if the Defendant is covered by sufficient insurance, the Plaintiff should have little difficulty being paid. On the other hand, if the Defendant refuses to cooperate or is judgment proof, the Plaintiff must look to postjudgment procedures to determine how to collect from the Defendant.

Postjudgment procedures include filing a **judgment lien** on the Defendant's real estate or, if appropriate, on his or her business (such as a corporation) at the Secretary of the State's Office.

Once a judgment lien is filed, one of two things could take place: The Defendant will not be able to sell or transfer the liened asset without first paying the judgment to the Plaintiff (because otherwise, the new buyer or transferee will become responsible for the Defendant's debt), or the Plaintiff may foreclose on the real estate that is liened and take the proceeds as payment of the judgment or attempt to sell off the assets belonging to the corporation. In addition, the Plaintiff may seek assistance from the court by filing a court-issued form that requests one of the following:

1. A **wage execution:** The court orders the Defendant's employer to deduct a specific amount of money each pay period from the Defendant's paycheck and send it to the Plaintiff until the judgment is paid.
2. A **bank execution:** The court orders a bank where the Defendant has an account to withdraw the funds in the account, up to the amount of the judgment (and permitted costs), and pay those funds to the Plaintiff.
3. A **property execution:** The court orders the Defendant's assets (other than real estate) to be seized and sold at auction. The proceeds are paid to the Plaintiff, up to the amount of the judgment.

Note that bank, wage, and property executions are usually handled by sheriffs or constables in their precincts. The money is paid first to them. They, in turn, will forward it to the Plaintiff. Their fee is usually 10 percent of the total amount received, above the amount of the judgment, which is paid by the Defendant. Therefore, it does not cost the Plaintiff any additional money.

VI. Conclusion

A. Key Issues in This Chapter

1. Motions for Mistrial and Motions for Directed Verdict are made during the trial.
2. Parties who are dissatisfied with a verdict may file one or more of several motions within (usually) ***ten days*** of the judge accepting the verdict. If necessary, file a Motion for Extension of Time to file these motions.

B. Appeal

The trial is over. Now what? Either side who is aggrieved by the final judgment may appeal the case to an appellate court. An appeal will **stay** the judgment (otherwise known as a stay of execution). This means that if judgment entered for the Plaintiff, the Defendant will not be required to pay the judgment until after the appeal is decided. In the appeal, the aggrieved party will allege that the trial court made an error during the trial that was contrary to the law. As a result, the party is entitled to a new trial or to judgment in his or her favor.

STATE SUMMARIES

Connecticut: Motions Made during and after a Trial

Pbs 16-35 through 17-3 address motions made during and after trial. Those that challenge the verdict must be served no later than ***ten days*** after the day the verdict is accepted.

Massachusetts: Motions Made during and after a Trial

Rules 50, 58, and 59 address motions that a party may bring during the trial and afterward. Those that challenge the verdict must be served no later than ***ten days*** after the court enters judgment. See also Super. Ct. Rule 26.

New Jersey: Motions Made during and after a Trial

Rules 4:40-1 and 2 as well as 4:49-1 and 2 address motions made during and after trial. Those that challenge the verdict must be served no later than ***ten days*** after the verdict. Rule 4:50 et seq. may also be helpful.

New York: Motions Made during and after a Trial

CPLR 4401 et seq. discusses motions made during and after trial. According to CPLR 4405, post-trial motions should be served and filed no later than ***15 days*** after the decision or verdict is entered or the jury is discharged.

Rhode Island: Motions Made during and after a Trial

Rules 50, 59, 60 and 62 discuss motions made during and after trial. Post-trial motions should be served and filed no later than ***ten days*** after the decision or verdict. Rule 54 discusses taxation of costs.

Example 21-1. Connecticut, Motion for Additur (presume the case did not settle)

DOCKET NO. CV 96-0333333 S	:	SUPERIOR COURT
SARAH A. DONAHUE	:	JUDICIAL DISTRICT OF TOLLAND
VS.	:	AT ROCKVILLE
RICHARD P. ANDREW	:	(date)

MOTION FOR ADDITUR

Pursuant to Connecticut Practice Book Section 16-35, the Plaintiff, Sarah A. Donahue, hereby moves the court to increase the jury verdict accepted on _________, _____________ on the ground that the award of noneconomic damages is inadequate as a matter of law, given the uncontroverted evidence at trial that the Plaintiff sustained permanent injuries.

Wherefore, the undersigned respectfully moves this court to increase the award of noneconomic damages consistent with the evidence at trial.

THE PLAINTIFF

BY ____________________________

Christine Kulas, Esq.
Law Offices of Christine Kulas,
her attorney
P.O. Box 2005
Ellington, CT 06066
Tele. #(860) 222-2222
Juris #989898

ORAL ARGUMENT REQUESTED
TESTIMONY NOT REQUIRED

ORDER

The foregoing Motion having been considered by the Court, it is hereby ORDERED: GRANTED/DENIED.

____

JUDGE/CLERK

CERTIFICATION

I hereby certify that a copy of the foregoing Motion for Additur was mail on _______ to all counsel and pro se parties of record, namely: Attorney Neil E. Clifford, of Michaels, Sabrina and Alexander, P.C., 259 Sage Road, Suite 200, West Hartford, CT 06080.

____

Commissioner of the Superior Court

Example 21-2. Connecticut, Objection to Motion for Additur

DOCKET NO. CV 96-0333333 S	:	SUPERIOR COURT
SARAH A. DONAHUE	:	JUDICIAL DISTRICT OF TOLLAND
VS.	:	AT ROCKVILLE
RICHARD P. ANDREW	:	(date)

OBJECTION TO MOTION FOR ADDITUR

The Defendant, Richard P. Andrew, hereby objects to the Plaintiff's Motion for Additur dated______________ on the grounds stated below.

The Plaintiff maintains that the verdict which awarded economic damages only is inadequate as a matter of law because the evidence introduced at trial demonstrated that she suffered permanent injuries. As a result, the Plaintiff is essentially asking the court to add noneconomic damages to the jury's verdict.

The evidence offered by the Plaintiff at trial indicated that she incurred medical bills in the amount of $9,035.00 and lost wages in the amount of $4,200. There was further evidence that she suffered a permanent partial disability to her _______.

In determining whether the verdict is inadequate as a matter of law, certain other evidence is pertinent. For instance, although Dr. Feller testified that the Plaintiff had been assessed with a permanent partial disability rating, the jury could have found that she nonetheless:

(a) was capable of working at three different types of employment within six months after the accident;
(b) earned $14,600 more during the year of her injury than she'd earned the previous year;
(c) earned $23,000 more the year following the injury which she has maintained for the past two years before trial.

As a result, the jury could have reasonably found that the Plaintiff suffered minimal pain as a result of her injuries. It is also possible that the jury did not credit the evidence suggesting that the Plaintiff would be compelled to undergo future surgery.

It is the function of the jury to award fair, just and reasonable damages. If the verdict does not fall outside the limits of what amounts to reasonable compensation, it is improper for the court to increase the verdict pursuant to a Motion for Additur. *Fox v. Mason,* 189 Conn. 484, 489, 490 (1983). Where the verdict does not go against the evidence and when there is no evidence that the jury was improperly influenced by prejudice, partiality, mistake or corruption, the verdict must stand. *Ricket v. Fraser,* 152 Conn. 678, 682 (1965); *Zarrelli v. Barnum Festival Society, Inc.*, 6 Conn. App. 322, 327 (1983). The jury had the right to accept part of the evidence presented and to reject the remainder. *Ricket v. Fraser,* supra, 581. Clearly, the jury in the instant case did not credit or believe that the Plaintiff's permanent partial injury justified noneconomic damages and the evidence introduced demonstrated that it could have reasonably and fairly reached the conclusion that it did.

Based upon the foregoing, the Defendant respectfully moves that his Objection to the Plaintiff's Motion for Additur be sustained.

THE DEFENDANT

BY ________________________________

Neil E. Clifford, Esq.
Michaels, Sabrina and Alexander, P.C.,
his attorney
259 Sage Road, Suite 200
West Hartford, CT 06080
Tele. # (860) 111-1111
Juris # 626262

ORDER

The foregoing Objection having been considered by the Court, it is hereby ORDERED: SUSTAINED/OVERRULED.

CERTIFICATION

I hereby certify that a copy of the foregoing was mailed on ______________ to all counsel and pro se parties of record, namely: Attorney Christine Kulas, Law Offices of Christine Kulas, P.O. Box 2005, Ellington, CT 06066.

____

Commissioner of the Superior Court

Example 21-3. New Jersey, Motion for Remittitur or New Trial

GRAVEY, MADISON AND PAUL, P.C.
190 Court Street
Newark, New Jersey 07102-5497
(201) 623-0000
Attorneys for Defendant/Third-Party Plaintiff,
Safety Insurance Co.

BIRCH REALTY COMPANY Plaintiff	:	SUPERIOR COURT OF NJ LAW DIVISION: BERGEN COUNTY
vs.	:	DOCKET NO.: BER-L-11111-98
SAFETY INSURANCE CO., Defendant	:	Civil Action
vs.	:	NOTICE OF MOTION FOR JUDGMENT NOTWITHSTANDING THE VERDICT
JOSEPH DEXTER Third-Party Plaintiff	:	

TO: Robert A. Hathaway,
Marsh & Marsh
2719 Bergen Street
Wayne, New Jersey 07470

COUNSEL:

PLEASE TAKE NOTICE that Defendant/Third-Party Plaintiff, Safety Insurance Company, through its undersigned attorneys, will move before the Superior Court of New Jersey, Law Division, Bergen County, at the Bergen County Courthouse, 119 Justice Center, 10 Main Street, Hackensack, New Jersey on _______ or as soon thereafter as counsel may be heard, for judgment notwithstanding the verdict (N.O.V.) dismissing Plaintiff's loss of business income claim or alternatively, for an order of remittitur and/or directing that a new trial be granted;

PLEASE TAKE FURTHER NOTICE that Safety Insurance Company will rely on the brief submitted herewith, together with the record of the trial of this action. A proposed form of Order is also submitted herewith;

PLEASE TAKE FURTHER NOTICE that Safety Insurance Company hereby requests oral argument.

GRAVEY, MADISON & PAUL, P.C.
Attorneys for Defendant/Third-Party Plaintiff
Safety Insurance Company

By: ______________________________
Walter Madison

CERTIFICATION OF SERVICE

I hereby certify that on _____ I have caused an original and one copy of the within Notice of Motion, Brief of Defendant/Third-Party Plaintiff Safety Insurance Company and a proposed form of Order to be filed via hand delivery with the Clerk, Bergen County, Superior Court of New Jersey, 10 Main Street, Justice Center, Hackensack, New Jersey and one copy was hand-delivered to:

Robert A. Hathaway, Esq.
Marsh & Marsh
2719 Bergen Street
Wayne, New Jersey, 07470

Dated: _______________ ______________________________

Walter M. Madison

22 THE APPEALS STAGE

TERMINOLOGY

Amicus Curiae
Brief
Record
Final Judgment
Petition for Certification
Articulation
Reply Brief
Advance Sheets
Appellee
Rectification
Preargument Conference
Aggrieved Party
Appellant

INTRODUCTION

This chapter provides a broad overview of Appellate practice. Appellate practice is extremely specialized and the rules can be quite technical. In fact, entire texts have been devoted to appellate procedure and some law firms handle only appeals, and no other types of litigation. Therefore, be sure to carefully read and follow all applicable court rules and statutes. Last, please note that when I refer to the Supreme Court, I am talking about any state's highest court.

I. THE TRIAL COURT AND APPEALS

A party who files an appeal disagrees with the outcome of his or her case in a lower court. In many instances, this lower court is the Superior Court and is usually referred to as the trial court when appeals are discussed.

The availability of the appeals process keeps trial judges in check when making decisions. It has caused trial court judges to constantly feel as if they are in the hot seat. Without warning, they are expected to make split-second decisions regarding all types of issues that arise. They don't have time to stop the trial and do hours of research or consult a law clerk. Instead, all eyes peer at these judges, expecting them to deliver instant pearls of wisdom. Afterward, if the case is appealed, the Appellate Court or Supreme Court will have several weeks or even months to review the trial record and the parties' briefs to determine if mistakes were made. Hence, trial court judges are at a significant disadvantage and work extremely hard to make proper rulings.

II. The Parties to an Appeal

The party who files an appeal is called the **Appellant.** The opposing party is called the **Appellee.** In many states, however, the courts prefer the parties to be referred to as Plaintiffs and Defendants whenever possible. Nevertheless, to avoid confusion here, we will use Appellant and Appellee.

In addition to the parties that were part of the trial court case, an individual or entity may be permitted to file a brief (see Section VII below) as an **Amicus Curiae,** translated as a friend of the court, to voice an opinion contrary to or in support of the issue(s) on appeal. In many instances, these individuals are acting on behalf of a governmental body such as the state's Attorney General's Office or an activist group.

III. The Appellate Court and the Supreme Court: Overview

As you read in Chapter 2, most states (except Rhode Island) have a three-tiered court system. The Superior Court is the trial court (except in New York) and the lowest of the three tiers. The Appellate Court (or Appeals Court) is often referred to as the intermediate court. Neither are trial courts. Instead, each appeal is usually decided by a panel of justices who refer only to the trial record, the parties' briefs, and the law. There are no witnesses or exhibits and no new evidence is presented.

In every state, the **aggrieved party** is entitled to at least one appeal. It is usually to the Appellate Court. Very few cases (except in Rhode Island) are appealed directly to the Supreme Court. If, after the appeal is decided, a party disagrees with the Appellate Court decision, he or she may file a **Petition for Certification** and ask the Supreme Court for permission to file an appeal. If the petition is granted, a new appeal begins. If the petition is denied, the Appellate Court's decision stands.

IV. Types of Civil Cases That May Be Appealed: Final Judgments

Most states agree that an aggrieved party may appeal from a **final judgment,** except as otherwise provided by law. Typically, the aggrieved party is the party who loses his or her case in the trial court. A final judgment means that the trial court case has been decided and is now finished. See the examples stated below.

A. Judgment on a Complaint

A party who loses on a Complaint is an aggrieved party and may appeal that judgment. In these cases, the judgment is a *final judgment* because the case is over, unless a Counterclaim, Cross Claim, or Third-Party action is still pending.

A final judgment on a Complaint may occur in one or more of the following ways:

1. after a trial, when a verdict is rendered in favor of either party;
2. when a Motion to Dismiss is granted;
3. when a Motion for Summary Judgment is granted;
4. when a nonsuit, default, or dismissal is granted and the court refuses to open the case or permit a new action.

B. Judgment on an Entire Counterclaim, Cross Claim, or Third-Party Action

Like a Complaint, a final judgment from a trial, a Motion to Dismiss, Motion for Summary Judgment, nonsuit, default, or dismissal can dispose of an entire Counterclaim or Cross Claim or Third-Party action. The case would then proceed at trial on the remaining Complaint.

C. Deferring an Appeal

When a part of a case is still ongoing, such as in the situations discussed in A. and B. above, an aggrieved party may defer his or her right to appeal a decision until the entire case is over. This can get very complicated. Therefore, be sure to check the applicable court rules.

D. Obtaining a Written Determination from the Appellate Court or the Supreme Court during a Trial

There are times when a trial court judge will permit a party to appeal regarding a decision made during a trial because the issue is of "such significance to the determination of the outcome of the case." Once the issue is decided, the trial will continue and the trial court will follow the Appellate Court or Supreme Court's decision. See applicable court rules for details.

V. Deadline to File an Appeal: 20 Days

Most states require an appeal to be filed within ***20 days*** from the date the notice of the judgment or decision is given. Be sure to check applicable court rules regarding how to calculate this deadline. Don't forget about post-trial motions and decisions that might delay the deadline, or that a party may file a motion for additional time to appeal.

VI. The Trial Court Record

As mentioned earlier and in Chapter 2, the Appellate and Supreme Courts base their decisions exclusively on the events that took place at trial. Therefore, the parties must present an adequate trial court record to be reviewed. This record includes relevant transcripts of the proceeding, the court's written memorandum of decision, if it is part of the appeal, relevant pleadings, motions, and related documents, objections, exhibits, etc. If an adequate record is not provided, the court will not be able to address the issue(s) on appeal.

A. Motion for Articulation

If the trial court decision on appeal is unclear, the Appellant must ask the trial court to explain it in writing by filing and serving a **Motion for Articulation.** For instance, if a judge grants a Motion to Dismiss from the bench with little or no explanation, or if he or she issues a written decision that is confusing or conflicting, the Motion for Articulation will ask the trial court to clarify and explain the legal basis for the decision in the form of a Memorandum of Decision.

In most cases, the trial court will comply with the Motion for Articulation. If not, or if the Memorandum of Decision is still unclear, the Appellant may ask the Appellate or Supreme Court to order the trial court to cooperate.

B. Motion for Rectification

If the Appellant believes the trial court record is inaccurate, he or she may file and serve a **Motion for Rectification** to correct any errors. As with a Motion for Articulation, most trial courts will comply. If not, the Appellant may ask the Appellate or Supreme Court for assistance.

VII. Briefs

The parties' briefs are crucial to an appeal and must be served and filed by Appellants and Appellees in each case. Typically, the Appellant will file his or her brief by a specific deadline stated in the applicable court rules. In most instances, this deadline is determined by the date the Appellant receives the relevant transcripts from the court reporter.

Upon receipt of the Appellant's brief, the Appellee will calculate when his or her opposing brief is due. Once it is served and filed, the Appellant has a specific number of days to serve and file a **Reply Brief.**

Essentially, briefs include the following:

1. the issues on appeal, i.e., the errors claimed to have occurred in the lower court;

2. specific references to these issues in the transcripts, pleadings, motions, etc.;
3. case law and statutes that support a ruling in favor of the party who drafted the brief.

VIII. Preargument Conferences

As in the trial court, the parties will have the opportunity to settle an appeal on their own or at a Preargument Conference in front of an Appellate or Supreme Court judge who will not be on the panel deciding the case. In many instances, these judges are retired from the Appellate or Supreme Court bench.

IX. Oral Argument

Most states permit the parties to orally argue the points raised in their briefs in front of the panel of justices who will ultimately decide the appeal. During this argument, the parties should be prepared to answer questions posed by the justices. Often, they are limited to no more than an hour each to present their arguments.

X. Decisions

Appellate and Supreme Court decisions are issued in writing as part of each state's reporter system. (See Chapter 2.) Usually, they are released once per week in **advance sheets** that may be placed in a loose-leaf type binder until a hardbound volume is published.

In addition to the advance sheets, some states permit the clerk's office to notify the parties by telephone of the decision and will fax it or permit them to pick up a copy a day or two before the advance sheet is available.

XI. Certification to the Supreme Court

This section focuses on cases that have been appealed to a state's Appellate Court. Dissatisfied with that decision, one of the parties decides to attempt to appeal it to the state's Supreme Court.

A. There Is No Right to a Supreme Court Appeal

As stated earlier, an appeal to a state's highest court is usually not automatic. Instead, the party who is aggrieved by an Appellate Court decision must ask permission to file a Supreme Court appeal in a **Petition for Certification.**

B. Possible Reasons Why the Supreme Court May Accept Certification

Below is a list of some of the reasons a Supreme Court may agree to hear an appeal. The list is not exhaustive, nor is a Supreme Court bound to it. Instead, it has sole discretion to accept or deny any appeal, for any reason.

1. When the Appellate Court has determined an issue that has not previously been addressed by the Supreme Court, or decided a case in a way that may not follow applicable Supreme Court precedent;
2. When the Appellate Court decision conflicts with other Supreme Court decisions;
3. When the Supreme Court believes the Appellate Court may have acted in a manner that may require Supreme Court supervision;
4. When issues of great public importance are involved;
5. When the Appellate Court judges agree on the end result of a case, but do not agree on the grounds for that decision;
6. When, prior to deciding an appeal, the Appellate Court informs the Supreme Court that it believes a transfer to the Supreme Court is appropriate.

XII. Filing a Petition for Certification

A. Time to File

In most instances, a Petition for Certification must be filed by the aggrieved party by the earlier of:

1. within a specific time period, often ***20 days*** from the date the Appellate Court decision is officially released; or
2. within a specific time period (again often ***20 days***) after issuance of notice of any order or judgment by the Appellate Court that finally determines the case.

Note: If a motion such as a Motion to Reargue or a Motion for Waiver of Fees and Costs is filed within that initial time period, a new time period will usually begin to run, as of the date that notice of a decision on the motion is issued by the court. In addition, a party who needs more time may usually file a Motion for Extension (or Enlargement) of Time.

B. Content of the Petition for Certification

A Petition for Certification is usually limited to a specific number of pages, exclusive of the index, and shall contain something similar to the following sections, in the order listed:

1. Statement of the Questions Presented for Review;
2. Statement of the Basis for Certification;
3. Summary of the Case (material facts);
4. Argument: state the reasons relied upon to support the petition; no other memorandum of law will be accepted;
5. An Index containing:
   a. a copy of the Appellate Court opinion or order at issue;
   b. a copy of any motion that would stay or extend the time for filing the petition;
   c. a list of all parties to the appeal in the Appellate Court, including names, addresses, telephone and fax numbers, and Juris Numbers.

C. Opposition to Petition for Certification

1. Statement of Opposition to Petition

A party who opposes certification must file a Statement in Opposition to Petition. This pleading should disclose any reasons why the Supreme Court should not grant certification and respond to the Petition for Certification, in form and content. This is not a Motion to Dismiss, but any jurisdictional challenges should be included. No other memorandum of law on this issue will be accepted.

2. Where and When to File

The Statement in Opposition must be filed in the clerk's office within a specific deadline and contain no more than a specific number of pages.

XIII. When Certification Is Granted or Denied

A. A Vote

A Petition for Certification will be granted by an affirmative vote, determined by applicable court rules. At this stage, the petitioner will become the Appellant. If the petition is denied, the Appellate Court's decision stands as the final decision.

B. The Appellant: Filing Fees

An Appellant who is granted certification must next pay the applicable Supreme Court filing fees within a specific time period and file any necessary documents.

C. Briefs, Preargument Conferences, Oral Arguments, and Decisions

Many of the rules relating to briefs, preargument conferences, oral argument, and sanctions are similar to those for the Appellate Court. Be sure to check deadlines, etc.

XIV. Sanctions

As stated earlier, specific court rules determine Appellate and Supreme Court procedures. Be sure to follow them carefully. For instance, if a party neglects to file a brief within the deadline and fails to obtain an extension of time, or intentionally fails to attend the Preargument Conference without permission, the applicable court could fine the party or, if the Appellant is at fault, even dismiss the appeal.

XV. Conclusion

Key Issues in This Chapter

1. Appeals may be taken from *final judgments* only.
2. The *Appellant* is the party who brings the appeal. The *Appellee* is the opposing party who defends the lower court's actions.
3. An appeal must be filed *within a specific time after notice of the final judgment or decision was given.* This deadline may be affected by motions that delay the commencement of the appeal period.
4. The parties must present an adequate trial court record. In most instances, this burden falls on the Appellant. Be sure to file a *Motion for Articulation* or a *Motion for Rectification* if more information or a correction is needed.
5. This chapter only highlights some of the more common issues that arise in appellate practice. Because Appellate and Supreme Court practice is so complicated and diverse, I have not added State Summaries at the end. Nevertheless, I feel confident that those of you who have mastered understanding how trial court rules are applied will have no difficulty deciphering the Appellate and Supreme Court rules that apply to your state.

XVI. Some Final Words

As I've said many times in this text, when practicing litigation in any court, always double check the court rules and statutes. Also check the case law to determine how these laws and statutes are interpreted. Laws and rules are amended every year and it's necessary to stay current.

Finally, good luck, keep your chin up, and remember: Law is an argumentative profession. If everyone got along, there would be no need for litigation. Don't fight the conflicts. Instead, allow them to stretch the limits of your imagination as you perfect the art of persuasion.

Appendix A: Litigation Checklist for Superior Courts in Massachusetts, New Jersey, and Rhode Island

Name of Case: ______________________________

Date of Incident: ____________ Statute of Limitations: ____________

Superior Court address and telephone #: ______________________

I. The Complaint

Causes of action: ______________________________

Draft Summons and Complaint and make sufficient copies: ____________

Jury Demand or court trial?: ______________________

Date case is filed in court:____________ Case number: ____________

II. Serve Defendant

Name and Tele. # of Proper Officer: ______________________

Deadline to make service: ______________________

Approve Return of Service: ______________________

Date, type of service, and location: ______________________

Date Return of Service is filed in court: ______________________

III. Defendant's Appearance

Name, address, telephone, and fax of defense attorney: ______________________

____

IV. The Pleadings: Defendant's 1st Pleading Due: ________

A. Answer: ______________ Jury Demand?: ______________________

Affirmative Defenses__________ *Counterclaim: ______________________

*Cross Claim against: ______________________

*Third-Party Action against: ______________________

____

(*If yes, create a separate list to address these claims.)

B. Motion to Dismiss: ______________ Obj. due: ______________________

Name of judge and date of decision: ______________________

Court's Decision: ______________________

C. Motion for More Definite Statement: ______________________

If no obj., compliance due:____________ Obj. due: ______________________

Judge's name and date of decision: ______________________

Decision/compliance due: ______________________

D. Motion to Strike: ____________________

If no obj., compliance due:__________ Obj. due: ____________________

Judge's name and date of decision: ____________________

Decision/compliance due: ____________________

V. Plaintiff's Discovery and Defendant's Compliance

A. Interrogatories and Requests for Production

Directed to: ____________________

Date Served: ____________ Responses/Obj. Due: ____________________

Motion to Extend Time?: ______New deadline: ____________________

Date responses received:______________ Objections?: ____________________

Discovery conference dates and results: ____________________

Name of judge, date and decision on objections: ____________________

____

Date to comply: ____________________

B. Requests for Inspection/Examination

Directed to: ____________________

Date Served:________________ Responses/Obj. Due: ____________________

Motion to Extend Time?: ______________ New deadline: ____________________

Date responses received: ___________ Objections?: ____________________

Discovery conference dates and results: ____________________

Name of judge, date and decision on objections: ____________________

____

Date to comply: ____________________

C. Disclosure of Defendant's Expert Witnesses

Date disclosed: ____________________

Names, addresses of experts: ____________________

D. Requests for Admission

Directed to: ______________________________

Date served: __________ Responses/Obj. due: ______________

Motion to Extend Time?: __________ New deadline: __________

Date responses received: __________ Objections?: ______________

Discovery conference dates and results: ______________

Name of judge, date and decision on objections: ______________

____

Date to comply: ______________________________

E. Request for Mental or Physical Exam (usually needed only if Defendant asserts a personal injury Counterclaim against Plaintiff)

Directed to: ______________________________

Date served: ______________ Name of doctor: ______________

Objection?: ______________________________

Discovery conference dates and results: ______________

Name of judge, date and decision on objections: ______________

Date to comply: ______________________________

F. Depositions: For each deposition:

1. Deponent's name and Address: ______________________________

Date and location of deposition: ______________________

Name of attorney conducting deposition: ______________

Name and telephone number of Court Reporter: ______________

Transcript received: __________ Transcript verified by deponent: __________

Copy of transcript sent to other parties: ______________

2. Deponent's Name and Address: ______________________________

Date and location of deposition: ______________________

Name of attorney conducting deposition: ______________

Name and telephone number of Court Reporter: ______________________

Transcript received: _________ Transcript verified by deponent: __________

Copy of transcript sent to other parties: ________________________

G. Other Discovery and Compliance Issues:

VI. Defendant's Discovery to Plaintiff and Plaintiff's Compliance

A. Interrogatories and Requests for Production

Directed to: ______________________________________

Date Served: __________ Responses/Obj. Due: ____________________

Motion to Extend Time?: _______ New deadline: ____________________

Date responses received: ____________ Objections?: ______________

Discovery conference dates and results: ______________________

Name of judge, date and decision on objections: ________________

Date to comply: ____________________________________

B. Requests for Inspection/Examination

Directed to: ______________________________________

Date Served: ____________ Responses/Obj. Due: __________________

Motion to Extend Time?: ____________ New deadline: ____________

Date responses received: _________ Objections?: __________________

Discovery conference dates and results: ______________________

Name of judge, date and decision on objections: ________________

Date to comply: ____________________________________

C. Disclosure of Defendant's Expert Witnesses

Date Disclosed: ____________________________________

Names, addresses of experts: ____________________________

D. Requests for Admission

Directed to: ______________________________

Date Served: __________ Responses/Obj. Due: ______________

Motion to Extend Time?: __________ New deadline: __________

Date responses received: __________ Objections?: ______________

Discovery conference dates and results: ______________

Name of judge, date and decision on objections: ______________

____

Date to comply: ______________________________

E. Request for Mental or Physical Exam (usually needed only if Defendant asserts a personal injury Counterclaim against Plaintiff)

Directed to: ______________________________

Date served: __________ Name of doctor: ______________

Objection?: ______________________________

Discovery conference dates and results: ______________

Name of judge, date and decision on objections: ______________

____

Date to comply: ______________________________

F. Depositions: For each deposition:

1. Deponent's name and address: ______________________________

Date and location of deposition: ______________________________

Name of attorney conducting deposition: ______________

Name and telephone number of Court Reporter: ______________

Transcript received: __________ Transcript verified by deponent: __________

Copy of transcript sent to other parties: ______________

2. Deponent's name and address: ______________________________

Date and location of deposition: ______________________________

Name of attorney conducting deposition: ______________________

Name and telephone number of Court Reporter: ______________________

Transcript received: __________ Transcript verified by deponent: __________

Copy of transcript sent to other parties: ______________________

G. Other Discovery and Compliance Issues:

VII. Pretrial

Date: ______________ Judge: ______________________

VIII. Trial

Date :______________ Judge: ______________________

IX. Conclusion

A. Settlement terms: ______________________

B. Verdict: ______________________

C. Appeal: ______________________

Appendix B: Litigation Checklist for Superior Courts in Connecticut

Name of Case: ______________________________

Date of Incident: ______________ Statute of Limitations: ______________

Superior Court address and telephone #: ______________________

I. The Complaint

Causes of action: ______________________________

Draft Summons and Complaint: ____________ Return Date: ____________

II. Serve Defendant

Name and tele. # of Proper Officer: ______________________

Deadline to serve: ____________ Approve Return of Service: ____________

Date, type of service, and location: ______________________

Deadline to file Summons, Complaint, Return of Service, and entry fee: ______

Date of filing: ______________________________

Docket Number: ______________________________

III. Defendant's Appearance

Deadline for Defendant to file Appearance: ____________________

Date filed: ____________________

Name, address, telephone, and fax of defense Attorney: ____________________

____

IV. The Pleadings: Defendant's 1st Pleading Due: _____

A. Motion to Dismiss: ____________________ Obj. Due: ____________________

Judge's name and date of decision: ____________________

Decision: ____________________

B. Request to Revise: ____________________

If no obj., compliance due: ____________________ Obj. due: ____________________

Judge's name and date of decision: ____________________

Decision: ____________________

Compliance due: ____________________

C. Motion to Strike: ____________________

If no obj., compliance due: ____________________

Obj. due: ____________________

Judge's name and date of decision: ____________________

Decision: ____________________

Compliance due: ____________________

D. Defendant's Answer: ____________________

Special Defenses: ____________________ Reply Due: ____________________

*Counterclaim: ____________________ *Cross Claim against: ____________________

*Third-Party action against: ____________________

(*If yes, create a new list to address these claims.)

E. Closed Pleadings: Certificate of Closed Pleadings

Filed by: ____________________ Date filed: ____________________

Court Trial: ________________ Claim for Jury and fee: ____________________

V. Plaintiff's Discovery and Defendant's Compliance

A. Interrogatories and Requests for Production

Directed to: ____

Date served: ________________ Responses/Obj. Due: ____________________

Motion to Extend Time?: __________ New deadline: ____________________

Date responses received: ________________ Objections?: ________________

Discovery conference dates and results: ____________________

Name of judge, date and decision on objections: ____________________

Date to comply: ____

B. Requests for Inspection/Examination

Directed to: ____

Date Served: ______________ Responses/Obj. Due: ____________________

Motion to Extend Time?: ______________ New deadline: ________________

Date responses received: __________ Objections?: ____________________

Discovery conference dates and results: ____________________

Name of judge, date and decision on objections: ____________________

Date to comply: ____

C. Disclosure of Defendant's Expert Witnesses

Date Disclosed: ____

Names, addresses of experts: ______________________________

D. Requests for Admission

Directed to: ____

Date Served: ________________ Responses/Obj. Due: ____________________

Motion to Extend Time?: _______________ New deadline: _______________

Date responses received: _______________ Objections?: _______________

Discovery conference dates and results: _______________

Name of judge, date and decision on objections: _______________

____

Date to comply: _______________

E. Request for Mental or Physical Exam (usually needed only if Defendant asserts a personal injury Counterclaim against Plaintiff)

Directed to: _______________

Date Served: _______________ Name of Doctor: _______________

Objection?: _______________

Name of judge, date and decision on objections: _______________

____

Date to comply: _______________

F. Depositions: For each deposition:

1. Deponent's name and address: _______________

Date and location of deposition: _______________

Name of attorney conducting deposition: _______________

Name and telephone number of Court Reporter: _______________

Transcript received: __________ Transcript verified by deponent: __________

Copy of transcript sent to other parties: _______________

2. Deponent's name and address: _______________

Date and location of deposition: _______________

Name of attorney conducting deposition: _______________

Name and telephone number of Court Reporter: _______________

Transcript received: __________ Transcript verified by deponent: __________

Copy of transcript sent to other parties: _______________

G. Other Discovery and Compliance Issues:

VI. Defendant's Discovery to Plaintiff and Plaintiff's Compliance

A. Interrogatories and Requests for Production

Directed to: ______________________________

Date Served: ____________ Responses/Obj. Due: ____________

Motion to Extend Time?: ____________ New deadline: ____________

Date responses received: ____________ Objections?: ____________

Discovery conference dates and results: ____________

Name of judge, date and decision on objections: ____________

Date to comply: ______________________________

B. Requests for Inspection/Examination

Directed to: ______________________________

Date Served: ____________ Responses/Obj. Due: ____________

Motion to Extend Time?: ____________ New deadline: ____________

Date responses received: ____________ Objections?: ____________

Discovery conference dates and results: ____________

Name of judge, date and decision on objections: ____________

Date to comply: ______________________________

C. Disclosure of Defendant's Expert Witnesses

Date Disclosed: ______________________________

Names, addresses of experts: ______________________________

D. Requests for Admission

Directed to : ______________________________

Date Served: ____________ Responses/Obj. Due: ____________

Motion to Extend Time?: ____________ New deadline: ____________

Date responses received: _______________ Objections?: ____________________

Discovery conference dates and results: ________________________________

Name of judge, date and decision on objections: ________________________

____

Date to comply: ____

E. Request for Mental or Physical Exam (usually needed only if Defendant asserts a personal injury Counterclaim against Plaintiff)

Directed to: ____

Date served: _________________ Name of doctor: _______________________

Objection?: ____

Name of judge, date and decision on objections: ________________________

____

Date to comply: ____

F. Depositions: For each deposition:

1. Deponent's name and address: ____

Date and location of deposition: ______________________________________

Name of attorney conducting deposition: _______________________________

Name and telephone number of Court Reporter: ___________________________

Transcript received: __________ Transcript verified by deponent: ___________

Copy of transcript sent to other parties: _______________________________

2. Deponent's name and address: ____

Date and location of deposition: ______________________________________

Name of attorney conducting deposition: _______________________________

Name and telephone number of Court Reporter: ___________________________

Transcript received: __________ Transcript verified by deponent: ___________

Copy of transcript sent to other parties: _______________________________

G. Other Discovery and Compliance Issues:

VII. Pretrial

Date: ____________________ Judge: ______________________________________

VIII. Trial

Date: ____________________ Judge: ______________________________________

IX. Conclusion

A. Settlement terms: ____

B. Verdict: ____

C. Appeal: ____

Appendix C: Litigation Checklist for Supreme Courts in New York

Name of Case: ______________________________

Date of Incident: ____________ Statute of Limitations: ____________

Superior Court address and telephone #: ____________________

I. The Complaint

Causes of action: ______________________________

Draft Summons and Complaint and make sufficient copies: ____________

Date case is filed in court: ____________ Index number: ____________

II. Serve Defendant

Name and Tele. # of Proper Officer: ____________________

Deadline to make service: ____________________

Approve Return of Service: ____________________

Date, type of service, and location: ____________________

Date Return of Service is filed in court: ____________________

III. Defendant's Appearance

Name, address, telephone, and fax of defense attorney: ____________________

____

IV. The Pleadings: Defendant's 1st Pleading Due: ______

A. Answer: ____

Affirmative Defenses ______________ *Counterclaim: ____________________

*Cross Claim against: ____

*Third-Party Action against: ____________________________________

(*If yes, create a separate list to address these claims.)

Date Demand for Bill of Particulars served: ______________________

Date responses due: ____

B. Motion to Dismiss: ______________________ Obj. due: ____________________

Name of judge and date of decision: ______________________________

Court's Decision: ____

C. Motion for More Definite Statement: ______________________________

If no obj., compliance due: ______________ Obj. due: ____________________

Judge's name and date of decision: ______________________________

Decision/compliance due: ____

D. Motion to Strike: ____

If no obj., compliance due: ______________ Obj. due: ____________________

Judge's name and date of decision: ______________________________

Decision/compliance due: ____

V. Plaintiff's Discovery and Defendant's Compliance

A. Interrogatories and Notice to Produce

Directed to: ____

Date Served: ________________ Responses/Obj. Due: ____________________

Motion to Extend Time?: ______________ New deadline: __________________

Date responses received: ____

Objections?: ____

Discovery conference dates and results: __________________________________

Name of judge, date and decision on objections: ___________________________

____

Date to comply: ____

B. Notice to Inspect/Examine

Directed to: ____

Date Served: ________________ Responses/Obj. Due: ____________________

Motion to Extend Time?: ______________ New deadline: __________________

Date responses received: ______________ Objections?: ____________________

Discovery conference dates and results: __________________________________

Name of judge, date and decision on objections: ___________________________

____

Date to comply: ____

C. Disclosure of Defendant's Expert Witnesses

Date disclosed: ____

Names, addresses of experts: ____

D. Notice to Admit

Directed to: ____

Date served: ________________ Responses/Obj. due: ____________________

Motion to Extend Time?: ______________ New deadline: __________________

Date responses received: ______________ Objections?: ____________________

Discovery conference dates and results: __________________________________

Name of judge, date and decision on objections: ___________________________

____

Date to comply: ______________________________

E. Notice of Mental or Physical Exam (usually needed only if Defendant asserts a personal injury Counterclaim against Plaintiff)

Directed to: ______________________________

Date served: ____________ Name of doctor: ______________

Objection?: ______________________________

Discovery conference dates and results: ______________

Name of judge, date and decision on objections: ______________

____

Date to comply: ______________________________

F. Depositions: For each deposition:

1. Deponent's name and address: ______________________________

Date and location of deposition: ______________________________

Name of attorney conducting deposition: ______________________________

Name and telephone number of Court Reporter: ______________________________

Transcript received: __________ Transcript verified by deponent: __________

Copy of transcript sent to other parties: ______________________________

2. Deponent's name and address: ______________________________

Date and location of deposition: ______________________________

Name of attorney conducting deposition: ______________________________

Name and telephone number of Court Reporter: ______________________________

Transcript received: __________ Transcript verified by deponent: __________

Copy of transcript sent to other parties: ______________________________

G. Other Discovery and Compliance Issues:

VI. Defendant's Discovery to Plaintiff and Plaintiff's Compliance

A. Interrogatories and Notice to Produce

Directed to: ______________________________

Date Served: ____________ Responses/Obj. Due: ____________

Motion to Extend Time?: ____________New deadline: ____________

Date responses received: ____________ Objections?: ____________

Discovery conference dates and results: ____________

Name of judge, date and decision on objections: ____________

____

Date to comply: ______________________________

B. Notice to Inspect/Exam

Directed to: ______________________________

Date Served: ____________ Responses/Obj. Due: ____________

Motion to Extend Time?: ____________ New deadline: ____________

Date responses received: ____________ Objections?: ____________

Discovery conference dates and results: ____________

Name of judge, date and decision on objections: ____________

____

Date to comply: ______________________________

C. Disclosure of Defendant's Expert Witnesses

Date Disclosed: ______________________________

Names, addresses of experts: ______________________________

D. Notice to Admit

Directed to: ______________________________

Date Served: ____________ Responses/Obj. Due: ____________

Motion to Extend Time?: ____________ New deadline: ____________

Date responses received: ____________ Objections?: ____________

Discovery conference dates and results: ____________

Name of judge, date and decision on objections: ____________

Date to comply: ____________

E. Notice for Mental or Physical Exam (usually needed only if Defendant asserts a personal injury Counterclaim against Plaintiff)

Directed to: ____________

Date served: ____________ Name of doctor: ____________

Objection?: ____________

Discovery conference dates and results: ____________

Name of judge, date and decision on objections: ____________

____

Date to comply: ____________

F. Depositions: For each deposition:

1. Deponent's name and address: ____________

Date and location of deposition: ____________

Name of attorney conducting deposition: ____________

Name and telephone number of Court Reporter: ____________

Transcript received: ____________ Transcript verified by deponent: ____________

Copy of transcript sent to other parties: ____________

2. Deponent's name and address: ____________

Date and location of deposition: ____________

Name of attorney conducting deposition: ____________

Name and telephone number of Court Reporter: ____________

Transcript received: ____________ Transcript verified by deponent: ____________

Copy of transcript sent to other parties: ____________

G. Other Discovery and Compliance Issues:

VII. Note of Issue and Certificate of Readiness

Filed: ______________ Jury Trial: ______________ Court Trial: ______________

VIII. Pretrial

Date: ____________________ Judge: ______________________________________

IX. Trial

Date: _____________________ Judge: _____________________________________

X. Conclusion

A. Settlement terms: ____

B. Verdict: ____

C. Appeal: ____

GLOSSARY

abode service Involves *service of process.* A *proper officer* may serve a Defendant a lawsuit by leaving copies of a *Summons* and *Complaint* **inside** the Defendant's home or inside any other residence where the Defendant currently lives and is most likely to receive notice of the action. **Note:** In some states it is sufficient to slip the documents under the door. In others, the documents must be handed to someone of a specific age or capacity who lives at the location.

affidavit A written statement, sworn to or *affirmed* under oath to be true to the best of one's knowledge. A third person such as a notary public administers the oath and signs and stamps the document under the person's signature.

affirmative defenses Called *special defenses* in Connecticut. Legally recognized grounds Defendants may rely upon to justify their actions alleged in a Plaintiff's Complaint to reduce or eliminate their liability. If applicable, these defenses should be made part of the Defendant's Answer to a Complaint.

Agent for Service An individual or entity who agrees to accept service of process on behalf of a corporation. The name and address of an Agent for Service should be on file at the applicable Secretary of State's Office. The Agent does not become liable for the corporation's actions. Instead, it merely accepts service and informs the corporation of the lawsuit.

agreement for representation See *retainer letter.*

amended pleadings New *pleadings* (documents) filed in court that the author alters by adding, deleting, or correcting the information set forth in the original pleadings.

Answer The Defendant's required response to the Plaintiff's *Complaint.* In addition to an Answer, the Defendant may include *Defenses* to the Complaint and/or a *Counterclaim, Cross Claim,* or *Third-Party Complaint.*

Answer (or Reply) to Counterclaim The Plaintiff's required response to the Defendant's Counterclaim. See *Answer.*

Appellant The party in a case who files an appeal to the appellate court or the supreme court.

appellate court Often referred to as the intermediate appeals court. In most states, appeals of cases from the trial court must first be filed in the state's appellate court. A party who is dissatisfied with the appellate court's decision may then ask the state's highest appeals court, often called the Supreme Court, to hear the appeal. Appellate court is also a term used to refer to courts that are above the trial court, where there is no jury, no witnesses, and no new evidence presented. Instead, this court makes its decisions based on what took place in the lower court.

Appellee The party in a case who did not file the appeal and finds himself or herself responding to the appeal by defending the trial court or intermediate appellate court decision.

articulation See *Motion for Articulation.*

bank execution A postjudgment collection procedure: a court-ordered attachment of a party's funds in a bank account that are used to pay a judgment the party owes to another. See also *property execution* and *wage execution.*

bench trial A trial in which a judge instead of a jury acts as the finder of fact and decides a case.

brief A document that is filed in court and addresses specific issues, by providing case law and arguments, regarding issues that have arisen in a case. See *memorandum of law.*

burden of proof The standard a Plaintiff must meet in order to prevail in court. In most civil cases, the Plaintiff's burden is by *preponderance of the evidence.* In a few types of civil cases, the burden of proof is *clear and convincing evidence.* In criminal cases, the burden of proof is *beyond a reasonable doubt.*

case caption Also known as a case heading. A case caption should appear at the top of the first page of every document filed in court. It contains the parties' names, the location of the court, the *docket number,* and the title of the document.

Certification of Service A specific statement that is required at the end of all documents after the Complaint is filed. Its purpose is to confirm that a copy of the pleading has been mailed or delivered to all other parties (or their counsel, if represented) of record.

challenges Pertains to *jury selection.* Each individual party in a lawsuit is given four challenges to use to excuse potential jurors from sitting on their case at trial.

charge Also known as the *judge's charge* or *jury instructions.* At a jury trial, after all the evidence and arguments have been presented, the judge will explain the law to the jury and instruct it regarding its role as a fact finder and in reaching a *verdict.*

civil litigation Proceedings and lawsuits that usually involve claims for money from Defendants for their noncriminal but harmful acts to Plaintiffs.

closed pleadings The status of the court's file on a case when the Defendant has filed an Answer and there are no other outstanding responsive pleadings that must be filed, such as a *Reply to Special Defenses,* an *Answer to Counterclaim,* etc.

closing argument Takes place at the end of the trial. After each party finishes introducing its evidence, it will have the opportunity to address the jury one last time and make a short statement concerning the case. The court will determine how long such arguments may be. Typically, each party has approximately one hour. The Plaintiff goes first. When the Defendant is finished, the Plaintiff will have one last, brief opportunity to speak.

Complaint A written document that sets forth, in paragraph form, a Plaintiff's cause of action against a Defendant. The *Complaint* is usually the first pleading filed in court in each lawsuit.

constable A proper officer who has the authority to perform service of process in a specific jurisdiction within a state.

continuance A postponement of a scheduled event or deadline.

Counterclaim An action a Defendant brings against a Plaintiff in the Plaintiff's lawsuit. The Counterclaim often contains allegations that relate to the allegations in the Plaintiff's Complaint. All rules that apply to a Complaint apply to a Counterclaim; the Plaintiff must file an *Answer* to the Counterclaim. In addition, he or she may assert *Special Defenses*, etc.

counts Each cause of action against each Defendant should be stated separately. A count is the term used to designate each cause of action, for instance, Count One: Breach of Contract; Count Two: Unjust Enrichment. In addition, in those cases that involve more than one Plaintiff or Defendant, it is common to have separate counts for each of them.

court filing fees Fees the court requires a party to pay if that party wishes to file certain documents such as a Complaint. Contact the clerk's office in the applicable courthouse to verify current fees.

court monitor Similar to a *court reporter* in that the individual provides a transcript of deposition or trial testimony. Note, however, that a court monitor uses a recording device rather than a stenograph machine or computer to record such testimony.

court reporter An individual who is qualified to properly record entire court proceedings and, if requested, transcribe that recording into a *transcript*.

Cross Claim In an attempt to reduce or extinguish liability to the Plaintiffs, if a lawsuit involves more than one Defendant, he or she may file a Cross Claim stating that the other Defendant(s) in the lawsuit is liable for all or part of the damages the Plaintiff seeks.

cross examination Occurs after *direct examination* of a party or witness. It is testimony of a witness (including a party) taken under oath during a *deposition*, a pretrial court argument, or during trial, pursuant to questions asked by the opposing party. Usually, these questions are closed-ended, requiring only a yes or no answer, and must relate to the witness' testimony that was elicited during *direct examination*. Often cross examination is used to challenge what a witness said during direct examination.

damages A sum of money the Plaintiff claims he or she has lost or is entitled to as a result of the Defendant's wrongful actions.

default A penalty against a Defendant who has failed to comply with a court order or rule. Once a default is obtained, the Plaintiff may attempt to proceed to judgment, rather than wait for a trial.

Defendant An individual or entity named in a lawsuit as a wrongdoer and who is being sued by the Plaintiff.

defense Grounds relied upon to explain a Defendant's actions (or a Plaintiff's actions if there is a Counterclaim) to reduce or eliminate the Defendant's liability. See *affirmative defenses.*

Demand for Relief In Complaints, the relief is actually the damages the Plaintiff seeks against the Defendant. It should be stated at the end of the Complaint and addressed to each count. (Caution: In most instances, the Plaintiff may not state a specific dollar amount.)

denied with prejudice When a court denies a motion and will not consider changing its mind if the issue or motion is raised again at a later time in the case.

denied without prejudice When a court denies a motion but may be willing to reconsider its decision if the motion is brought again at a later date.

deny When a court declines to grant what a party asks for in a *motion.*

deponent A person who testifies at his or her *deposition.*

deposition A type of discovery in which a person (a party or a nonparty) appears out of court, to testify regarding what he or she knows about a case. The testimony is made under oath and is recorded by a stenographer, such as a court reporter, or may be videotaped. The proceeding usually takes place in an attorney's office, with all attorneys and clients present. If requested, the court reporter will create a *transcript* of the testimony which can be used later at trial. A party who intends to take a *deposition* must notify all other parties in the action by serving them with a *Notice of Deposition.*

deputy sheriff A proper officer who is authorized to serve legal process in a specific jurisdiction within a state.

diarying Also called calendaring. Using one or more calendars to record important dates, as reminders for each case.

direct examination Questions asked of a witness by the party who called the witness to testify. For instance, during the Plaintiff's case in chief, the Plaintiff will conduct a direct examination of each witness he or she calls. Afterward, the Defendant will have the opportunity to challenge what the witness said through *cross examination.*

Disclosure of Expert Witnesses Formal notification to an opposing party regarding the identity of any experts, such as doctors, engineers, etc., a party intends to call at trial to support his or her claims. This information may be disclosed through answers to interrogatories as well as by other means.

discovery A formal investigation of a case, made pursuant to applicable court rules. Discovery includes: *Interrogatories, Requests for Production, Request for Admissions, Request for Mental or Physical Exams, Inspection of Property, Depositions* of parties and other witnesses. Discovery takes place during the Pretrial Stage, simultaneously with filing *pleadings* and *motions.*

dismissal A Plaintiff's case may be dismissed due to his or her failure to prosecute it with reasonable diligence.

docket number Also called a case number, index number, civil action number, etc. A series of numbers assigned by the court where the action is filed that is used to identify each case. The docket number must be included in the case caption of every document filed in court.

en banc When all the judges appointed to the Appellate Court or the Supreme Court sit at the same time to hear and decide a case.

Et Al An abbreviation used in case captions when there is more than one Plaintiff or Defendant.

Et Seq An abbreviation used to indicate more than one consecutive statue or rule.

evidence Testimony and exhibits; the information presented in court to support an argument or prove a case at trial. This information can be presented through witness testimony and through exhibits such as documents, photographs, records, etc. that are admitted into evidence through a specific witness who has a direct connection to the exhibit, unless the parties otherwise *stipulate.*

exception Pertains to disagreeing with a court's ruling on an objection. In certain circumstances, the party must inform the court that he or she takes *exception* to the court's ruling in order to preserve the right to appeal that ruling after the trial.

exhibits At trial, exhibits are tangible items that a party introduces to the trier of fact to prove his or her case. Exhibits may include photographs, documents, records, etc.

ex parte Communications or court orders that take place between one party and a judge, without the knowledge and/or consent of the other parties in a case.

expert witness A witness who possesses significant knowledge, education, and experience in a specific field that is not common knowledge to the average person. An expert witness is hired by a party to examine a situation and provide an opinion based upon his or her knowledge, education, and experience. See *Disclosure of Expert Witnesses.*

file Two definitions: **1.** As a noun, a file is a folder that contains information about a case. **2.** As a verb, to file something means to deliver a document to court to be accepted by the clerk who date and time stamps it, then adds the title of the document to the courthouse computer system and eventually places the document in a manila folder (the court's file) that contains all the documents filed under that case's *docket number* and *case caption.*

grant When a court agrees to order what a party is asking for.

hearing A mini trial in front of a judge, to resolve contested issues regarding the lawsuit. In most instances, hearings take place during the Pretrial Stage to address *motions.*

Independent Medical Exam (IME) A physical or mental medical examination, performed by an independent physician hired by the opposing party, to provide an objective opinion regarding the Plaintiff's mental or physical injuries or condition.

in hand service Occurs when a proper officer actually gives a copy of a *Summons* and *Complaint,* or any other type of document or pleading, to the party or person named in the document.

insufficiency of process Occurs when there is some type of mistake pertaining to the documents that are served upon a party or other person not named in a lawsuit, for instance, if a *Complaint* was served upon a Defendant without a *Summons* attached to it. In some states, it may also include a situation in which a Defendant is not served a copy of the Summons and Complaint within the time permitted under the applicable court rules.

insufficiency of service of process Occurs when there is some type of mistake pertaining to the way a party or other person not named in the lawsuit is served a specific document, for instance, if a *proper officer* failed to properly serve a *Summons* and *Complaint* upon a Defendant. See also *insufficiency of process.*

Interrogatories Two types: **1.** *Discovery:* written questions from one party that are directed to the opposing party to be answered under oath within a specific time period. **2.** At *Trial:* written questions directed to a *jury,* to be answered after it has reached a verdict in order to identify to the parties and the court the facts it relied upon to reach that verdict.

judge's charge See *charge* and *jury instructions.*

judgment A final decision in favor of one party and against the other in a case.

judgment proof When a Defendant party has little or no assets with which to pay a judgment that was entered against him or her.

jurisdiction The authority of a court to hear, decide, and enforce a judgment in a particular case.

Jury Claim When a party indicates, according to applicable court rules, that he or she wishes a jury to hear the trial and determine the outcome, rather than a judge.

jury instructions Also known as the *charge.* At a jury trial, after all the evidence and arguments have been presented, the judge will explain the law to the jury and instruct it regarding its role as a fact finder and in reaching a verdict. See *Requests to Charge.*

Jury List Part of the *Trial List.* A list of cases that are ready for trial before a jury and are waiting to be assigned a trial date.

jury selection Also known as *Voir Dire.* The process by which the parties select individuals to sit as jurors on their case. See also *challenges.*

lawsuit A civil court proceeding initiated by a Plaintiff against a Defendant seeking damages. Also called a case, an action, a suit, etc.

Lis Pendens A notice that a specific piece of real estate is involved with litigation. The document is filed on the land records in a town or city hall where the real estate is located and served on the owners of the property. It warns potential purchasers that they will be placed under the court's jurisdiction if they purchase the property without the court's consent.

litigants The parties involved in a lawsuit; the Plaintiffs and the Defendants.

litigation The art of persuading the trier of fact in court, pursuant to specific procedures and laws.

Mechanic's Lien A type of *Prejudgment Remedy* that may be used by a party who has performed specific types of work (such as construction or repairs) or who supplied materials for work on real estate. This lien may be foreclosed on if the owner of the property does not pay for the work or materials supplied. In addition, the lien must be paid before the property can be sold or transferred to someone else. If it is not paid, the new owner will be held liable for the sum stated in the lien.

memorandum of decision A judge's written decision regarding a pleading or a trial.

memorandum of law Also called a brief in some states. A document that is attached or included with a *motion* or *objection* and contains case citations and legal arguments to support the motion or objection.

military affidavit A written statement made under oath that states whether or not a specific Defendant is in the military or naval service in the United States. This document is needed in most states before a court will enter a *default judgment* against a Defendant who has not appeared in an action.

monitor See *court monitor.* Similar to *court reporter.*

motion A document that asks the court to rule on an issue in a particular way. In many states, the party filing the motion must include some type of written order.

Motion for Additur A document that asks the court to increase the amount of a *jury verdict.*

Motion for Articulation A document that requests a trial court to provide a written explanation of its decision. This decision is usually an issue on appeal.

Motion for Default A document filed by a Plaintiff when a Defendant has failed to appear or file a pleading according to applicable court rules.

Motion for Default for Failure to Appear A document filed by a Plaintiff when a Defendant has failed to respond to the Summons and Complaint.

Motion for Default for Failure to Plead A document filed when a party (usually the Defendant) has failed to file a pleading according to applicable court rules. The consequences may be judgment against the Defendant.

Motion for Disclosure of Assets A document usually filed by Plaintiffs that asks the court to order a party to provide a list of all his or her assets and their location.

Motion for More Definite Statement A pleading filed during the *Pretrial Stage* by a Defendant who is asking the Plaintiff to correct or clarify a portion of his or her *Complaint.* Plaintiffs may file this motion directed at a *Defendant's Answer, Special Defenses, Counterclaim,* or *Cross Claim.* This motion is called a Request to Revise in Connecticut.

Motion for Nonsuit A document filed by the Defendant against a Plaintiff who has failed to comply with a court rule, statute, or court order. The consequences may result in the case being dismissed and judgment entering in favor of the Defendant.

Motion for Order of Compliance A pleading filed by either party against the other who fails to comply with discovery requests.

Motion for Protective Order A document filed by a party who believes justice requires that they not be required to disclose certain information requested through discovery by the opposing party. Reasons can include to protect a party from annoyance, embarrassment, oppression, or undue burden or expense, etc. As an alternative to granting the motion, the court may limit the information to be disclosed and require the party requesting the information to pay any costs incurred in its reproduction.

Motion for Remittitur A document that asks the court to reduce the jury verdict to comply with the evidence presented or due to a mathematical error.

Motion for Summary Judgment A document filed by either party that states that there is no issue of material fact in the case. As a result, judgment should enter in his or her favor.

Motion in Limine A document filed by either party to prevent the opposing party from introducing specific evidence during the trial, or to limit the introduction of specific evidence to within certain parameters. In most cases, this motion is filed before trial and is decided by the judge assigned to the trial.

Motion to Dismiss A document filed by the Defendant in the Pretrial Stage, usually before the Answer, seeking to dismiss the Plaintiff's *Complaint* for one or more of the following reasons: *lack of subject matter jurisdiction, lack of personal jurisdiction, insufficiency of process, insufficiency of service of process, improper venue,* and except in Connecticut, *failure to state a claim upon which relief can be granted,* etc.

Motion to Open Default A document filed by a Defendant who has been defaulted for failing to appear or failing to plead, yet judgment has not yet entered. In the motion, the Defendant is seeking the court's permission to void (open) the default, correct the error, and allow the case to proceed as usual, rather than directly to judgment.

Motion to Open Default Judgment A document filed by a Defendant who has had a judgment entered against him or her as a result of a default. This motion must be filed within four months of notice sent of the judgment and asks the court to void (open) the judgment, restore the case to the docket, and allow it to proceed as if no judgment were entered.

Motion to Open Judgment A document filed by a party within four months of notice sent of a judgment against him or her that asks the court to void (open or set aside) the judgment due to mistake, fraud, new evidence, a change of circumstances, etc.

Motion to Open Nonsuit A document filed by a Plaintiff who has been nonsuited. In the motion, the Plaintiff is asking the court to void (open or set aside) the nonsuit, restore the case to the docket, and allow it to proceed as if no nonsuit had been entered.

Motion to Quash Subpoena A document filed by any party or person who has been served a subpoena and wishes to avoid appearing in court or at a deposition to testify. In the motion, the party asks the court to void the subpoena and release him or her from its authority.

Motion to Set Aside Default See *Motion to Open Default.*

Motion to Set Aside Dismissal A document filed by a Plaintiff whose case was dismissed and asks the court to remove (set aside) the dismissal and permit the case to continue.

Motion to Set Aside Judgment See *Motion to Open Judgment.*

Motion to Set Aside Verdict A document filed after a jury has reached a verdict which asks the court to void (open or set aside) the *verdict* and render judgment in his or her favor, or order a new trial.

Motion to Strike Two definitions: **1.** In Connecticut, a document filed by the Defendant before the Answer, that alleges that the Plaintiff's Complaint, or a part thereof, fails to state a "claim upon which relief can be granted" or other similar allegation. As a result, the challenged document or part thereof should be stricken. **2.** In other states, this motion is filed to remove scandalous, repetitive, or harassing language from a pleading.

Motion to Transfer A document filed by either party asking the court to transfer the case to another court. This motion may be used to address a *Motion to Dismiss* based upon *improper venue* or a *Motion to Dismiss* based upon *lack of subject matter jurisdiction.*

Motion to Withdraw Appearance A document filed by an attorney asking the court to permit him or her to withdraw as a party's attorney. This motion is necessary if a client refuses to voluntarily hire another attorney to represent him or her or refuses to file a pro se Appearance, in lieu of the attorney's Appearance.

nonparties Persons or entities who are not named as parties in a lawsuit but who may have information relating to the case that could require a deposition or for them to testify as witnesses at trial. Nonparties should be *subpoenaed* to attend court or their deposition, to ensure their cooperation and compliance.

nonsuit See *Motion for Nonsuit.*

Notice of Deposition A document that informs all parties in a case that an opposing party intends to take someone's deposition on a date and at a place specified in the notice.

Notice of Lis Pendens See *Lis Pendens.*

objection An oral announcement or written document made by a party who contests an opposing party's motion or request or a situation that occurs during a trial.

Offer of Judgment A written offer to settle a case for a specific sum.

open default See *Motion to Open Default.*

open default judgment See *Motion to Open Default Judgment.*

open judgment See *Motion to Open Judgment.*

oral argument When the parties appear in court to orally argue a *motion* or *objection* before a judge. Also takes place during trials.

order A court ruling that grants or denies motions and sustains or overrules objections.

Order of Notice A document often filed by Plaintiffs, rather than Defendants, asking the court for permission to allow a *proper officer* to serve a nonappearing, out-of-state Defendant or a Defendant who cannot be located. Service may be through certified mail, if an address is known, or by publication in a newspaper, etc. If the application is granted, the court will issue an *Order of Notice.*

overrule A court ruling which indicates it disagrees with a party's objection to a *motion* or *request.* The result is that the initial motion or request is granted.

parties Plaintiffs and Defendants in a lawsuit. Also known as litigants.

penalties See *sanctions, Motion for Nonsuit, default.*

personal jurisdiction The authority of a court to enforce a judgment against a party. See *Motion to Dismiss.*

Petition for Certification A document drafted by a party who wishes to bring an appeal to the Supreme Court. Once received, the Supreme Court will determine if it will deny the petition or grant it and permit the party to file the appeal.

Plaintiff The person, individual, entity, corporation, etc., that brings a lawsuit against a Defendant claiming damages.

pleadings Documents filed in court that pertain to a specific lawsuit. In most cases, the *Complaint* is the first pleading filed in a lawsuit.

Prejudgment Remedy (PJR) An attachment (also called a lien) against a Defendant's assets, up to the amount of the Plaintiff's claims in his or her case, that is obtained prior to judgment, in order to ensure that the Defendant will not be *judgment proof* if the Plaintiff wins the case. Note that a Defendant who files a *Counterclaim* may obtain a PJR against a Plaintiff's assets for the same purpose. A *Mechanic's Lien* and a *Lis Pendens* are other types of PJRs.

pretrial conference A court-scheduled meeting between the parties and a judge (or other person authorized by the court) to help parties settle their lawsuit rather than go to trial. These meetings are also used to narrow down contested issues and determine discovery schedules. Most courts require the attorneys to bring their clients with them to these meetings at the courthouse, or at least have them available to discuss settlement, and also to draft a pretrial memo.

privileged cases Cases that are given priority for a quick trial date due to a specific circumstance.

probate An area of law that addresses issues such as administering estates, wills, and trusts, adoption and other matters relating to children, guardianships, and conservatorships.

Pro Hac Vice Also known as a Pro Hac Vice Appearance. This term is used to describe an out-of-state attorney who has permission to appear in a specific state court and represent a client although he or she is not licensed to practice law there. This attorney must usually work under the guidance of or in conjunction with an attorney licensed to practice in that state.

proper officer *High Sheriffs, deputy sheriffs, constables,* and other individuals who are elected or appointed to serve civil process such as a Summons and Complaint, etc., within their precincts.

property execution A postjudgment collection procedure: a court-ordered attachment of a party's (usually a Defendant's) assets. The assets are auctioned by a *proper officer* who then gives the proceeds to the person (usually a Plaintiff) who is owed the judgment. See also *bank execution* and *wage execution.*

pro se A party who files an Appearance in court indicating he or she will represent himself or herself, rather than hire an attorney.

protective order See *Motion for Protective Order.*

record A list and contents of all documents filed and the proceeding that took place in the trial court pertaining to a case.

Reply Brief or Memo In most states, any party in a trial court case may reply in writing to a party's opposing brief or memorandum of law before the issue is decided by the court. In addition, in appeals, the Appellant is often permitted to file, in addition to his or her initial brief, a reply brief directed at the Appellee's brief.

Reply to Special Defenses The Plaintiff's response to the *Defendant's Special Defenses,* which is filed as part of an *Answer* to the *Plaintiff's Complaint.* Not all states require this responsive pleading.

request A document that asks a party to take a specific action. If the opposing party does not object within a specified period of time the request is automatically granted and the opposing party is required to comply. A request does not require an *order.*

Request for Admission A type of *discovery* that requires a party to admit or deny specific statements. Do not confuse this with an *Answer.* An Answer is a mandatory pleading. All discovery is optional. The responses to Requests for Admission often narrow down *contested issues* between the parties and may provide grounds to file a *Motion for Summary Judgment.*

Request for Mental Exam A type of *discovery* that permits a Defendant to request a Plaintiff who is claiming damages for mental harm and suffering to submit to a mental examination performed by a physician selected by the Defendant at the Defendant's expense. If a *Counterclaim* for mental injuries is filed by a Defendant in an action, the Plaintiff may make this same request of the Defendant. This exam is also known as an *IME:* an independent medical exam.

Request for Physical Exam A type of *discovery* that permits a Defendant to request a Plaintiff who is claiming damages for physical injuries to submit to a physical examination performed by a physician selected by the Defendant at the Defendant's expense. If a *Counterclaim* for physical injuries is filed by a Defendant in an action, the Plaintiff may make this same request of the Defendant. This exam is also known as an *IME:* an independent medical exam.

Request for Production A type of *discovery* that permits a party to request to examine specific original documents, or to receive copies of these documents from the opposing party. This type of discovery also enables a party to request to examine tangible items that may be subjects of the suit.

Request to Charge A document prepared by each party that contains suggestions for the trial judge to incorporate when delivering its charge (also known as jury instructions) to the jury after all the evidence has been presented and all the parties' arguments are concluded.

Request to Inspect Property Similar to a Request for Production, this type of *discovery* enables a party to request to examine large tangible items or real estate itself that is the subject of the suit and is owned or located on the opposing party's property or within his or her control.

Request to Revise See *Motion for More Definite Statement.*

responsive pleadings Documents filed in response to the Plaintiff's Complaint. They include the Answer, Reply to Affirmative or Special Defenses, Answer to Counterclaim, Answer or Reply to Cross Claim, and Answer to Third-Party Complaint.

retainer Legal fees paid by the client to his or her attorney usually at the time the client agrees to hire the attorney and the attorney agrees to accept the case. The attorney's work is then billed against the amount of the retainer.

retainer letter An agreement for representation. This letter or agreement confirms in writing the understanding between the client and the attorney regarding legal services and fees. It should be signed by both prior to the attorney beginning work on the case.

Return of Service A document, similar to an affidavit, from a *proper officer* that verifies he or she delivered (served) a specific document to a party or nonparty, as directed by the attorney or pro se. A Return of Service is needed for every document that is served by a proper officer. See also *service of process.*

sanctions Penalties imposed by the court due to a party's failure to comply with court rules or orders.

service To deliver copies of documents that are filed in court to all parties in a lawsuit.

service of process This term pertains to delivering (serving) a copy of a *Summons* and *Complaint* to the Defendants named in these documents in order to inform them that there is a lawsuit pending against them. Service must be made by a *proper officer,* either *in hand* or *abode.* If in hand or abode service is not possible, service must be made according to the language of the applicable statutes.

set aside default See *Motion to Open Default.*

set aside judgment See *Motion to Open Judgment.*

Special Defenses See *affirmative defenses.*

stenographer Also known as a *court reporter,* a person who records testimony in court or during a *deposition.*

stipulation An agreement by the parties. Usually, it is written and filed in court, or placed orally on the court record. The agreement can pertain to the entire case as a settlement or discovery deadlines, or to one or more contested issues in the case.

subject matter jurisdiction A court's authority to hear, decide, and enforce a particular type of case.

subpoena A document that compels the person named in the document to appear and testify in court or at a *deposition* on a specific date and time. The subpoena must be served to the person by a *proper officer* which may include anyone who is 18 years old or older and is not related to the parties or the attorneys or involved in the case. See the applicable court rules or statutes.

subpoena duces tecum A document that compels the person named in the document to appear and testify in court or at a *deposition* on a specific date and time and to bring with them certain documents that are listed in the document. The subpoena duces tecum must be served to the person by a *proper officer* which may include anyone who is 18 years old or older and is not related to the parties or the attorneys or involved in the case. See the applicable court rules or statutes.

Summons Also called a *Writ* or *Writ of Summons.* A document that is attached to a Complaint and contains the names of the parties, the address of the court where the lawsuit will be filed, and instructions for the Defendant.

sustain A court ruling indicating it agrees with a party's *objection* to a *motion* or *request.* The result is that the initial motion or request is denied.

taxation of costs A party who prevails at trial is entitled to be reimbursed by the opposing party for certain costs expended to prosecute or defend the lawsuit.

testimony Oral answers to questions posed by either party to a witness (a party or nonparty) during a trial or *deposition.* At *trial,* testimony is part of the *evidence* each party presents to the trier of fact.

Third-Party Action When a Defendant attempts to reduce or extinguish his or her liability to a Plaintiff by bringing a third person, who is not currently a party in the lawsuit, into the lawsuit and claiming that he or she is somehow liable for damages claimed by the Plaintiff. (Third-party actions may also be brought by Plaintiffs faced with a Counterclaim and Defendants faced with a Cross Claim.)

tort An act or lack of action by an individual or entity that causes another individual or entity to suffer *damages.*

tortfeaser One who commits a tort; a wrongdoing against another.

transcript A court argument, *testimony,* or *deposition* that has been reduced to a typewritten (or computer generated) document by a *court reporter.*

trial A legal proceeding that usually takes place in a courtroom that is located in a courthouse whereby Plaintiffs and Defendants have the opportunity to present their *evidence* (*testimony* and *exhibits*) in order to convince a *trier of fact* (either a judge or a jury) to resolve a dispute by ruling in their favor.

trier of fact A judge or jury who is designated to determine the facts in a case, based upon the evidence presented by the parties during a trial, and who reaches a *verdict* based upon those facts and the law.

venue The proper court location where a case should be filed. See *Motion to Dismiss* and *Motion to Transfer.*

verdict The outcome of a trial that is determined by the *trier of fact.*

voir dire Jury selection.

wage execution A postjudgment collection procedure: a court-ordered attachment of a party's employment wages that is applied to pay a judgment the party owes to another. See also *bank execution* and *property execution.*

witness A party or nonparty who has information concerning a case and who will testify during a *deposition* and/or at trial.

witness fees Fees the *proper officer* will give to a nonparty witness when serving any type of *subpoena* that compels him or her to appear at a *deposition* or at trial. The fee is based upon the mileage the witness will need to travel.

Index